WOMANWORDS

JANE MILLS

A Vocabulary of Culture and
Patriarchal Society

LONGMAN

Longman Group UK Limited,
Longman House, Burnt Mill, Harlow, Essex CM20 2JE England
and Associated Companies throughout the world.

First published 1989

British Library Cataloguing in Publication Data

Jane Mills
    Womanwords.
    1. Women – Thesauri
    025.4'93054

    ISBN 0-582-89232-5

Typset by Flairplan Phototypesetting Ltd.
Printed and bound in Great Britain by
Mackays of Chatham PLC, Chatham, Kent

For Elizabeth (Betty) Mills
and Alice Rachel Hayes

Contents

Abbreviations

OED – Murray, J A H, Bradley, H, Craigie, W A and Onions, C T, *The Oxford English Dictionary* OUP, Oxford. 1933, Supplements 1972–86

Webster's – Gove, Philip Babcock (ed), *Webster's Third New International Dictionary of the English Language*. G & C Merriam Co., Springfield, Mass. 1961

Brewer's – Evans, Ivor H (ed), *Brewer's Dictionary of Phrase and Fable*. Book Club Associates/Cassell, London. 1981

Fowler's – Fowler, H W, *A Dictionary of Modern English Usage*. OUP, Oxford. 1983

Cross-references are indicated by SMALL CAPITALS.

Introduction

"When I use a word", Humpty Dumpty said, in rather a scornful tone, "it means just what I choose it to mean – neither more or less." "The question is," said Alice, "whether you can make words mean so many different things." "The question is," said Humpty Dumpty, "which is to be the master – that's all."
Lewis Carroll, Alice Through the Looking Glass, 1872

When we speak or write few of us are aware of the history of our language. Not that this matters ordinarily since one of the most important functions of language is to communicate ideas. If both the speaker and hearer, or writer and reader, share a similar understanding need it concern either that a word which is now female-specific and opprobrious was once non-gender-specific and non-abusive? The answer is eloquently supplied by Deborah Cameron: "It is often said that the most distinctively human quality we possess is the ability to communicate with each other by means of languages, and that linguistic communication is crucial to the organisation of human societies. So people with an interest in the workings of any society must also concern themselves with its language. . . . Feminists are deeply interested in the workings of their societies, since in order to fight their oppression they must first understand it. Much feminist effort is directed, therefore, to re-analysing society as a partriarchy, a system in which men have power over women. Language is part of patriarchy. If it plays a crucial part in social organisation it is instrumental in maintaining male power, and feminists must study its workings carefully." (*Feminism and Linguistic Theory*)

Language is not solely a means of communication. It is also an expression of shared assumptions and transmits implicit values and behavioural models to those who use it. When, for example, such ordinary words for a female person as *woman* or *girl* acquire the additional commonly understood meanings of 'mistress' and 'prostitute', as they once did, an attitude towards women held by some members of society becomes part of the experience of all that society's members. Language is at once the expression of culture and a part of it. Just as changes in language may be understood by an examination of the social and historical context in which it is used, so may social attitudes be illuminated by a study of language change.

Changes in language occur for a variety of reasons: vowels or consonants can get dropped; the meaning of a similar-sounding word becomes attached; members of a specific group may make a conscious attempt to use or avoid certain words and thus influence both structure and meaning, a dialectal usage comes to dominate; foreign words are borrowed, and so one. Meaning is never simple: earlier and later senses often coexist, or one meaning can drop out and, on occasions, reappear.

In their methodology some linguists adopt a synchronic approach to language by disregarding time as a relevant factor and attributing to the data a uniform status of simultaneity. Historical linguists investigate and describe the way in which languages change or maintain their structure during the course of time, thus their domain is language in what is called its diachronic aspect. The advantage of this approach is that it provides an historical context for an interpretation of semantic change.

In *Womanwords* I concentrate on the semantic histories of words rather than other aspects of language because, as Theodora Bynon writes, "the lexicon is the part of a language which has the most direct links with the spiritual and material culture of its speakers and . . . semantic developments may only be comprehensible by reference to the cultural background". (*Historical Linguistics*) By selecting certain words, all of which relate to women and exploring how, when and perhaps why these words changed their meaning, I found a means by which to examine the balance of power between the genders within anglo-phone society.

In order to explore what it has meant, and means today, to be a women in patriarchal society I have selected a number of key words in a vocabulary which best reveal how, over the years, radical change, discontinuity and conflict as well as continuity and acceptance have affected women's lives. The process of selection inevitably reflected my own interests and concerns as a feminist passionately interested in language and in the past and present history of the woman's struggle. I began this process first by reading feminist linguistic theory, then general linguistic theory. This provided me with a framework in which to 'glean' yet more words from the works of both feminist and non-feminist and of male pro- and anti-feminist writers from the translations of early Greek authors to the present day. This gave me over 500 words for which I traced the etymological and semantic histories.

By the time it came to make the final selection a number of criteria had evolved. Clearly not all woman-related words could be included: I had to confine my semantic detective-work to words which best enabled me to explore the history of changing (and sometimes relentlessly unchanging) attitudes towards women. This then, became another criterion: the words generally had to possess a sufficiently long semantic history to allow me to explore the past and the present. *Womb* and *clitoris*, for example, are included because they have a rich semantic history, but *ovary* and *fallopian tube*, although clearly both woman-related, did not provide much semantic history with which to analyse patriarchal society.

This inevitably meant that I excluded many recent neologisms and slang terms while I included other words which are now perhaps obsolete or obsolescent. It also meant a bias towards British English rather than North

American or Antipodean English. Inclusion of more recent words may simply reflect personal idiosyncrasy: *wimp* is in because I was genuinely surprised to find that it was once female-specific; *blurb* is in because I was amazed to discover that such an innocuous word denoting a piece of writing widely considered to be mindless was woman-related. (After researching *babble, chatter, gossip, nag, scold,* etc. I was considerably less amazed.) The sheer number of slang terms which define woman as sexually promiscuous (there are comparatively few for men) meant that I had to draw an arbitrary line lest *Womanwords* turned into a dictionary of slang.

A desire to provide a critique of lexicography was something else that influenced my selection. Dictionary-bashing is currently enjoying something of a vogue, especially among feminists. This is nothing new: Samuel Johnson defensively defined a lexicographer as "a harmless drudge". Early dictionaries of the C17th were deliberately intended to exploit a new female market as the more enlightened began to accept that a woman's education did not have to comprise only needlwork and basic skills in housewifery. Dictionaries were aimed at "the class intermediate between the educated gentleman and the illiterate peasant, a class defined on one title page as consisting of 'Young scholars, Tradesmen, Artificiers, and the female Sex', on another as 'Ladies who have a turn for Reading and Gentlemen of no Learned Profession'". Yet another dictionary was "chiefly intended for the more-knowing Woman and less-knowing Men". (Ernest Weekly, *The Atlantic Monthly,* 1924).

It is clear to me that until very recently dictionary definitions largely reflected male rather than female experience and language-use. Writing of "The myth of lexicographic objectivity", Alleen Pace Nilsen points out that "dictionaries, like the bible, are treated as absolutes, yet are full or prejudice: more space is given to male items, sex-stereotyped examples are used to illustrate sentences, the masculine is presented first in a sequence where the feminine is also present, more insulting terms are included for women than men, prejudiced comments are included and there are more drawings of men and male animals." (cited in Thorne and Henley, *Language and Sex*).

Lexicographers deserve much of the criticism levelled against them. But not all of it. When it is said that a word first entered the English language this, until recently when cinema, television and radio became sources to plunder, refers to the first *written* example of usage; the basic source material of a lexicographer has been the written word, and most books have been, and still are, written and published by men. Dictionaries which chronicle usage are not necessarily prescriptive. If in the past a dictionary failed to refer to a young woman as a 'girl' the lexicographer would have been failing in his job had he not used the term which the rest of society used and understood.

The desire to reveal something of the breadth of linguistic – especially feminist – theory was another criterion I applied when making my final selection of words. Some feminist linguists such as Casey Miller and Kate Swift believe that sexist language is symptomatic of cultural attitudes which may well be unconscious. Others, like Dale Spender believe that language actually causes women's oppression. These beliefs are not incompatible: both are true.

A helpful insight into language is the distinction between what Noam Chomsky termed 'competence' and 'performance'. 'Competence' refers to the knowledge of grammar internalised by the speaker of which she or he is not conscious, as distinct from 'performance', or the use made of this knowledge. What this means in effect is that internalised language itself can never be racist, sexist, ageist, etc. In the same way, for instance, that a scientific theory can only ever be neutral; it's not the theory which makes possible the splitting of an atom that is morally despicable but the humans who use this theory to make nuclear weapons. There is a difference between the lexicon of a language which is never neutral and the basic grammar structure which is. Social change affects the way in which we use words and the meanings we give to them. It is humans who invest their prejudices and biases into the words and their meanings.

Take, for example, the vexed question of gender. The word itself is derived from the Greek word meaning 'class' or 'kind'. It was used to divide Greek nouns into three classes labelled 'masculine', 'feminine' and 'neuter'. But if Protagoras (who is credited with this area of linguistic scholarship) had used totally different words, for example A, B and C, which have no values associated with them, we would not, perhaps, be quite so confused or think in terms of one class/gender being 'better' than another. The same could be said of Freud's labelling or passivity as 'feminine' and aggression as 'masculine'. These labels reflect contemporary cultural attitudes towards feminity and masculinity. We may conclude that Freud was sexist, but it does not have to be concluded that all women are necessarily passive and weak and all men are active and strong, or that strength is 'better' than weakness.

Some feminists claim that usages such as the grammatically possible but semantically meaningless 'Man is unique among the apes in that he grows a long beard', or 'Man breast feeds his children', supposedly 'prove' that English gender is only natural if you are a male. But all we can learn from this is that sexism is expressed in linguists' analyses of language.

An overwhelming impression gained from the words in this book is that the term for the female is likely to become pejorative, likely to acquire negative sexual connotations and, once it is attached to the female is unlikely to be transferrable to a male (unless to express contempt). Some linguists have concluded that this constitutes a definitive semantic rule. This, however, is simplistic. The semantic derogation of woman-related words does indeed constitute a very strong tendency, but a linguistic rule requires there to be no exceptions. There are exceptions: *crumpet* has recently been appropriated by women to refer to men; *dowager* and *bride* have never had negative sexual connotations; *jilt*, once female specific, has ameliorated and become non-gender-specific; *bat* has lost its negative sexual connotations.

Another so-called semantic 'rule' that has been proposed claims that langue defines woman as 'negative' meaning that women, as well as being defined pejoratively, are excluded from the meaning or reference of general terms.

However, the term 'pejorative' cannot be understood as synonymous with 'negative'. Linguistically, woman is certainly not the norm, but this does not mean she is not defined. As Maria Black and Rosalind Coward have pointed out, "Women are precisely *defined*, never general representatives of human or all people ... The curious feature is exactly the excess of (sexual) definitions and categories for women. A similar profusion is not found for men, whose differentiation from one another comes not through sexual attributes and status, but primarily through occupation or attributes of general humanity, eg decent, kind, honest, strong. Men remain men and women become specific categories in relation to men and to other categories." (*Screen Education*, 1981)

No word can be totally isolated from another any more than it can from the context in which it is used; the interconnections between words are as important as the semantic history of each individual word. While writing *Womanwords* I discovered certain themes of categories which reveal the ways in which women have been, and still are, defined and stereotyped. I hadn't for instance, realised quite how many words the English language possesses which define woman as edible – usually for male consumption, eg *cheesecake, cherry, crumpet, dish, honey, meat, mutton, tart*, etc. The passivity implicit in this concept provides an interesting contrast to words which define her as powerfully destructive or castrating, eg *banshee, crone, crow, fate,* hag, *harpy, siren, snatch, termagant, vamp*, etc. Some words crop up in several different categories: *mutton*, for example, has been used to define woman as edible, animal, whore and (huge crime) old. To share some of these interconnections and stereotyped definitions I include a list of the main themes and categories on page xiii.

One problem I faced in selecting words to reflect the width and depth of female experience and language-use was the absence of certain words. For instance, it has been noted that the English language has no word to name the female experience of penetration. (*Enveloping* has been adopted by some women but, as yet, shows no sign of catching on.) Another example is *uxorious* which means 'overly loving one's wife'; there is no word which denotes 'overly loving one's husband'. From this, however, I do not conclude, as do some, that the English language is the result of some sort of male conspiracy to silence women or that a concept cannot exist simply because the word doesn't exist. Sexism, for example, clearly existed long before the word entered the English language in the late C19th.

Many women today are making a conscious attempt to reform the English language. Even a cursory dip into *Womanwords* will reveal the ways in which English insults, excludes, and trivialises women with universal male pronouns, misogynist insult words, patriarchal personal names, trivialising suffixes for women in professions, *girl* being used in contexts where *boy* would not be acceptable, the part objectification of women by the use of words like *skirt* standing for the whole woman and so on.

Suggestions for reform include the reclamation and rehabilitation of words and meanings: some believe that *cunt* for example, may have had an old connexion with *cunning* which had notions of wisdom; *virago* had early positive associations of strength. Neologisms to 'name' concepts which don't have a word to describe female experience (as with *enveloping* mentioned above) and altered spellings (*wimmin*, herstory, etc) are recommended by feminists such as Adrienne Rich and Mary Daly. The rejection of what has become called 'he/man language' (ie the use of male pronouns as generic or unspecified terms) is another suggestion. The rejection of certain pronouns – such as the use of *she* for ships and cars – is yet another. One reform, originally widely derided, is now in fairly widespread use: the recasting of words and sentences to make all terminology neutral so that *forefathers* becomes *ancestors*, and the use of *they* as a singular pronoun – something Shakespeare wasn't afraid to do.

These reforms have met with resistance from conservatives such as the English philosopher Roger Scruton: "Each of us inherits in language the wisdom of many generations. To mutilate this repository of human experience is to mutilate our most fundamental perceptions." Deborah Cameron notes that "The cause of such conservatism is only partly anti-feminism, fear of social and political upheaval. Resistance to language change is also related to the way in which people conceptualise language itself as a fixed point in the flux of experience, providing names (their essential correctness guaranteed by history) for phenomena which would otherwise elude our collective grasp." This, as Cameron ably argues, is an erroneous view of language, an illusion from which people take comfort, but ultimately untenable as a theory of language precisely because social change does affect the meaning of words.

There are many problems about the attempts to reform language. I might, for example, wish to impart a positive sense when using the word *cunt*, but if this meaning is not understood by my reader then we're back to square one: in the minds of sexists, language can always be sexist.

But this is not to believe that there can be no change in either language or society. For me, one of the main reasons for studying the history of word meaning, as well as to analyse the way in which patriarchal society defines and thus controls women, was to draw attention to the past and present masculist bias of conventional usage. Definitions are not static and closed, they are possible subjects for rational discourse. With almost every word we utter we always have a choice. To understand the relationship between patriarchal society and the language of its members is to begin to understand the nature of power. Language can be a tool of oppression. It can also be a weapon in the struggle against patriarchy.

* * * * * *

Many readers will have their own personal favourite 'womanwords' which, for the reasons stated, haven't been included; they should write to me c/o the publishers for possible inclusion in any future editions.

Woman Defined

Perhaps the question 'What do women want?' would be easier to answer if patriarchal society didn't possess an excess of definitions and lexical categories for women. Many of the definitions are sexual and many of the categories are apparently contradictory or mutually excluding. As many a woman will testify, while she can expect to be fragmented into wife, mother, daughter, cook, nurse, listener, shopper, cleaner, plumber, wage-earner, lover, etc, all of which add up to 'woman', she finds herself narrowly defined in ways which divide her – one part of herself from another, from other women, and from men. To define a woman narrowly constitutes an attempt to limit her desires and needs, and to deny her the possibility of living life to its fullness.

As I stated in the introduction, no word can be totally isolated from another; the interconnections between words are as important as the semantic history of each individual word. While writing this book I discovered certain categories which reveal some of the many ways in which women are stereotyped. These categories (in capitals in these paragraphs) provide the means to make some connexions and to explore the way in which women experience great fragmentation. Some are well known, eg the VIRGIN/ WHORE dichotomy. Others came to me as something of a surprise.

Woman can be no more than a dumb ANIMAL (see BIRD, BITCH, FILLY, MOUSE, etc), and/or she can be elevated to the position of GODDESS (see APHRODISIAC, VESTAL, SHEILA, etc). She can be CONTAINER and/or contents (see DISH). For centuries women have known that their 'rightful' place is in the HOME where, as MALE PROPERTY, they are either or both the good INFANTILISED child-WIFE and the good MOTHER. As a WORKER inside another's home she may be defined as morally suspect (see SCRUBBER, SLUT, WENCH, etc), or, if EDUCATED, asexual and beyond moral reproach (see GOVERNESS, BLUESTOCKING, etc). If she takes care of her outward APPEAR- ANCE she may gain approval as a LADY – but too much make-up and she becomes a JEZEBEL; too little and she's a DRAB or a SLATTERN. Her CLOTHING can signify the whole woman (as in MUFF, SKIRT, PETTICOAT, etc) and woman as PART OBJECT, as in an expression like 'a bit of skirt'. A woman feels her VAGINA to be just one part of her body but words like CUNT, TWAT, BEAVER, etc. are used to denote all of her.

Once outside the home a woman is in danger of being negatively defined as WITCH or WHORE with POWER disruptive to the male order. An angry woman is BELLICOSE (see AMAZON, VIRAGO, etc), but she can be PLIABLE too (see BUXOM, LESBIAN, TART, etc). Her WORDS can be dismissed as mere BABBLE, GOSSIP or CHATTER, or feared (see SCOLD). When CHASTE she may fit the FEMININE IDEAL (see LADY, MAIDEN, VIRGIN) or she may find herself defined pejoratively (see NUN, SPINSTER, STRAIT-LACED, etc). The CHASTE woman clearly can't be PROMISCUOUS – or can she? (See VIRGIN.) Her SEXUALITY has always been subject to make ambivalence: but while a woman might feel herself to be part both TEMPTRESS and VIRGIN, often it's as if she has to choose between one or other. The non-passive or powerful woman is defined as DESTROYER, DECEIVER, EMASCULATOR, SNATCHER, or UNRULY. Stripped of her POWER she is dismissed as OLD (see ANILE, MAID, MUTTON, etc).

The attempt to control and dominate woman by defining her could be interpreted as evidence of female passivity and collusion. This cannot be totally denied; but few women have had either the social or economic power to 'be' anything other than prostitutes, housewives, mistresses, and so on. But for every negative definition there have existed women who refused to accept these stereotypes, LIBERATED women who, despite the societal pressures, rejected the narrow patriarchal definitions of femininity and were proud to be MOTHERS and SEXUAL, edible by night and workers by day, FEMININE and TERMAGANT, SIREN and SPINSTER. Increasingly, women are claiming the right to define themselves on their own terms in their own words.

The following list of categories, drawn up with the assistance of Sandra Ferguson, provides the means to explore the significance of inter-connections between the words in this book and between the various stereotypes of women as perceived and experienced by women and men in a society in which men define and thereby attempt to control women.

WOMAN AS ANIMAL
bat; beast; beaver; bevy; bird; bitch; bunny; cat; chick/chicken; cow; crow; cuckquean; dog; ducky; filly; fish; hack; haggard; harridan; hen; jade; minx; mount; mouse; nag; nightmare/mare; pig; pussy; shrew; sow; tit; vixen

WOMAN AND HER APPEARANCE
anile; bag; battle-axe; beast; blowzy; broad; cow; crow; dish; dog; doll/dolly; dowdy; drab; floozy; gorgon; hag; haggard; Jezebel; lady; pig; pin money; porcelain; pretty; scrubber; slag; slattern; slut; sow; strait-laced; stuff; tart; tawdry; trollop; wanton

WOMAN AS BELLICOSE
aegis; amazon; battle-axe; bully; circean; virago

WOMAN AS CHASTE
aegis; chasity; lesbian; maid/maiden; nubile; nun; strait-laced; vestal; virgin; widow

WOMAN AS CLOTHING
bloomer; bluestocking; muff; petticoat; skirt; slattern; slut; strait-laced

WOMAN AS CONTAINER
bag; dish; honey; matrix; porcelain; vessel

WOMAN AS DECEIVER
cocktease; coquette; cunning; cute; floozy; glamour; Jezebel; jilt; metetricious; muliebrity; nan; pornography; quaint; siren; tart; wanton; witch

WOMAN AS DESTROYER
banshee; circean; crone; crow; fate; hag; harpy; siren; snatch; termagant; vamp

WOMAN AS EDIBLE
cheesecake; cherry; crumpet; dish; fish; honey; madeleine; meat; mutton; (spare) rib; tart; tit

WOMAN AS EMASCULATOR
cotquean; effeminate; emasculate; fag/faggot; female; feminine/femininity; feminism/feminist; gay; hen; hermaphrodite; molly; pretty; pussy; quean/queen; Sheila; sister; squaw; tart; uxorious; wimp

WOMAN AND THE FEMININE IDEAL
amazon; androgyne; anima; bad; ball; battle-axe; beast; bluestocking; butch; chastity; coy; cute; doll/dolly; dyke; Eve; female; feminine/femininity; feminism/feminist; flower; frail; hermaphrodite; hysteria; lady; lesbian; maid/maiden; maternal; matriarchy; maudlin; misandry/misogyny; muliebrity; nice; nymphomania; other; petticoat; pretty; sex; sexism/sexist; sister; tribade; uxorious; vessel; virgin; woman

WOMAN AS GODDESS
admonish; aegis; Albion; amazon; anathema; anima; aphrodisiac; April; August; banshee; Cassandra; circean; cow; crone; crow; delphic; Easter; Europe; fate; focus; Friday; gorgon; governess; harpy; hermaphrodite; June; matriarchy; May; money; mother; nymph/nymphet; Sheila; siren; suttee; termagant; trivia; venereal; vestal; weird; womb

WOMAN AND THE HOME
cotquean; focus; housewife; hussy; lady; maid/maiden; mistress; spinster; vessel; vestal; wife

WOMAN AS HORSE:
filly; hack; harridan; jade; mount; nag; nightmare/mare; tit

WOMAN INFANTILISED
babble; babe/baby; chick/chicken; cute; daughter; doll/dolly; girl; lass; moll; nubile; pretty

WOMAN AND EDUCATION

bluestocking; glamour; governess; midwife; spinster; witch

LIBERATED WOMAN

bachelor (girl); bloomer; butch; clitoris; female; feminism/feminist; flapper; Ms; prude; shrew; sister; spinster; suffragette/suffragist; woman

WOMAN AS MALE PROPERTY

baggage; maid/maiden; Mrs; paraphernalia; pin money; rape; suttee; virgin; widow

WOMAN AS MOTHER

anima; April; authoress; beget; breast/bosom; cow; dame; Eve; mammy; maternal; matriarchy; matriculate; matrix; matron; womb

WOMAN AND NATURE

belladonna; harpy; maternal; May; mother; virgin

WOMAN AS OLD

anile; bag; battle-axe; beldam; biddy; dame; dowager; girl; gorgon; gossip; hag; haggard; hen; jade; maid/maiden; matron; mother; mutton; spinster; witch

WOMAN AS PART OBJECT

bit; crack; fluff; hole; Jane; nooky; piece; screw; stuff; tail; tit; twat

WOMAN AS PLIABLE

buxom; lesbian; tart; wench

WOMAN AND POWER (or lack of)

aegis; amazon; beget; dame; delilah; distaff; emasculate; feminine/femininity; frail; girl; glamour; governess; housewife; hussy; lady; madam; maid/maiden; matriarchy; mistress; muliebrity; petticoat; pussy; quean/queen; sister; witch

WOMEN AS PROMISCUOUS

actress; adventuress; babe/baby; bad; besom; bit; bunny; buxom; fully; flapper; floozy; frail; hen; housewife; jade; jezebel; jilt; loose; madam; meat; minx; mistress; moll; mount; muff; nice; piece; scrubber; Sheila; skirt; slag; slattern; slut; sow; tail; tart; tit; tramp; trollop; virgin; wanton; wench; whore; wife; woman

WOMAN AND SEXUALITY

aphrodisiac; ball; breast/bosom; butch; clitoris; cunt; dildo; dyke; fag/faggot; femme; frigid; hysteria; lesbian; nymph/nymphet; nymphomania; other; prude; tribade

WOMAN AS SNATCHER
circean; hag; harpy; hooker; snatch

WOMAN AS SPINNER
distaff; fate; spinster

WOMAN AS TEMPTRESS
charm; circrean; cocktease; coquette; coy; delilah; enchant; sorceress; vamp; wanton

UNRULY WOMAN
blowzy; filly; haggard; hoyden; hussy; hysteria; jilt; loose; minx; nymphomania; scold; shrew; termagant; tomboy; vixen; wanton

WOMAN AS VAGINA
beaver; berk; cat; cheesecake; crack; cowry; cunt; Eve; fanny; fish; flower; gash; hole; honey; housewife; Jane; lady; meat; minge; moll; money; mouse; muff; mutton; nag; nooky; pussy; quaint; (spare) rib; skirt; snatch; tail; tit; twat; vagina; woman

WOMAN VIOLATED
cherry; crack; deflower; gash; maid/maiden; rape; vagina; virgin

WOMAN AS VIRGIN
chastity; cherry; damsel; flower; girl; lass; maid/maiden; miss; nubile; nun; nymph/nymphet; spinster; vestal; virgin; wench

WOMAN AS WHORE
adventuress; bag; baggage; bat; bawd; biddy; bint; blowzy; broad; brothel; charity; concubine; courtesan; delilah; dog; doll/dolly; doxy; drab; ducky; fag/faggot; fornicate; frail; gray; girl; hack; harlot; harridan; hooker; hussy; jade; Jane; jezebel; jilt; lady; loose; madam; maid/maiden; maudlin; meat; meretricious; minx; miss; mistress; moll; mother; mouse; muff; mutton; nag; nan/nanny; nun; piece; pig; pin money; pornography; prostitute; quean/queen; screw; scrubber; street-walker; strumpet; succubus; tail; tart; tit; tomboy; tramp; trollop/trull; whore; woman

WOMAN AS WIFE
bride; Mrs; nubile; paraphernalia; rib; uxorious; widow/relict

WOMAN AS WITCH
besom; cat; circean; crone; crow; enchant; Friday; glamour; hag; haggard; hysteria; mascot; nightmare/mare; quaint; sorceress; succubus; vamp; weird; wicked; witch

WOMAN AND WORDS
anathema; authoress; babble; biddy; bitch; blurb; broad; Cassandra; cat; chatter; cotquean; delphic; fate; fishwife; flibbertigibbet; glamour; gossip;

hack; harpy; herstory; madrigal; mother(tongue); nag; nice; pretty; pussy; scold; Sheila; shrew; siren; termagant; testify; trivia; virago; vixen

WOMAN AND WORK
actress; authoress; biddy; distaff; fate; fishwife; governess; housewife; maid; matron; midwife; nan/nanny; prostitute; scrubber; seamstress; slut; spinster; wench; wife

Acknowledgments

This book was conceived with Sue Hayes, with whom I shared an ambivalent mixture of anger and hilarity towards the many dictionaries and reference books for which we have a passion. It is to our mothers that this book is dedicated. The gestation period has been long and many people have been involved in helping me. Sue Hayes, Christina Burnett, Kate Swan and Sandra Ferguson all helped me with the research — the main onus fell to Kate and Sandra, especially Sandra, whose work was exemplary and who also gave me a loyalty and support way beyond anything I could have hoped for when the going got rough. My thanks also to Jean MacDonald and Claire Davis for their typing.

The following have helped me in a variety of ways — advice, encourage-ment, ideas, references, words, definitions, criticism and support: Jessica Fraser, Charlie Hayes, Kate Owen, Ruthie Bundey, Geoffrey Robertson, Rosalind Delmar, Francine Wynham, Bill Webb, Steve Hawes, Paula Kahn, Ursula Owen, Elaine Steel, Margaret Mulvihill, Mick Gold, Joan Ashworth, Karen Altman, Barry Cox, Lawrence Moore, Michael Hatfield, David Hanley, Peter Thompson, Eleanor Randolph, Barry Cox, John Slater, David Line, Charles Onion, Fern Fraser, Kathy Lette, Susie Figgis, Luisa Passerini, Judith Herron and Denis MacShane.

For their editorial work and assistance I would like to thank Lucinda Montefiore at Virago Press and Jenny Hicks and Brian O'Kill at Longman.

For reading the manuscript and giving both support and necessary criticism I give sincere thanks to Dee Dee Glass, Aslí Göksel and Laura Mulvey.

I wish to thank Ronnie Fraser for giving me an understanding of language within a context of time and space. And my thanks too, to Jennifer Silverstone for helping me realise that a preoccupation with etymology can be a means of evading meaning and feeling.

Womanwords could not have been written without any of these friends but, of course, I accept full responsibility for the final product. The concept owes much to Raymond Williams' *Keywords: A Vocabulary of Culture and Society*, a book I much admire and which helped me to an understanding of the relationship between society, culture and language.

Actress

The girl who has half a mind to become an actress, doesn't realise that that's what it requires.

William Hazlitt, 1778–1830

Actor, deriving from the Latin *agere*, meaning to drive, carry on, do, or act, entered English in the C14th for a manager, overseer, agent or actor. In the late C16th it denoted a performer or stage-player and, by the early C17th, it was used in the wider sense of someone who acts, or performs any action or takes part in any affair. *Actress*, occasionally *actrice*, did not appear until 1589, when it was used to denote what Henry Cockeram's *English Dictionarie or interpreter of hard English words* (1626) defined as "a woman doer". By the early C18th the word in this sense was replaced by *actor*.

Actress, meaning a female stage performer, entered English in 1700, some 40 years after a licence of Charles II had proclaimed: "Whereas, women's parts in plays have hitherto been acted by men in the habits of women. . .we do permit and give leave for the time to come that all women's parts be acted by women." But the monarch had been beaten to it two years earlier when Margaret Hughes, MISTRESS of Prince Rupert, played the role of Desdemona in a London theatre on 8 December 1660, becoming the first woman to perform in public. At first, however, *actor* was used for both females and males.

In Old English the suffix *-estre* designated a female agent. From this developed the suffix *-ster*, which, in Middle English, came to refer primarily to a male agent, often with a pejorative sense. (SPINSTER is the sole feminine survivor.) The feminine-gender suffix *-ess* was a result of the French influence upon the English language following the Norman invasion of 1066. Casey Miller and Kate Swift point out in *Words and Women* that "as the old native female-occupation titles ending in -ster were taken over by males, and the need was felt for different words to label females within the occupations, the -ess suffix was ready at hand".

Although some words with the feminine *-ess* ending are still used (*waitress*, *goddess*, GOVERNESS, *stewardess*, etc), many have become obsolete or are disappearing: for example, we no longer talk of a dictatress (1784), a doctress (1549), or an oratress (1586). The OED explains: "the tendency of modern usage being to treat the agent-nouns in *-er* and the substantives indicating profession or occupation, as of common gender, unless there be some special reason to the contrary". Thus a woman who directs films is a director, a female head of government is a prime minister and so on.

Fowler's finds this curious: "we are dropping these words at the very time when it might be thought, as was said in the first edition of this book (1926) that 'with the coming extension of women's vocations, feminines for vocation-words are a special need of the future.' Perhaps the explanation of this paradox is that it symbolises the victory of women in their struggle for equal rights; it reflects the abandonment by men of those ideas about women in the professions that moved Dr Johnson to his rude remark about women preachers. Modern woman justifiably resents any such implications." (In 1763, Samuel Johnson said: "A woman's preaching is like a dog's walking on his hind legs. It is not done well; but you are surprised to find it done at all.") Rebecca West was one modern woman who did resent the implications of words with the -ess suffix. Reviewing a book by a male anti-feminist she wrote: "He attempts to quash the argument that a woman ought to have a vote because she pays taxes by stating that in return for her taxes she is a 'citizeness' – which sounds like something odd out of a menagerie. . ." (*The Freewoman*, 1912)

Miller and Swift believe that "since authors, poets, Negroes, sculptors, Jews, actors, etc may be either female or male, the significance of a word like authoress is not that it indicates a female but that it indicates deviation from what is consciously or unconsciously considered the standard". The *actor–actress* distinction, they suggest, might seem at first glance to be as valid and necessary as the male–female distinction. But *actor* is the generic term and one which is used, for instance by their trade union (Actors' Equity) and by theatres (Actors' Playhouse) etc. They apply the following formula: "if the group as a whole is called A, and some of its members are called As and others Bs, the Bs cannot be full-fledged".

Women in the acting profession increasingly prefer to use the term *actor*. Not only, one suspects, because the distinction between *actor* and *actress* is the difference between the norm and a deviation. Perhaps because of the widely known love-life of Margaret Hughes, England's first leading LADY (in this phrase 'lady' may be something of a euphemism), women stage performers have never gained general public approval: during the 18th, 19th and early 20th centuries *actress* was a synonym for a promiscuous woman and the profession is still considered by many to be morally dangerous for a woman. This is not true for male actors – although many homophobes dismiss them as effeminate or gay. In the late C19th *actressy* began to be used, both as a homophobic gibe and to signify someone of either gender who is affectedly theatrical, ie, the opposite of a good actor.

Acute See CUTE

Admonish See MONEY

Adventuress See GLAMOUR

Aegis

There is some disagreement among the major dictionaries about the mythological origins of the aegis, which derives from the Greek *aix* meaning goat. Most of them state it was a shield owned by Zeus. But the OED gives "A shield or defensive armour; applied in ancient mythology to that of Jupiter or Minerva." Webster's, on the other hand, tells us that it is "a shield or breastplate emblematic of majesty that was originally associated chiefly with the god Zeus, but later bordered with serpents and set with a GORGON head, associated mainly with the goddess Athena". From its symbolic significance of divine protection and power, *aegis* began to be used figuratively in the late C18th to mean "a protection or impregnable defence; a set of favourable circumstances; controlling or conditioning influence; patronage, backing or sponsorship; leadership; control, guidance, direction". (OED) At the time, of course, the aegis was believed to be symbolic of male power. It is worth sorting out the mythological origins of the aegis since there is every indication, as Robert Graves author of *Greek Myths* believes, that it was once a powerful symbol of MATRIARCHY or female power later usurped by a male god whose patriarchal rule was more acceptable to patrilineal times.

The aegis was originally owned not by Zeus, but by Athena to whom it was a symbol of her divine power and protection. The earliest sources describe it as a magical goatskin bag containing a serpent and protected by a gorgon mask. This evolved into a goatskin breastplate or shield, ornamented with serpents around the perimeter, with a gorgon's head in the centre; Gorgon or 'grim one', was Athena's title in her aspect as a death goddess. According to Plato, Athena was the Greek counterpart of the Libyan goddess Neith (Also known as Anath, Anat and Ath-enna), whom Graves believed belonged to an epoch when the male function in procreation was not known, although more recent research suggests such an epoch probably never existed. Anath was herself the gorgon mask surrounded by serpents, which some scholars have identified as the penises of her many male sacrificial victims. She was served by priestesses who wore the aegis, which was something like a fringed goatskin apron. It had a function of symbolic CHASTITY since it meant castration – or death – for a man to remove it without the owner's consent. The proximity of the gorgon's head to Athena's aegis may have been a relic of this ancient North African myth; any man who gazed upon the Gorgon's face was instantly petrified.

Later Homeric myths considered the aegis so essential to sovereignty that not even Zeus could rule the other gods without it. By seizing the aegis – previously denied to all males – from Athena, Zeus was able to become the Olympic–Platonic patriarch; he even claimed to give birth to Athena from his own head. Robert Graves interprets this myth in terms of male usurpation of female rule: "With the spread of Platonic philosophy, the hitherto intellectually dominant Greek woman degenerated into an unpaid worker and breeder of children wherever Zeus and Apollo [his son] were the ruling Gods." (*The Greek Myths*)

Albion

An ancient and poetical name for Britain, *Albion* probably derives from the Latin *albus*, meaning white, a reference to the white cliffs on its south-eastern shores. Another theory is that it comes from *alp*, the Celtic word for Britain. An ancient legend provides a third folk-etymological theory: the fifty daughters of the King of Syria were all married off on the same day. Presumably in protest against their arranged marriages, each one murdered her husband on her wedding night. As punishment for their treacherous behaviour, their father set them adrift in a ship which eventually reached the islands now known as Britain, where they duly wed native men of their own choice. Albia, the eldest of the defiant daughters, is said to have given her name to her new country.

Amazon

The Amazons, a tribe of warrior women, are first mentioned in the *Iliad* (C8th BC). They allegedly lived in Scythia on the south-eastern shores of the Black Sea. It has been suggested that Scythia gave its name to the scythe with which the Amazons supposedly castrated and killed their male enemies; *scyth*, however, derives from the Indo-European root *sek*, meaning to cut. Led by their two best-known QUEENS, Hippolyta and Penthesilea, the Amazons were the chief votaries of the goddess Diana at her temple in Ephesus. The only time they came into contact with men was for purposes of procreation and as opponents in war. All sons born to Amazon women were promptly dispatched back to their fathers. The main sign of their predilection for inverting biology was their custom of burning off their right breast in childhood, so that they could draw the arrows in their bows more easily in their many battles. Although worthy opponents for male warriors (how much acclaim can a man earn by fighting a weak coward?), ultimately the Amazons were defeated and subdued by all-conquering heroes such as Bellepheron, Heracles and Theseus.

Amazon first appears in English in a 1398 translation of a text by

Bartholomaeus Anglicus: "They were calyd Amazones, that is understonde wythoute breste." Towards the end of the C16th any female warrior was called an *amazon*, and the word began to be used in a transferred sense by the mid-C18th for "a tall, brawny, masculine, VIRAGO of a woman, one who assumes habits and occupations usually regarded as masculine". (OED) It is generally used pejoratively, such a woman being far removed from the FEMININE ideal of passive, subservient and home-bound (see HOUSEWIFE).

Did the Amazons ever exist? Some scholars, JJ Bachofen, Robert Briffault, Robert Graves and Merlin Stone among them, have suggested that most societies were originally matrilineal, (see MATRIARCHY) and possibly polyandrous before becoming patriarchal and monogamous. Merlin Stone believes that these earlier matriarchal societies, in which a goddess as valiant warrior was worshipped "seem to have been responsible for the numerous reports of female soldiers, later referred to by the classical Greeks as the Amazons. More thoroughly examining the accounts of the esteem the Amazons paid to the female deity, it became evident that women who worshipped a warrior goddess hunted and fought in the lands of Libya, Anatolia, Bulgaria, Greece, Armenia and Russia and were far from the mythical fantasy so many writers of today would have us believe." (*The Paradise Papers*) Whether or not they ever did actually exist, one thing does become clear: the construction of the Amazon myth, and the figurative use of *amazon* at different times in history, cannot be separated from the context of patriarchal dominance.

The myth flourished in ancient Greece, particularly among the Athenians, who stressed the defeat of the Amazons by Theseus whom they revered above all other heroes. Athens at this time was a patriarchy distinguished both by its fascination with female dominance and by its extreme degree of institutionalised female subordination. The Amazon myth, with its reiteration that women did not know how to handle power when they possessed it, reaffirmed dogmatically women's inferior position and provided the Athenians with a justification for their treatment of them. Further justifications can be seen in the folk etymologies invented by the Greeks in explanation of a word for which the derivation was lost. It was variously proposed that *a-mazon* meant breastless, not brought up by the breast, beings with strong breasts or with one breast, suggesting both the unnatural and unfeminine aspects of women who challenged the 'natural' order of things (as dictated by patriarchal society). Another retrospective etymology was *a-maza*, meaning without barley bread, again implying the monstrous nature of female warriors who could not be feminine and capable of providing the basic staple if they took it upon themselves to defend their own culture or land. *Azona*, meaning CHASTITY belt, was another theory. *Amazosas*, meaning opposed to men, was yet another. They all lend weight to the proposition that the Amazon myth can be interpreted as an expression of the unease and tension between the Athenian State and its female members.

The tradition of the seared breast appears to have been a late invention; no vase from classical times portrays an Amazon mutilated in this way, thus making the 'breastless' etymological theory highly unlikely. Robert Graves suggests that the *A* may be emphatic, so the word could mean many breasted, as certain scholars interpret certain statues of Diana of Ephesus. But Graves considers it more likely that the word originates from an Armenian word meaning 'moon women' – again a possible reference to Diana in her moon aspect. He posits that since the priestesses of the moon-godess on the south-eastern shores of the Black Sea bore arms, the accounts of them brought back by travellers became confused with certain Athenian icons depicting half-female half-male ANDROGYNES.

The Athenian use of the Amazon myth was used to confirm the historicity of the patriarchal state – portraying Amazon women as fearsome warriors but ultimately conquerable by a male hero, such as Theseus. The Romans, however, preferred to stress the chaste aspect of the Amazon, adapting the iconography of the fierce fighter to represent *virtus*, meaning strength, power, courage and worth. In *Joan of Arc*, Marina Warner outlines how the work of Italian Renaissance poets reveals a profound metamorphosis of the classical Amazon. She points to "a particular development of significance [which] was their treatment of the warrior MAID as a romantic heroine". When Joan of Arc was first written about, it was principally as an Amazon that she was presented. ("Her name, 'Arc' meaning 'bow', 'arch' and 'curve' places her at the centre of a web of imagery associated with the power of women since antiquity.") But this Amazon was no longer to be feared – except in battle where her aim was true and her character noble. Although Joan of Arc's masculine dress, cropped hair and fighting prowess was much feared and reviled by her enemies, she also remained the ideal feminine. Amazons were interpreted as living like knights, "but their knightliness, like their chastity no longer expresses rejection [of the female mode of life] but invitation within the special context of the love ideal centering on non-fulfillment, which is one of Christianity's most important legacies to European society". Thus Joan of Arc's amazonian likeness had to be softened to be at all acceptable: "her transvestism, her armour, her inviolability, had to seem something that in the final conclusion was offered on the altar of male supremacy".

The Amazon was to remain a figure of bewitchment in European literature for nearly two hundred years. Throughout the C16th, travellers to the Americas, to Ethiopia and to present-day Zimbabwe sighted societies of alluring, untamed – but ultimately tameable – Amazons. As the Spanish conquistador Francesco de Orellana made his way down the great river of South America in 1541 he expected to meet fierce tribes of women armed with bows and arrows. One of his prisoners recounted that his rulers lived without men but in order to propagate their race they raided neighbouring villages to carry off men who were only released when the women had conceived. Any sons were either killed or sent back to their fathers, while daughters remained to be instructed in the arts of war. To those who knew the ancient Greek texts, the story must have seemed very familiar. But far from casting doubt on the highly romantic tales of the conquistadors, this knowledge only served to 'prove' their tales to be true. Such stories gave their name to the great river on which Orellana travelled and to the surrounding lands. Spanish explorers also named what is now the state of California from the name of an island of the same name that appeared in the romance *Las Sergas de Esplandian* by Ordonez de Montalvo, published in 1510. The author had called his fictional island by this name after Califia, a fictional Queen of the Amazons.

By the C17th the image of the fierce, noble, chaste Amazon began to be replaced by a less romantic one. In his study of C17th English drama, Simon Shepherd describes how the image of the amazon at that time was applied to the supposedly sexually frustrated or overly independent woman: "the loading of the name amazon is pejorative; it can indicate aggressive lust, unbridled will, disobedience. On the stage it is frequently used as an insult, applied to women who fight and drink, especially wives who are aggressive and women who refuse traditional submission to men." (*Amazon and Warrior Women. Varieties of Feminism in 17th-Century Drama*)

The dual implications of an Amazon – masculine and therefore unnatural, but strong and therefore worthy of respect – continue to be a part of male erotic fantasy. Of C19th white male racism, the Black feminist bell hooks writes: "the black female was depicted by whites as an amazon because they saw her ability to endure hardships no LADY was supposedly capable of enduring as a sign that she possessed an animalistic sub-human strength". The 'animalistic' in women in misogynist fantasy has always been a bewitching attraction to men, although there was little of the erotic in the use of *amazon* as a scornful epithet to describe the early SUFFRAGISTS of the late C19th. By the mid-C20th, however, the image of the amazon gave way once again to male erotic fantasy; as Marina Warner points out in *Monuments and Maidens*, Wonder Woman is no simple feminist alternative to Superman. This popular American comic strip featured a series of fabulous full-breasted, armed maidens from an Amazon-like colony in outer space, with names such as Diana Prince that echo the ancient myths of androgynes and men-spurning warrior priestesses. Wonder Woman first appeared after World War 2 when women were feared – not as soldiers, perhaps, but clearly as equals when it came to traditionally 'male' jobs in factories and on the land. Such competition was unacceptable; governments and trade unions worked together to dispatch or seduce these modern amazons back to the home where they could revert to an idealised feminine – and non-bellicose – 'norm'. Some, however, stayed put and laid the foundations for the re-emergence of the women's movement in the late 1960s when, once again, women who fought against patriarchal domination earned the abusive epithet of 'amazon'.

Today, some feminists use *amazon* positively to mean a powerful woman, one who fights patriarchal institutions and assumptions. This definition reflects a new etymological theory for the word, proposed by Carol F Justus who has studied myth and syntax in Anatolian Hittite. Noting that *magh-*, one of the hypothesised roots for *amazon*, is very problematic and probably not of Indo-European origin, she suggests: "A non-Indo-European root *mag-*

may be responsible not only for Gothic *magan* meaning 'to have power, be able' . . .but also for Gothic *magus* 'son'. In contrast to the Indo-European word *sunus*, which meant the 'son' in the paternal line, the non-Indo-European *magus* and its relatives refer to the son in the maternal line. These non-Indo-European words suggest the linguistic traces of a pre-patriarchal social organization." (quoted in Kramarae and Treichler, *A Feminist Dictionary*).

Anathema

If any man love not the Lord Jesus Christ, let him be Anathema Maranatha.
1 Corinthians 16:22

In Latin, *anathema* is both an excommunicated person and the curse of excommunication. Its origins lie in a variation of the Greek word for an offering or a thing set up (to the gods), from *ana*, meaning up, and *tithenai*, meaning to set, becoming, in later usage, a thing devoted to evil, or an accursed thing. John Wycliffe (1329–84) translated it as 'cursid' in his English version of the Bible; William Tyndale kept the whole Latin phrase *anathema maranatha* in his 1526 translation, a policy followed by the 1611 King James version. The 1961 translation of the New Testament rendered the verse as: "If anyone does not love the Lord, let him be outcast. *Marana tha* – Come, O Lord!". In Catholic and Calvinist churches, to be anathematised became a more extreme form of denunciation than excommunication because it carried with it an official curse.

In English, *anathema* is used to mean anything accursed or consigned to perdition (since 1526); the formal act of consigning to damnation and, from this sense, the curse of God (since 1619), and subsequently any curse or imprecation (since 1691); since 1581 the word has also been used to mean a thing devoted or consecrated to divine use.

Barbara G Walker suggests that *anathema* derives from *Anath*, one of the names of the mother goddess worshipped by Canaanites, Amorites, Syrians, Egyptians and the early Hebrews. Each year she cast her death-curse – or anathema – on her son–husband Mot, who was the castrated 'sterility' aspect of the fertile Baal. He was sacrificed each year to enable Anath to use his body and blood during the barren winter months to re-fertilise the earth for the spring crops, when she would resurrect him. Anath's death-curse involved telling Mot that he was forsaken by his heavenly father El. Walker claims that "The words attributed Jesus, 'My El, my El, why hast thou forsaken me?' (Mark, 15:34) apparently were copied from the ancient liturgical formula, which became part of the passover ritual at Jerusalem." (*The Woman's Encyclopedia of Myths and Secrets*) Mot was consigned to a holy purpose at the same time as he was cursed to suffer death – thus providing Walker with an explanation for the two, and apparently opposite, meanings of *anathema*.

Androgyne

Originating in the Greek *androgynos*, meaning male and FEMALE into one, from *andro-*, meaning man or male (from a base meaning strong), plus *gyne*, meaning female, *androgyne* entered English in 1651 to mean having both FEMININE and masculine characteristics or nature, a similar meaning to HERMAPHRODITE.

Anile

A man is as old as he's feeling; A woman is as old as she looks.
                                        Mortimer Collins, 1827–76

Anile comes from the Latin word *anus*, meaning old WOMAN. The masculine counterpart is *senile* from *senex*, meaning old man. In English, *senile* is applied to both sexes to mean characteristic of old age, especially showing a loss of mental faculties associated with old age. *Senile*, in a nonmedical context, is used pejoratively of both sexes, reflecting a general discrimination towards the elderly, but *anile* entered English in the mid-C17th with grotesque misogynistic connotations. Dictionary definitions include: "a doddering old woman"; "old womannish"; "imbecile"; "a silly old woman". The term *old man* cannot be applied to both sexes and is generally a term of affection; *old woman*, when applied to a man, is a harsh insult. The disparity between *senile* and *anile* reveals a double standard in which elderliness in women is judged with special severity.

In her study *Old Age*, Simone de Beauvoir chronicles male fear and disgust for old women; "Since, as men see it, a woman's purpose in life is to be an erotic object, when she grows old and ugly she loses the place allotted to her in society: she becomes a *monstrum* that excites revulsion and even dread." The same is not true for a man: "A time will come that will dry yellow and wither your full-blown flower", wrote François Villon in the C15th. "I shall be old, you ugly and without colour." Ageing is perceived differently for men whose wrinkles, seen to be a sign of 'character', indicate emotional strength and maturity and show that he has 'lived' – qualities revered in men rather than women. An awareness of no longer being considered attractive often makes life extremely hard for the elderly: the problem is intensified for women for whom FEMININITY is identified with being young, sexually potent and attractive. "Thus, for most women", writes Susan Sontag, "ageing means a humiliating process of gradual sexual disqualification." (*The Double Standard of Ageing*)

Muriel R Schulz points out that there are not many terms in English for middle-aged or older women, and those which have occurred have taken on unpleasant connotation: "Even a relatively innocuous term like DOWAGER [a dignified elderly lady. 1531] is stigmatized. BELDAM [1581] is worse. Formed by combining the English usage of *dam* 'MOTHER' with *bel* indicating the relationship of a grandparent, it simply meant 'grandmother' in its earliest usage. It was later generalized to refer to any 'woman of advanced age' and, as so frequently happens with words indicating 'old woman', it pejorated to signify 'a loathsome old woman; a HAG'. Hag, itself, originally meant simply 'a WITCH' and was later generalized as a derisive term for 'an ugly old woman', often with the implication of viciousness or maliciousness." She notes that there are few terms for old people of either sex in English, "however, the few terms available to denote old men. . .are less vituperative than are those denoting women". (*The Semantic Derogation of Women*)

Anima

Anima and *animus* probably derive from a proto-Indo-European root which appears in Latin as *anima*, meaning air, spirit, breath, related by common descent to the Greek *anemos*, meaning breath, and in Sanskrit *aniti*, meaning s/he breathes. Robert Graves suggests that the roots of *anima*, or female soul, lie in *an*, meaning heavenly, and *ma*, meaning MOTHER. According to *The Woman's Encyclopedia of Myths and Secrets*, these syllables are found in the names of ancient creation mother-goddesses such as Anath, Anahid, Anna-Nin, and "in Anne, the mythical mother of the VIRGIN Mary, from the Middle-Eastern Goddess Anna, or Hannah, or Di-Ana, mother of Mari". *Ma*, according to the same source, is the: "basic mother-syllable of Indo-European languages, worshipped in itself as the fundamental name of the Goddess"; and it gives as example the names of ancient goddesses such as Matt, Madri, Maia, and Mari.

The concept of the female soul was not alien to ancient religions. Christian philosophy, however, rejected the concept – the Council of Nantes in AD66 decreed that women were "soulless brutes". One reason why alchemists were accused of heresy during the Middle Ages was because of their notion that the world-soul was a female anima.

Webster's defines *anima* as "soul, life; *specif* the passive or animal soul", and as "an individual's true inner self reflecting archetypal ideals of conduct – used especially in contrast with persona in the analytic psychology of Karl Gustav Jung". Jung, himself, used *anima*, and its masculine form, *animus*, to refer to the intuitive and reasoning parts of the mind respectively. The anima was the inner personality which he believed was in communication with the unconscious; the FEMININE principle as present in the male unconscious. In its most basic form, the anima was defined as an inherited collective image of WOMAN, finding its first incarnation in one's MOTHER. The artist's muse, with its feminine creative and inspirational, rather than logical, connotation, is another Jungian representation of the anima.

Aphrodisiac

Aphrodisiac first entered English in the early C18th for a drug or preparation that was believed to induce VENEREAL desire. It derives from *Aphrodite* (meaning foam-born), the name of the Greek goddess of love, who also ruled over birth, life, death, time and fate, reconciling humankind to all of them through her powers of sensual and sexual mysticism. She was born naked from the foam of the sea and came ashore riding on a scallop shell, first on the island of Cytherea. Finding the island too small, she travelled on to Paphos in Cyprus (which was later claimed to be her actual birth-place). Aphrodite was also called Mari ('the sea'). Christians on Cyprus later converted her temple into a sanctuary for the Virgin Mary – who, to this day, is hailed as *Panaghia Aphroditessa* at Paphos, according to Barbara G Walker.

In the mid-C19th, without any scientific empirical foundation, various foods believed to be sexually stimulating began to be called *aphrodisiacs*. Over the years these have included: nuts, truffles, potatoes, mushrooms, tomatoes, the powder of rhinoceros horn and most shell-fish – the last may be an echo of Aphrodite's scallop shell. In the 1980s *aphrodisiac* came to be used figuratively, eg, "Power is the ultimate aphrodisiac." (Henry Kissinger, US Secretary of State 1973–77).

April

From the Latin *aperire*, meaning to open, *April* is the name of the fourth month of the year when the buds open, leaves unfold and the womb of MOTHER nature is said to open with new life. In ancient Greece it was the month dedicated to Aphrodite (also known as *Aprilis* or *Aphrilis*), the VIRGIN/MOTHER/CRONE goddess who ruled birth, life and death (see APHRODISIAC).

The tradition of tricking someone on 1 April, or All Fools' Day, is widespread in Europe (in India it occurs on 31 March at the Holi Festival). This may be a relic of a Roman festival known as the Cerealia, named after the goddess Ceres, which used to be held at the beginning of April. When her daughter, Proserpina, was abducted to the lower world by Pluto, Ceres thought she heard her screams and went in search of the voice. But she was fooled into going in the opposite direction: it was only the echo of Proserpina's screams that she heard. Looking for the 'echo of a scream' proved to be a fool's errand.

August

According to most dictionaries, the month of August was named after Gaius Julius Caesar Octavianus Augustus, the 1st Roman emperor. The Christian Church claimed it was named after St Augustine – a theory somewhat difficult to sustain since the name had been given to the month centuries before the saint was born. Yet another theory is that it was named after the oracular mother–priestess goddess Juno Augusta, and that oracles were first known as *augustae* – a term later applied to male priests and then to emperors. It has been suggested that Gaius Octavianuis took his title from the goddess who was presumed incarnate in his wife Livia Augusta.

Authoress

As some day it may happen that a victim must be found,
I've got a little list – I've got a little list
of society offenders who might well be underground,
And who never would be miss'd – who never would be miss'd
....

And that singular anomaly, the lady novelist
I don't think she'd be miss'd – I'm sure she'd not be miss'd!
Sir William Gilbert (1836–1911), *The Mikado*

Author comes from Middle English *autour*, via Old French from the Latin masculine noun *auctor*, meaning one that gives or increases, from *auctus*, the past participle of *augere*, meaning to increase, make grow or originate. *Augere* probably comes from the Indo-European root *aug-*, meaning to increase, from which *augment* derives. The earliest, now obsolete, use of *author* signified one who begets, a father or ancestor (1300). Three other obsolete or archaic uses from the same century were: he who authorises or instigates, he who gives rise to or causes an action and a circumstance, state or condition of things. *Author* in the sense of one who sets forth written statements, ie, the composer or writer of a treatise or book, was standard English by the late C14th. *Authoress* entered English in the late C15th to mean a FEMALE originator or causer, a female leader, a MOTHER or creator, or a female literary composer. Today, *authoress* is usually replaced by *author*.

It was not always so. Fowler's (1926 edition) castigated women writers who refused to accept the description or title of *authoress*: "Their view is that the female author is to raise herself to the level of the male author by asserting her right to his name." The 1965 edition of Fowler's had a change of heart: "*Authoress* is a word that has always been disliked by authoresses themselves, perhaps on the ground that sex is irrelevant to art and that the word implies disparagement of women's literary abilities. They had good reason to be sensitive: as recently as 1885 a Savoy audience was invited to applaud the sentiment that 'that singular anomaly the LADY novelist' would never be missed. When the OED was published the authoresses seemed to be getting their way for the opinion given there is that *authoress* 'is now only used when sex is purposely emphasised; otherwise in all senses, and especially in the last [to wit, a female literary composer] *author* is now used of both sexes.' But *authoress* is dying slowly. Seventy years after the OED's pronouncement a book reviewer still finds it natural to say *The authoress does not much discuss the quality of acting in Garrick's theatre,* and a High Court judge to say *The wife was in several respects the authoress of her own wrong because of her nagging.*" (See NAG.)

There are signs that words with the FEMININE *-ess* suffix are disappearing from the English language or, like *actress* and *governess* have acquired connotations or meanings which indicate substantially less potency than the equivalent male terms.

Babble

In 1362 *babble* entered English, meaning to make imperfect attempts at speech like a child, and to utter inarticulate or indistinct sounds. It was probably formed on the repetition of the syllable *ba, ba* – one of the earliest sounds made by infants. There is no direct etymological connexion with the biblical town of Babel, a city in Shinar, where, according to Genesis, the building of a tower was interrupted by the confusion, or babble, of tongues, although it is likely that this affected the sense development of the word. In the C15th the meaning of *babble* extended to mean idle, foolish or unreasonable talk. A *babbler* was a chatterer (SEE CHATTER), a prater or a GOSSIP and a teller of secrets. Although *babble* is used of both sexes or mixed crowds, the talk of women is often dismissed as babble. It is a subtle way of suggesting not only that the subject matter of women's conversations is TRIVIA but also of infantilising women by implying that they are only capable of BABY-talk.

Babe/Baby

[Women suffer from]. . .writers of all descriptions, from the deep thinking philosopher to the man of. . .gallantry, who, by the bye, sometimes distinguishes himself by qualities which are not greatly superior to those he despises in women. Nor can I better illustrate the truth of this observation than by. . .the polite and gallant Chesterfield. 'Women', says his lordship, 'are only children of a larger growth. . . A man of sense only trifles with them, plays with them, honours and flatters them, as he does an engaging child; but he neither consults them, nor trusts them in serious matters.'
Catherine MacCaulay (1731–1791), Letters on Education

Although *baby*, or *babe*, are often terms of endearment used of a loved one of either sex, from the late 1890s, *babe*, later *baby*, have been slang terms for a young woman or a woman of any age (often referred to as a GIRL), specifically one considered by a male to be sexually attractive and/or available. The terms have also denoted a high-spirited or 'sporty' woman – which implies she is morally 'LOOSE'. Use of the terms carries both censure and ridicule as they reduce a woman to the state of childishness. The OED lists the following unflattering and infantilising senses and connotations of both *babe* and *baby*: DOLL, puppet, foolish or childish, innocent, little, tiny (as in mind), babyish, silly, ignorant, trusting, guileless, immature.

Should anyone be in any doubt about the negative patriarchal connotations, the *Dictionary of American Slang* states that *baby* is used of "Anything which. . . is the object of one's special attention, interest or masculine admiration or affection; anything that gives a man pride or a feeling of power to possess, create or build; that with which familiarity or association gives a man a feeling .of masculine pride or power." The ultimate in infantalising terms for a woman considered to be sexually attractive – and therefore available to become the property of a man – is *baby doll*.

Bachelor

The origins and sense development of *bachelor* are uncertain, but the Old French *bacheler* may be connected with the Late Latin *baccalaris*, meaning a division of land, a term which was applied to both female and male tenants in the C8th. From an early sense of an inexperienced person or novice, the term *Knight-bachelor* was applied to a knight of the lowest rank, one who would probably have been unmarried. This may explain how, by the C14th, *bachelor* denoted an unmarried man.

SPINSTER is no simple female equivalent, since it denotes not only an unmarried woman but also one regarded as being beyond the age of marriage, or unmarriageable for whatever reason. In the C17th *spinster* pejorated, becoming a euphemism for a MISTRESS or PROSTITUTE, which probably explains why *bachelor* was (briefly) applied to a single woman at around the same time. In the C20th, *bachelor*, which carries positive connotations of independence, was resurrected to be used of women, especially in the USA. *Bachelor-girl*, (despite the unflattering infantilising connotations of GIRL) is often used in preference to *spinster*, which acquired the negative connotations of sexless, frustrated, unemployed, unpropertied, unendowed, uneducated and economically dependent on others. Although when applied to men *bachelor* can imply a positive image of sexual licence, the term seems to have avoided this connotation when used of a woman, for whom sexual licence is seldom acceptable.

Bad

The Oxford Dictionary of Etymology traces the origins of *bad* to the Old English word *baeddel*, meaning HERMAPHRODITE – a person combining characteristics of both sexes. Hermaphroditos, the child of Aphrodite (see APHRODISIAC, APRIL) and Hermes, united both parental sexual characteristics equally, as well as combining their names, but he was considered basically male with FEMININE tendencies. Hence the word *baedling*, or *badling*, used from the C10th to C17th, meaning originally a sodomite and later an

EFFEMINATE fellow or womanish man. The FEMALE equivalent would presumably have been the Greek mythological bearded woman, or ANDROGYNE, from *andros*, meaning man, and *gyne* meaning woman, but this word is also defined as an effeminate or womanish man.

By association, Old English *badde* originally meant a male homosexual. By the C13th it had come to mean something or someone of defective quality or worth, of whom one does not think much, or anything, or who was below par, worthless, wretched, miserable. In the C17th it was also used to mean evil. Today, *bad* has many shades of meaning including unfavourable, decayed, disobedient, disastrous, etc. The examples of usage given by Webster's shows that when used of men, it is more likely to mean having an evil, depraved or vicious character ('a thoroughly bad man'), but when used of a woman, it tends to imply that she is sexually immoral ('GOSSIP had it that she was a bad GIRL').

In C20th Black slang many words have come to mean the exact opposite (antonym) of their usual meaning, without any pejorative implications. Thus what was once described as 'hot', connoting good, swinging or fashionable is called 'cool'. Similarly, something wonderful or good is described as 'mean' or 'bad'. Hence the title *Bad* for superstar Michael Jackson's smash-hit album and video in 1987. These antonyms usually also contain the suggestion that the object being praised will not be valued by conventional white society.

Bag

Early Middle English *bagge*, meaning bag, pack or bundle, probably derives from Old Norse *baggi*, and may be related to the medieval Latin *baga*, meaning chest or sack. There is a possible etymological connexion with the Old English words *belg*, *baelg* and *balig*, from which *belly* and *bellows* derive. In the C17th it acquired the sense of an udder or BREASTS, eg: "Those wicked HAGS. . .whose writhled bags foul fiends oft suck." (Henry More, 1642) In the 1890s it denoted a middle-aged or elderly SLATTERN, later a slatternly or part-time PROSTITUTE. In the C20th *bag* ameliorated although it is still used derisively to refer to an unattractive woman (or 'GIRL', as most dictionaries persist in calling young women), or an ugly or bad-tempered woman. Other definitions include 'old SHREW' and 'good-for-nothing woman'. *Old bag* is a term used by a man in Britain to refer to his WIFE. This present day usage, most dictionaries assure us, is jocular or humorous. The objects of this derision may be forgiven if they fail to see the joke.

Bag is one of several words in the English language used to suggest a woman is an empty container or VESSEL – one presumed available to be 'filled up' by a man.

Baggage

Baggage, meaning portable property, entered English in the C15th; it was probably formed on the French *baguer*, meaning to tie up, or *bague*, meaning bundle or pack. At first, it was used to denote the Latin word *impedimenta*, from the Latin *impedere*, meaning to impede. In the C16th *baggage*, in one sense, degenerated to mean rubbish, refuse, purulent or corrupt matter, and was contemptuously used by Protestants to refer to the rites and accessories of Roman Catholic worship. Hence its figurative use for dregs and riff-raff applied to a worthless or vile fellow. In this sense it became female-specific and was used to denote a saucy young woman or, more pejoratively, a morally worthless woman or a STRUMPET. In the C17th the sense of an army's portable property combined with that of a morally disreputable woman, causing the word to be used to denote a camp follower – in other words a PROSTITUTE who travelled with the army. The phrase *heavy baggage* came to mean women and children – suggesting that they were regarded as both impediments and the personal property of men. Since the late C17th *baggage* has been "Used familiarly or playfully of any young woman, especially in conjunction with artful, cunning, sly, pert, saucy, silly, etc (cf. WENCH, MINX, HUSSY, gipsy, rogue etc)". (OED) By the beginning of the C18th *baggage* began to show signs of amelioration; it was more frequently used in a playful sense of a flirty young woman, but, as Webster's points out, *baggage* usually implies "gentle criticism or a somewhat patronizing attitude".

Ball

Many women object to most slang terms for sexual intercourse: to *fuck*, *screw*, *lay*, *poke*, *shaft*, etc, all suggest that sex is something that a man does *to* a woman while she passively has it done to her. They may like to consider one theory as to the origins of the chiefly US slang term *to ball*, which has nothing to do with testicles as is generally thought and is put forward by some dictionaries. The word in this sense comes via the French *bal*, from the Latin *ballare*, meaning to dance.

Balls, a slang term for courage or 'guts', is a metaphoric reference to the male genital organs. Courage in a woman is assumed to be rare, remarkable and no part of her FEMININE nature. It is clearly an absurd and pejorative term when used of a woman, eg: "Give a woman a job and she grows balls." (Jack Gelber)

Banshee

The OED defines *banshee* as a "supernatural being supposed by the peasantry of Ireland and the Scottish Highlands to wail under the windows of a house where one of the inmates is about to die". The word comes from the Old Irish *ben side*, meaning female or woman of the fairies or elves. The first syllable is akin to the Greek *gyne*, meaning WOMAN, the last is the genitive of *sid*, meaning fairy abode.

In Irish mythology the woman of the fairies was identified with Macha, Queen of the Phantoms, the CRONE aspect of Morrigan's trinity (the others being the VIRGIN Ana and the MOTHER Badb) who summoned her children to death. To some she came full of horror; to others she gave a soft low chant (see ENCHANT), bringing notice of death tenderly to reassure the one destined to die and comfort the relatives – a welcome rather than a warning.

In the USA in the 1970s the wail of a police car SIREN became known as a banshee.

Bat

The 1811 edition of *Dictionary of the Vulgar Tongue* defined *bat* as "a low WHORE: so called from moving out like bats in the dusk of the evening". In the C20th the word lost its sexual connotations but remained a pejorative term for a woman; it is a generalised expression of abuse – used particularly of the mothers-in-law of husbands rather than of wives. In the 1960s *bat* as an epithet for a woman was banned on US television.

Battle-Axe

In the C14th *battle-axe* denoted a broad axe used as a weapon of war. In the C19th the term began to be used for a quarrelsome domineering WOMAN. Although no dictionary makes it explicit, it is assumed that such a woman is one who quarrels with, and dominates, men. The *Dictionary of American Slang* is lyrical in its definition of *battle-axe*: "an old, or elderly woman who is resentful and vociferous, thoroughly unpleasant, usually arrogant and no beauty".

After the re-emergence of the woman's movement in the late 1960s, feminists understood the term to be: "One of the American male's favorite put-down words for the strong, fist-shaking, foot-stomping, rights-demanding woman." (Barbara Miles, 'Amazons and Battle Axes: Herstory', in *Everywoman*. 1971) In 1983 the term was redefined in the British feminist magazine *Spare Rib* as "Aggressive woman, HARRIDAN, VIRAGO, AMAZON, LESBIAN — all those women who don't comply with conventional ideas of femininity."

Feminists have not successfully rehabilitated the word: like BAT, it is still a favourite term of abuse, often employed by a husband to refer to his mother-in-law.

Bawd

Bawd is first found in *Piers Plowman* (1362). It originally denoted someone of either sex who was a pander or go-between in a sexual intrigue. By the C17th bawd had become female-specific and pejorated to denote a procuress or female BROTHEL keeper. Today it is occasionally used to mean a female PROSTITUTE.

The origin of *bawd* is uncertain. It may be an abbreviation of *bawdstrot* — possibly formed on the Old French *baud*, meaning GAY and lively, and the Anglo-Norman *trote*, meaning old. woman (see ANILE) or HAG. Another suggestion is that the *-strot* was formed on *strutt*, meaning strut, giving *bawdstrot*, denoting one with an inviting walk. It is also possible that *bawd* became confused with the now obsolete *baude* (lively) which, when applied to women, acquired the sense of a morally promiscuous woman. *The Dictionary of English Etymology* states it is unlikely that *bawd* originated in *ribaude* (later *ribald*), meaning scurrilous, obscene or irreverent, and suggests that the connection with *bawd*, a C16th word meaning dirty or filthy, is undetermined. Another etymological theory suggests that the word may be compared with the Welsh *bawaidd*, meaning dirty, from *baw*, meaning mud; the French *boue*, meaning mud, possibly coming from the same origin.

Bawd is an example of the many words in the English language which began as non-insulting when applied to both sexes, but which became associated with women and acquired negative sexual connotations. It eventually came to be an abusive term meaning PROSTITUTE. Other such examples are TART, HARLOT, WHORE, WENCH, etc. Muriel R Schulz believes that this came about through a systematic process of language change which she calls 'semantic derogation'. She cites Stephen Ullmann who suggested three possible reasons for the degeneration of terms designating women: association with a contaminating concept, euphemism and prejudice. Of these, Schulz suspects "prejudice is the most likely source for pejorative terms for women. They illustrate. . .'the labels of primary potency' with which an in-group stereotypes an out-group. Certain symbols, identifying a member of an out-group, blind the prejudiced speaker to any qualities the minority person may have which contradict the stereotype. . . . And what is the source or cause of the prejudice? Several writers have suggested that it is fear, based on the supposed threat to the power of the male. . .fear of sexual inadequacy. A woman knows the truth about his potency; he cannot lie to her. Yet her own performance remains a secret, a mystery to him. Thus, man's fear of woman is basically sexual, which is perhaps the reason why so many of the derogatory terms for women take on sexual connotations." (*The Semantic Deragation of Women*) In the end it is uncertain whether words like *bawd* degenerate because they are associated with women or whether they become female-specific because they have acquired negative sexual connotations.

Beast

Of all the wild beasts on land or sea, the wildest is woman.

Menander, *Supposititio*, c300 BC

Originating in the Latin *bestia*, via the Old French *beste*, when *beast* first entered English it specifically included all humankind and can be found in this sense in .Chaucer (c1374). (In Old English *deor* – from which *deer* derives – was the general word for animal.) By the C16th *beast* was applied to the lower animals as distinct from humankind. Since the C17th *beast* has been used to denote the animal nature in a human and employed opprobriously to express disgust or aversion. In the C20th it became a US slang term for a young woman, especially one considered (presumably by males) to be coarse and unattractive. It is one of a long list of words used pejoratively of women who arouse male disgust or fear because they do not conform to a concept of the FEMININE ideal.

Beaver

The *Dictionary of American Slang* states that in the C20th *beaver* became a taboo word for the female genitals, "so-called because the triangle of pubic hair resembles the beaver (slang for a beard since c1850)". Another theory maintains that the "dark and hairy shape of this part of the body looks from above much like a beaver when swimming". (*The Slanguage of Sex*) Of the many euphemisms for the VAGINA, many of which connote male repulsion or fear, eg, *bite*, *ditch*, GASH, *gutter*, *nasty*, *snapper*, *stink*, etc, *beaver* seems to be fairly innocuous – although not quite as positive as CHERRY, *golden doughnut*, honeypot, etc. But it is just possible that the word was influenced by another slang use of *beaver* to mean one who works diligently (since the C19th). If so, a woman's genitalia are reduced to an organ for constant male use.

Two 'beaver'-compound terms reflect male sexual aggression: a *split beaver* is a vagina openly displayed in PORNOGRAPHIC pictures; a *beaver-shooter* is "a Peeping Tom. . .I've seen guys chin themselves on transoms, drill holes in doors, even shove a mirror under a door". (Jim Benton, *Ball Four*, 1970)

Beget

The OED states that the verb *to beget*, meaning to procreate or generate, is usually said of the father and only rarely of the MOTHER. Early examples of usage, show that originally the word did not exclude women: "Thus was Maerlin bigeten and iboren of his modr" (1205); "Begetare, as a fathyr, genitor. . .as a mothere, genetrix" (1440). Webster's gives the following early, now obsolete, definitions: "to make (a woman) pregnant", and "to give birth to, breed," with the example: "excellent COWS do not beget only excellent daughters". But it reveals that the word is now lost to women, defining it as "to procreate as the father: sire" (see SURNAME). Casey Miller and Kate Swift point out: "The English word fails to convey here [in King James Version of Deuteronomy] the full sense of the original Hebrew verb, which means either the begetting of a father or the bearing of a mother." (*Words and Women*)

Beldam See ANILE

Belladonna

Another name for the highly poisonous *Atropa belladonna* plant is deadly nightshade. In Italian, from which the term is adopted, *belladonna* literally means a beautiful or fair LADY. It gets its name, not from any fears or fantasies about the toxic or intoxicating propensities of women, but either because "The Italian ladies make a cosmetic from the juice" (1757), or, more dramatically, because it was employed by an infamous Italian poisoner named Leucota to murder beautiful women.

Berk

Berk, or *burk* is C20th British slang for a foolish, incompetent or irritating (usually male) person. This male specificity is interesting since the word derives from rhyming slang *Berkshire Hunt*, or *Berkeley Hunt*, meaning CUNT (absurdly referred to as 'the unprintable' in the 1960 *Dictionary of Rhyming Slang*). Other examples of rhyming slang for *cunt* are: *Grumble, Gasp* (or *Groan*) and *Grunt*; *Joe Hunt*; *Sharp and Blunt*. In all cases these slang terms denote both a woman's genitalia and a woman as a whole, thus reducing her to a mere part of her anatomy.

Besom

A besom, or broom made of twigs (originally often from the Broom, or *Genista* plant) tied around a stick, has long been popularly associated with WITCHES. Well before the witchhunts of the C14th–C17th, the besom figured in pagan rituals of marriage and birth and was the symbol of Hecate, Greek goddess of childbirth and marriage, labelled 'Queen of the Witches' in medieval Europe. *Besom-rider* was a C17th synonym for a witch, from the popular notion that witches used their broomsticks to fly. Christian Inquisitors subjected the besoms of alleged witches to close scrutiny. A French description of how witches flew reveals that Hecate's besom was put to very personal use: "with an ointment which the devil had delivered to them they anointed a wooden rod. . .and their palms and their whole hands likewise; and so, putting this small rod between their legs, straightway they flew where they wished to be. . .and the devil guided them". Female masturbation was condemned by the medieval Church as an abhorrent and unnatural practice.

In the C19th *broom* became a vulgar expression for the female pudenda, and the role of the male in the sexual pleasuring of the female was re-established in the coarse use of *broomstick* for the penis.

The pagan wedding ritual of jumping over a besom survived into Christian times, especially among the medieval peasantry; when the priesthood took over all nuptial rites, unions said to be *by the broom* were those not sanctified. Brooms, or besoms, became associated with illicit sex outside marriage hence the old English saying "If a GIRL strides over a broom-handle, she will be a MOTHER before she is a WIFE". The C18th expression *to hang out the besom* meant for a man to have a sexual encounter when his wife was away – it was adopted from the French phrase *rotir le balai* ('to roast the besom'), meaning to go on the razzle. From 1700 to the early 1800s *to jump the besom* meant to go through a mock marriage and live as common-law husband and wife. The same broom-jumping ritual was a feature of the churchless marriages of Black slaves, forbidden to wed by their white slave-owners in the USA in the C19th. In the C20th, *to jump the broomstick* is a euphemism for extra-marital sex, a woman who gives birth to a bastard child is said to have *jumped over the besom* and *living over the brush* is used of an unmarried cohabiting heterosexual couple in northern England.

In northern English and Scottish dialect since the early C19th *besom* has been a derogatory term for a woman, especially a woman considered BLOWZY, slovenly, shrewish (see SHREW) or morally unacceptable, ie, LOOSE. It is likely that this sense was influenced not only by the association with witches and illicit sex but also by connotations of working women, who use brooms to clean the houses of the wealthy. The same applies to the word SCRUBBER. This is a fairly common process in the English language. MOLLY and DOLLY, for example, were firstly pet names which became popular among the serving or peasant classes as personal names, and which subsequently degenerated, acquiring connotations of unruliness, sluttishness (see SLUT) and sexual immorality. An upper or middle class WOMAN or LADY, was, of course, always scrupulously tidy in her personal appearance as well as beyond moral reproach.

Bevy

In the C15th *bevy* originally denoted a company or group of MAIDENS or LADIES, roes, quails or larks. It subsequently came to mean company. Its derivation and early history is unknown but it has similarities in the Old French *bevee*, or *buvee*, meaning drink or drinking, and the Italian *bevuta*, meaning a drinking bout. In Middle English a *bever* was a drink or a time for drinking, from the Latin *bibere*, to drink. It has been suggested that *bevy* may have developed from the sense of a drinking party to a party or company in general. When applied to a group of women, *bevy* has an aura of disparagement about it. This may be because of a lingering association with drinking which has never been acceptable as a female pastime. When Milton wrote of "A Beavie of fair women, richly GAY" (1667) he used the word 'WOMAN' as distinct from a refined or 'feminine' LADY, as in 'woman of pleasure', a euphemism for a PROSTITUTE. In the C20th the situation has been reversed and, in some circumstances, lady is used to denote a woman of low character. It is not clear from the major dictionaries which all refer to 'lady' in their definitions of *bevy* whether they are making this distinction or not.

None of this provides any explanation why female humans, female deer and quails and larks of both sexes should all share the same umbrella term (in the C17th *quail* was used figuratively for a COURTESAN: "An allusion to the supposed amorous disposition of the bird" – OED), but the association of young, unmarried women (*maiden* in the sense of VIRGIN) with game – ie, animals to be hunted, killed and eaten – has not endeared the use of *bevy* to women.

Biddy

Biddy is the diminutive of *Bridget*, a female personal name which, like many women's names – eg, *Kitty*, DOLLY, *Jill*, *Polly* and others – became a general pet name, or term of endearment for a woman and then degenerated to mean a PROSTITUTE. There are no examples of a male personal name passing through the same process of pejoration – although in the USA *John* (ie,

Doe) became a prostitutes' slang term in the C20th for a male client (and *JANE* became slang for a prostitute).

An especially popular name in Ireland, Brigit, Brigid or Bridgit was originally an early triple goddess of the Celtic Irish, who appeared as Brigantia in England and BRIDE in Scotland. She is one of the clearest examples of the survival of an early pagan goddess into Christian times: "So entrenched was the devotion of the Irish to their Goddess that the Christians 'converted' her along with her people, calling Brigit the human daughter of a Druid and claiming she was baptized by the great patriarch St Patrick himself. Brigit took religious vows, the story went, and was canonized after her death by her adoptive church, which then allowed the 'saint' a curious list of attributes [goldsmithery, blacksmithery, poetry, inspiration, healing, medicine, whistling and keening], coincidentally identical to those of the earlier goddess." (Patricia Monaghan, *Women In Myth and Legend*)

The 1811 edition of the *Dictionary of the Vulgar Tongue* defines *biddy* and CHICK-a-*biddy* as a chicken and, figuratively, a young PROSTITUTE. It is possible that in this sense *biddy* developed from *birdy*. During the C19th the word ameliorated, losing its sexual connotations to become used of a hired GIRL or MAID-servant, and, especially, an elderly housemaid or cleaning woman in a dormitory. This may be connected to the times of famine in the C19th, when Irish women were forced to emigrate and flooded the cheap-labour market in more prosperous countries. *Biddy* is still used in the USA, chiefly of an Irish maid-servant.

Webster's defines *biddy* as a disparaging epithet for "an elderly and often gossipy [see GOSSIP] or dissolute woman". This derogatory use may have been influenced by racist attitudes towards the Irish and also perhaps because the low pay of domestic workers meant that many became part-time prostitutes as a means of economic survival.

Other definitions of *biddy* give "interfering" and "busy-body": this may explain the US and Australian slang use of the word for a female schoolteacher. The education and relatively high status of female teachers often resulted in their getting involved in family and local politics. But whereas this would usually be valued in male teachers, in female ones it was more likely to be resented.

Bint

Bint is British–English slang for a woman or girl adopted directly from the Arabic. Among British soldiers in Egypt in the late C19th it was the term used for PROSTITUTE. Such women were called *saida bint*, literally "a 'good-day!' daughter". It has ameliorated slightly although it can still contain connotations of immorality.

Bird

In 1880, *bird* began to be used as a slang term, chiefly in the UK, for a young woman, often referred to as a GIRL. In the 1890s it became a military term of endearment for a female sweetheart. Like many female terms of endearment it degenerated to mean a PROSTITUTE (1900). *Bird* subsequently ameliorated slightly in the UK: it was a word very much in vogue in England during what became called 'the swinging '60s' for a young woman who epitomised the sexually liberated times when contraception and abortion became more easily available.

In the USA, a *birdcage* is slang for a BROTHEL and also Black slang for an experienced, tough, female prostitute. When applied to a male, perhaps because it has become so identified with women, *bird* has somewhat patronising connotations implying a man who is a bit peculiar, inconsequential or EFFEMINATE.

Etymological speculation suggests that the origins of *bird* in this sense have nothing to do with the feathered flying animals. In the C13th *burde* was a poetic word for WOMAN or LADY, probably originally an embroideress. *Burde* later became used chiefly of a young woman or MAIDEN (ie, VIRGIN). It corresponds with the masculine *berne* which, before 1400, meant a warrior, hero or man of valour, and later became used poetically for a man.

Burde has been variously identified with both bird and BRIDE. The Old English adjective *byrde*, meaning wealthy lady, or perhaps well-born, is phonetically identical and these senses make it a suitable female equivalent for *berne*. The identification with Old English *bryd* makes no phonetic sense, but many etymologists consider it to be a possible connexion since BRIDE may derive from the root *bru*, meaning to cook, brew, or make broth – the traditional duty of a young woman or daughter-in-law in the primitive family.

Whatever its actual origins it seems likely that in the C19th *bird* was understood to be a figurative use of the feathered animal – and it may well have developed independently from early standard English.

Columbine (from Latin *columba*, meaning dove), *quail*, BEVY, CHICKEN, CHICK, HEN, BIDDY, FLAPPER, *sea-gull*, as well as *bird* itself, are all examples of 'bird'-words which originated as metaphors for young women, used as terms of endearment, and which later pejorated to become abusive or disparaging epithets. Muriel R Schulz notes: "If the derogation of terms denoting women marks out an area of our culture found contemptible by men, the terms they use as endearments should tell us who or what they esteem. Strangely enough, in English the endearments men use for women have been just as susceptible to pejoration as have the terms identifying the supposedly beloved object itself."

With connotations of unintelligence (*bird-brained*) and personal property (the proverb "a bird in the hand is worth two in the bush") it is not a term which has endeared itself greatly to women who value themselves and their gender.

Bit

In the mid-C19th *bit* became a colloquial term for a young woman or GIRL, especially one regarded sexually. Like PIECE, it is an example of how the whole woman is frequently indicated by just a small part. Two other senses of *bit* demonstrate just how disparaging a term it is: Samuel Johnson defined it as "as much meat as is put into the mouth at once" (1755); and the OED gives "something small or unimportant of its kind". Since the 1850s women have been called 'bits of' the following: *black velvet*, *crumb*, CUNT, *ebony*, FLUFF, *grease*, *jam*, *muslin*, MUTTON, *raspberry*, SKIRT, *soap*, STUFF, *tripe*, *crackling*, and *spare* (see RIB). Almost all were, or, in some cases, still are, used derogatorily and with negative sexual connotations – *a bit of cunt, fluff, jam, muslin, mutton,* and *stuff* have all denoted a PROSTITUTE or a sexually available woman. According to *The Penguin Dictionary of Historical Slang*, the following 'bits ofaf04' were not derogatory: *crumb*, denoting a pretty plump young woman, and, almost unbelievably, *grease*, which in 1909 was Anglo-Indian military slang for a stout, smiling Hindu woman. If these must be considered affectionate terms rather than derogatory, it has to be assumed that the opprobrium (and racism in the case of *bit of grease*) was unconscious.

There exist only three examples of phrases employing *bit* for men: a *bit of red* was a soldier (late C18th–C19th); in the early C19th a *bit of stuff* was used of an over-dressed man and a *bit of haw-haw* of a fop (see EFFEMINATE). Admittedly, none are particularly flattering, but none are as derogatory as those used of women. These terms are all now obsolete. Several 'bit'-terms continue to be applied to women especially in British English.

That the use of *a bit* is very largely female-specific, and a term which implies the male fetishisation of woman as a sexual part-object, is made clear by the phrase *to have a bit* which, since the late C19th, has meant to copulate with a woman. Likewise, a *bit of black velvet* meant not simply a Black woman but was also a military term for coitus with a Black woman. A *bit on the side*, once a gender-specific term meaning sexual intercourse with a woman who was not the man's wife, has now been adopted by women since the 1960s for their own extra-marital dalliances.

Bitch

A woman is but an animal, and an animal not of the highest order.
Edmund Burke (1729–97)

Old English *bicce*, meaning a female dog, first appeared c1000. By the early C15th it had become standard English as a term used opprobriously of a woman, strictly one considered to be lewd or sensual. At this time it was also applied to men, but in this case, according to the OED, it was "less opprobrious and somewhat whimsical – like the modern use of 'dog' ". Towards the middle of the C16th, influenced by the sense of lewdness, *bitchery* was used to denote harlotry (see HARLOT) and in 1675 the verb *to bitch* meant both to call any one 'bitch' and to frequent the company of lewd women. Both these last two senses were obsolete by the early C18th and Samuel Johnson's rather mild definition of *bitch* in 1755 as a term of reproach for a woman – it was no longer applied to men – might suggest that the term had ameliorated. But the 1811 edition of the *Dictionary of the Vulgar Tongue* reveals the extent to which the word had actually derogated: "A she dog, or doggess; the most offensive appellation that can be given to an English woman, even more provoking than that of WHORE, as may be gathered from the regular Billin[g]sgate or St Giles answer – 'I may be a whore, but can't be a bitch.' " (*Billingsgate* and *St Giles* were euphemisms for the abusive language of working women, the language of a FISHWIFE.) And yet in the same dictionary, the phrase *to stand bitch* is less pejorative as it is defined as "to make tea or do the honours of the tea-table, performing a female part". It is impossible to gauge whether the compiler of this dictionary was being ironic, or attempting to redress the balance, when he added to this definition: "bitch there standing for woman, species for genius". This sense was obsolete by the early C19th but the association with female social gatherings may have influenced the C19th – present-day slang uses of *bitch* to mean complaint or grumbling and a malicious, spiteful and domineering woman (see SHREW).

Today *bitch* does not seem to have lost its early associations of lewdness. In *Words and Women* Casey Miller and Kate Swift cite a 1972 sex discrimination case brought by a New England woman which revolved around "whether the word 'bitch' used by a male in reference to a woman carries any inference of bias or prejudice against women". The woman's counsel argued that a bitch is a female dog which, when in heat, actively seeks insemination; judged by the cultural standards of the time, such a dog is considered 'lewd' – one of the meanings of *bitch* when applied to women. During gestation and immediately after giving birth, continued counsel, a female dog develops a behaviour pattern which by prevailing human standards may be said to be spiteful, malicious, unpleasant and selfish, to the point of stopping at nothing to achieve her aim. *Bitch* conveys the same connotative meanings when used of a woman as it does when used of a female dog, and in using the word a speaker "betrays a preconceived judgement that a woman's behaviour is directed by her reproductive function; it also repudiates her for want of docility to the male". Therefore use of bitch "does manifest prejudice and a discriminatory attitude towards women as a group and. . .conversely, betrays prejudice toward the woman of whom it is said because of her sex." The woman won her case.

In 1970 a US FEMINIST tract, *The Bitch Manifesto*, attempted to rehabilitate the word, claiming that it is used to put down 'uppity' women who refuse to submit to male domination. They argued that "John may think Mary is a bitch because she is aggressive but since he would praise the same quality in James, his use of bitch is in fact a compliment". (Miller and Swift) This sort of linguistic reform ignores the intention of the speaker: when John calls Mary a bitch it is most definitely not a compliment. Bitchiness is widely regarded as a negative FEMININE trait and a sign of effeminacy (see EFFEMINATE) in any male.

Although *bitch* no longer means a harlot there are few signs of any further amelioration. The US linguist Alleen Pace Nilsen points out that *bitch* "has taken on such negative connotations – children are taught it is a swear word – that in every day American English, speakers are hesitant to call a female dog a bitch. Most of us feel that we would be insulting the dog."

Bloomer

I'll be a Bloomer
Their husbands they will wop
And squander all their riches
Make them nurse the kids
And wash their shirts and breeches.

Popular broadsheet, 1850

Today, bloomers are women's baggy knickers or underpants that are gathered together just above the knee. They owe their name to Amelia Jenks Bloomer (1818–94), the American editor of *The Lily*, a woman's suffrage and temperance newspaper (see SUFFRAGETTE). The 'bloomer costume' was designed by Elizabeth Smith Miller, cousin of Elizabeth Cady Stanton, one of the founders of the C19th women's movement in the USA. Bloomers initially consisted of an all-in-one jacket, skirt and Turkish-style trousers gathered together at the ankles, first worn by Amelia Bloomer as part of the 'rational dress' campaign which was supported by women's-rights campaigners at the time.

By 1857 the word *bloomerism* reflected the prevailing hilarity about women's-rights campaigners. *Bloomer* was a term of ridicule for womanists (as FEMINISTS were then called), eg: "She then burst out crying, which was an unfair advantage the bloomer took over Reginald." (Charles Reade, *The course of true love never did run smooth*, 1857) The women were soon forced to abandon their bloomers as they realised that they brought ridicule to the whole of the women's movement.

The advent of cycling in the 1890s, however, caused bloomers, which by then had lost the jacket and skirt, to be readopted – although the campaign for female suffrage, with which they once had been so closely connected, still had a good few more years to run.

Blowzy

Blowze, originally meaning a beggar's TRULL or a WENCH, entered English in the C16th, coming to mean, later that century, "A fat, red-faced, bloted wench, or one whose head is dressed like a SLATTERN" (Nathan Bailey, *A Universal Etymological English Dictionary*, 1791). *Blowzy* appeared in the C18th to denote having a bloated face, of red or coarse complexion (1778) or having dishevelled, slatternly dress or hair (1770), being occasionally applied to men.

Etymologists are uncertain about the origins of *blowzy*. It may come from various Dutch and Low German words with the sense of red or flushed, eg: "Thinking herself too ruddy and blowzy, it was her custom to bleed herself three or four times". (Madeleine d'Arblay. 1778) A red face on a woman has always been considered an indication that she has dubious moral standards. Chaucer's satirical portrait of the Wife of Bath is an early example:

Bold was hir face, and fair, and reed of hewe,
She was a worthy woman al hir lyve,
Housbondes at chirche-dore she hadde fyve,
Withouten other companye in youthe,
But thereof nedeth nat to speke as nouthe.

Another theory is that the development of *blowzy* was influenced by *blow*, in the sense of a windswept appearance, eg. "Long his beard and blouzy hair". (Thomas Erskine, 1770) Other senses of *blow* which may have affected *blowzy* or *blowze* include: a harlot (early C19th); a breath of fresh air or a considerable exposure to wind, as in the phrase 'to get a blow' (C19th–C20th); and in the C20th, from a male standpoint, sexual intercourse. *Blow-job* is C20th slang for fellatio.

In some senses *blow* may also have been influenced by *blowen*, which is defined in the 1811 edition of the *Dictionary of the Vulgar Tongue* as "A MISTRESS or WHORE of a gentleman of the scamp [highway man]." It gives as an example of use "The blowen kidded the swell into a snoozing ken, and shook him of his dummee and thimble", which it translates as "the GIRL inveigled the gentleman into a BROTHEL and robbed him of his pocket book and watch".

Blowzy has also had connotations of coarse rusticity: "I cannot fancy the blousy wisdom of the country". (*Help's Complete Solitude*, 1851) In the C18th, *blowzelinda* was a common name applied to a rustic young woman. Combining several senses, late C18th definition of a *blowse* or *blowsabella* is "A woman whose hair is dishevelled, and hanging about her face: a slattern (late C17th). *A Dictionary of Slang and Unconventional English* defines *blowsabella* as an C18th colloquialism for a country wench and *blowse*, or *blowze*, (late C16th–C18th) as a beggar's trull.

Yet a further theory, less likely, is that BLOWZY may derive from the French *bluson*, meaning a loose, ill-fitting over-garment worn by workmen, artists and peasants. One definition of the verb *to blouse* is to droop or BAG. In the C17th *bag* was a widely used slang term for a pregnant woman and later a slang term for a middle-aged or elderly slattern. Like *blowzy*, the word *slattern* – from the German *schlottern*, meaning to hang loosely, waddle or slouch – also orginally denoted either a woman or a man but degenerated to mean a sluttish female prostitute, ie, a blowze.

Webster's indicates that *blowzy* had ameliorated by the 1950s to mean merely "a person who is negligent of his [sic] appearance or surroundings, esp. an untidy slovenly woman". But the example of usage which it gives demonstrates the extent to which negative connotations of female sexuality continue to be atttached to the word: 'A big blowzy JEZEBEL from the docks.' It defines *Jezebel* (from the wife of Ahab in the Old Testament who pressed the cult of Baal upon the Israelites) as an impudent, shameless, or abandoned woman (since C16th).

Bluestocking

When a woman inclines to learning, there is usually something wrong with her sex apparatus.

F W Nietzsche (1844–1900)

Bluestocking entered general use in the 1750s when it was used derisively to refer to the convention-defying sartorial habits of those who frequented the literary soirées of the wealthy London hostess Elizabeth Montagu. One of her guests, an amateur poet named Benjamin Stillingfleet, wore grey, or blue, worsted stockings instead of the silk ones that etiquette demanded of a gentleman of his position. He may have borrowed the idea from a Venetian literary society of the early 1400s called the *Della Calza*, to which the few educated women of the city were invited and whose male members wore the blue worsted stocking of the peasantry to symbolise their rejection of the frivolous. In English, the term had also been used contemptuously to describe Cromwell's radical 'Little Parliament' of 1653 because its members wore plain clothes. But the most obvious source for Stillingfleet's taste in stockings would have been the aristocrats who attended the Parisian salons of educated hostesses, such as Mme de Polignac in the 1590s, and who formed a literary society called the *Bas Bleu*.

These famous salons, which were to flourish for two hundred years, played their part in persuading C18th women and men of letters that a woman's education should comprise more than those arts – music, needlework and dancing – traditionally deemed sufficient for a young woman's raison d'être: the acquisition of a husband. Elizabeth Montagu and her female friends deliberately sought to replace the mindless card-playing and TRIVIAL conversation expected of them as women with intellectual and literary ways of expressing themselves.

Among the British and French intellectuals *bluestocking* did not have any risible connotation – Elizabeth Montagu is said to have adopted the badge of the *Bas Bleu* with pride, and the Parisian salons became a focal point for serious radical debate in which women played an active part in the century which culminated in the French Revolution. But when the term came to be applied specifically to women it acquired a totally pejorative meaning. By the end of the C18th it was used to refer to women who were thought to ape men by affecting to understand intellectual and literary matters. These, clearly, were topics which only the male brain could grasp. The French philospher Jean-Jacques Rousseau (1712–78), whose concept of radical egalitarianism excluded women, warned of the 'over' education of women. In direct reference to the *Bas Bleu* he wrote: "But I would a thousand times rather have a homely GIRL, simply brought up, than a LADY and a wit who would make herself a literary circle and install herself as its president. . . She is very rightly a butt for criticism as we always are when we try to escape from our own position into one for which we are unfitted."

In the early C19th any woman who displayed signs of learning was suspected of unnatural longings to escape from her god-given place – the home. The English campaigner for women's rights Harriet Martineau, who received an unusually good education for a member of her sex, recalled: "When I was young it was not thought proper for a young woman to study very conspicuously. . .young ladies were expected to sit down in the parlour to sew. . .or practice their music; but so as to receive callers without any signs of bluestockingism which could be reported abroad." (*Autobiography*, 1855)

While *bluestocking* connoted masculine traits of intelligence, it also acquired pejorative implications of a supposedly very feminine use of wile and guile. The original bluestockingers had deliberately turned their backs on accepted husband-attracting pastimes, but ironically, a century later, the term came to mean a flirt, a woman who pretended to learning in order to attract potential husband-fodder. Martineau, most anxious not to be considered a bluestocking, using the term disparagingly in the sense of the trumpery of a COQUETTE. In 1845 the American writer Edgar Allan Poe revealed just how pejorative a term it had become: "When we think very ill of a woman and wish to blacken her name we merely call her a bluestocking." By then the word was totally female-specific.

C19th FEMINISTS (or womanists as they were then called) persisted in challenging the prevailing notion that women were incapable of serious intellectual activity and its underlying assumption that they only needed to be taught how to catch a husband, run a home and bring up children. The schools and colleges founded by some formidable women education reformers in the 1850s were far removed from the glittering social salons of the earlier bluestockingers, and may have influenced an amelioration of the word. In 1858 the writer Thomas de Quincy noted – possibly with more optimism than accuracy: "The order of ladies called Bluestockings by way of reproach has become totally extinct among us."

The word may have lost its connotations of coquetry but it began to acquire negative connotations of unfemininity. When the teenage Simone de Beauvoir and her friend informed her father of their intention of going to university in the 1920s, she recalled later: "Though my father liked intelligent and witty women he had no time for bluestockings. When he announced 'My dears you'll never marry; you'll have to work for your livings' there was bitterness in his voice." (*Memoirs of a Dutiful Daughter*, 1959)

The OED claims that the pejorative sense of *bluestocking* is "now nearly abandoned" due to the "general change of opinion on the education of women". Sadly, not so: the introduction to the 1983 edition of Beatrice Webb's diary makes it clear that the term is still derogatory: "she described an eclectic education in which speculation about religion and philosophy played as large a part as the study of literature and the classics, modern languages, history, mathematics, and science. She was not merely the earnest bluestocking that such highmindedness suggests. She was strikingly handsome. . .and sociable." *Bluestocking* continues to imply that learning diminishes a woman's FEMININITY and makes her less attractive – to men, that is.

Blurb

We owe the origins of this word for the promotional description found on book covers to one Miss Belinda Blurb. A character in a novel by the US humorist Gelett Burgess (1866–1951), her name appeared on its cover. *Blurb* became standard English in the 1920s.

Bosom See BREAST

Boston Marriage See LESBIAN

Breast

Brest, denoting the human mammary glands of both women and men, first made its written appearance in English c1000. Old English *breost*, akin to Old High German *brust*, may be related to Old Saxon *brustian*, meaning to bud. The first figurative use of *breost* (c1000) was non-gender-specific: "the seat of the affections and emotions, the repository of consciousness, designs and secrets, hence the affections, private thoughts and feelings". (OED) *Bosom* entered English at about the same time in the singular, meaning the breast of a human being. One theory claims it is based on an Indo-European word for arm; the word, like the then partially synonymous *fathom*, primarily meaning the space embraced by two arms. Another theory, however, traces it to an Indo-European root *ben-* or *bhen-*, meaning to swell. Today, *bosoms* denote a woman's breasts. Marina Warner maintains that *breast* and *bosom* did not become female-specific until "possibly very recently" (*Monuments and Maidens*), but the tendency to associate them more closely with the female body rather than that of the male can be seen in the figurative use of *breast* to mean a source of nourishment from as long ago as 1611.

A plethora of euphemistic slang terms exist for female breasts. In the C19th the word was so closely identified with the (naked) female body that in 'polite' circles it was taboo. The term *white meat* was used to allow gentlemen to ask for CHICKEN breast and spare the blushes of the LADIES present. (Likewise, *dark meat* denoted a chicken leg or thigh.) In the C20th the circle was completed: *white* and *dark meat* became jocular, but clearly offensive, euphemisms for both a woman's breasts or VAGINA, or for the vagina of either a white or a Black woman. Another euphemism, *bust*, first appeared in 1691 as a non-gender-specific sculptural term for the upper front portion of the human body, but by the C18th it was slang for a woman's breasts, since when it became standard English.

In *The Female Eunuch*, Germaine Greer wrote: "The degree of attention which breasts receive, combined with the confusions about what the (male) breast fetishist wants, make women unduly anxious about them. They can never be just right; they must always be too small, too big, the wrong shape, too flabby." The long list of slang terms also suggests a male confusion about what they want. Some of the euphemisms over the centuries suggest men find them variously: appetising – *apples, cakes, lollies, grapefruits*; too small – *pellets, lemons, cupcakes, grapes*; too large – *mountains, headlights, melons, superdupers*, and in the USA during World War 2 a lifejacket was known as a *Mae West,* rhyming slang for *breast* and a reference to the large breasts of the film star; reproductively functional – *dairies, jugs* (ie, for milk), *milkers, norks* (Australian, from 'Norco' the name of a brand of butter in New South Wales with a wrapper carrying a picture of a cow's udder on it), *TITS*, or *titties* both deriving from *teat*; play objects – *balloons, Mary Poppins*; warm, soft and comforting – *tremblers, big brown eyes*; hard – *racks, wallopies, coconuts*; jokes – *Tale of Two Cities* (rhyming slang for *titties*). There are many, many more.

One of the functions of euphemism is to "avoid the direct naming of an unpleasant, painful, or frightening reality". (Webster's) What is it about breasts that is so threatening? Susan Brownmiller suggests that the American male's breast fixation dates from the war years of the 1940s and remains unmatched throughout the world (British male sexual obsession, as reflected in the majority of PORNOGRAPHY, apparently relates to the female buttocks). "Perhaps," she writes, "it can be partially understood as symptomatic of a new imperialist nation's desire to overcome or transform the childhood experience of nestling in dependence against the mother's bosom, or perhaps in the theory that Americans were fighting a Puritan heritage that believed all displays of sex and sexuality to be shameful. But we must admit that the national breast obsession is often less than amicable and frequently is downright unfriendly. The phantasmagorical spectre of the engulfing super-breast that has appeared in the work of Philip Roth and Woody Allen is more alarming than sexual, and slangy familiarities such as boobs, jugs and titties are basically hostile appraisals, despite attempts by some women to incorporate these contemptuous descriptions into their own vocabulary as hip terms of demystified endearment." (*Femininity*)

No slang or euphemistic term exists for male breasts, almost as if they don't exist at all. But then, phallocentric heterosexuality has meant that few men have discovered the erotogenic qualities of their own breasts. That this is culturally inculcated was emphasised by the findings of the US sex researchers Masters and Johnson: "As a source of erotic stimulation male breasts and nipples seldom are manipulated during heterosexual activity. However, breast stimulation does constitute a significant segment of male homosexual activity. As a result, the nipples and even the anterior chest wall develop erotogenic qualities seldom found in the heterosexually oriented male." (*Human Sexual Response*, 1966)

That *breasts* and *bosoms* have come to denote specifically the female mammary organs with the lack of any slang vocabulary for men's breasts might, perhaps, indicate a male denial of the FEMININE in themselves as well as a male psychological denial of the intimacy of the early mother–child suckling relationship.

Bride

It has been suggested that *bride* originally meant daughter-in-law from the Germanic root *bru*, meaning to cook, brew or make broth – once the traditional job of the daughter-in-law living with her husband's family in patrilocal society. Old English *bryd* denoted the betrothed person who was pledged but not yet married. This pledge was sealed with a cup of ale called *brydealu*, which by the C16th was *brideale*, from which *bridal* is derived. During the C15th and C16th, *bride* was applied to men as well as women, with the C17th bride-couple denoting a newly wedded pair. Therefore, the C16th *brydegrome* was perhaps the bride-lad, the lad who was a bride. *Bridegome*, however, appeared in the C14th, being a northern English and Kentish dialect word from the Old English *bryde* and *guma* meaning man. *Guma* is akin to *omage*, the Old French origin of *homage*, which has led some etymologists to suggest that BRIDEGROOM originally meant the male servant of the bride. Radford and Smith put forward another theory, however, basing *groom* on the Old Norse *gromr*, meaning a boy. (*To Coin a Phrase: A Dictionary of Origins*). In the C16th the spelling of *gome* changed to *groom*, probably due to a confusion with the Middle English term for a male attendant or man-servant. Some etymologists believe that BIRD, used to denote a woman, may have developed from *bryd*.

Bride is one of the few words in the English language which, originally denoting someone of either sex, never acquired derogatory and negative sexual connotations as it became female-specific, thus disproving a supposed rule of semantic derogation which some feminist linguists have posited from the development of words such as WHORE, HARLOT, WENCH, SLATTERN, etc.

Broad

In the 1920s *broad* became US slang for a promiscuous woman considered unworthy of respect. It may derive from BAWD or from a couple of derogatory C19th expressions applied to women with large hips: *broad in the beam* (originally a nautical term for a ship or VESSEL with a wide base); and *broad-gauge* LADY (a railway officials' expression). Some obsolete senses of *broad* suggest that it was a particularly appropriate word for anyone wishing to express opprobrium to women: wide and open (C10th–C17th); outspoken – often in a bad sense (C16th–C19th); coarse, unrefined, vulgar (C15th–C16th); and LOOSE, gross, indecent (C15th–C19th).

By the 1930s *broad* had slightly ameliorated and was, at least according to the US writer Damon Runyon, an acceptable term for all women: "He refers to MISS Penny as a broad, meaning no harm whatever, for this is the way many of the boys speaks of the DOLLS." But the *Dictionary of American Slang*, shows that although in the 1960s *broad* could be used neutrally, it had still retained the highly derogatory sense of "a promiscuous woman, a PROSTITUTE, a woman whom the speaker does not respect". In the 1980s *broad* degenerated even further, becoming US slang for a male homosexual prostitute and/or a large, powerful self-opinionated woman (also called a *Big Ass*).

Against this tide of pejoration *A Feminist Dictionary* defines *broad* as "a woman who is liberal, tolerant, unconfined and not limited or narrow in scope".

Brothel

From Old English *breodan*, meaning to go to ruin, *brothel* is a variant of *brethel*, meaning a worthless or abandoned fellow, a scoundrel or wretch. It was used mostly of men, although *fellow* originally meant a person of either sex. It was not always used totally opprobriously – the C15th York Mystery Plays refer to Christ as a *brethell*. As this sense became obsolete, *brothel* pejorated and came to be applied only to women: in the C16th it denoted an abandoned woman or common PROSTITUTE. By the end of the C16th, the word, no longer used in a personal sense, had become a euphemism for a bordello. This sense development appears to be the result of a confusion with an entirely different word: *bordello*, meaning brothel, was adopted in the late C16th from Italian, derived from the Old French *bordel*, meaning cabin, hut or small farm. The combinations of *bordel-house* and *brothel's* (ie prostitute's) *house* ran together, ending up shortened to *brothel*.

Brothel has remained the standard word for a house etc, where prostitutes may be visited, but many other euphemisms have been used, eg, a *house of ill-fame* or *ill-repute* (*ill* has been a euphemism for moral depravity since c1300), BAWDY *house*, *sporting house*, CHICKEN *ranch* (allegedly from a brothel in Gilbert, Texas, where poor local farmers paid for their illicit sex with chickens), BIRD *cage*, *shooting gallery* (ie, where a man ejaculates), CAT *house*, *hook shop* (see HOOKER), *knocking shop* and many more.

Bully

Derived from the Dutch *boel*, meaning a lover of either sex, in the C16th *bully* meant sweetheart and was a term of endearment and familiarity applied to both females and males, eg; "Though she be sum what olde, It is myne owne swete bullye." (1538) By the late C17th it was only rarely applied to women in its original sense, and developed through the senses of a fine chap, then a blustering, browbeating fellow, especially one who is habitually cruel to others weaker than himself, and finally it became a colloquialism for a pimp. *Webster's Ninth New Collegiate Dictionary* defines *bully* as "a protector for a PROSTITUTE". A protector is one who keeps safe, defends or guards against danger, injury, disadvantage, etc; whether the prostitutes themselves felt safe with men defined as being habitually cruel is a moot point.

Samuel Johnson's attitude towards pimps can be detected from his definition of *bully*: "A noisy, blustering, quarrelling fellow: it is generally taken for a man that has only the appearance of courage." As an example of usage he quoted the English essayist Joseph Addison (1672–1719): "A scolding hero is, at the worst, a more tolerable character than a bully in PETTICOATS." Since Johnson defined a SCOLD as "a clamorous, rude, mean, low, foul-mouthed woman" (ie, a FISHWIFE), *bully* had clearly degenerated far indeed. On the derivation of *bully* Johnson muses that it may be a corruption of the pronunciation of *burly* or, less probably, from *bulky* or *bull-eyed*. Alternatively, "May it not come from *bull*, the pope's letter, implying the insolence of those who came invested with authority from the papal court?"

C20th etymologists suspect that the present meaning of *bully* in the sense of one who uses strength or power to coerce others by fear was probably influenced by two Dutch words: *bul*, meaning both a bull and a clown, and *bulderen*, meaning to bluster.

During the early C19th a *bully boy* was a hired ruffian, and *bully back* was a euphemism for both a pimp and a whoremonger. This last term is of interest as one of the relatively few words in the English language for the male customer of a female prostitute; *Slang and its analogues* (1965) gives over five hundred synonyms for prostitute but only sixty-five for whoremonger. On this Muriel R Schulz comments: "Women are generally acknowledged to be – for whatever reasons – the more continent of the two sexes, the least promiscuous, and the more monogamous. Nevertheless, the largest category of words designating humans in sexual terms are those for women – especially for loose women. I have located roughly a thousand words and phrases describing women in sexually derogatory ways. There is nothing approaching this multitude for describing men." (*The Semantic Derogation of Women*)

In the C20th, in the sense of one who possesses the characteristics of a pimp, ie, one who persecutes and/or oppresses physically or morally by threat of superior force *bully* is once again used of both sexes.

Bunny

It is not known why rabbits (and squirrels) first acquired the name of *bun*, and later the diminutive *bunny* which mostly denoted a young rabbit. Perhaps from the association of the reputed intense sexual activity of rabbits, and, possibly, because they are soft and furry, *bun* became slang for the female pudendum in the C17th. The 1811 edition of the *Dictionary of the Vulgar Tongue* defined *bun* euphemistically as "the monosyllable" (ie, CUNT) and refers to "a practice observed among sailors [before] going on a cruise called 'To touch bun for luck' " (ie, to have sexual intercourse). *Bun* in this sense was superseded by *bunny* in the early C20th when its meaning changed to buttocks.

In the 1960s a chain of US-owned dining and gambling clubs, known as Playboy Clubs, pushed their waitresses and female croupiers, called *Bunny Girls*, into ridiculous costumes complete with a fluffy tail and a head-dress comprising large floppy ears.

Alleen Pace Nilsen points to a linguistic principle about the use of animal metaphors: "If both the animal and the woman are young, the connotation is positive, but if the animal and the woman are old, the connotation is negative. [See ANILE] Hugh Hefner might never have made it to the big time if he had called his girls rabbits instead of bunnies." The clubs, much criticised and ridiculed by feminists, went bankrupt in the 1980s – even after trying to accommodate the comparatively less sexist times by persuading male employees to adopt the ludicrous costume.

Butch

Butch is used to mean a tough (male) youth or man, a mannish woman, a masculine-looking LESBIAN, sometimes called a DYKE, or a masculine GAY. Before it was adopted into homosexual slang in the C20th, *butch* was northern British dialect for the youngest male child of a family, and UK slang for a rough, tough young man. It was also used to describe a type of man's haircut, from the verb *to butcher*, ie, to cut up or hack. When used pejoratively of a lesbian, the term denotes the lesbian stereotype of a woman with short-cropped hair, who wears boots and working or 'mannish' clothes, or the counterpart to the fem, or FEMME, the supposedly passive partner in a lesbian relationship. In the 1970s many lesbians reclaimed the word and among them it has ameliorated to mean an assertive and strong-minded lesbian.

Buxom

The adjective *buxom* conjures up the image of the warm, plump, large-breasted (see BREAST), female stereotype. This current sense may appear to be a long way from the original Old English verb *bugan*, meaning to bow, yield or bend. From this the Middle English word *buhsum*, meaning tractable, obliging, and obedient was formed. This sense remained until the 1890s but three other branches of meaning emerged in the late C16th which influenced later senses and resulted in the present meaning of the word. From the sense of obedience, *buxom* came to denote yielding to pressure, unresisting and, figuratively, easily swayed morally (see LOOSE). *Buxom* also acquired the senses of blithe, gladsome, bright and lively, perhaps from the notion that something which, or someone who, yields to pressure is seen to be flexible, accommodating and (in the case of a person) easily yielding to pleasure. Before becoming obsolete both these senses degenerated, and by the mid-C18th Samuel Johnson gave "obsequious" and "WANTON" as two further definitions of *buxom*. The third C16th sense of plump, comely and comfortable-looking is the one which survives today. Originally used of both sexes it was female-specific by the late C18th – perhaps because of associations with obedience and wantonness. In the US the various archaic senses of pliancy and liveliness may have influenced the current sense of full-bosomed. The similarities in spelling and pronunciation of *buxom*, *bust* and *bosom* may have been a further influence on the meaning of the word.

Although not exactly pejorative, *buxom* is not exactly complimentary either. This may be because the large-breasted female runs counter to the fashionable slim boyish-looking female ideal of today. A bar-MAID (whose morals are inevitably considered suspect) may be described as buxom, but never a 'LADY'.

Cassandra

Cassandra, whose name meant 'she who entangles men', was the daughter of Hecuba and Priam, the QUEEN and king of Troy at the time of the Trojan war. Apollo fell in love with her and gave her the power to foretell the future. When Cassandra refused to 'pay' for his gift by making love with him, the scorned Apollo bade her farewell with a kiss, ensuring that although her prophecies would be accurate she would never be believed. Among Cassandra's unheeded accurate predictions were that Paris would cause the fall of Troy and that the Greeks would use a wooden horse to fool the Trojans.

In the English language a *cassandra* is one who prophesies misfortune or disaster, applied to pessimists and those who take a delight in gloomy predictions. Webster's calls Cassandra "the prophetess of evil or disaster". But the point about her is that, had she been believed, the Trojans might have been able to avert disaster. Cassandra only earned respect after her death: in Laconia she was worshipped as the goddess Alexandra, whose name means 'helper of men'. Cassandra symbolises a patriarchal refusal to trust in the words of women – their talk is more likely to be dismissed as idle TRIVIA or GOSSIP than it is to be taken seriously.

Cat

In ancient Rome the cat was a symbol of liberty. The Goddess of Liberty was represented with a cat at her feet. No animal is so opposed to restraint as a cat.
Brewer's Dictionary of Phrase and Fable

The cat may have noble origins but over the centuries the word has tended to have extremely negative connotations when specifically associated with women. From a prehistoric German word, probably borrowed from the late Latin *cattus, catta, cat* had entered English by the C12th. In the C13th, in a figurative sense, *cat* was used of any human being who scratches. This non-gender-specific sense persists today, although over the centuries scratching has been regarded as a childish, and therefore FEMININE, characteristic (see DOLL, GIRL).

The old superstition that the Devil's favourite form was that of a black cat, and the subsequent association of black cats with WITCHES may have influenced another sense of the word which, by the C15th, denigrated to become slang for a common female PROSTITUTE. By the C19th this sense had pejorated even further and *cat* was used colloquially for the VAGINA – as was PUSSY. In the USA *cat house* became a slang term in the C19th for a BROTHEL – especially a cheap one.

The 1811 edition of the *Dictionary of the Vulgar Tongue* reveals several derogatory and specifically female uses of *cat*: an *old cat* was a cross OLD WOMAN; *catamaran* was slang for a scraggy old woman or a cross-grained, vixenish old woman (perhaps a corruption of 'cat o' mountain', which in America, since c1830 meant a SHREW; *cat-witted* meant small-minded, obstinate and spiteful which, although used of both sexes, when used specifically of a man means he had a brain like that of a woman. This was not complimentary.

In the C20th *cat* mostly lost its sexual connotations but continued to be a denigrating epithet when used of a woman: *cat* is a mean spiteful woman; to be *catty* is to be given to malicious GOSSIP – usually regarded as a female characteristic; like BITCH, or *bitchy*, to apply these terms to a man is to imply he is EFFEMINATE. When applied specifically to a man, *cat* can have positive connotations: a *hep-cat* is a man who dresses in the latest style and who pursues women for sexual purposes; or *cat* can simply denote a man, fellow or guy. One UK C20th slang phrase in which sexual connotations are not absent, referred to in *The Slanguage of Sex* as "possibly the most violent image in slang referring to the female body", is *cat with its throat cut*, meaning the female genitals.

Charity See WHORE

Charm/Charming

The women who want women's rights
Want mostly women's charms.

Punch, 1870

Charm has undergone considerable change since its origins – in the Latin *carmen*, meaning song, verse, oracular response or incantation. The key to its subsequent development in English lies in another Latin sense of the word: a magical formula or spell. Some etymologists suggest that *carmen* derives from *Carmenta* (meaning 'Car the wise'), the name of a Roman divinatory goddess. It was Carmenta who invented the fifteen-letter Latin alphabet and, according to Pliny, also invented augury. However tempting it might be to see the alphabet as some sort of female magical charm, it seems more likely that the root of both charm and incantation is the Latin *canere*, meaning to sing. The English cognate of *canere* is *hen*, once meaning singer, referring to 'the bird that sings in the morning'. A similar semantic development can be found in the Medieval French word *chauntecleer*, literally, a clear singer. The French *chaunte* entered English as *chant*. The Latin *carmen* became the French *charme* with the extended sense of magical incantation or song with occult powers, especially to cure or heal. In English, *charm* was directly borrowed from the French, first appearing in 1300 with this same meaning. The sense of occult power meant that it became associated with the black magic of WITCHES. By the C15th *charm* was used to refer to the power possessed by women to fascinate, bewitch or seduce. The connotation of seduction may have developed as a result of the widespread belief in the ability of witches to seduce the devil and mortal men. Witches were said to cast a particularly evil form of charm, called GLAMOUR, which deprived a man of his penis.

Towards the end of the C16th *charm* began to ameliorate (although the witch hunts were to continue into the C17th); it came to denote an amulet or object that either brought good luck or that had the power to avert bad luck, ie, an object with which it was possible to resist the seductive black magic or charms of a witch. Perhaps because *charm* now meant something positive it developed the sense of any quality, attribute, trait, feature, etc which exerts a fascinating or attractive influence, exciting love or admiration. When used in the plural, *charms* referred especially to female beauty.

By the early C19th charm was very definitely considered an entirely positive female characteristic denoting attractiveness or delightfulness. In the C20th a charm school was an establishment where the daughters of the middle class paid to learn the rules of social etiquette with which they could charm young men into becoming their husbands. In one sense only there remains an echo of the diabolical ability of witches to enslave and seduce men with their spells and devilish VAGINAS: in US slang *charms* is a euphemism used in pornographic (see PORNOGRAPHY) magazines, strip-joints, etc for naked female BREASTS and genitalia.

Chaste/Chastity

Patriarchal civilization dedicated woman to chastity; it recognised more or less openly the right of the male to sexual freedom, while woman was restricted to marriage.

Simone de Beauvoir, *The Second Sex*, 1947

According to dictionaries, *chastity* has always been applied equally to both sexes, apart from a short period in the late C16th when *chaste* had the male-specific sense of gelded. From the mid-C13th until today, *chaste* has denoted someone who is pure from unlawful sexual intercourse, continent and virtuous. But this dictionary definition ignores the overwhelmingly feminine associations of the word: the pure virginal MAIDEN is the image that springs more readily to the mind than that of the virtuous male who abjures illicit sex.

The development of *chastity* is related to the history of Christianity and to that of women's economic position – when that has been vulnerable, chastity has become her most valued possession in a patrilineal, propertied society. *Chastity* derives from the Latin *casta, castus*, meaning morally pure or holy. Originally there was no sense of virginity attached to the concept of chastity. The parthenogenic love-goddesses of ancient mythology, such as Venus, Ishtar, Astate, Anath etc were called 'VIRGIN', but their many lovers are witness to their lack of chastity. It was only with the advent of Christianity and the cult of mariolatry that *chastity* and *virginity* became confused and used as virtual synonyms.

Several factors contributed towards the elevation of chastity as an essential female virtue: an awareness of the male role in procreation (if this knowledge was ever lacking); the change from matrilineal to patrilineal succession (see MATRIARCHY) and the spread of Christianity. Of this last factor, Marina Warner writes: "Sometimes this long and durable obsession with chastity perpetuated by the Church appears to be an incomprehensible attack of mass lunacy. When applied to women, however, it served an evident purpose which was reinforced by chastity's correlative among Christian virtues: humility interpreted as submissiveness." (*Alone of All Her Sex*) This evident purpose was the need – presumably both psychological and economic – for men to have no legal doubts about the legitimacy of their heirs to property and title.

Women were generally considered to be the more lascivious of the two sexes (men had reason to control their sexual appetites), hence the chastity belt, imported from the semitic East by C13th crusaders. Little more than joke objects for tourists to giggle at today, it should not be hard to imagine the pain and infection once caused by these blood, urine and faeces-encrusted instruments of torture. They continued to be sold up to the C19th – in 1880 a French merchandising company advertised the *camisole de force* as follows: "The advantages are manifold. Not only will the purity of the virgin be maintained, but the fidelity of the WIFE exacted. The husband will leave the wife without fear that his honour will be outraged and his affections estranged. Fathers will be sure of their parenthood and will not harbour the terrible thought that their children may be the offspring of another, and it will be possible for them to keep under lock and key things more precious than gold."

Secular society during C16th–C18th adopted the Church's obsession with female chastity. Whereas the honour of a man was damaged if he was called a liar, "the worst thing a woman could say of another was that she was unchaste – which might well result in a law suit for slander in an ecclesiastical court". (Lawrence Stone, *The Family, Sex and Marriage in England 1500–1800*) Furthermore, it was not only a woman's honour that was perceived to be at stake: the honour of a married man was severely damaged if he got the reputation of being a cuckold (see COTQUEAN). His wife's lack of chastity cast a slur on his virility and on his ability to rule his own household. The value of his sexual property – his wife – was diminished by being used by another and he, in turn, suffered a loss in honour. Stone cites examples of men who were not only defamed by their wive's lack of chastity but even considered unfit for public office.

Of the double standard by which chastity was expected of women but discouraged in men, Stone found only one period, the 1630s and 1640s, in which this was seriously questioned. "Courtiers like Sir Kenelm Digby claimed that breach of chastity 'is no greater fault in them than in men'. The puritan John Milton (1608–74) adopted a similar position."

Not so Samuel Johnson (1709–84), who considered that upon female chastity "all the property of the world depends" and that "confusion of progeny constitutes the essence of the crime [of adultery]". Consequently, "wise married women don't trouble themselves about infidelity in their husbands" whereas wifely unchastity was "unpardonable". This support for a double standard was challenged by an unnamed woman friend of Johnson's: "I argued that the chastity of women was of much more consequence than that of men, as the property and rights of families depend upon it. 'Surely' said she, 'that is easily answered for the objection is removed if a woman does not intrigue but when she is with child.' I really could not answer her. Yet she was wrong, and I was uneasy. . ."

This double standard, which for centuries has clung to the concept of chastity, survives today. Whereas a chaste male is often regarded as an object of pity, an unchaste one is deemed worthy of admiration or, at worst, amusement. For women, however, there exist countless terms of abuse which cast opprobrium upon those who are suspected of unchastity.

Chatter

Women and sparrows twitter in company.

Japanese proverb

In the early C13th *chatter* entered English as an onomatopoeic word for the twittering sound of birds. Within the century the sense transferred to denote the rapid, incessant talk of humans. Today, the phrase 'the chattering of a magpie' is commonly held to be a simile drawn from the sound of human chatter.

Chatter and *chat* have had both negative and positive connotations since the C15th when they denoted idle, unimportant, TRIVIAL talk, and the C16th when they could also denote light, familiar talk without stiffness or ceremony.

As the Spanish proverb "Men speak, Women chat" suggests, *chatter* and *chat* have strong feminine associations. The OED makes an oblique reference to this in its definition of chatter: "to talk rapidly, incessantly and with more sound than sense, esp. said of children; but often applied vituperatively to speech which one does not like". The 'one' referred to here can only mean a woman as men's talk is seldom, if ever, referred to as chatter.

Several compound terms reveal much about male attitudes towards women who do not defer silently to male conversation, towards the content of women's talk and towards verbal interaction between women. *Chatterbox*, meaning "one whose tongue runs twelve score to the dozen" (*Dictionary of the Vulgar Tongue* 1811 edition) fits perfectly the stereotype of the verbally incontinent female whose subject matter is considered inconsequential. Women, after all, are like children – best seen and not heard (see BABE, DOLL). This term may derive from the C17th *prattle-box*, meaning an incessant childish chatterer. This was probably modelled on *sauce-box*, a C16th term for an impudent person at a time when *saucy* denoted insolence towards superiors and was a term much used of both children and women. In the C17th a *chatterhouse* was a place "for women to meet and determine of their attires". *Chatter-broth*, *chatter-water*, *prattle-broth* and *scandal-broth* all denoted tea, both in the sense of the beverage and of a party in the C17th, C18th and C19th, when tea was considered a woman's drink and tea-parties as all-women or women-dominated gatherings (see BEVY).

Samuel Johnson defined *chitchat* as "Prattle; idle prate; idle talk. A word only used in ludicrous conversation" and gave as an example of use: "I am a member of a female society, who call ourselves the *chitchat* club. *Spectator*, No. 560." (1755)

Chat, *chatter* and *chit-chat*, like the terms *girl's talk*, SHEILA-*talk*, HEN-*party*, *prattle*, BABBLE, GOSSIP and *twitter*, are all words which are used to denigrate women and devalue their verbal interactions. Of this Deborah Cameron notes: "Women's talk is not subversive per se: it becomes subversive when women begin to attach importance to it and privilege it over their interactions with men. . . Men trivialize the talk of women not because they are afraid of any such talk, but in order to make women themselves downgrade it. If women feel that all interaction with other women is a poor substitute for mixed interaction and trivial compared with the profundities of men's talk, their conversations will indeed be harmless." (*Feminism and Linguistic Theory*)

Cheesecake

For five hundred years *cheesecake* meant a cake or TART made of cheese or curdled milk, eggs and sugar. During World War 2 it joined the long list of slang words which refer to women as edible and sexually available to men. At first, American GIs used the term for "photos (as in advertisements or publicity) featuring the natural curves of shapely female legs, thighs or trunk, usually scantily clothed, also called a PIN-UP or leg art". (Webster's) From this sense *cheesecake* developed to mean any sexually attractive young woman.

The term was probably influenced by the US slang use of *cheese* to mean easy, and the Black American slang use of *cake* as a euphemism for the VAGINA. These terms reveal a common male fantasy about the supposed availability of women whom they find sexually exciting, as well as male contempt for any woman who is no more CHASTE than many men are.

Another theory about the origins of *cheesecake* is that it derives from the request of photographers to say 'cheese' in order to simulate a smile. A more fanciful explanation is that it derives from the practice of restaurants in New York's entertainment district of displaying a large cheesecake in their windows. The word then supposedly became transferred to the main publicity photos outside cinemas and theatres which displayed the naked or nearly naked 'CHARMS' of ACTRESSES and chorus-GIRLS, ie, women regarded as morally incontinent or LOOSE.

Cherry

Since the beginning of the C16th *cherry* has been a term of endearment, usually used to a woman, possibly from the French *chérie*, meaning beloved, and from which *cherish* derives. In the second half of the C19th *cherry* and *cherry pie* began to be used colloquially for an attractive young woman. By the mid-C20th *cherry pie* came to mean something easily attainable, easy or pleasant to accomplish, perhaps influenced by the notion that a young woman who was considered attractive was sexually promiscuous, ie, a ripe fruit ready for picking and for (male) consumption. This probably influenced the development of *cherry* as a euphemism for the HYMEN and a female VIRGIN (since the C19th). Germaine Greer points out in *The Female Eunuch*, "The basic imagery behind terms like HONEY, sugar, DISH, sweety-pie, cherry etc. is the imagery of food. If a woman is food, her sex organ is for consumption also."

Barbara G Walker suggests that "the use of cherry for virginity may be traced to a mythic past. Like other red fruits, such as the apple and pomegranate, the cherry symbolized the VIRGIN Goddess: bearing her sacred blood colour and bearing its seed within, like a WOMB." (*The Woman's Encyclopedia of Myths and Secrets*)

Contempt for virginity in a male can be seen in the C20th US military slang use of *cherry* for a new recruit – a young man who has yet to be 'blooded'. *Cherry* was also adopted in the 1950s as a gay slang term for a virgin who had not yet been anally penetrated. Heterosexual expressions for the deflowering of a virgin include *to cop*, *pop*, or *crack a cherry*. US gay slang of the 1950s used *cherry-splitter* for a long thin penis.

Chick/Chicken

Chick, when applied to humans, began as a term for a child or young GIRL (c1400). In the C15th it became a term of endearment applied to a female sweetheart. It degenerated to mean a young promiscuous woman in the early C20th, but ameliorated and acquired connotations of a liberated or independent female in the 1930s, as a Black male or jazz slang term for a hip young woman. A little outdated today, *chick* is still used of women, usually ones who are young and sexually attractive.

The late C17th *Dictionary of the Canting Crew* defined *chicken* as "a feeble little creature of mean spirit". *Chicken-* and HEN-*hearted* (since C18th) means cowardly; *chicken-feed* (C20th) means small change or something of low value; *chicken-shit* has been used since the C19th of anything considered to have absolutely no value at all. The cockerel has, on the whole, been held in higher esteem than his female counterpart. Although the phrase *cock-and-bull* (c1700) describes an idle, silly or incredible story, most cock-terms have positive masculine connotations: *cock of the walk* (C15th) means a dominant person, one in charge; *cock* has denoted a plucky fighter, a penis, a chief or leader, and in ancient oaths it signified God. *Cockish* (c1800) is the single 'cock'-related word which has been applied specifically to women; it was a derogatory term denoting WANTON, uppish and forward.

Exploring the implications of this and other words for women drawn from the chicken metaphor, Alleen Pace Nilsen illustrates how they can tell us the whole history of a woman's life: "In her youth she is a *chick*, then she marries and begins feeling *cooped* up, so she goes to HEN-parties where she *cackles* with her friends. Then she has her *brood* and begins to *hen-peck* her husband. Finally she turns into an old BIDDY."

Many women object to being called by a word which originally meant a child and which also denotes, however adorable, the small, FLUFFY, offspring of a species not known for its great intelligence.

Circean

Circean entered English in the mid-C17th, meaning to have the quality of a fascinating sorceress and to be dangerously or fatally attractive or misleading. The word derives from *Circe*, the name of a Greek goddess, meaning 'she-falcon'. In one of her identities, Circe was the falcon death-bird Circos (or Kircos) whose name means 'circle', from the circling movements falcons make when flying. *Circos* may derive onomatopoeically from the 'circ, circ' cry of these birds. Circe ruled all the stars that determined human fate and was said to turn men into animals. According to Homer she was unable to use her magical power, or sorcery, on Odysseus since he was protected by a special herb, but she turned all his crew into pigs.

Sorcery, from the Latin *sors, sortis*, meaning lot or fate, once the revered and feared power of pagan goddesses, was reviled by Christian theologians. In English, sorcery has always been closely associated with WITCHES, and hence with women. *Sorcery* entered English in c1300 as a synonym for witchcraft, whereas *sorcer* (C14th–C16th) and *sorcerer* (C16th onwards) were other words for a wizard or male magician. *Sorceress* entered English in the late C14th. The development of *sorceress* is very similar to that of two other witch-related words, CHARM and GLAMOUR, in that as the widespread belief in witches waned it began to acquire positive connotations of female sexual seductiveness.

Simone de Beauvoir pointed out that: "the threadbare vocabulary of the serial novels describing woman as sorceress, an enchantress, fascinating and casting spells over man, reflects the most ancient and universal of myths . . . In societies where man worships these mysteries, woman, on account of these powers, is associated with religion and venerated as priestess; but when man struggles to make society triumph over nature, reason over life, and the will over the inert, given the nature of things, then woman is regarded as a sorceress. The difference between a priest and a magician is well known; the first controls and directs forces he has mastered in accord with the gods, and in the name of all members of the group; the magician operates apart from society, against the gods, and the laws, according to his own deep interests. Now, woman is not fully integrated into the world of men; as the OTHER, she is opposed to them. It is natural for her to use the power she has, not to spread through the community of men and into the future the cold emprise of transcendence, but, being apart, opposed, to drag the males into the solitude of separation, into the shades of immanence. Woman is the SIREN whose song lures sailors upon the rocks; she is Circe, who changes her lovers into beasts, the undine who draws fishermen into the depths of pools. The man, captivated by her charms, no longer has will-power, enterprise, future; he is no longer a citizen, but mere flesh enslaved to its desires, cut off from the community. . .the perverse sorceress arrays passion against duty, the present moment against all time to come." (*The Second Sex*)

Clitoris

Clitoris makes its first appearance in written English in a 1615 anatomy book entitled *A Description of the Body of Man*: "These ligaments. . .do degenerate into a broad and sinewy slendernes. . .upon which the Clitoris cleaveth and is tyed." The word was adopted from the Greek *kleitoris*. *The Oxford Dictionary of Etymology* maintains that it derives from the Greek word meaning to shut. *The American Heritage Dictionary*, however, suggests that it derives from a Greek word meaning little hill – a theory which might at first appear to be more likely.

The Woman's Encyclopedia of Myths and Secrets claims that *kleitoris* meant "divine, famous, goddess-like", and that Greek myth personified the clitoris as an AMAZON queen named Kleite, ancestral mother of the Kleitae, a tribe of warrior women who founded a city in Italy. It points to Clytie, one of Pandareus' orphaned daughters, whom Artemis made grow tall and strong, as an allegory of Clytie's erection. Clytie, whose name means 'famous', was also a NYMPH (*nymph* is a Greek synonym for *clitoris*) who loved the phallus of the sun and always followed his motion with her head. Transformed into a sunflower, or heliotrope, "she still worshipfully follows his movement across the sky" (Patricia Monaghan, *Women In Myth and Legend*)

The definition of *clitoris* in most dictionaries is, to many, bewildering: "a homologue of the male penis". There is, of course, some similarity between the tip of the penis and the clitoris – called in both the 'glans' (from the Greek word meaning acorn): both are located in the genital region; both are the outermost tips; and both are erotically sensitive to tactile stimulation. But the similarities between the clitoris and the penis stop there. In her book *Eve's Secrets*, Josephine Lowndes Sevely argues that the clitoris/penis analogy is not only wrong, but that the belief came about only in the C16th as a result of an ingrained male perspective that viewed the female as inferior, and an unquestioning acceptance of incorrect translations of ancient texts.

According to Lowndes Sevely, the Greeks saw the VAGINA, not the clitoris, as the homologue of the penis. This idea had been introduced to the ancient world by the Greek-born physician Galen (129–c199) who described the vagina as "a penis turned inside out". In keeping with the masculist assumptions of his time, Galen saw the female genitals as a less than perfect and mutilated version of the male's, thus the penis was the norm and the vagina was the inferior female homologue. By inverting the penis it becomes the vagina and the foreskin becomes the skin that is the appendage to the vagina. By appendage, Galen was referring to the skin that forms the inner folds, ie, the labia minora, or little lips. It was these that the Greeks called the clitoris, for which they also used the names 'nymphae' (see NYMPH) and 'fruit of the myrtle'.

This vagina/penis homologue theory went unchallenged until the C16th when Italian anatomists suddenly began to call the clitoris a female penis without apparently noticing that they were contradicting ancient Greek theory. The Paduan professor of anatomy Gabriel Fallopio – who bequeathed his name to the uterine tubes – wrote: "Avicenna. . .mentions a part positioned in the female pudendum and calls it 'a penis' or rather '*al bathara*' [the Arabic synonym for what the Greeks called the clitoris]. . .It can sometimes reach a growth so remarkable in some women that they can have coitus with each other, like men fornicating. This part is still called by the Greeks the clitoris, and from this term is still found the verb 'clitorizing' used in an obscence sense. . .This small part corresponds to the male penis. . ."

In fact, Fallopio failed to realise that Avicenna (or Ali Ibn Sina, to give him his Arabic name) had described the female genitalia exactly as had Galen – with the vagina as the homologue of the penis, the scrotum as the part which in a woman turns into the outer folds (or labia majora) and the foreskin as the parts corresponding to the external parts of the vagina, ie, the labia minora or, as the Greeks had called it, the clitoris. Furthermore, Avicenna had used the Arabic word *al bathara* to refer to those parts which "are to the vaginal opening what the foreskin is to the penis", ie, the labia. It seems highly unlikely that the Arabs would have perceived the glans (the only part of what we now call the clitoris they then knew about) as a vaginal foreskin.

Lowndes Sevely asks: "How *did* the penis/clitoris idea come about? A painstaking scrutiny of medical texts that span the intervening fourteen hundred years between Fallopio and Galen reveals that a seemingly inconsequential little slip was made in the translations of some early texts that resulted in a confusion of some magnitude. As the relevant texts were translated from Greek into Latin, from Latin into Arabic, then back again from Arabic into Latin, somehow the clitoris/penis idea got locked into medical thinking, and it was never questioned because everyone apparently believed that the idea represented the word of Galen – everyone, even including Fallopio, who was otherwise one of Galen's critics."

Thus it would appear that what we now call the clitoris was not what the Greeks called the clitoris, and that the penis/clitoris homologue was a C16th notion based on a misapprehension of ancient Greek anatomical theory which, in fact, had proposed a penis/vagina homologue. If Lowndes Sevely is correct, the etymological theory that *clitoris* comes from the Greek word meaning to shut begins to make sense, since the labia could conceivably be seen as some kind of 'shut' doors behind which is the vagina. The theory that *clitoris* derives from 'little hill', however, becomes totally baffling if Lowndes Sevely is correct.

Historically, the function of the clitoris has been subject to about as much confusion as its etymology. In her book on witchcraft, Barbara Rosen mentions a witch trial in 1593 at which the investigator – a married man – discovered a clitoris for the first time. He concluded that this "little lump of flesh, in a manner sticking out as if it had been a teat, to the length of half an inch" could only be a devil's teat. So amazed was he by his discovery that although at first he determined not to show it to anyone "because it was adjoining to so secret a place which was not decent to be seen; yet in the end, not willing to conceal so strange a matter" he exposed the woman's genitals to others who, likewise, were astounded. On the strength of this evidence the woman was convicted of being a WITCH.

By the C19th some within the almost exclusively male medical profession had begun to understand the role of the clitoris a little better. In the 1840s, describing it in his book *On Single and Married Life*, Dr R J Culverwell wrote: "It is exquisitely sensitive, and believed to be the seat of pleasure in the sexual embrace." And it was clearly sufficiently understood by those C19th surgeons who performed clitoridectomies upon women who were judged hysterical nymphomaniacs (see HYSTERIA, NYMPHOMANIA) as a result of their masturbatory habits. But generally the clitoris continued to be regarded as some sort of failed penis.

During the C20th the clitoris competed with the vagina as the contender for the focus of female sexual response in the arguments that raged among sex reformers, sexologists, psychoanalysts and FEMINISTS. Freud maintained that in little girls, during the pre-oedipal phallic phase, all sexual interest focused on the clitoris. The transition from immaturity to maturity entailed the transfer of sensitivity of her clitoris to her vagina. Although Freud was writing primarily about a psychological process rather than a physiological one, many sexologists and feminists understood him to be denying the function of the clitoris altogether during orgasm and claiming a vaginal orgasm as the real thing. It is true that although he thought the later importance of the clitoris to be infinitely variable, he did believe that clitoridal sex alone indicated an arrestation of the development of FEMININITY. To feminists, of course, clitoridal sex indicates an independence of men. Writing of these debates Beatrix Campbell has argued: "It is not so much denial of the clitoris that is striking as its appearance and disappearance in theories of female sexuality and, where it is acknowledged, its displacement in favour of the mythologized vagina, in defence of the penis as the organizing principle of the sexual act." (*A Feminist Sexual Politics: Now You See It, Now You Don't*, 1980)

Clinical evidence produced by William H Masters and Virginia E Johnson in 1966 apparently concluded the debate: "Conceptualisation of the role of the clitoris. . .has created a literature that is a potpourri of behavioural concept unsupported by biologic fact. Decades of 'phallic fallacies' have done more to deter than to stimulate research interest in clitoral response to sexual stimulation. Unfortunately, the specific roles previously assigned clitoral function in female sexual response were designated by objective male consideration uninfluenced by and even uninformed by female subjective expression." And they finally stated what many women, at least, had often suspected: "clitoral and vaginal orgasms are not separate entities". (*Human Sexual Response*)

Clearly, the clitoris has been the source of centuries-old debates on several levels but, by the 1980s, at least one thing can be stated without contention: enough is now known for dictionary compilers to eschew the traditional definition of the clitoris as a homologue of the penis in favour of entries which are both more accurate and less masculist, eg, "a small erectile organ at the front or top part of the vulva that is a centre of sexual sensation in females". (*Longman Dictionary of the English Language*, 1984)

Cocktease

Since the late C19th *cockteaser* has been a vulgar term of contempt for a woman who "displays affection and sexual interest in a male, assumes sexually inviting postures, speaks intimately, allows petting or necking, and perhaps indulges in sexual foreplay, but does not allow coitus or satisfy the male". (*Dictionary of American Slang*) In the UK, *prickteaser* is more common.

Cock, a vulgarism for penis since the early C18th, probably derives from *cock* denoting tap (UK) or faucet (USA). *Prick*, from the basic sense of anything that pricks or pierces, was initially standard English for penis from the late C16th–c1700, when it became a vulgarism and later a low colloquialism. *Tease* originates in the Anglo-Saxon spinning term *taesan*, meaning to pull, tear, comb or card. Spinning has always had strong female associations (see SPINSTER). Since the C10th *to tease* has meant to pull the fibres apart in preparation for spinning; from this developed the sense of to tear to pieces, later to worry or annoy persistently, and finally, since the C18th, to bother slightly in mischief or sport. The definition of *cockteaser* quoted above, however, suggests that cockteasing is one sport which is singularly unappreciated – by males, that is.

Male contempt for a woman who says 'no' is, of course, nothing new. But it is strongly rivalled by the contempt felt towards women who say 'yes', as evidenced by the huge number of derogatory words in the English language for sexually active experienced females or even those simply considered attractive by males. *Pricktease* and *cocktease* are the product of a double sexual standard. This insists upon women being sexually attractive, exciting and, most of all, available (to men) and, at the same time, remaining idealised, CHASTE, VIRGINS. One result of this confusion is the masculist myth that all women say 'no' when they really mean 'yes', providing a male justification for RAPE.

Cocktease and *pricktease* appeared towards the end of the C19th when an increasing number of women were openly questioning male sexual domination and rejecting penile penetration as an essential aspect of sexual activity. They were widely dismissed as hysterical (see HYSTERIA) PRUDES. The terms also reveal possible gender differences in attitudes towards heterosexual sex. A woman can be sexually satisfied by what is often dismissively referred to as foreplay since it involves stimulation of the CLITORIS. The term *foreplay* suggests that clitoral stimulation is a mere game which takes place before the 'real' action. It has tended to be viewed less dismissively by women since, as well as being the major source of orgasm, it minimises the risks of venereal disease and unwanted pregnancy. Male sexual fulfillment, however, is often dependent upon penetration and notions of overpowering female resistance.

The double standard means that a woman is damned if she does (SLUT, WHORE, TART, etc) and damned if she doesn't (COCKTEASE, COQUETTE, JILT, etc). No term today exists for the male who leads a woman to expect sexual satisfaction but fails to satisfy her.

Concubine

Concubine derives from the Latin *con-*, meaning together, and *cubare*, meaning to lie down. Since the late C13th *concubine* has denoted a woman who cohabits with a man without being his WIFE, and from the C15th–C16th it was also used of a male paramour. According to Webster's, it is still used of a man who cohabits with either a woman or another man, but to most minds, it is female-specific and the word reflects the weak position of women in a society which does not insist upon legal marriage as a precondition to cohabitation and yet does insist upon the legal protection of patrilinial inheritance.

Under Roman law, concubinage meant the permanent cohabitation of a man and woman which was recognised in addition to a formal marriage. It was commonly considered an inferior form of marriage, the offspring of which were entitled to support but did not come under the *potestas* (authority, control, power) of the father but might under the laws of Justinian be legitimated by a subsequent formal marriage. The concubine, or kept MISTRESS, today finds herself in much the same position: her children are usually recognised as the offspring of her lover and yet they are not his legal heirs. The problems experienced over the years by such women is, perhaps, reflected in the metaphoric sense of *concubinage* to mean a state of mental subserviency or bondage.

Coquette

In French *coquet*, literally, 'little cock', was applied to a macho male from the image of a cockerel strutting and flaunting himself in front of HENS. *Coquet* entered English in the C17th to refer to both sexes with a range of connotation: gallantry; wantonness; immodesty; pretty; pertness. But although the word was non-gender-specific the senses differed according to the gender of the person the word was applied to: male coquets were gallant; female ones (eventually spelled *coquette*) were WANTON, immodest or prettily pert.

During the C18th the word was more or less synonymous with what would today be called a 'flirt'. Samuel Johnson defined the verb *to coquet* as "To entertain with compliments and amorous tattle; to treat with an appearance of amorous tenderness." (He defined *flirt* as "To jeer; to gibe at one" and "To run about perpetually; to be unsteady and fluttering" and *flirtation* as "a quick sprightly motion. A cant word among women."

Coquet began to lose its male application and to pejorate. By 1770 the London gentleman's literary magazine *Monthly Review* was oblivious to the masculine origins of the word, referring deprecatingly to "One of those narcissus-like, or lady-like, gentlemen called a male-coquet." Coquetry was regarded as a very specific female trait which, although 'Women were deceivers ever', ran counter to the feminine ideal and so aroused moral indignation and wrath, eg, "A coquet commonly finds her own perdition in the very flames which she rallies to consume others" (1790). The 1811 edition of the *Dictionary of the Vulgar Tongue* defined *coquet* as a JILT, which it defined bitterly as "A tricking woman who encourages the addresses of a man whom she means to deceive and abandon".

The OED echoes the moral indignation of the C18th and C19th; its definition reads strangely passionate in an otherwise relatively value-free work of scholarship: "A woman (more or less young) who uses arts to gain the admiration and affection of men, merely for the gratification of vanity or from a desire of conquest, and without any intention of responding to the feelings aroused: a woman who habitually trifles with the affection of men: a flirt." Of a male flirt, the OED is content to say blandly "one who plays at courtship".

The English language possesses few terms which apply specifically to men who seduce and abandon women. *Womaniser, lecher, profligate, lady-killer* etc, while fairly damning, also carry positive connotations of a highly sexed and therefore totally normal and even attractive masculine, or manly, man; they suggest none of the moral indignation which lurk within the senses of *flirt, jilt* and *coquette*. An even angrier term to describe a woman who fails to 'give' herself totally to a man is COCKTEASE.

What is it that arouses so much passionate male anger? It is clearly not simply their toes that are being trodden on (or, presumably, not trodden on). Is there any reason to suppose that fear of rejection and abandonment is greater in males than it is in females? Our cultural history certainly provides every indication that men have less difficulty in expressing their anger at rejection. Definitions of masculinity also suggest that it is difficult for a man to project himself in the world as manly if woman, his intellectual, social and economic inferior, has the upper hand (see EFFEMINATE, EMASCULATE).

Cotquean See HOUSEWIFE, QUEAN

Courtesan

From the Old Italian *cortigiano*, meaning a courtier, *courtesan* entered

English in the C15th to mean one attached to the court of a prince, and, until the end of the C16th, it was commonly used to refer to a member of the papal curia, or court. As papal courtesans became objects of suspicion in Protestant England, *courtesan* became a euphemism for a female PROSTITUTE. Thus contaminated, the original sense dropped out of use and *courtesan* became pejorative and female-specific. But connotations of high birth remained with it: the *Dictionary of the Canting Crew* of the 1690s defined 'curtesan' as "a gentile fine MISS or quality WHORE". and Webster's states that such a female prostitute may have "a clientele drawn from the wealthy or upper class".

Cow

From the C16th to the early C17th, *cow* was applied to a timid, faint-hearted person of either sex. By the 1690s it was no longer used in this sense; it had degenerated and become female-specific for a lazy, dronish, BEAST of a woman and by the C18th was simply an abusive epithet for any WOMAN. In the mid-C19th *cow* pejorated further to mean a female PROSTITUTE. In the C20th it acquired yet further negative connotations of coarseness, obesity and general loathsomeness: the very antithesis of the delicate, slim, FEMININE ideal. There have been signs of some amelioration, particularly in the UK, since it is also used fairly light-heartedly of a woman, especially a MOTHER, mother-in-law or WIFE. This is reflected in the cockney rhyming slang *cow and kisses*, ie, 'MRS', for a woman or a wife, and, although they may not sound so complimentary, the expressions *silly cow* and *silly moo* usually contain an element of affection. In Australia and New Zealand *cow* or, more strongly, *fair cow* denotes a very despicable or objectionable person, a most unworthy act or an obnoxious thing.

The link between cows and women has not resulted in such derogatory and misogynistic language and ideas in other cultures. The ancient Egyptian moon goddess known as Io, later Isis, who was worshipped for more than a millennium longer than the life, to date, of Christianity, was best known in her aspect as a white, winged cow goddess of creation. Her udder produced the Milky Way constellation, and her body was the firmament which gave daily birth to the sun, her golden calf. The cow, as creatress, also existed in the myths of the Greeks, northern Europeans and Hindus to whom the milk-giving moon-cow is still sacred. The *Dictionary of Historical Slang* also points out that the *cu* in CUNT "apparently is the equivalent to quintessential femineity and partly explains why, in India, the cow is a sacred animal".

The English language, however, reveals little reverence for the concept of woman as cow. The C19th *cow-cunted* shows the very depths to which MISOGYNY can sink; it meant "a woman deformed by child-bearing or by harlotry" [see HARLOT]. (*Historical Slang*)

Why should the cow be singled out to express contempt for women who are considered obese, clumsy, ugly, immmoral and beastly? They are, after all, also gentle, fairly obedient, easily domesticated, maternal and nurturing. Could it be that our society breeds contempt for the females of a species which so obviously, after the initial fertilisation, have no need of male company during the pregnancy, birth and suckling process?

Cowry See PORCELAIN

Coy

The Latin *quietus*, meaning calm, quiet, gentle, gave the Old French word *quei* and Middle French *coi*, from which the English *coy* was adopted in the C14th. Until the C17th it was applied to women (mostly an OLD WOMAN), men and things – such as thoughts – in the sense of quiet and still. This sense survives in the present use of the word to mean undemonstrative, shyly reserved or retiring. But its main use today is in the sense of a woman who is the very opposite of calm and quiet, ie, one who displays modest backwardness or shyness precisely in order to attract attention.

The double-bind situation that women find themselves in is clearly shown by the connotations of *coy*. If they are loud and immodest they are accused of being a COQUETTE or HUSSY. If, on the other hand, they are modest, shy and retiring, they run the risk of being accused of being coy as defined by Webster's: "archly affecting shy or demurred reserve, marked by CUTE, coquettish, or artful playfulness", ie, they are flirtatious hussies.

Crack

Since the C16th, *crack* has been a euphemism for VAGINA. It was also used of a lively lad, a rogue (playfully) or a wag. But negative associations with female genitalia presumably influenced the word to become female-specific and to degenerate to become slang for a woman of broken reputation, a WENCH or PROSTITUTE (c1670–1820). In the C20th *crack* became slang for any woman. In the sense of vagina, *crack* is one of several crude and belittling terms which describe a woman as a gap, HOLE or orifice carrying with it the implication that her total function is to be penetrated, filled or plugged up by a man. Indeed, in the C19th *crack-hunter* was briefly popular slang for penis. This term also suggests that a woman is perceived as game to be tracked down, shot and cooked for male consumption. It draws upon the same violent imagery as does the slang *to shoot*, meaning to ejaculate.

Crone

Since 1386 *crone* has denoted a withered OLD WOMAN, an old ewe or sheep whose teeth are broken off and the obsolescent sense of "an old man useless or womanish from senility" (Webster's). Its etymology is uncertain. In the sense of old ewe, the word may be related to Middle Dutch *karonje*, from Old Northern French *carogne*, meaning carrion or carcass. This may have derived from the Latin *caro, carnis*, meaning flesh, (from which *carnal* derives) which is akin to the Greek *keirein* meaning to cut. In the sense of an old woman, *crone* may be a derogatory figurative transferral from old ewe or, as one theory proposes, it may have come directly from *carogne* in the sense of a cantankerous or mischievous woman.

Some feminist linguists have suggested that the word originates in the name of the ancient Greek goddess Rhea Kronica, the destroyer aspect of the triple goddess who represented old age, death, winter, the waning moon and other symbols of the inevitable destruction or dissolution that must precede regeneration.

It has proved tempting for some etymologists to connect *crone* with *crony*, meaning an intimate friend or associate, or chum. But *crony* appears to be C17th university (and therefore male) slang, possibly from the Greek *chronios*, meaning long-lasting.

Crow

Crow derives from a West Germanic verb of imitative origin. The Greek word *coronis*, which was probably a title of the goddess Athene in her death aspect. In northern European mythology the crow was a common symbol of the death-goddess, and the valkyries often took totemic form as ravens or crows. In Middle English *walkyry* was an occasional synonym for a WITCH.

Because of the folk association of crows with death and witches, and their black malevolent appearance and characteristics, it was perhaps highly predictable that in the C16th *crow* should become a term of abuse for an OLD WOMAN, and later, a woman who was considered to be particularly unpopular, unattractive or ugly.

Crumpet

A crumpet is a small round bread or cake made of unsweetened dough which is cooked on a griddle. The word derives from *crump*, or *crumb*, meaning baked. As it is little known outside the UK, the application of *crumpet* (since the 1880s) to a woman viewed as an object for male sexual gratification is not widespread outside Britain. In this sense *crumpet* ameliorated slightly in the late 1890s to become a term of endearment for a woman, originally chiefly among the working class. Like most terms applied to women which employ the imagery of food, *crumpet* carries the implication that a woman's value lies in her availability for male consumption.

In the 1980s women appropriated the word to refer to men: *The Longman Register of New Words* defines *crumpet* as British slang for "a man or men considered solely from the point of view of being sexually attractive", giving us the example: "It's Paul Newman – the older woman's crumpet. *Double First*, BBC 1, 13 Sept 1988."

Cuckquean

During the C16th and C17th the wife of an unfaithful husband was called a *cuckquean*. The word was formed from *cuckold*, the husband of an unfaithful WIFE, from *cuckoo*, the bird which lays her eggs in the nest of another. QUEAN derives from the Old English *cwene*, meaning WOMAN, related to the Greek *gyne*, meaning woman.

Cuckold entered English in the C13th and has remained, although it is used relatively rarely today. That *cuckquean* should have become obsolete after only two centuries of use reveals something of the double standard attached to fidelity and CHASTITY. Fornication (see FORNICATE) and adultery have long been seen as exclusively a male prerogative. Laurence Stone pointed out that "The honour of a married man was. . .severely damaged if he got the reputation of being a cuckold, since this was a slur on both his virility and his capacity to rule his own household." (*The Family, Sex and Marriage in England 1500–1800*). The cuckquean, on the other hand, did not become the subject of derision or shame to quite the same degree as the cuckold: her husband's infidelity was to be expected and certainly overlooked and her FEMININITY was in no way impaired. Commenting on the disappearance of *cuckquean* from our vocabulary, *A Feminist Dictionary* makes the succinct point that the husband of an unfaithful wife is a cuckold, but "the wife of an unfaithful husband is just a wife".

Cunning

To make women learned and foxes tame has the same effect: to make them more cunning.
King James I (1566–1625), upon hearing the suggestion that his daughter should learn Latin.

From the Old English *cunnan*, meaning to know, *cunning* meant wisdom or learning when it first entered English in the C14th. This sense was gradually replaced by that of ability and skill. By the C16th its meaning had deteriorated to mean deceit and craftiness. The reason for this deterioration is probably because the word had begun to acquire connotations of a type of knowledge considered evil – the occult and black magic. A cunning woman or man, for example, was simply another name for a WITCH or a wizard in the C15th and C16th. Thus the definition of the English essayist Francis Bacon: "We take cunning for a sinister or crooked wisdom." (1612) Although the belief in witchcraft faded from around the turn of the C18th, *cunning* retained connotations of the supernatural. The 1811 edition of the *Dictionary of the Vulgar Tongue* defined a *cunning man* (sic) as "a cheat, who pretends by his skill in astrology to assist persons in recovering stolen goods: and also to tell them their fortunes, and when, how often, and to whom they shall be married. . . This profession is frequently occupied by LADIES."

Like several other words once connected with witchcraft (eg, CHARM, GLAMOUR, CROW, etc), *cunning*, in the sense of deceit and craftiness, came to be associated with women: in the USA in the mid-C19th *cunning* was applied especially to women to mean charming, pretty or engaging. The word sums up the problem for those – women and foxes alike – who have no real power: "Women are told from their infancy, and taught by the examples of their mothers, that a little knowledge of human weakness, justly termed cunning, softness of temper, outward obedience, and a scrupulous attention to a puerile kind of propriety, will obtain for them the protection of man. . .." (Simone de Beauvoir, *The Second Sex*)

Cunt

In the C14th *cunt* was Standard English for the female pudendum (which derives from the Latin *pudere*, meaning to be ashamed). Since the C19th the word has also been used to denote a woman regarded as a sex object, a dysphemism for sexual intercourse, and to describe a particularly unpleasant, stupid or disliked person of either sex.

Its origins are obscure: etymologists dispute whether it is related to the Latin *cunnus*, meaning vulva, which was related to *cuneus*, meaning wedge. It may derive from the Germanic *kunton*, via the Middle Low German *kunte*, meaning female pudenda, and Old High German *Kotze*, meaning PROSTITUTE. Another theory is that its roots lie in a Greek Macedonian dialect work, *guda*, the basic meaning of which was round or curved, and from which the Old English word *cot*, meaning den, derives (see COTQUEAN). In Old English is it cognate with *cwithe*, meaning WOMB. It has been suggested that *cunt* derives from the Old English *coint*, *coynte* or *qwaynt*, etc, eg "Pryvelyhe caught her by the queynte" (Chaucer, *The Miller's Tale*, 1386).

The earliest sense of QUAINT was wise and ingenious as well as crafty and cunning, subsequently elegant, clever, cleverly wrought and hence beautiful. This theory, an attractive idea to many woman, is currently discounted.

Partridge, the author of *A Dictionary of Slang and Unconventional English*, finds it difficult to explain the *nt* part of the word but suggests that: "The main root would seem to be the *cu* (*cwe* in old English) [from which QUEEN derives] which is apparently equivalent to quintessential physical femineity [see FEMININE] and partly explains why, in India, the COW is a sacred animal." Partridge also explains why the word dropped out of Standard English: "owing to its powerful sexuality the term has since the C15th been avoided in written and polite English: though a language word, neither colloquialism, dialect, cant nor slang, its associations make it perhaps the most notable of all vulgarisms. . .and since 1700 it has, except in the reprinting of old classics, been held obscene, ie a legal offence to print it in full; Rochester spelt it *en toutes lettres*, but Cotgrave [author of the first English–French dictionary in 1611], defining *con* went no further than 'A woman &c', and the dramatist Fletcher, who was no PRUDE, went no further than 'They write sunt with a c, which is abominable' in the *Spanish Curate*. Had the late Sir James Murray courageously included the word, and spelt it in full, in the great OED, the situation would be different; as it is, neither the *Universal Dictionary of English* (1932) nor the SOD (1933) had the courage to include it. (Yet the OED gave prick: why this further injustice to women?)" However, Partridge seems to have been unaware that cunt was included in Nathan Bailey's *A Universal Etymological English Dictionary* (1791). The first modern dictionary to include the word was the *Penguin English Dictionary* in 1965.

The 1811 edition of the *Dictionary of the Vulgar Tongue* demonstrated a mixture of legality and misogyny in its definition: "C**T: the *xovvos* of the Greek and the *cunnus* of the Latin dictionaries; a nasty name for a nasty thing: *Un con miege*." But, presumably, not all males found cunts nasty; the same dictionary defines 'Nickumpoop or Nincumpoop' as "A foolish fellow; also one who never saw his wife's ****."

As a term of abuse *cunt* has been applied to people and things considered worse than either excrement (*shit-face* is considered less abusive than *cunt-face*) or the penis which, as *prick*, was a term of endearment in the C16th and C17th. As Germaine Greer wrote in *The Female Eunuch*, "the worst name any one can be called is a cunt". *The Slanguage of Sex* suggests that, as a term of abuse it "reflects the deep fear and hatred of the female by the male in our culture. It is a far nastier and more violent insult than 'prick' which tends to mean foolish rather than evil. This violent usage is a constant and disturbing reminder to women of the hatred associated with female sexuality and leaves women with few positive words to name their own organs."

Cute

In the C18th *cute* was shortened from *acute*, which derives from the Latin *acuere*, meaning to sharpen. Both *cute* and *acute* were applied to persons of either gender with the sense of clever, keen-witted, shrewd or intellectually sharp. By the mid-C19th, however, while *acute* retained its original sense, *cute* had pejorated and become associated with women. In the USA it became a colloquial and schoolboy (the OED fails to tell us if schoolgirls used it) slang term meaning CUNNING. *Cunning* by this time had deteriorated from its original sense of knowledge and learning to mean a sort of underhand or sly skill, chiefly used of women. *Cute* became used to describe a Victoran stereotype of the FEMININE ideal that survives to this day: "a generalized expression of approval suggesting daintiness, fine features, deftness, or delicacy". (Webster's)

When used of a man, however, the feminine implications of the word cast very definite aspersions on his masculinity, eg: "Young, dark and small with pretty features as regular as if they'd been cut by a die. 'He's cute'. I said." (Dashiell Hammett, 1894–1961) Since the 1930s, combining the senses of pretty, cunning and perhaps COY, *cute* further deteriorated absorbing a distrust of supposedly feminine CHARM to denote "artificial, straining to impress". (*The Oxford American Dictionary*)

Seldom used of men, *cute* is also seldom used by men according to Cheris Kramerae: "A number of sources I consulted for this paper indicated that women do not use the same adjectives as men do, or they are used in different contexts or with different frequency. Native speakers will recognise 'NICE', 'pretty', 'darling', 'charming', 'sweet', 'lovely', 'cute', and 'precious', as being words of approval used more frequently by women. As one male student in my speech class said, 'If I heard a guy say something was "cute", I'd wonder about him'. That is, his masculinity would be in question." (*Quarterly Journal of Speech*, 1974)

Dame

Adopted from Old French in the early C13th, *dame* originated in the Latin *domina*, meaning LADY or MISTRESS of the house, the feminine of *dominus*, meaning lord or master, from which *dominate* derives.

At first, *dame* was used to express relation or function in the sense of a female ruler, superior or head, synonymous with *lady*, the feminine equivalent of *lord*. It was also used as a form of address to a lady of rank or woman of high position, the feminine equivalent of *sire*. *Dame*, or *dam*, was also used to denote a mother. In 1330 it acquired the sense of the 'lady' of the house, or the mistress of the household – ie, a HOUSEWIFE – and was prefixed to her name to indicate her function. This was at a time when *mistress* had no sexual connotations and *housewife* indicated a position of an altogether much higher status than it does today. *Dame* was also the prefix of an elderly MATRON as a mark of respect.

As the power of the household declined, notably from the C14th onwards, so did the position of its female ruler and, like *lady*, *mistress* and *housewife*, *dame* came to denote a woman of insignificant power. Unlike these other synonyms, however, *dame* never acquired negative sexual connotations.

By the mid-C17th *dame* was obsolete in its earlier sense of a female ruler. In the sense of the lady of the house it was replaced by *housewife*, and humorously applied to an elderly housewife. As a form of address used to a lady of rank it gradually extended to women of lower rank and, after the C16th, was left solely to these. This 'democratic levelling' did not affect *lord* which retained its original connotations of high status. *Dame* was no longer used as a prefix to the name of a woman of rank except in personifications such as Dame Fortune or Dame Nature (see MOTHER), when science had proved to man that nature was controllable and notions of fortune, fate, luck, etc held little sway. In its sense of mother it became a disparaging term except when used of animals. Earlier connotations of elderliness probably influenced its development as a term for a schoolmistress in an elementary school (mid-C17th to early C20th) – usually an OLD WOMAN or WIDOW, neither being highly valued members of society.

In 1611 *dame* was revived as the legal title prefixed to the name of the WIFE of a knight or baronet. But it was not until 1917, when it was bestowed upon the first women admitted to membership of the Order of the British Empire (OBE), that *dame* was once again applied to a woman in her own right.

In the USA, where no titled aristocracy exists, *dame* lost all connotations of rank, power or status. There, since the beginning of the C20th, it has been chiefly a slang term for a young woman, as noted by G H Knight: "In the vocabulary of modern youth, chivalry is dead. . .A GIRL is a JANE, a dame, a MOLL. . .." (*English Words*, 1923) In 1988 the word was used to express contempt by First Lady Nancy Reagan towards her Soviet counterpart Raisa Gorbachev: "Who does that dame think she is?" (*Time* magazine)

In 1902 the term *pantomine dame* first appeared. In this comic character, traditionally an elderly or middle-aged woman played by a male actor, all female power, status and even dignity is portrayed as one big joke. This character can be contrasted with another pantomime figure, that of Prince Charming, traditionally played by an attractive young ACTRESS. For a man, generally considered virile and powerful until very old, to portray an ageing and therefore ugly and sexually unattractive woman is very much what the joke of the pantomime dame is all about. When a woman dons the trousers of Prince Charming her character acquires male potency, but when a man puts on skirts it is the notion of a male losing his power that, in the eyes of the audience, is so funny.

Damsel

Like DAME, *damsel* originates in the Latin *domina/dominus*, meaning LADY/lord or MISTRESS/master. In Old French *demoiselle* and *damoisel* denoted persons of high status: the *domicellus* or *damoiseaux* was the son of a king, prince, knight or lord before he entered the order of knighthood. The king's young knights were called *damoiseaux* or *damsels*. The female equivalent, *demoiselle*, was used of young unmarried women of noble birth and it was with this meaning that *damsel* entered English in the late C13th.

Like *dame*, it extended downwards and lost all implications of high rank or noble birth becoming, by the late C14th, synonymous with MAID, MAIDEN, GIRL and country LASS. The 1611 King James translation of the Bible undoubtedly played a part in this development of the word: "Now David was old and stricken in years; and they covered him with clothes but he gat no heat. Wherefor his servants said unto him, Let there be sought for my Lord the King a young virgin. . .and let her lie in thy bosom, that my Lord the King might get heat. So they sought for a fair damsel. . .And the damsel was very fair, and cherished the King, and ministered to him: but the King knew her not." (1 King's 1:4)

Consequently, during the Restoration (1660) a *scotch warming-pan* was a euphemism for a 'female bed-fellow'. In 1727 *damsel* became a colloquial term for a hot iron or warming pan. During the C19th *warming pan* was a euphemism for a fart; whether this is in any way connected to male attitudes towards female bed-fellows is uncertain.

Daughter

Joseph T Shipley derives *daughter* as "ultimately from The Sanskrit *duhitri*, from *duh*, from *dhugh*, to milk (Eng. *dugs*): the milker of the family". (*Dictionary of Word Origins*) The OED, however, states that daughter derives from the Indo-European *dhughater*, whence also Sanskrit *duhitar*, and generally refers to the verbal root Indo-European *dhugh*, Sanskrit *duh* – to milk. The origins of many kinship terms lie in the function traditionally performed by the person denoted by the word.

With one exception *daughter*, which has been in the English language since at least 1000, never degenerated, and never developed negative sexual connotations. Not even any of the rhyming slang terms – *bottle of water*, *soap and water*, *bricks and mortar* – carry negative implications.

The exception is the use of *daughter* in names given to instruments of torture, such as *Duke of Exeter's daughter* and *Scavenger's daughter*, invented by the Duke of Exeter and Sir Leonard Skevington, Lieutenant of the Tower of London respectively, and *Gunner's daughter*, the gun to which seamen were lashed to be flogged.

This lack of negative terms does not apply to some proverbs which suggest that daughters have not always been unreservedly appreciated: "Two daughters and a back door are three arrant thieves" (1670); "Daughters and dead fish do not keep well" (C18th); "Daughters pay nae debts" (Scottish).

Deflower See FLOWER

Delilah

I have a lot of respect for that dame. There's one lady barber that made good.
                                        Mae West, in *Goin' to Town*, 1935

From the biblical story (Judges 16) of the woman who betrayed her lover, Samson, to the Philistines by cutting off his hair, *Delilah* has been used colloquially since the C19th to denote a seductive false temptress or HARLOT.

Delphic

Since the late C16th *delphian*, or *delphic*, has meant obscure, ambiguous or enigmatic. This sense derived from Delphi near Mount Parnassus where the most famous oracle of ancient Greece was reputed to have been. Like all oracles it revealed the truth and foretold the future in complicated riddles.

Delphi (cognate with the Greek word for WOMB) was considered by the ancient Greeks to be the centre or navel of the earth: it was where Hera, the MOTHER earth goddess, was worshipped in her prophetic form as Delphyne. In her temple was a white stone, or omphalos, bound with a red ribbon to represent the navel and umbilical cord. Delphyne was killed by Apollo on whose temple were reputedly engraved the words "Keep woman under rule", and the oracle was taken over by him.

Dildo

The origins of *dildo* are unknown but this has not prevented lexicographers from making some imaginative guesses. The *Dictionary of Early English* suggests that it was a nonsense word used in the refrains of popular risqué songs in the C16th and C17th. Hence *dildo* became a name for a phallus. This begs the question because these songs may have been considered risqué precisely because they had the word in their refrains. Two other theories were put forward in Nathan Bailey's *A Universal Etymological English Dictionary* and echoed in the 1811 edition of the *Dictionary of the Vulgar Tongue*: "From the Italian *diletto*, a woman's delight; or from our word *dally*, a thing to play withal."

In the C17th *dildo* was used for a sausage-shaped curl, usually of a wig or hairpiece, a long cylindrical glass tube, and a phallus-shaped tree or shrub of the genus *Coreus*. It also became the term for a penis substitute for insertion in the VAGINA, a contemptuous or reviling appellation used of a man or lad, and, in the USA, it came to denote a weak or EFFEMINATE man. In this last sense *dildo* developed to become a slang term for a foolish, stupid person, also called a prick, and is popular among boys aged between ten and fourteen.

Dish

The imagery of food is frequently drawn upon in the English language to portray women and their external sexual organs as edible objects for male consumption. The concept of woman as an empty container to be filled or plugged up by a man, his sex organ or his semen, is another common image. *Dish*, C20th slang for a sexually alluring young woman, combines both. Although also used of an attractive male, its development explains why it is more frequently used of a woman.

In Old English *dish* denoted a BROAD shallow VESSEL; in the C15th it also denoted food ready to be served. In *Antony and Cleopatra* Shakespeare made use of these two senses: "I know that a woman is a dish for the gods." The 1811 edition of the *Dictionary of the Vulgar Tongue* defines *dishclout* (ie, dish-cloth) as "a dirty greasy woman" and explains that the phrase "He has made a napkin of his dishclout" means "One who has married his cook MAID".

Distaff

In the traditional method of spinning by hand, a distaff was the cleft stick, or staff, on which wool or flax was wound. The word first appeared around 1000. The first syllable, *dis*, or *dise*, is akin to the Low German *diesse*, meaning a bunch of flax, and connected with *dize*, *dizen*, meaning to put tow on a distaff.

By the late C14th *distaff* was synonymous with women's work. *To have tow on one's distaff* meant to have serious work in hand, or trouble in store – a figurative use of *distaff* which takes women's work seriously and does not dismiss it as a frivolous way of merely passing time.

Until the C18th, the day after Twelfth Day (January 7th) was known popularly as 'St Distaff's day', as this was the date when women supposedly returned to their spinning or other regular employment after the Christmas and New Year festivities.

Give St Distaff all the right
Then give Christmas sport goodnight,
And next morrow every one
To his own vocation

Popular rhyme, 1657

In *Concerning Famous Women*, Boccaccio (1313–75) used the distaff to symbolise the castrating effects of female power. He describes how Iole, in revenge for being forced to submit to the domination of Hercules, induced this mighty Amazon-slayer to renounce his spear: "she brought that man. . .to such a pass that he would sit like a woman among the other common women and tell the story of his labours. Taking the distaff he would spin wool, and his fingers, which had been hard enough to kill serpents when he was still a baby. . .now at a vigorous age, in fact his prime, were being softened by spinning wool." Boccaccio clearly knew nothing of the callouses that this method of spinning caused to the hands of women which, of course, had to be fair, gentle and soft if the SPINSTER was to live up to the FEMININE ideal.

Towards the end of the C14th the distaff stood symbolically for the FEMALE sex and for female authority and dominion – hence Hercules' humiliation (at least AMAZONS were fearsome and worthy opponents for all-conquering heroes). The word was also used to denote the female branch of a family: the 'spindle-side' as opposed to the 'spear-side'.

Dog

You will find that the woman who is really kind to dogs is always one who has failed to inspire sympathy in men.

Max Beerbohm (1872–1956)

The more I see of men the more I love dogs.

Marie de Rabutin-Chantal, Marquise de Sévigné (1626–96)

Late Old English *docga*, of unknown origin, probably originally denoted a large or powerful kind of what was known generically as *hund*, a term which was eventually displaced by *dog*. In distinguishing gender, a dog was once the male of the species, eg: "The Dogge is thought better than the Bitche" (1577), up until the end of the C19th, eg: "The man who knows and loves his hound only uses the word dog, as he does the word BITCH, to denote sex." (1890) It is possible that because *bitch* pejorated to such a great extent the once masculine *dog* became more acceptable as the norm for both sexes.

Dog is used pejoratively in many different contexts with connotations of inferiority or unattractiveness, eg, *dog cheap*, *dog's body*, *dog-tired* etc. But when applied specifically to women it usually means something a whole lot worse. In US slang, for example, *dog's dinner* denotes a mess or an unattractive person, but a *dog-lady* is an ugly PROSTITUTE. And whereas *dog*, when used of a man, can mean merely disreputable or untrustworthy, when used of a woman it means ugly, unrefined or sexually disreputable, or a woman who is boring and does not have the compensation of beauty.

Doll/Dolly

She was created to be the toy of man, his rattle, and it must jingle in his ears whenever, dismissing reason, he chooses to be amused.

Mary Wollstonecraft, *A Vindication of the Rights of Woman*, 1792

Both *doll* and *dolly* were late C15th pert forms of *Dorothy*, and later became generic terms for a female pet or favourite. Thereafter their etymological histories differ slightly.

By the beginning of the C16th *doll* had degenerated to become a euphemism for a MISTRESS – like so many other names of women which were popular among rural or working women (see also MOLLY). In the C18th a child's imitation baby play-thing was called a doll. This presumably influenced a C19th sense of a pretty but unintelligent or empty-headed person, especially when dressed up; mostly it was used to denote a pretty but silly or frivolous woman. In the mid-C19th *doll* was also used among the working classes as a term of contempt for a 'LADY', or well-dressed woman of the upper and monied classes (the female equivalent of a 'toff'). *To get dolled up* meant to dress showily and extravagantly. At the same time *doll* was used in the sense of a female companion: the *New Swell's Guide to Nightlife* (1846) refers to "sailors and their dolls", suggesting strong sexual connotations. Most of these senses survived into the C20th. The *Dictionary of American Slang* gives the following definitions: "1. A pretty GIRL or woman; esp. a pretty girl or woman whose main use in life seems to be to grace the scene rather than to make an active contribution; esp. a clear complexioned blonde, blue-eyed girl with regular features. 1920: 'If a blonde girl doesn't talk we call her a "doll".' (Scott Fitzgerald, *This Side of Paradise*.) 2. Any female especially a pert or saucy one. 1932: *Guys and Dolls*, title of a book by Damon Runyon."

This led to the slang use of *doll* for any attractive, sweet person; a pleasant generous person of either sex. And, thus freed from its female specificity and denuded of its connotations of sexuality, *doll* ameliorated and since the 1940s has been commonly used by teenage girls to refer to an attractive, popular boy.

In the C19th British essayist Thomas Carlyle (1795–1881) understood well the conflict between ideals of FEMININITY and what it meant for a woman to be fully adult. Influenced by woman's-rights campaigners such as Mary Wollstonecaft, Harriet Martineau and his wife, Jane, he wrote of woman: "There is much for her to do. . .her whole sex to deliver from the bondage of frivolity, dollhood and imbecility."

Similarly, Henrik Ibsen wrote of his play *The Doll's House*: "A woman cannot be herself in today's society, which is an exclusively male society, with laws written by men and with prosecutor and judge who judge woman's conduct from a male point of view." In the famous ending, Nora rejects the role of child-WIFE which has been forced upon her and, slamming the door behind her, leaves her husband and children in her erstwhile doll's house. This was totally unacceptable to German audiences in the 1880s for whom Ibsen agreed to rewrite the ending so that Nora returned to her doll-like status.

Dolly fared less well than *doll*. In the C16th it pejorated to denote a SLATTERN – the very opposite of a well-dressed woman. And, like *slattern*, it also acquired negative sexual connotations. Between the C17th and C19th it meant first a mistress, then a drab, useless woman and eventually a HARLOT. A *dolly-mop* was first a harlot and then an amateur PROSTITUTE. Presumably influenced by *doll* in the sense of a child's play-thing, in the mid-C19th *dolly* came to mean silly, foolish or babyish. In the 1960s *dollybird* (see BIRD) arrived on the scene of 'swinging London'. It was a demeaning, albeit complimentary, term for the stereotypical slim, attractive, trendily dressed and sexually liberated young woman.

Despite one or two periods of amelioration during their histories, the re-emergence of the woman's movement in the late 1960s has ensured that even though many of the earlier negative connotations are now obsolete, few people can be unaware of the demeaning and infantilising aspects of reducing a woman to a man's toy implicit in these terms.

Dowager

This word entered English in the C16th from the Old French *douagere*, meaning a WIDOW who owns some title or property bequeathed to her by her deceased husband. In the late C19th the term was used familiarly to denote an elderly LADY of dignified demeanour. These positive connotations probably result from the belief that money bestows dignity, thus a 'lady' is perceived to be a woman of means and no woman without means can have dignity. In the USA *dowager* is even more positive as it denotes "an elderly woman of imposing appearance or dominant personality; *often*: one of the elder women of assured position who tend to set the tone of an assembly, social group, or community". (Webster's) It is one of the few words in the English vocabulary which is actually positive about an OLD WOMAN.

Dowdy

In the C14th *doude*, of unknown origin, denoted an ugly woman. By the C17th *dowdy* had replaced *dowd* and was a derogatory term for a badly dressed woman. Samuel Johnson defined a *dowdy* as "an awkward, ill-dressed, inelegant woman". (1755) *Dowd* made a brief reappearance in the C18th for a woman's mob-cap. This term derived from the woman's personal name *Mabel*. In the late C17th *mab*, (a name popular among serving and working class females) denoted a SLATTERN or an untidily-dressed woman. By the C18th it had pejorated and acquired an overtly negative sexual sense: *The New Canting Dictionary* (1725) defined *mob, or mab*, as a WENCH or HARLOT. In the C19th the obsolete dialect verb *to mabble* was defined in *North Country Words* as "to dress carelessly. Hence mab-cap, generally called mob-cap. A cap which ties under the chin – worn by elderly women."

If a woman did not keep her hair in place overnight with her mob-cap or dowd, she would look dowdy the next day. Or perhaps she was not considered too elegant in her dowd – something that was echoed in C20th advice books to women which warned them they would lose their husbands if they wore curlers and hairnets in bed at night. (How they could keep their spouses if their hair was a mess during the day because they did not wear their curlers and nets at night was yet another problem.) By the beginning of the C19th *dowdy* had pejorated; The 1811 edition of the *Dictionary of the Vulgar Tongue* defined the word as "a coarse vulgar-looking woman". A dowdy woman was also termed a *frump* which was probably shortened from the C14th dialect word *frumple*, meaning to wrinkle, although in the C16th *frump* denoted a sneer, jeer or hoax and had developed by the C17th to denote ill humour and sulks.

Dowdy ameliorated slightly in the C20th, but it continues to reflect an almost obsessional need for women to be tidy and well-dressed if they are to gain societal approval. The OED defines *dowdy* as "a woman or GIRL shabbily or unattractively dressed, without smartness or brightness; (almost always of a woman or her dress)."

In *The Female Eunuch*, Germaine Greer cites DRAB, *slommack*, SLUT, slattern, COW, *douchebag*, *ragmop* and *sleaze* in "the vocabulary of reprobation which refers to a woman's lapse in neatness". *The Slang Thesaurus* lists no words which refer derogatorily to an untidily dressed man. Indeed, his masculinity is enhanced by a little carelessness or a pair of 'manly' working or dirty jeans; a dowdy woman, however, does not live up to the FEMININE ideal.

Doxy See DUCKY

Drab

Drab was probably a low or cant word for a dirty and untidy woman (also called a DOWD, SLUT or SLATTERN), which first entered English in the early C16th. Its derivation is uncertain but it may be connected with the Irish *drabog* and Scottish Gaelic *drabag*, both meaning a dirty female. A connection with Low German *drabbe*, meaning dirt or mire, has also been suggested. By 1630 *drab* had degenerated to mean a female PROSTITUTE. In its sense of dull, *drab* derives from the hempen, linen or woollen cloth of natural undyed colour which was known as drab or drap.

Ducky

Of all the animal metaphors used of a woman – most of them insisting upon her role as a sexual object – *ducky* (or *ducks*) might seem to be the least offensive. However, it was probably first used as a euphemism for *doxy*, which was C16th and C17th slang for a beggar's trull, a WENCH, or a female beggar. Until the C20th a doxy also meant a female paramour, MISTRESS or PROSTITUTE. The root of *doxy* may be the Dutch *docke*, meaning DOLL.

Dyke

"Are you really a dyke Harriet?"
"I rather thought of myself as the Hoover Dam".

Rita Mae Brown, *Sudden Death*, 1983

Dyke, which is often used to denote the stereotypical mannish LESBIAN, was originally an early C20th US slang term of abuse either for any lesbian or for any woman who rejected male advances. Its origins are unknown, although one suggestion is that it began as -*dite*, from HERMAPHRODITE, on the grounds that heterosexist orthodoxy insists that a woman whose sexuality is independent of a man must be part male. By the 1980s many lesbians, refusing to accept the myth that they are either BUTCH or FEMME, began to use *dyke*, without any negative connotations, to refer to all lesbians.

Effeminate

From the Latin *effeminare*, meaning to make feminine, *effeminate* entered English in the C15th with the sense, according to the OED, of "that has become like a WOMAN" which it claims was used "of persons". This suggestion that the term was non-gender-specific is misleading – for how could someone who is a woman become like one? But the real question to be asked is what is a woman like? On this, the etymological history of *effeminate* is very revealing.

In the C16th the word could be used of men, without reproach, to mean they had acquired qualities of gentleness, tenderness and compassion. Until the late C17th it was used of things such as music and odours to mean soft and voluptuous. This notion of voluptuousness was also present in another obsolete C17th usage which had the more negative connotation of self-indulgence, as in the declaration of Charles 1 to his army at Southampton in 1642: "Avoid excessive drinking and effeminacy (by some esteemed the property of a soldier)." From this developed the sense of a devotion to women or, as Webster's reveals, "degraded by subjection to women".

The sensuous pleasure of woman was dangerous to man, as John Milton (1608–74) warned:

> But foul effeminacy held me yok't
> Her Bond-slave; O indignity, O blot
> To Honour and Religion! servil mind
> Rewarded well with servil punishment!
> The base degree to which I now am fall'n,
> The rags, this grinding, is not yet so base
> As was my former servitude, ignoble,
> Unmanly, ignominious, infamous,
> True slavery, and that blindness worse than this,
> That saw not how degenerately I serv'd.
>
> Samson Agonistes

Yet another obsolete sense of *effeminate* possessed connotations of woman as physically weak and delicate – and since woman had the contaminating power to EMASCULATE obviously any man worried about his masculinity would do best to steer well clear of female company. Similarly, a man also had to be on his guard against too great a love for his wife, since the word *UXORIOUS* carries the same connotations of degradation. (Could it be that masculinity, for all its manliness, strength and courage, was/is actually more frail than femininity?)

Today *effeminate* is a totally derogatory word used of a man who is thought to possess "qualities more characteristic of and suited to women than to men". (Webster's) According to the OED these qualities are: "womanish, unmanly, enervated, feeble, self-indulgent, voluptuous, unbecomingly delicate, or over-refined". Webster's definition is no less opprobrious towards women: "lacking manly strength and purpose: exhibiting or proceeding from delicacy, weakness, emotionalism".

Christian theologians appear to have been confused about effeminacy. The 1609 Donai version of the Bible translated the Latin *effeminati* as 'effeminates'. The 1611 King James version preferred 'sodomites'. The 1952 Revised Standard Version gives 'male PROSTITUTES'. (1 Kings 14:14)

Emasculate

Emasculate comes the from Latin *emasculare*, meaning to castrate, from *e*, meaning out, and *masculus*, the diminutive of *mas*, meaning male. Today the word used literally means to deprive a male person or animal of his virility or, used figuratively, to censor or deprive something such as language, law, literary composition, film, etc of its strength and vigour, ie, to weaken, make EFFEMINATE and cowardly, to enfeeble or impoverish. This raises an interesting question. Since, presumably, a feminist book or film 'lacks manliness' (a definition of *effeminate*), could a censor ever be said to be able to emasculate, for example, this book?)

Like *effeminate*, there is no corresponding FEMININE word in our vocabulary for *emasculate*. The word WOMAN, itself, connotes weakness and feebleness. Whereas a man can only be weakened by femininity, a woman can only be strengthened by masculinity.

Enchant/Enchantress

The Latin stem *can*, meaning sing, is the root of CHARM, *incantation* and *enchantment* (*incantatus*). *Charm* and *enchant* followed very similar etymological paths.

Since the C13th *enchantment* has meant the employment of magic or sorcery. From the C14th–C17th, coinciding with a period in which several million women throughout Western Europe and North America were persecuted and killed for being witches, it meant to influence irresistibly or powerfully, as if by a charm, or to hold spell-bound. An enchantress during the C14th–C16th was a woman who used magic: a WITCH, a SORCERESS. But by the C17th when belief in witchcraft was waning, *enchant* ameliorated to mean to delude or befool, and *enchantment* to refer to the delusive appearance of beauty; *enchantment* subsequently softened to mean merely an alluring or overpowering charm. *Enchantress* denotes no more than a charming or bewitching woman.

Today, most of the old connotations of the evil power of women have disappeared from *enchant* (as they have in *charm*, GLAMOUR and other witch-related words). It has become regarded as a fairly trivial word (see TRIVIA) which, like CUTE, PRETTY, NICE, etc is used mostly by, and/or of, women.

Europe

The continent of Europe owes its name to the Greek mythological daughter of Telephassa, also called Argiope, and Agenor, who was Libya's son by Posidon. Her name means 'broad-faced', a synonym for the full moon and a title of the moon-goddess Demeter at Labadia and Astarte at Sidon. If, however, the word is not *eur-ope* but *eu-rope*, it may mean 'good for willows' – that is, 'well-watered'. The willow ruled the fifth month of the ancient sacred year and was associated with witchcraft (see WITCH) and fertility rites throughout the continent of Europe. The Greeks first applied the name *Europe* to central Greece, then to the whole of the Greek mainland and later to the land-mass behind it.

Eve

Although the OED has an entry for *Adam* – "the first man, father, of the human race" – there is no entry for *Eve*, the first MOTHER. Webster's, however, does not discriminate and gives: "[Middle English, after *Eve*, the first WOMAN in the Bible]: a woman having qualities typically associated with womankind; woman," with an example of use from *Newsweek* "an effortless-ly FEMININE creature whose personal career never interferes with her role as a charming eternal *Eve*".

Eve was one of the common Middle-Eastern names for the mother–goddess of all living things. To the Hittites she was *Hawweh*, meaning life; to the Persians she was *Hvov*, or 'the earth'. A Semitic root of her name was *Hayy*, a matrilineal (see MATRIARCHY) kinship group once considered the 'life' of every tribe by direct descent from the first mother-creatress. *Eve*, *serpent* and *life* all derive from the same root in Arabic. The association with the serpent may also be present in *Harreh*, Hebrew for Eve, which meant life, life-giving and, possibly, snake.

Several English compound terms and phrases are revealing about attitudes towards women and concepts of FEMININITY. Brewer's gives *Daughter of Eve* as a synonym for *woman*, which is "often used in reference to feminine curiosity". The 1811 edition of the *Dictionary of the Vulgar Tongue* defines the phrase *Eve's custom house* as "where Adam made his first entry. The monosyllable." (see CUNT). *The curse of Eve* was a late C19th–C20th euphemistic or jocular colloquialism for the menses, which was shortened to *the curse* in the mid-C20th.

Eve was not the first woman in Jewish tradition, as Patricia Monaghan explains in *Women in Myth and Legend*: " 'Male and female He created them', proclaims Genesis in its first version of humanity's creation. But the Bible later changes its mind, explaining the creation of woman as Jehovah's afterthought. Jewish tradition outside the Bible understood the disparity: there *was* a female created simultaneously with Adam, and her name was Lilith. . . When the first man suggested intercourse to the primal female, she enthusiastically agreed. Adam then instructed Lilith to lie down beneath him. Insulted, she refused, pointing out that they had been created equally and should mate so." Adam immediately requested God to provide him with a more submissive mate: Eve was provided for Adam and Judaeo-Christianity was provided with a very different model of archetypal woman.

Some feminist linguists suggest that both the word *adam* and the biblical character may be more feminine than Jews and Christians have been prepared to accept: "The root Hebrew word for 'ADAM is 'ADAMAH (soil or earth). 'ADAMAH is a feminine noun, and it could be argued that 'ADAM is a derivation both linguistically and symbolically from an arch-type 'Mother Earth' Hebrew concept." (American Jewish Committee, cited in Casey Miller and Kate Swift, *Words and Women*)

The American theologian Dr Phyllis Trible has shown that *'adham* was a generic term in ancient Hebrew for humankind. This, she suggests, throws a different light on the second (but older) story of creation in Genesis 2 in which God formed man(kind) from the dust of the ground and later made woman from the rib of *'adham*. She sees this original person as an androgynous being with the potentialities of both sexes. To enable procreation to take place God then performs surgery on the sleeping ANDROGYNE. Up to this point in the story the ancient Hebrew storyteller consistently used the generic term *'adham*. "Only after the rib episode are the Hebrew words specifying the human male *'ish* and the human female *'ishshah* introduced. *'Adham*, whose flesh and bones have now been sexually identified as female and male, speaks of the two sexes in the third person. 'She shall be called woman (*'ishshah*) because she was differentiated from man (*'ish*)' provides a valid alternative for the Hebrew term usually rendered 'taken out of'." (Miller and Swift)

When the 1611 King James version of the Bible translated *'adham* as 'man', the original Old English sense of *man* as a person of either sex, although still recognised, was already ambiguous and increasingly becoming interpreted as a male person. Referring to the biblical story of creation, Miller and Swift conclude that it is "far different from the male-oriented interpretation. . .that has embedded itself in our conscious understanding and our less conscious use of language. In English the once truly generic word man has come to mean male, so that males are seen as representing the species in a way females are not."

The English language does not divide nouns into feminine, masculine and neutral genders as do some languages. The fact that some languages do has provided some feminist linguists with material which they suggest indicates that a language itself can be sexist or patriarchal. But linguistic descriptions such as *gender*, *feminine* and *masculine* were chosen arbitrarily by linguists themselves. That nouns with weak vowel endings are designated 'feminine' and those with strong consonant endings are designated 'masculine' reflects only the cultural associations of linguists. Language cannot be sexist but linguists have been and are.

Fag/Faggot

Of unknown origin, *fag(g)ot* was adopted from French in the C14th for a bundle of twigs bound together used as fuel. Until the C17th it was also used as a pejorative slang term applied to women, a synonym for BAGGAGE, in the sense of a LOOSE woman or HARLOT. Until the mid-C19th, generally preceded by *little*, it was also a term of abuse for a child (*heavy baggage* was a far from complimentary term used of women and children as the property of a man). In the C19th it became a slang verb meaning (for a man) to copulate, and to frequent harlots. A *faggot-master* was a whoremonger. During the C18th and C19th *faggot* was also military slang for a "man hired at a muster to appear as a soldier" (*Dictionary of the Vulgar Tongue*, 1811 edition), ie, a raw recruit or a dummy soldier.

In the late C18th *fag* came to mean hard work or drudgery, possibly influenced by the use of the word in English public schools for a boy who was made to do menial work for an older boy. This may have derived from a perversion of *fatigue*. During World War 1 *fag* came to mean a cigarette. There are a number of theories on the origin of this sense. Partridge, in *A Dictionary of Slang and its Origins*, suggests that fag was an abbreviation of fag-end, literally the coarse end of a piece of cloth, and originally, from about 1887, it meant an inferior cigarette. Brewer's *Dictionary of Phrase and Fable*, posits that it was possibly connected with *vag* a Devonshire term for a turf for burning. Another theory is that it was an acronym from the wording on cigarette tins sent to soldiers on the western front in World War 1 which proclaimed 'For a Good Smoke'. *Fag hag* was then used pejoratively of women who did the most unfeminine thing of smoking cigarettes.

In the 1920s *fag* became slang for an EFFEMINATE man and, by the 1940s, specifically for a male homosexual. The *Dictionary of American Slang* states that: "It has been suggested that 'fag' meaning homosexual comes from 'fag' meaning cigarette, since cigarettes were considered effeminate by cigar and pipe smokers when they were first introduced at the end of World War 1. Although this may have reinforced the use of the word, 'fag' meaning a boy servant or lackey has been common English schoolboy use since before 1830, and may be the origin of 'fag' meaning homosexual."

Interestingly, a US marine reported the re-emergence of the earlier connotations of *fag* in the sense of an army recruit: "While in basic training, one is continually addressed as a faggot or a GIRL. These labels are usually screamed into the face from a distance of two or three inches by the drill instructor, a most awesome, intimidating figure. During such verbal assaults one is

required, under threat of physical violence, to remain utterly passive."
(quoted in H Michaelowski, *The Army Will Make A Man Out Of You*, 1982)
Female and homosexual images are thus combined to represent the weak
qualities in a recruit, stressing the ineffectiveness and passivity of FEMININITY
or non-masculinity, and the power and aggression of masculinity.

Fag BAG denotes a woman married to a gay and the even more derogatory
term *fag* HAG has come to be used of a heterosexual woman who seeks out
the company of gays, eg: "I'd hazard a guess that you're simply a Faggot's
Moll, Fag Hag, or Fruit Fly. . .a girl who enjoys the company and attention
of males-who-go-to-bed-with-males is generally quite hung up about sex
and afraid of getting fucked, not to mention a more complicated relationship." (Una Screw, *Screw*, 1969)

Fanny

The woman's name *Fanny* became a slang term in the C19th (possibly
earlier) for the female pudendum or VAGINA. This may have been influenced
by John Leland's novel, *Memoirs of Fanny Hill* (1749), whose eponymous
heroine was a PROSTITUTE. *Fanny-fair* and *fanny-artful* were also C19th
euphemisms for the same thing. In the USA *fanny* changed its anatomical
position in the 1920s, becoming a non-gender specific slang term for "the
human rump" as the *Dictionary of American Slang* somewhat quaintly
calls the backside or bottom.

In the UK *fanny* is also used to denote something of no value, as in the
phrase 'You're talking a lot of old fanny.' This may seem a particularly
offensive dismissal of this part of a woman's anatomy but in fact it derives
from another source entirely. In 1812 eight-year-old Fanny Adams was
murdered in a hop garden at Alton, Hampshire in southern England. Her
body was gruesomely dismembered, cut up into small pieces and thrown
into a river. By 1889 British sailors with a macabre sense of humour used
her name for their rations of tinned lumps of mutton. Hence *Fanny Adams*
or *Sweet Fanny Adams* became terms denoting nothing at all. The
expression *Sweet F.A.* refers either to Fanny Adams or 'Fuck All'. *Fanny* is
one of the least objectionable UK euphemisms today for CUNT; it is so mild
that many young British girls, if they use any name at all for their genitalia,
are encouraged to use it.

Fate

In early Greek mythology, Fate, the goddess of destiny, was known as
'Moira'. *Moira* originally signified a person's 'lot' or 'portion'. In later Greek
mythology the *Moirae* were aspects of the triple creator–preserver–destroyer

goddess named respectively, Clotho, Lachesis and Atropos. Clotho bore the DISTAFF and spun the thread of life; Lachesis measured out the life span of every creature as the thread came off the spindle; Atropos (whose name meant 'she who cannot be turned aside or avoided') snipped the thread of life with her shears. It is thought that this myth is based on an ancient Greek custom of weaving family and clan marks into the swaddling bands of each newly born baby to indicate the child its allotted place in society.

In Roman mythology the *Moirae* were known as the Parcae, or the 'Fates', the latter being from the Latin *fari*, meaning to speak. Literally, *fate* meant 'that which has been spoken'; its primary sense was first 'sentence of doom of the gods' and later, with the demise of pagan worship, the impersonal power by which events are determined.

Via the Italian *fato*, *fate* was incorporated into the English language by the end of the C14th with the sense of "the principal power or agency by which, according to philosophical and popular systems of belief, all events and some events in particular are unalterably predetermined from eternity". (OED) An Old English synonym was *wyrd*, from which WEIRD derives. Because of associations with death and with pagan practices, *fate* also had negative connotations in the sense of what a person was destined to suffer or, as a verb, to ruin irrevocably.

By the C16th the adjective *fatal* meant producing or resulting in death or destruction, or irreversible. But hyperbolic use led to a weakened sense so that by the C17th *fatal* also came to mean the causing of harm or evil, specifically less grievous than death or ruin, or merely mischievous. This influenced the use of the term *femme fatale*, adopted from the French, which means literally 'disastrous woman' but is generally used in the sense of a seductive woman who lures men into dangerous or compromising situations.

Thus the once immortal power of the original Fates which controlled the destinies of all humankind was reduced to little more than the cheap CIRCEAN CHARM of a VAMP or a SIREN.

Female

The female is a female by virtue of a certain lack of qualities; we should regard the female nature as afflicted with a natural defectiveness.

Aristotle (384–322BC)

Female is a Middle English variant of the Old French *femelle*, a development from the Latin *femella*, meaning young or little woman, from *femina*, meaning WOMAN. Its original C14th spelling *femal* or *femall* persisted until the C17th – its present spelling is probably the result of the mistaken belief that the word was derived from male, and that the *fe-* was a FEMININE prefix.

By the C15th *femal* was used to denote precious stones which were inferior or different on account of paleness or some colour flaw. *Male* was applied to various things, both material and immaterial, to denote their superiority, strength or greatness. Thus from the late C16th–C18th *female* was also used to mean womanish, EFFEMINATE or weakly – that is, non-masculine and therefore inferior. In another now obsolete sense of the word, in the C17th *female* designated something that was simple, plain or undisguised. This did not, however, herald any significant amelioration since it continued to denote inferiority.

As a synonym for woman, *female* was a term of contempt by the mid-C19th eg, "The 'Totty' (from Hottentot, meaning Black [man]) of the present day and his female (for the creature can scarcely be dignified by the name of woman)" (E E Napier, *Excursions in Southern Africa*, 1849). And it remained a degrading epithet in the C20th. In *The Mothers Recompense* (1925), by Edith Wharton, a young woman is reproved for including the word in her vocabulary: " 'Female' – she murmured – 'is that word being used again? I never thought it very nice to apply to women, did you?' ".

Fowler's 1983 edition notes that "to call a woman a female is resented as impolite; the noun has acquired the same kind of disparaging overtone as individual. It is not reasonable to extend this resentment to the adjective use of female; but this is what probably accounts for the apparent avoidance of the natural phrase *f. suffrage* and the use of the clumsy *woman suffrage* instead. . . In the first edition of this book [1926] the hope was expressed that when the way women were going to vote came to be a common theme of discussion it would be called the *female vote* and not the *woman vote*; for to turn *woman* into an adjective with *female* ready made would be mere perversity. In the event we have been neither impolite enough to call it the *female vote* (though we still speak of the *male vote*) nor perverse enough to turn *woman* into an adjective; we have evaded the dilemma by calling it the *women's vote*."

Although *female* has, undoubtedly, retained some disparaging connotations, Casey Miller and Kate Swift point out that "Ruth Todasco's *An Intelligent Woman's Guide to Dirty Words*, documents from standard dictionaries the extraordinary fact that with the possible exception of *female*, the everyday words for a female person have acquired either directly or in combinations the additional meaning of PROSTITUTE: woman of the streets, fancy woman, fruit woman, fallen woman; GIRL, girlie, call girl, joy girl, bad girl, working girl; LADY of pleasure, lady of the evening. Like MISTRESS, the titles QUEEN, MADAM, and DAME, all have debased meanings unmatched by masculine-gender counterparts." (*Words and Women*)

Although women in the late 1960s also eschewed *female* in the phrase 'Women's liberation', a slogan such as 'The Future is Female' suggests that some women, at least, are no longer prepared to accept that there is anything disparaging about the use of the word any more than there is about being female.

Feminine/Femininity

The latin *femininus, femina* was formed on *femina*, meaning woman or, properly, 'the suckling one' or 'the sucked one'. This was formed on an Indo-European root from which the Latin *felare*, meaning to suckle, *filius*, meaning son, and *felix*, which originally meant fertile, also derive.

Feminine, adopted from the Latin, first entered English c1384 as an adjective applied to persons and animals merely to denote FEMALE. Sometime in the C15th it acquired its most common present-day sense: characteristics of, peculiar, or proper to, women; womanlike or womanly. From c1430 to 1651 it was used opprobriously to mean womanish or EFFEMINATE. In the late C16th, as a verb, it was used to mean to make feminine, in the sense of to weaken. In the late C17th, implying a female incapacity, it was also used in the sense of "such as a WOMAN is capable of" (OED), eg, "Some dreams I confess may admit of easie and feminine exposition" (Sir Thomas Browne, *A Letter to a Friend*, 1672)

Femininity, meaning feminine quality, or the characteristic quality or assemblage of qualities pertaining to the female sex, entered English c1386. In early use it also denoted female nature. Like masculinity, it was often referred to as the essential aspect of gender, eg, "What she [the American woman] conspicuously lacks, . . .is essential femininity." (*Westminster Gazette*, 1893) These essential characteristics of femininity have generally been understood to be passivity, docility, and weakness; when applied to a man *femininity* has denoted the EMASCULATION of his essential masculinity, ie, virile strength, vigour, assertiveness, etc, eg "There is. . .a decided note of femininity in his genius; a want of manly strength". (J Forster, *Academy*, 1890)

This equation of femininity with weakness and masculinity with strength has spilled over into transferred uses: when applied to music *feminine* denotes "having the final chord occurring on a weak beat" (OED); in linguistics a final syllable is said to be *masculine*, denoting stressed or strong, or *feminine* denoting the opposite. One of the best, most easily understood definitions of *femininity* (an area in which clarity is frequently lacking) appears in Lisa Tuttle's *Encyclopedia of Feminism*: "The socially determined expression of what are considered to be innately female attributes, virtues and deficiencies, as dispayed through costume, speech, posture, behaviour, bodily adornments and attitude." Susan Koppelman Cornillon makes the helpful observation that although femininity is a concept shared by both sexes it has very different meanings for the two sexes: "in a male culture, the idea of the feminine is expressed, defined and perceived by the male as a *condition* of being female, while for the female it is seen as an *addition* to one's femaleness and a status to be achieved". (*Images of Women in Fiction: Feminist Perspectives*)

Not everyone is agreed that femininity is culturally determined: Freud made the unfortunate statement that "anatomy is destiny" and Janet Sayers quotes a British housewife Yvonne Stayt: "Men are naturally more suited to be aggressive and assertive and dominant and women more suited to be submissive and give way and be the peacemakers." (*Sexual Contradictions*, 1984)

This issue of whether to define femininity as biologically or culturally determined was one Simone de Beauvoir confronted: "Most assuredly the theory of the eternal feminine still has its adherents who will whisper in your ear: 'Even in Russia women still are *women*.'

"It would appear, then, that every female human being is not necessarily a woman; to be so considered she must share in that mysterious and threatened reality known as femininity. Is this attribute something created by the ovaries? Or is it a Platonic essence, a product of the philosophic imagination? Is a rustling petticoat enough to bring it down to earth? Although some women try zealously to incarnate the essence, it is hardly patentable. It is frequently described in vague and dazzling terms that seem to have been borrowed from the vocabulary of the seers, and indeed in the times of St Thomas it was considered an essence as certainly defined as the somniferous virtue of the poppy." (*The Second Sex*)

One of the conclusions de Beauvoir came to was that no essence can define woman once and for all; femininity, like "the 'true woman' is an artificial product that civilization makes, as formerly eunuchs were made. Her presumed 'instincts' for coquetry [see COQUETTE] and docility are indoctrinated, as is phallic pride in man." She also writes of the devaluation of femininity, reflected in the dictionary definitions: "woman feels inferior because, in fact, the requirements of femininity *do* belittle her. She spontaneously chooses to be a complete person, a subject and a free being with the world and the future open before her: if this choice is confused with virility, it is so to the extent that femininity today means mutilation." "Thus femininity", as Tuttle writes, "is also the term used to represent the OTHER, where masculinity or maleness is seen as the norm. Because our culture (all patriarchal cultures) is male-centred, women are the outsiders, and femininity is in opposition to whatever is considered to be important to civilization."

Susan Brownmiller also shows how femininity is defined in terms of mutilation: "Femininity, in essence, is a romantic sentiment, a nostalgic tradition of imposed limitations," and believes that "Femininity pleases men because it makes them appear more masculine by contrast." (*Femininity*) De Beauvoir referred to Balzac's belief that femininity involves treating a woman as a slave while persuading her she is a queen. Brownmiller puts it like this: "The world smiles favourably on the feminine woman: it extends little courtesies and minor privilege. Yet. . .one works at femininity by accepting restrictions, by limiting one's sights, by choosing an indirect route, by scattering concentration and not giving one's all as a man would to his own, certifiably masculine, interests. It does not require a great leap of the imagination for a woman to understand the feminine principle as a grand collection of compromises, large and small, that she simply must make in order to render herself a successful woman."

Definitions of femininity and masculinity, although they change – in the last century a woman who displayed a stockinged ankle would have been considered unfeminine, today a woman bare-legged in a mini-skirt can be considered feminine – have always supported male domination. Thus feminists who challenge this sexual inequality have been found lacking in femininity. As Janet Sayers writes: "Anti-feminist propaganda has repeatedly sought to achieve its ends by discrediting feminists as deviating from the norms of their sex, as unfeminine – as 'unsexed'. . .as evincing 'masculo-femineity (viraginity)' and 'psycho-sexual aberrancy'. . . as seeking 'unisex rest-rooms' and a generally 'desexed society'. . .".

Sayers examines the three main theories which inform current discourse on gender, in an attempt to explain or understand the sexual inequality which is built into definitions of feminine and masculine. One theory holds that femininity and masculinity are biologically determined, that women's subjection is determined by the biological fact of women's childbearing, and by their being physically weaker than men. Although Sayers accepts some involvement of the sex hormones she convincingly argues that "the evidence that sex *differences*. . .are directly determined by the endocrine system or by some other aspect of biology [childbearing, for instance] is far less convincing".

Another theory is that gender behaviour is shaped by the child's under-standing of sex and gender. According to this cognitive–developmental theory, within the first two years of life little girls become aware that femininity means passivity and that masculinity means aggression simply from their surroundings.

Sayers outlines another theory which suggests that our preference for gender conformity is an effect of the material benefits it brings. De Beauvoir was one who supported this view of social conditioning: "the passivity that is the essential characteristic of the 'feminine' woman is. . .a destiny imposed upon her by her teachers and by society. . .she is taught that to please she must try to please, she must make herself an object; she should therefore renounce her autonomy. . . If she were encouraged in it, she could display the same lively exuberance, the same curiosity, the same initiative, the same hardihood as a boy." (In which case she would be called a TOMBOY).

Sayers explores the various different psychoanalytic theories which also inform this discourse. Karen Horney was probably the first well-known critic of Freud's views on the subject of femininity – but her own views are also deeply rooted in a biologically deterministic standpoint. Since Horney, other feminists (eg, Kate Millet, Eve Figes, Germaine Greer, Adrienne Rich, Luce Irigaray, Mary Daly, etc) and psychoanalysts (Melanie Klein, Wilhelm Reich, Jacques Lacan, W R D Fairbairn, Donald Winnicott, etc) have attacked or modified classical Freudian theory on, among other things, the concept of penis-envy which Freud believed was the major influence on femininity, his apparently biologically deterministic position, and his definition of feminine as passive and masculine as active.

On this last point Freud wrote: "It is essential to realise that the concepts of 'masculine' and 'feminine', whose meaning seems unambiguous to ordinary people, are among the most confused to occur in science. . . Every individual. . .displays a mixture of the character-traits belonging to his own and the opposite sex; and he [sic] shows a combination of activity and passivity whether or not these last character-traits correspond with his biological ones." (1905) But, as Juliet Mitchell, a feminist and a psychoanalyst (influenced by Lacan), has pointed out, classical psychoanalytic theory has the value of showing psychoanalysis to be "an incipient science of the ideology of patriarchy – of how we come to live ourselves as feminine or masculine within patriarchal societies." (*Women: The Longest Revolution*) In *Psychoanalysis and Feminism* she wrote: "Under patriarchal order women are oppressed in their very psychologies of femininity; once this order is retained only in a highly contradictory manner this oppression manifests itself. Women have to organise themselves as a group to effect a change in the basic ideology of human society. To be effective, this can be no righteous challenge to the simple domination of men (though this plays a tactical part), but a struggle based on a theory of the social non-necessity at this stage of development of the laws instituted by patriarchy."

Psychoanalytic theory has deeply influenced feminist linguistic theory. Deborah Cameron explains why: "The connection lies in the notion of a 'symbolic order' or set of meanings which define culture. In contemporary theory of the subject this symbolic order is not only to be understood in the same way as. . .a system of differences [called *langue* by Saussure], it is very frequently equated with language itself." Rosalind Coward and John Ellis explain it like this: "Because all the practices that make up a social totality take place in language, it becomes possible to consider language as the place in which the social individual is constructed." This clearly has an important bearing upon understanding the concepts of femininity and masculinity and the argument about whether they are socially constructed or not.

According to Cameron the main problem with much of the psychoanalytic approach to language, as with some other feminist approaches, is that, "they all subscribe to some degree of determinism, to the idea that men control language and (especially) to the notion that women are alientated from it to a degree that men are not. They stress the inauthenticity of women's language at present, the difficulties women have in talking about their experience, or sexuality. They trace back to this linguistic disadvantage important elements of symbolic language or the forging of an authentically female code. . . On the one hand theories of alienation and inauthenticity seem to me misguided because they locate us in a linguistic utopia which never has existed, and never will exist; on the other, I find them politically dubious because they are remote from the lived experience of women, and indeed, reject the validity of much of that experience."

Psychologist Jean Baker Miller, among others, has suggested that the way forward for feminists (linguists and non-linguists) is to interpret essential feminine traits such as emotionalism, vulnerability and intuition (the example of feminine given by *The Concise Oxford Dictionary*) not as the weaknesses that patriarchy has defined them, but as strengths which may be essential to the development of a new and better society. Although this may represent some sort of resolution to a deadlock, there is a huge problem in this proposal for reform: while language may reflect SEXIST attitudes it can never, in itself, be separated from the viewpoint of the speaker. Freda may mean something wonderfully positive when she utters the phrase 'feminine intuition', but when Fred utters it he may be implying something totally derogatory.

Dictionaries, so far, have only ever provided definitions based upon the written word. Until relatively recently most words have been written and published by men (they still are but it is possible to envisage a position of equality). It may be, as more and more women write – and as the spoken word (radio, television, film) increasingly reflects and influences meaning, and as dictionaries come to accommodate this change (as they are beginning to) – female experience as expressed in language will come to be acknowledged in dictionaries to an extent that it never has before.

Another area in which concepts of feminine and masculine are connected with language is that of the grammatical category of gender. This originated in the linguistic scholarship of Greece. Gender (the term derives from a word meaning class or kind) was used to divide nouns into three classes, labelled 'feminine', 'masculine' and 'neuter'. As Cameron points out, not all languages exhibit this kind of noun classification. English, for instance is said to be a type of language called natural gender. This means that only those words which refer to something with a biological sex can be feminine or masculine. But "Feminists, contemplating such usages as 'Man is unique among the apes in that he grows a long beard, and it is to this that he owes his superior intelligence' have pointed out that English gender is natural only if you are a man." Cameron believes that "This observation marks a step in the right direction: some aspects of, say, pronoun replacement (eg that ships [or VESSELS], and cars are *she*) cry out for a cultural rather than nature/grammar explanation."

Grammarians insist that, for instance, the use of *he* is a rule of grammar which has nothing whatsoever to do with ideology. This rule, known as 'marking theory' and referred to by Cameron as "the newest red herring in the gender debate", is a technical spell under which even feminists fall. She cites a patronising statement which two such linguists made to their non-linguist sisters: "they may be forgiven for failing to understand the theory of marking, which explains that *he* can be unmarked for sex in certain contexts but marked for it in others. Even now, statements about the 'essential absurdity of using the same symbols for all the human race in one breath and for only half of it in the next' betray ignorance of this principle widely operative in languages." (Betty Lou Dubois and Isobel Crouch, *American*

Minority Women in Sociolinguistic Perspective)

Cameron cannot accept that grammar and ideology can be separated. "One of the most thoroughly documented phenomena in feminist research has been the rise of sexist practices in prescriptive grammar, and it is this which turns out to be at the bottom of unmarked *he*. Since at least 1553, when one Thomas Wilson asserted the precedence of masculine nouns and pronouns, grammarians have been attempting to eliminate the tendency still present in ordinary speech to use *they* as a singular for generic or unspecified referents (as in 'you can't blame a person if they get angry about sexist grammar'). John Kirkby's *Eighty Eight Grammatical Rules* of 1746 stated that the masculine is more comprehensive than the feminine, and this view found its way into the statute books by 1850, when *he* was held legally to stand for *she*." (Although it didn't when it came to the female franchise and women – even freehold-owning ones – found themselves excluded from the category of citizen or person.)

Maria Black and Rosalind Coward argue that this attitude originates in a general 'discursive practice' within our culture whereby there is a discourse available to men of masculine sexuality as well as one "which allows them to represent themselves as people, humanity, mankind. This discourse, by its very existence, excludes and marginalises women by making women the SEX." ('Linguistic, Social and Sexual Relations: A Review of Dale Spender's Man Made Language') Thus men may obliterate their masculinity, but femininity can never be effaced. This produces the effect that women are an exception to the male norm.

As Cameron points out, "Unmarked *he* is indeed a feature of grammar – of prescriptive grammar, reinforced by male grammarians for avowedly ideological reasons."

Feminism/Feminist

I myself have never been able to find out precisely what feminism is: I only know that people call me a feminist whenever I express sentiments that differentiate me from a doormat or a prostitute.

Rebecca West, 1913

The word *feminism* dates from the 1850s. It originates in the Latin *femina*, meaning woman, or, properly, 'the suckling one' or 'the sucked one'. This will have strong resonances for childless females (whether by choice or not) who find that in patriarchal society they are treated as if they are not 'real' women because they are not mothers.

Feminism was used in the last half of the C19th to mean an expression or idiom peculiar to women, and the tendency in a man to feminine habits. This last sense was taken over by *effeminancy* (see EFFEMINATE). *Feminism* (with the associated *feminist*), meaning the faith in women, the advocacy of the rights of women, or the prevalence of female influence, did not appear until the 1890s following the 1892 First International Woman's Congress in Paris which used the label *feministe*. Before then, *womanism* had been briefly popular during the 1860s, '70s and '80s for the advocacy (by both females and males) of the rights, achievements, etc of women. Other terms which had been applied to those who campaigned for women's rights include *emancipators*, *reformers*, SUFFRAGISTS, etc.

Feminist first appeared in print in the English national newspaper *The Daily News* in 1894: "What our Paris correspondent describes as a 'feminist' group is being formed in the French Chamber of Deputies" – a reference to the female suffrage movement in France. *Feminism* made its debut a year later in the journal named *The Athenaeum*. An anonymous review of *The Grasshoppers* by the popular novelist Miss Sedgwick described how the main 'delicately nurtured' women characters were plunged into "an abyss of poverty, privation and dependence". The reviewer referred to one of these characters "whose intellectual evolution and. . .conquettings [see COQUETTE] with the doctrines of 'feminism' are traced with real humour, while the poignancy of her subsequent troubles is enhanced by the fact that. . .she, alone. . .has in her the capacity of fighting her way back to independence". By 1897 the self-conscious apostrophes around the neologism were abandoned and *feminism* had arrived in the English language to stay.

A precise, or even meaningful, definition of *feminism* has perplexed many lexicographers, writers both female and male, and feminists themselves. The OED defined it at first as being used only rarely to mean: "The qualities of females or the state of being female." Its 1933 supplement told its readers to "delete rare" and came up with a new definition: "The opinions and principles of the advocates of the achievements and claims of women; advocacy of women's rights." Webster's gives a more materialist definition: "the theory of the political, economic, and social equality of the sexes", as well as the more generalised "organized activity on behalf of women's rights and interests; specifically, the C19th and C20th movement seeking to remove distinctions that discriminate against women".

None of these definitions is incorrect, but all fail to capture what for many feminists today is the essence of feminism: the pluralism of the ideology. As Rosalind Delmar writes: "The fragmentation of contemporary feminism bears ample witness to the impossibility of constructing modern feminism as a simple unity in the present or of arriving at a shared feminist definition of feminism. Such differing explanations, such a variety of emphases in practical campaigns, such widely varying interpretations of their results have emerged, that it now makes more sense to speak of a plurality of feminisms than of one." (*What is Feminism?*)

Thus *The Feminist Dictionary* (1985) attempts to solve the problem while at the same time, perhaps unconsciously, arriving at a definition which reflects this pluralism, by providing as many as thirty definitions of the word from different women all over the world; it also includes entries under several headings which reflect different types of feminism, eg Black, radical, socialist, marxist, lesbian, etc.

The problem – for feminists – of defining what is meant by feminism has been further complicated by the strong negative reaction that the ideology, and the word arouses. In the introduction to *New French Feminisms* (1981), Elaine Marks and Isabelle de Courtivron point out that "Women concerned with the woman question in France use the word 'feminism' and 'feminist' less often than do their counterparts in the United States. The ridicule to which 'feminists' were subjected has always been more aggressive in France; this may be one reason why the words do not appear as frequently. . .we have nonetheless decided to place 'feminisms' in our title because there is as yet no better word to account for the phenomenon. . ."

This problem has not been confined to French feminists, giving rise to the much used phrase "I'm not a feminist, but . . .". A Woman's Liberation poster of the early 1970s cheerfully listed some of the masculist attempts to define feminism: "BITCHY, CATTY, DYKEY, frustrated, FRIGID, bitter, intuitive, petty, NYMPHOMANIAC – We are the women that men have warned us about."

But perhaps one of the simplest definitions remains the best:

"Mother, what is a Feminist?"
"A Feminist, my daughter,
Is any woman now who cares
To think about her own affairs
As men don't think she oughter."

Alice Duer Miller, 1915

Femme See BUTCH, FATE

Filly

Filly, meaning a young mare or female horse, dates from the C15th or possibly even earlier if, as most etymologists believe, it was adopted from the Old Norse *fylja.*

In the C17th, *filly,* like so many horse-related words, was applied to a GIRL or young woman. In 1665 Samuel Pepys used the phrase *slipping her filly* to refer to a miscarriage. The connotations of skittishness presumably influenced its subsequent development as a euphemism for a WANTON woman. By the early C19th *filly* had ameliorated slightly; it lost the negative sexual connotations present in wantonness and became used to describe any young woman who was lively and high-spirited.

How much it ameliorated depends very much on one's point of view. To *The*

Penguin Dictionary of Historical Slang the term is "an entirely inoffensive word for a woman used by the upper classes". For this, Pierce Egan the Elder, "a very close observer of the speech of his day", is cited: "This phrase [*fillies of all ages*] is now so commonly used in a sporting point of view, without meaning any offence to the fair sex, that it would be almost *fastidious* to make any objections to it." (1828)

Noting this, *The Slanguage of Sex* comments with commendable sternness: "But today's 'young girls' are likely to find the term not at all 'unobjection-able' with its overtones of the woman as an animal, valued for its breeding, youth and qualities as a 'ride'. The only comparable name for a male is a 'stallion' which has quite different implications of power and virility."

Members of the fair sex of Pierce Egan the Elder's acquaintance may well have observed some fastidiousness had they been aware of the phrase *filly-hunting*, which from C19th–early C20th meant searching for an amorous, obliging or mercenary woman.

Fish

In the 1850s *fish* became an insulting term for VAGINA. At the same time the now obsolete phrases *a* BIT *of fish* and *to go fishing* were euphemisms for coition (with a woman), and to seek for an obliging or mercenary woman (ie, a PROSTITUTE), respectively. A *fish-market* was a term for a BROTHEL. However, *fish* may have had similar connotations from a much earlier period. From mid-C16th to C17th, *fishmonger* was a term for a BAWD, possibly being a corruption of *fleshmonger*, while a *fishmonger's daughter* was a whore. In current US gay slang *fish* is a contemptuous term for both a woman and a vagina, and *to have a fish dinner* is to have sex with a woman. In straight slang, a *fish* QUEEN, meaning a gay, expresses heterosexual contempt for male homosexuality and male disgust for women. In contrast, when *fish* is used of men, as in *he's a queer* (or *poor*) *fish* there are no female connotations and it is less derogatory. In US and Canadian male prison slang *fish* is a term for a new inmate; in this usage the connotations of freshness or newness are in striking opposition to those of slimy, smelly, carrion-like flesh when the word is used of a woman and/or her genitalia.

The Dictionary of Contemporary Slang suggests that the use of *fish* to denote a woman derives from the "alleged smell of the vagina". According to *The Woman's Encyclopedia of Myths and Secrets* this association has had a long history: "A world-wide symbol for the Great Mother was the pointed-oval sign of the yoni; known as the *vescia piscis*, VESSEL of the Fish. It was associated with the 'fishy smell' that Hindus made a title of the yonic Goddess herself, because they said women's genitals smelled like fish. In Greek *delphos* meant both fish and womb. Christian theology adopted the fish claiming that *ichthys*, Greek for fish, was an acronym for 'Jesus Christ, Son of God': the fish became a phallic symbol."

Although cunnilingus has had its male advocates over the centuries, and the belief in the APHRODISIAC powers of the oyster suggests positive male attitudes towards the smell, taste and feel of the vagina, Susan Brownmiller points to a way in which use of the term *fish* reinforces an insecurity in women about themselves and their genitalia: "I can never convince myself that perfume is just a harmless pleasure. I've heard too many jokes, I suppose, like the one about the blind man who tips his hat and says 'Good morning ladies' when he passes a fish market. Dread that the female scent needs a mask for sexual confidence is frankly exploited in commercials for vaginal deodorants, or feminine hygiene sprays as they are called euphemistically. (Perhaps not so euphemistically. Hygiene refers to the practice of health and cleanliness: in the context of a douche-like product the word conveys the age-old charge against women, 'unclean, unclean'.)" (*Femininity*)

Fishwife

In the C16th *fishwife* denoted a woman who sold fish. Towards the end of the century *a fishmonger's daughter* was a euphemism for WHORE; by the mid-C17th *fishwife* had degenerated to mean a scurrilously abusive, foul-mouthed, vulgar, scolding (see SCOLD) woman; in the early C19th a *fish-FAG* was slang for a vixenish (see VIXEN) or foul-mouthed woman. The 1811 edition of the *Dictionary of the Vulgar Tongue* defined *Billingsgate Language* as "Foul language, or abuse. Billingsgate is the [London] market where the fishwomen assemble to purchase fish; and where, in their dealings and disputes, they are somewhat apt to leave decency and good manners a little on the left hand".

Brewer's states that the phrase *to swear like a fishwife* came about because "women who sell or hawk fish are renowned for their invective". This expression tells us something about the extent to which speech is integrated into a basic notion of FEMININITY. The idea that women should be 'NICE' and 'ladylike' (see LADY), that is, they should carefully monitor their langauge and behaviour, functions as a strong mechanism of social control. The fishwife, selling her produce in the markets and streets of British towns and cities, clearly offended C16th susceptibilities when, as Joan Kelly has pointed out, "a new gender construction of the domestic lady was emerging and the post-Renaissance male conception of ladylike behaviour was assuming its more modern form". (*Women, History and Theory*) Fishwives – originally women married to fishermen rather than those married to urban retailers of fish – may not have been subject to the same degree of stringent male control as other women traders since their menfolk spent long periods away at sea: it is possible that their language and behaviour was indeed less 'ladylike' as a result. The 'language of the streets' was taboo for women: they were not supposed to hear it because they were not supposed to be there – their place was in the home.

C20th sociolinguists have noted that the fishwife stereotype is a relatively rare phenomenon. In the 1920s, Otto Jespersen commented in his study of language differences between the sexes: "Among the things women object to in language must be specially mentioned anything that smacks of swearing ... Such euphemistic substitutes for the simple word 'hell' as 'the other place', 'a very hot' or 'a very uncomfortable' place, probably originated with women." He concluded "there can be no doubt that women exercise a great and universal influence on linguistic development through their instinctive shrinking from coarse and gross expressions and their preference for refined and (in certain spheres) veiled and indirect expression". (*Language: Its Nature, Development and Origin*)

Shulamith Firestone doubted that 'instinct' had anything to do with it: "As for the double standard about cursing: a man is allowed to blaspheme the world because it belongs to him to damn – but the same curse out of the mouth of a woman or a minor, ie an incomplete 'man' to whom the world does not yet belong, is considered presumptuous, and thus an impropriety or worse."

Socialised to use special 'polite' or 'indirect' means of expression, women are considered unfeminine if they don't use it. They suffer from a double bind since they are then castigated for the indirectness of their speech and accused of being unable to speak precisely or express themselves as forcefully as men do.

Ignoring the originality, imagination and sheer inventiveness of the euphemistic style of language of women who are constrained from using the language of the supposedly 'mannish' fishwife stereotype, Jespersen warned: "Men will certainly and with great justice object that there is a danger of the language becoming languid and insipid if we are to content ourselves with women's expressions."

Flapper

The Dictionary of Modern Slang defines *flapper* as "the popular female type of the 1920s, typically, a young woman, characterized by a cynical attitude, a frank interest in sex, a penchant for daring fashion, including short straight dresses, no petticoats, bobbed hair, stockings rolled below the knee etc. together with the use of bright lipstick and eyeshadow, cosmetics introduced after World War 1".

The word was commonly assumed to be a figurative use of the onomatopoeic word *flapper* which, since the early C18th, has meant a young wild duck or partridge. Etymologists now believe it derives from an early C17th English dialect use of *flap* to denote a woman or girl of light or LOOSE character. This theory is supported by the modern northern British dialect term *flap*, meaning an unsteady young woman. An 1889 dictionary of slang gives "Flippers, flappers very young girls trained to vice". A certain lack of 'ladylike' decorum is implicit in the 1890s use of *flapper* for a girl in her teens, from her plaited pigtail tied at the end with a large bow which flapped against her back as she walked along. And a Northumberland glossary of 1892 gives "A young giddy girl is called a flap, or a woman who does not settle down to her domestic duties."

Flap and *flapper*, then, are terms which express societal disapproval of the independent or unsubdued woman – the flighty young 'bird' who refuses to settle down in her father's or husband's nest.

In Britain in the 1920s *flapper vote* was used contemptuously of the parliamentary vote for women at twenty-one rather than thirty, presumably in an attempt to suggest that women were too immature to vote, eg: " 'Flapper' is the popular press catchword for an adult woman worker, aged twenty-one to thirty, when it is a question of giving her the vote under the same conditions as men the same age." (*Punch*, 1927)

Flighty young women in their twenties were given the vote in 1929; it has to be said all fears that this would change the existing (im)balance of power between the sexes proved to be unfounded.

Flibbertigibbet

This word may derive from an onomatopoeic representation of senseless chatter. The OED states that it means a chattering or gossiping person and cites a 1549 sermon of the English Reformation preacher Hugh Latimer who warned young King Edward VI to ignore the "flatterers and flibbergibs" who would try to seduce him away from his studies. Although GOSSIP and CHATTER are both strongly associated with women it would seem that at first a flibbertigibbet was conceptualised as masculine. In the *Declaration of Egregious Popish Impostures* (1603) the English theologian Samuel Harsnet named Fliberdigibbet as one of the four devils cast out by Jesuits. Six years later Shakespeare named the "foule flibbertigibbet" as one of the five fiends from hell which possessed 'Poor Tom' in *King Lear*. In its masculine form *flibbertigibbet* ameliorated to a synonym for the devilish, but not evil, Puck. In the C19th, after Sir Walter Scott called the boy Dickie Sludge a flibbertigibbet in his novel *Kenilworth*, the word came to mean merely mischievous and impish-looking.

When applied to women the term was far less complimentary; "a flighty or frivolous woman" (OED); "a light-minded or silly restless person, esp. a pert young woman with such qualities" (Webster's).

Floozy

Webster's states that the origins of *floozy* (also spelled *floozie*, *floosie* and *floosy*) are unknown and defines the word as an attractive young woman of LOOSE morals and, in slang, as a dissolute and sometimes slovenly woman. Defining *floosie* as naval slang for a "GIRL [read young woman] as a companion" in use since c1940, *A Dictionary of Slang and Unconventional English* believes the word originated in South Africa and is formed on *flossie*. The *Dictionary of American Slang* defines it as "An undisciplined, prom- iscuous, flirtatious, irresponsible girl or woman, especially a cynical, calculating one who is only concerned with having a good time or living off the generosity of men; a cheap or loose girl or woman." It defines *flossy* as over fancy, over shiny and over elegant.

From this a picture emerges of the deceiving woman whose attractive exterior hides an evil, immoral or filthy interior, ie, the JILT, flirt, COQUETTE or COCKTEASE. In the C16th she was the WANTON who, seduced by the devil, wore fine clothes, the JEZEBEL who wore makeup and eschewed the home in favour of gadding about abroad, in order to seduce men who were powerless to resist her alluring CHARM or GLAMOUR.

The notion of woman as a VESSEL containing filth has a long history. Reflecting C16th puritan ideas, Shakespeare summed up the floozy of his time as follows: "Virtue is beauty, but the beauteous evil/Are empty trunks, ore-flourish'd by the devil." (*Twelfth Night*, 1601)

Flower

From the Old French *flor*, *flour*, from the Latin *flos*, *flower* entered English in the early C13th. Because, perhaps, the flowers of most plants contain both the female and the male reproductive organs, the etymological history of the word over the centuries is informative about perceived notions of both FEMININITY and masculinity.

Presumably because of the beauty and natural perfection of a flower, the word has been used in a non-gender-specific sense since 1200 to mean the choicest individual or the 'pick' of the 'bunch'. In fact, this is the earliest recorded sense in English. Since the late C16th it has also meant the most attractive or desirable part or product of anything, the essence, quintessence or 'gist' of a matter. Applied to males, the phrase *flower of chivalry* was given to several knights in the C14th–C16th at the height of their manly powers, denoting their vigour, strength and maturity. With masculine connotations of strength, virility, fame and prosperity, the prime of life was also known as the 'flower' of an individual's life.

At the same time a flower also symbolised the supposedly feminine qualities of delicacy, frailty and immaturity. This identification with the feminine is apparent in the C14th use of the word to denote virginity (see VIRGIN). This may have influenced the mid-C15th sense of *flower* to denote an adornment, ornament, a precious possession or a 'jewel' – all euphemisms for maidenhead (see MAIDEN). It is possible that this sense also influenced the word *flowers*, denoting menses (c1400–1859), although this is thought to have derived from a totally different root: the Latin *fluor*, meaning flowing.

An obvious identification of flowers with the feminine is in the use of the names of flowers for women's personal names. *Flora* was the name of an ancient Roman goddess, in fact the patron of PROSTITUTES. *Rose*, *Poppy*, *Pansy*, *Iris*, *May* and *Rosemary* are some of the many flower names bestowed upon females. The symbolic meaning of several flowers represents the embodiment of desirable feminine values: lily for purity; violet for modesty, innocence and faithful love; jasmine for amiability; veronica for fidelity. There are no personal names of males which derive from flowers. But the flower image has not always reinforced the masculist tendency to idealise women as beautiful fair maidens. The virgin/WHORE dichotomy is clear from the C19th slang use of *flower*, *flower-pot*, and even *flower of chivalry* (a pun alluding to the 'ride' of the sexual act), as vulgar colloquialisms for the VAGINA. A *flower-fancier* was slang for a frequenter of prostitutes.

Of all the terms that have been used as euphemisms for the female genitalia, *flower* might seem to be the least opprobrious. But *deflower*, meaning to deprive a woman of her virginity (since the late C14th) hints at something darker. Although *The Sydenham Society Lexicon* (1883) defines *deflower* as "term for sexual connection for the first time without violence in distinction to RAPE", the OED's definition of it leaves us in no doubt as to the underlying connotations of male violence: "to violate, ravage, desecrate, to rob of its bloom, chief beauty or excellence (since 1486)".

Fluff

The origins of *fluff* seem to be connected with *flue*, meaning softy downy material, and are thought to be an onomatopoeic modification of that word, imitating the action of puffing away some light substance. Since the 1790s *fluff* has meant light, feathery, downy, flocculent stuff. In the 1890s it came to be used figuratively with reference to personal character or intellect. At around this time *fluff* became a slang term for female pubic hair (see BEAVER). By 1903 the expression *a little* BIT *of fluff* was first Australian and subsequently US and UK slang for a young woman – presumably because she was considered, in Webster's definition of *fluff*, "something essentially trivial (see TRIVIA] and lacking in importance or solid worth".

Fluff is also used in modern speech to denote an error, fault or blunder. Although there would seem to be no direct link, a view of woman as some sort of mistake or failed male has influenced Western thinking for centuries. Aristotle, for example, wrote: "We should look upon the female state as being as it were a deformity. . .the female, in fact, is female on account of an inability of a sort, viz it lacks the power to concoct semen."

Focus

The origins of *focus*, the centre or common point of anything, throws light on a period of ancient European history when women may have played a more central role in society than they were to do subsequently. The Latin *focus* meant hearth, fireplace, pyre, altar or, used figuratively, a home.

Vesta (see VESTAL) was the Roman goddess of the hearth whose name was adopted from the Greek goddess Hestia, whose name itself meant hearth. Robert Graves has pointed out that: "The centre of Greek life, even at Sparta, where the family had been subordinated to the State – was the domestic hearth, also regarded as a sacrificial altar; and Hestia, as its goddess, represented personal security and happiness and the sacred duty of hospitality." (*Greek Myths*) More information is provided by Patricia Monaghan: "Living at the centre of every home [Hestia] further symbolised family unity and, by extension, as goddess of the public hearth, she embodied the social contract. In the beginning of her worship, matrilineal succession seems to have been the rule, and traces of it survived in the custom of classical Greece whereby a new home was not considered established until a woman brought fire from her mother's hearth to light her own. In the same way, Greek colonists brought fire from the mother city's public hearth to assure the cohesion of their new communities." (*Women in Myth and Legend*) This custom continues today in the house- or hearth-warming party.

With the focus of succession completely shifted away from the matrilineal to the patrilineal and women's work in the kitchen long since devalued, it may seem a cruel irony to a modern HOUSEWIFE, as she slaves over her hot stove, that one definition of focus today is "a vital or creative centre". (Webster's)

Fornicate

Behind the Latin word *fornax, furnus*, meaning oven, kiln or furnace, lies the Indo-European root for warm. A connotative extension of *fornax* resulted in *fornix*, meaning vault or arch, from the shape of Roman ovens. This later came to be applied to the arched underground vaults in Rome which were cheaply rented to the poor. *Fornix* then came to mean BROTHEL, because the vaults were used by many poor, unskilled women prostitutes who did not have the security or status as workers in official brothels. From this stem developed the word *fornatrix*, meaning PROSTITUTE. The masculine *fornicator* denoted the male client of a prostitute and their sexual activity was termed *fornication*. It was in this sense that *fornicate* entered English in the late C14th.

The Jungian scholar Erich Neumann has suggested another possible influence. In Rome, ovens and bakeries were associated with the goddess whose HARLOT-priestesses were often called 'Ladies of the bread'; their exuberant sexually licentious festivals were called *Fornicalia*, meaning oven-feasts, from *fornix*, meaning oven.

Ovens, dough and bread-making have always had close associations with women. The word LADY originally meant 'the kneader of dough'; *oven* was low slang for the VAGINA during the C18th and C19th, perhaps from the C16th–C19th proverb "He that has been in the oven knows where to look for a DAUGHTER/son". *Oven* has also meant, WOMB, as in the euphemism for pregnancy, *A bun in the oven*, popular since the C19th.

In England in the C14th, when *fornication* came into use, it was not officially compatible with Christian morality. Various translators of the Bible over the centuries have interpreted it with different shades of meaning but always with strong connotations of sinfulness. Coverdale's 1535 translation used *fornication* to mean adultery. The Douai (1609), incorporating an earlier translation of the New Testament (1582) and Authorised (1611) versions used *fornication* in the sense of sexual intercourse between unmarried people; the Revised Standard Version (1946) used it in the sense of unchastity and the New Catholic (1945) edition used it more generally to cover immorality, meaning all sexual intercourse except that between husband and WIFE or CONCUBINE. It is also used figuratively in scriptural texts to mean idolatry, hence the term *spiritual fornication* (since 1691) to mean the forsaking of God.

In the C19th a *fornicator's hall* was a vulgar colloquialism for vagina; *fornicator* and the terms *fornicating engine*, *member* and *tool* were all euphemisms for the penis. In the previous century trousers with a flap in the front had been called *fornicators*.

In current use *fornication* has two conflicting meanings: it can mean either sexual intercourse between a spouse and an unmarried person, ie, adultery, or sexual intercourse on the part of any unmarried person and not necessarily adultery.

Frail

Frailty, thy name is woman!

William Shakespeare, *Hamlet*, 1601

The Middle English *frele* or *freel* originates in the Latin *fragilis*, meaning fragile. Since the C14th when the word entered English the various different senses of it have all reflected concepts of FEMININITY, ie, "liable to break or be broken, easily crushed or destroyed; weak, subject to infirmities; wanting in power, easily overcome; morally weak, unable to resist temptation". (OED) The idea that women were morally weaker than men was a strongly held tenet of Christian belief in medieval EUROPE and an explanation to many for the existence of WITCHES. According to the C15th German authors of *Malleus Maleficarum* ('Witches Hammer') published c1486 the very word *female* derived from *fe*, meaning faith, and *minus*, meaning less than. It was this frailty that allegedly made so many women susceptible to the influence of the devil.

The only time *frail* reflected a positive notion of femininity was in the late C16th when it briefly acquired the sense of tenderness, eg: "That sight . . . smote deepe indignation and compassion frayle into his hart" (Edmund Spenser, *The Faerie Queene*, 1590). Otherwise it was to be the sense of weak and easily broken which prevailed.

The notion of moral weakness influenced the development of the word in the 1830s when *frail* became a euphemism for COURTESAN or a woman considered to live a 'fast' or LOOSE life. This sense continued into the C20th when it came to be applied – only half jocularly according to the OED – to a woman who lived unchastely (see CHASTE) or who had fallen from virtue. Expressing contempt for their victims, the word *fragile*, a synonym for *frail* (and defined in *The Concise Oxford Dictionary* as "easily snapped or shattered, weak, perishable, of delicate frame or constitution") was used by white slave traders in the 1920s of girls under the age of consent whom they exported to the Argentine as PROSTITUTES. By the late 1920s *frail* had become widespread US slang for a woman. In this sense it was partially anglicised by the writer Eric Linklater: "Without bullets whistling through the air to frighten him and threaten widowhood for the ravished frail". (*Don Juan in America*, 1931) In US Black slang, *frail* came to be used sympathetically for a weak person of either gender. In the 1950s a *frail eel* was Harlem slang for a 'pretty girl' as the *Dictionary of American Slang* infantilises an attractive young woman. Another Black slang term, a *frail job*, meant both a woman and intercourse with a woman. Many terms exist in the English language which denote both a woman and sexual intercourse with her; no terms exist which do the same to men.

The association of women with frailty is most tellingly revealed in the legal debates of the C19th concerning the struggle of women to enter the professions and obtain the right to vote. The supposed frailty of women was an important article of faith to the paternalistic judges who interpreted the law to deny women the vote and access to higher education. Both were thought to be dangerous in that they encouraged the removal of women from the domestic sphere of the home, and the entirely male legal profession protested that they needed to prevent this in order to protect the weaker sex from the harsh vicissitudes of public life. This dual myth – of frail woman and strong male protector – was exposed for the sham it was by women's rights reformers. John Stuart Mill (1806–73) demanded of the British government information on the number of women who were annually beaten, kicked or trampled to death by their so-called protectors. In 1874 the influential German reformer Hedwig Dohm insisted that the notion of inherent female frailty be more closely inspected: "A picture of women toiling in glassworks, papermills, glue and tobacco factories etc; working half-bare in fervid cotton mills with suffocating dust and dirt; destroying themselves, contracting consumption in the flaxmill. . .employed in brick-works or stamping down stones. . .metalworkers and miners. . .But the female constitution is too delicate – says the patriarch – for the universities to be open to women!"

Working-class women, of course, were not considered feminine precisely because they worked. According to Albie Sachs, "underlying C19th male legal and political arguments was a two-fold material interest structured around gender: first that woman should continue to serve men in the domestic sphere at home and secondly that they should not swell the ranks of competitors at work". (*The Myth of Male Protectiveness and the Legal Subordination of Women*)

Friday

Friday derives its name from *Frig*, the name of the Anglo-Saxon and Scandinavian goddess of creation. The source for this is Aelfric, the late period Anglo-Saxon chronicler who, in his homily *On False Gods*, wrote: "The sixth day they dedicated to the shameless goddess called Venus and Fricg in Danish." The Old English *Frigedaeg*, or Frig's day, is comparable to the Latin *Veneris dies* (day of Venus), from which the modern French *Vendredi* and Italian *Venerdi* derive. Frig earned the clerical disapproval of Aelfric as it seems likely that she was a manifestation of Freya, the Germanic goddess of fertility, sexual love and marriage, from whose name the Anglo-saxon noun *frig*, meaning love, probably in the sense of sexual intercourse, derived. In the C16th *frig* came to mean to copulate. It also meant to masturbate but this appears to originate in the Latin *fricare*, meaning to rub, from which the word *fricatrice*, meaning LESBIAN derives.

Friday was sacred to the creation goddess; it was the day on which fish was eaten as a fertility charm and was considered the most propitious day for marriage. Christian theologians anxious to stamp out pagan practices decided that Friday should be a day of fasting and sexual abstinence arguing that it was the day on which Adam and EVE ate the forbidden fruit as well as the day Christ was crucified. Friday 13th was considered especially unlucky: it combined the pagan creation-goddess's sacred day with her sacred number drawn from the pagan lunar calendar. In the Middle Ages Christian churchmen designated Friday the day of devil worship: "Above all other times they [WITCHES] confess on Fridaies": torturers can usually determine when their victims 'confess'.

Frigid

From the Latin *frigidus*, the word *frigid* entered English, meaning intense coldness, in the late C15th. Since the mid-C17th it has been used figuratively to mean "destitute of ardour or warmth of feeling, lacking enthusiasm or zeal; cold, indifferent, apathetic; formal, stiff". (OED) In this sense *frigid* was used for both women and men – perhaps more often of men: *A New Dictionary of Terms Ancient and Modern of the Canting Crew* (1700) defined *frigid* as, "a weak, disabled Husband, cold, impotent".

By the C20th *frigid* had begun to acquire female specificity. Webster's, for example, gives the following definition: "abnormally averse to sexual intercourse, used especially of a woman". Sheila Jeffries argues that, "The 'Frigide' [who] has marched through the pages of sexological and sex advice literature throughout the C20th, was 'invented' in the 1920s to explain the phenomenon of women rejecting marriage – or [their lack of] sexual response within marriage." She identifies these women as a small but influential group of FEMINISTS who argued, "that the sexual control of women's bodies was the basis of men's domination over women. They undertook a critique of male sexual behaviour within marriage and questioned the necessity of sexual intercourse as a sexual practice." (*The Spinster and her Enemies*)

The women who rejected heterosexual intercourse and/or marriage were regarded by the sex-reformers, psychologists, psychoanalysts and anti-feminists as hysterical (see HYSTERIA) and labelled LESBIAN, PRUDE and frigid. This response took place within the context of the 'surplus woman question' – ie, the increased number of SPINSTERS who were seen to be the mainstay of the SUFFRAGETTE movement; they were, to many, alarmingly independent of men and therefore dangerous.

The psychoanalyst William Stekel estimated that between 40% and 50% of all women were frigid. He proposed that female frigidity was a form of resistance to male dominance and suggested that a woman's capacity for sexual pleasure depended on the extent to which she was able to embrace joyfully the reality of her inferior status: "To be roused by a man means acknowledging oneself as conquered." (*Frigidity in Women in Relation to her Love Life*, 1926) Stekel and many like him believed that curing frigidity on a mass scale would aid the end of women's resistance to men in the battle of the sexes and ensure male dominance not just on an individual but on a societal plane.

The label *frigid* was a means of control – just as the label *nymphomaniac* had been in the C19th. No matter how orgasmic, the woman who could not reach orgasm solely through penetration was classified as neurotic, immature and frigid. By the early 1970s many women previously labelled frigid began to realise that sexual arousal was often no more than the failure on the part of their male partners to understand their sexual needs.

Charles Rycroft has helpfully redefined *frigidity*: "Although some writers use the word 'frigidity' to describe all sexual inhibitions in women, including the inability to have vaginal orgasms, it is best restricted to the inability to be in any way sexually aroused. Since many women enjoy sexual intercourse without coming to a climax, the wider definition leads to the absurdity of designating as frigid women who are sexually responsive. Frigidity can only be regarded as a neurotic sympton a) if it is persistent and b) if it occurs even under the most favourable circumstances; otherwise it is a sign of either inexperience or insincerity (on the part of either the women or her partner)." (*A Critical Dictionary of Psychoanalysis*)

Dale Spender suggests that frigidity "could perhaps be more aptly named (from a female point of view) as reluctance, a reluctance to respond to male sexuality rather than a recluctance to utilize one's own". (*Man Made Language*)

Frump See DOWDY

Gash

Garsh and garse, as gash was spelled from C13th–C17th, were adopted from the Old French garse, formed on garcer, or jarcer, meaning scarify, which originated in the Greek word for scratch. The change in the English spelling was probably helped by the analogy of slash.

Meaning "a cut, slash or wound, relatively long and deep made in the flesh; a cleft in any object such as would be made by a slashing cut" (OED), gash has also been a vulgarism for the VAGINA (as an object for male sexual desire), and a euphemism for sexual intercourse since the C18th.

The violent connotations of defloration, of sexual intercourse generally and of menstrual blood, clearly influenced the use of a word denoting wound for the vagina. This association is widespread as Kate Millett points out: "Primitive peoples explain the phenomenon of the female's genitals in terms of a wound, sometimes reasoning that she was visited by a bird or snake and mutilated into her present condition. Once she was wounded, now she bleeds. Contemporary slang for the vagina is 'gash'. The Freudian description of the female genitals is in terms of a 'castrated' condition." (Sexual Politics)

The violence underlying the imagery of gash – present in other slang terms for the vagina such as a CAT with its throat cut (C20th) – attests to the gender politics of notions of male sexual aggression and female passivity. Slang terms for the penis which reinforce these notions have included: CHERRY-splitter, chopper, dagger, driving post, gun, hammer, pistol, pork sword, prick (ie, to pierce), swack, swipe and weapon.

In the C20th gash has come to be used not only as a brutal term for a vagina, but also for a woman herself. The inference that a woman is valued as an object to satisfy male sexual aggression can be drawn from the fact that the very word vagina originates in a word meaning sheath or scabbard.

Gay

Since 1310 gay has meant "full of or disposed to joy or mirth; light-hearted, exuberantly cheerful, sportive, merry" (OED). It was adopted from the Old French gai but its earlier roots are disputed. One theory is that it derives from the Old High German gahi, meaning swift. Another theory is that it derives from the Old High German *wahi* meaning pretty. Other early senses of *gay* include: bright or lively looking, especially in colour; brilliant or showy; finely or showily dressed; brilliantly good; excellent or fine; in an immaterial sense, brilliant, attractive or charming; and, used of reasonings, specious or plausible. In the C13th *gay* GIRL denoted a female child.

By the beginning of the C17th *gay* had degenerated and was used to denote addiction to social pleasure and dissipations; in this sense it was often used euphemistically of LOOSE or immoral life. "Hence," the OED informs us, the slang application of *gay* in the early C19th "of a woman leading an immoral life, living by prostitution", eg: "As soon as ever a woman has ostensibly lost her reputation, we, with a grim inappositeness, call her 'gay'." (*Sunday Times*, 1868) An obsolete sense of *gay* meaning slack, not closely fitting, which exists in all the Romance languages, although not recorded very early in any of them, may be of etymological significance to this development.

In the C19th the *gaying instrument* was slang for the penis. From the mid-C19th to the early C20th *gay girl* was a slang term for a PROSTITUTE. The expression *gay in the arse, groin* or *legs* denoted a loose or immoral woman; *to gay it* was a colloquialism for sexual intercourse.

In 1925 the slang term *gay boy*, meaning a male homosexual, first appeared in Australia. The transference from a female-specific term of abuse to a contemptuous term for a male homosexual is not uncommon in the English language, eg, FAGGOT and QUEEN. But *A Feminist Dictionary*, suggests that a reason for this pejoration may lie in the Middle English theatrical use of *gay* to describe a saucy, prostituting or sexually promiscuous character played, of course, by a male actor, since a woman was not allowed to be an ACTRESS. Similarly, *gai* became popularised in Middle French burlesque theatre's description of EFFEMINATE, pretentious, male character roles.

It may have been both the connotations of FEMININITY and those of immorality that led American homosexuals to adopt the title 'gay' with some self-irony in the 1920s. The slogan 'Glad to be Gay', adopted by both female and male homosexuals, and the naming of the Gay Liberation Front, which was born from the Stonewall resistance riots following police raids on homosexual bars in New York in 1969, bear witness to a greater self-confidence.

By the end of the 1970s, many female homosexuals rejected the term *gay* eg: "I prefer to reserve the term LESBIAN to describe women who are woman-identified, having rejected the false loyalties to men on all levels. The terms gay or female homosexual more accurately describe women who, although they relate genitally to women, give their allegiance to men and male myths, ideologies, styles, practices, institutions, and professions." (Mary Daly, *Gyn/Ecology*)

Girl/Girlie

Men, indeed, appear to act in a very unphilosophical manner when they try to secure the good conduct of women by attempting to keep them always in a state of childhood.

Mary Wollstonecraft, *A Vindication of the Rights of Women*, 1792

The origins of *girl* are unknown but one theory is that the Old Scottish verb *to girl*, meaning to thrill, whirl or be giddy, may have been influential.

When *gurle*, *girle* or *gerle* entered English in the C13th it denoted a child of either sex. *Knave girl* was a boy; *gay girl* (see GAY) was applied to young women. In the C14th *boy* came to be used of male children as *knave* specialised to mean first a young male servant and later an unprincipled or dishonest (male) rogue. (Many terms designating females have denigrated (as *girl* did) but there are very few examples of words denoting males which have done so: *knave* is a notable exception.)

By the 1530s *girl* denoted a female child. By 1668 it was used to mean a MAID-servant – an implication of this term being virginal, which is not present in *boy*-servant. This use of *girl* for a female employed as a domestic labourer continued into the C20th when the word came to be applied to any female worker, such as a secretary or shop assistant, who was presumed to be unmarried and therefore a virgin. However economically unrealistic, these 'girls' were expected to quit paid work when they married to take up their 'rightful' place in the home. At this point, if they were lucky, they might earn the label 'WOMAN' – but not necessarily. Perhaps an unconscious reason for the application of *girl* to female workers was that by infantilising women, they were also subtly devalued as potential competitors in the labour market. A 'career girl' is less threatening than a 'career woman'. For, implicit in the word *girl*, are the notions of childishness, dependency, conformity, non-aggression, obedience and non-competitiveness.

Connotations of sexual innocence and inexperience in childhood – especially required of female children – became buried in the C18th euphemistic use of *girl* for a PROSTITUTE. This was probably an abbreviation of the expressions *girl about* (or *of*) *the town* (1711) and *girl of ease* (1756). In the late C18th the verb *to girl* was an Oxford University colloquialism meaning to consort, or have sexual intercourse, with a woman. In the 1850s, *girls* referred to HARLOTS in the mass. *To have been after the girls* was an expression used of men with syphillis or gonorrhoea (1860). A *girlery* was a BROTHEL (c1870) or, by 1880, a low musical-comedy revue theatre (where the ACTRESSES would most certainly have been called 'girls' as a euphemism for amateur prostitutes). In the 1870s *girlometer* and *girl catcher* were low, jocular colloquialisms for the penis.

Girlie went through a similar process of pejoration. Originally a term of endearment for a small female child it came to be used of a woman friend (of a man) to indicate affection or intimacy and finally to denote a harlot. This sense was obsolete by the early C20th but pejorative sexual connotations continued in the modern use of *girlie* to refer to scantily clothed young women who displayed their CHARMS in strip-clubs and in pornographic (see PORNOGRAPHY) magazines. In C20th US-drug-culture slang; "They call cocaine girl because it gives 'em a sexual job when they take a shot." (cited in *Dictionary of American Slang*)

Alongside this pejoration and negative sexual connotation *girl* also ameliorated. The word is a perfect example of the VIRGIN/WHORE double standard. In the late C18th *girl* was applied to a female sweetheart or 'lady-love'. The late C18th term *kind girl*, abbreviated to *girl* in the C19th and C20th, denoted a MISTRESS which, although a step down from sweetheart, was less pejorative than prostitute. Since the C19th *best girl* has been used for a man's fiancée.

Old girl (see ANILE) has been applied to a woman of any age since 1845 "either disrespectfully or (occasionally) as an endearing term of address". (OED) The degree of endearment bestowed upon a man's 'old girl' can perhaps be judged by the fact that the same term was also used at first to address a MARE. Both, presumably, were thought to have their uses in satisfying a male desire to 'ride' (see FILLY, HACK, JADE, NAG, etc).

Girl, in some senses, may have lost its earlier negative connotations but it remains impossible to deny the patronising and infantilising attitude behind referring to a woman as a 'girl'. The US writer Adrienne Rich noted that "a career open to C19th women was perpetual childhood". In return for the 'privileges' of economic dependency on a husband, white married women were subjected to "enforced 'FEMININE' helplessness, idleness, denial of competency and physical strength [see FRAIL] and the kind of girlishness Ibsen depicted in. . .the *Doll's House* [see DOLL]". In Black women, for whom *girl* was widely applied in the USA in the C19th–C20th, physical weakness, of course, was not permissible; "she would be 'infantilised' in a different sense by her white female employer, condescended to as one of an irresponsible, lazy, intellectually childlike race". (*On Lies, Secrets, and Silence*)

The control of those who might threaten your own economic status is achieved by the process of infantilisation. Robin Lakoff comments on this and other implications: "One seldom hears a man past the age of adolescence referred to as a *boy*, save in expressions like 'going out with the boys' which are meant to suggest an air of adolescent frivolity or irresponsibility. But women of all ages are 'girls': one can have a man, not a boy, Friday, but a girl, never a WOMAN or even a lady Friday; women have girlfriends, but men do not – in a nonsexual sense – have boyfriends. It may be that this use of girl is euphemistic in the sense in which LADY is a euphemism: in stressing the idea of immaturity, it removes the sexual connotations lurking in woman. Instead of the ennobling present in lady, girl is (presumably) flattering to women because of its stress on youth. But here again there are pitfalls: in recalling youth, frivolity and immaturity, girl brings to mind irresponsibility: you don't send a girl to do a woman's errand (or even, for that matter, a boy's errand). It seems that again, by an appeal to feminine vanity. . .the users of English have assigned women to a very unflattering place in their minds: a woman is a person who is both too immature and too far from real life to be entrusted with responsibilities and with decisions of any serious nature." (*Language and Woman's Place*)

That a girl child is generally valued less highly than a boy child in patriarchal society is apparent from countless proverbs and old saws (see also DAUGHTER), eg: "I wanted to see if it was a boy or a girl before marrying her. If it had been a girl, I might not have bothered." (*New Society*, 1983) The Aristotelian view of the female as some sort of mistake was made appallingly clear by the language of the nuclear bomb testers awaiting the result of the mission to bomb Hiroshima on 16 July 1945. If a success the coded message was to read "It's a boy"; if the bomb proved to be a 'dud' it was to read "It's a girl". In the event the scientists and politicians BEGAT a boy bomb – proving their virility by the mass slaughter and subsequent slow deaths of hundreds of thousands of Japanese civilians.

Glamour

An imaginative but improbable etymological theory about the origins of *glamour* proposes that it derives from the name of the Celtic mother goddess Morgan (or Muirgan), who re-emerged in Arthurian legend as Morgan le Fay, the evil ENCHANTRESS, sister of King Arthur and MISTRESS and pupil of the wizard Merlin.

The true explanation is that *glamour* developed from the Scottish spelling of the English *gramayre* or *gramarye*. This entered English in the C14th denoting grammar or learning, from the Anglo-Norman word *gramarie*, ultimately from the Greek *gramma*, meaning letter.

By the C15th *gramayre* denoted occult learning. This development was explained by the C19th American poet James Russell Lowell: "all learning fell under suspicion, till at length the very grammar itself. . .gave to English the word gramary". He was referring to the renewed interest of Renaissance society in secular learning and the break with traditional ways of thinking which incurred the suspicion of the Church. It would seem that suspicion extended also to the very word that had been used to denote traditional learning. One of the responses to secular learning and to the concurrent widespread decline in religious fervour at a time of societal instability was the Church's declaration of open war against witchcraft (see WITCH). By the end of the C15th *glamour* (to give it its modern spelling) had come to mean a specific form of magic spell, or CHARM, cast by devils through the agency of mainly female witches which supposedly caused the illusory disappearance of the penis.

In 1486 two intensely MISOGYNIST German Dominican Inquisitors, Jacob Sprenger and Hendrik Kramer, promoted the persecution of witches by fanning male castration fears. In their influential diatribe, called the *Malleus Maleficarum* ('Witches Hammer') they cited many examples of glamour including that of a luckless man who lost his "virile member" when he abandoned his sweetheart: "that is to say, some glamour was cast over him so that he could see or touch nothing but his smooth body". Another man similarly afflicted returned to the witch who had cast her glamour on him to demand the return of his member. Relenting, she showed him to a nest in which she had stored the penises of several victims but warned him from one in particular which belonged to the local priest. The authors overcame all practical objections to their theory by claiming that glamour worked "not indeed by actually despoiling the human body of it, but by concealing it". Their concern was not with the reality, which presumably could have been easily disproved, but with what the victims believed had happened: "for it is no illusion in the opinion of the sufferer", making a clear distinction between the lived experience and the real (non) event.

For academic support they quoted St Isidore who had written that "a glamour is nothing but a certain delusion of the senses, and especially of the eyes. And for this reason it is also called a prestige, from *prestingo* since the sight of the eyes is so fettered that things seem to be other than they are." (Their etymology in this instance was not far off the mark: *prestige* derives from the French word meaning a conjuror's trick or illusion, originally from the Latin *praestringere*, meaning to tie up or blindfold, based on *stringere*, meaning to bind tight. *Prestidigitation*, meaning sleight of hand – another conjuror's trick – is from the Italian *presto*, meaning nimble or quick, and the Latin *digitus*, meaning finger.)

On the basis of such 'evidence' several million women were persecuted, tortured and killed during the C14th, C15th, C16th and C17th throughout EUROPE and the New World. By the time the witch-hunts ceased and rationalism had asserted itself, the word *gramayre* had fallen largely into disuse. The Scottish novelist and poet Sir Walter Scott (1771–1832) is credited with reintroducing *glamour* in its Scottish spelling in his poem *The Lay of the Last Minstrel* (1805). By this time it meant merely a magic spell.

Glamour followed much the same path as other witch-related words, such as *charm*, *enchantment* and *bewitching*. Once denoting evil or black magic, their meaning subsequently ameliorated to denote a desirable form of 'magic' in women. By 1840, *glamour* was used mostly of women with the sense of a magical or fictitious beauty, a delusive or alluring charm. Thus the C19th 'witch' was no longer capable of such sleights of hand as her C15th predecessor, but the word continued to connote female deception or artificiality which cloaked her, presumably unglamorous, 'real' self.

That these connotations were still attached to the word in the C20th is apparent in the following definition by the American–French dress designer, business woman and writer, Lily Dache: "Glamour is what makes a man ask for your telephone number. But it is also what makes a woman ask for the name of your dressmaker." (quoted in *Woman's Home Companion*, 1955)

The illusory nature of Hollywood and its deceptive means of displaying the charms of its stars led to the terms *glamour* GIRL and *glamour boy*. The two have slightly different connotations. Webster's defines the former as an ACTRESS or model, and the latter as an actor or adventurer. (There is also a subtle distinction between adventurer and adventuress: the male of this species may earn some opprobrium for being "one who seeks unmerited wealth or position, especially by playing on some credulity or prejudice of others" (Webster's). But he is also generally admired for displaying such manly attributes; an adventuress, however, is "a woman who seeks position or livelihood by questionable means". It is his dubious business ethic which is open to criticism but it is her sexual morality which is questioned.)

In the 1920s glamour magazines appeared, so-called because they contained photographs of the movie glamour girls; the term was later applied to soft-core PORNOGRAPHY magazines which revealed even more of the charms of (female) models and PIN-UPS. The purpose of these magazines, which came to be called GIRLIE magazines, is to provide fantasy masturbatory material for men for whom glamour confirms that their members are virile and that their castration fears are groundless.

Today, a woman's spell-binding charm no longer results in gynocide but Webster's definition of *glamour* shows that although the word has none of the intense gynephobia of the *Malleus Maleficarum*, it still hints at male fear of the FEMININE: "an elusive, mysteriously exciting, and often illusory attractiveness that stirs the imagination and appeals to a taste for the unconventional, the unexpected, the colourful, or the exotic: a strangely alluring atmosphere or romantic attachment: a bewitching, intangible, irresistibly magnetic charm; *often*: personal charm and poise combined with unusual physical and sexual attractiveness".

Gorgon

Since the C16th *gorgon* has been used to denote a very terrible or ugly person, but especially an ugly, repulsive or terrifying woman. It is frequently applied to the stereotype mother-in-law figure (see BATTLE-AXE). In popular Greek mythology the Gorgons, whose name probably derived from the Greek *gorgos* meaning terrible, were a female trinity: Medusa ('wisdom' or 'ruler'), Stheino ('strength'), and Euryale ('wide sea' or 'universality'). They had beautiful faces and bodies but were as terrifying as they were lovely since their skins were scaly, their hair was made of hissing snakes and their gaze turned the beholder to stone.

Robert Graves (*Greek Myths*) saw the Gorgons as prophylactic priestesses of the triple moon-goddess who guarded the secrets of women's mysteries. The

Gorgon's head was used as a warning to pryers: Greek bakers mounted a Gorgon's head on their ovens to warn away anyone who might open the door and ruin the rising dough. Another interpretation of Greek mythology proposes that Gorgon was the name of a tribe of Libyan AMAZONS conquered by Greek warriors who 'proved' their exceptional military prowess by describing their female enemies as terrifying monsters.

The use of pejorative terms for women who are considered unattractive – and the comparative lack of such terms to describe men – indicates the extent to which a woman's outward appearance is considered important, eg: "A pretty girl will hardly be a gorgon as a step-mother". (Miss Braddon, *Joshua Haggard's Daughter*, 1876) An ugly man remains just that: he may be ugly but he is still a man and he retains his masculinity. An ugly woman, however, is denied her femininity and often her humanity, she is turned into a HAG, CRONE, BAT, WITCH, gorgon, etc. An old woman has always been particularly susceptible to such a transformation since femininity is idealised in the image of the young woman, fair of face, whose character conforms to her outward appearance (see ANILE). A double standard operates: since women are considered duplicitous, any GLAMOUR or CHARM warns that a HARRIDAN, or worse, lurks not far behind a pretty female face.

Gossip

Men have always detested women's gossip because they suspect the truth: their measurements are being taken and compared.
Erica Jong, Fear of Flying, 1973

Gossip, originally meaning a sponsor at a baptism, is a descendant of the Old English *God-sibb*, meaning a kinswoman or kinsman in the Lord, from *sibb*, meaning relationship. *Gossip* in this sense survived from the early C13th to the late C19th. In the mid-C14th the word also acquired the meaning of a familiar acquaintance, friend or chum. This sense formerly applied to both sexes but survives only in an archaic application to women. By the late C16th *gossip* came to mean a woman's female friends who were invited to be present at a birth – thus providing a negative association with MIDWIVES who at this time were commonly regarded as WITCHES.

In the mid-C16th *gossip* began to degenerate. By 1566 it denoted "a person, mostly a woman, of light and trifling character, especially one who delights in idle talk, a newsmonger, a tattler". (OED) At its worst, gossip was regarded as inevitably malicious and possibly 'devil's talk'; at its best, for there was some amelioration, it meant easy unrestrained talk or writing, especially about persons or social incidents. Such subjects were inevitably those which mostly concerned women since they were excluded from the elevated affairs of State or Church politics – unless they happened to be a QUEEN.

That women and men today, when conversing socially, talk about different subjects has been confirmed by several linguistic studies. Research into English working-class conversation conducted in 1971 concluded: "Just as men in their clubs talk mainly about their work and secondly about sport and *never* about their homes and families, so do their wives talk first of all about *their* work, ie their home and families." (J Klein, *The Family in 'Traditional' Working Class England*) A 1967 study of US blue-collar couples revealed that the subject-matter of women's conversations was not highly regarded: the husbands felt their wives gossiped about "silly" TRIVIAL matters (see TRIVIA), dismissed by one as "dirty diaper stuff". (Mirra Komarowsky, *Blue Collar Marriage*) In *Toward a Feminist Analysis of Linguistic Behaviour.* (1974) Nancy Faires Conklin noted that women's talk is often characterised as gossiping, an activity with low value; if women elevate themselves above gossip, they are said to carry out conversation, which is still regarded as a form of entertainment. In contrast, professional men are said to engage in discussions, conferences, meetings; their talk is described as 'business-like' and 'talking straight from the shoulder'. Elizabeth Drew has suggested that gossip is not always so little valued: "it is true that the inspired scribbler always has the gift for gossip in our common usage too; he or she can always transform the commonplace with an uncommon flavour, and transform trivialities by some original grace or sympathy or humor or affection". (*The Literature of Gossip*, 1973) Generally, however, any male considered a gossip is likely to find himself accused of being an 'OLD WOMAN', for gossip is part crime, part sin, against masculinity.

The English historian Sheila Rowbotham suggests that gossip, devalued by, and apparently threatening to, men, also performs a powerful function of social control as it both arises from and perpetuates the constraints of female dependency upon the male: "Gossip can determine who is within the protection of society and restrict other women from moving over into self-determination. . . It is specifically directed against any manifestation of liberation, sexual or otherwise, and is designed to prevent women scabs taking on the powers of men." But she also points out that gossip can provide "an important way of perceiving and describing the world. In an underground and rather subversive way it communicates through anecdote." (*Dreams and Dilemmas*) To put it more succinctly: "Gossip is an indispensable feminist weapon!" (Sona Osman, 1983)

Governess

Govern was adopted from the Old French *governer*, which was a development from the Latin *gubernare*, meaning to steer, direct or rule. This orginated in the Greek *kubernan*, meaning steer. The appearance in English of *governess* in the C15th was as a shortening of the C14th *governeress*.

Originally, *governess* was applied to a presiding or ruling goddess. It was also used from 1483–1875 of a woman who governed a kingdom, province, community or religious institution. From the late C16th until the late C18th it was used of a woman who had charge or control of a person, especially a young one. From this last sense, since 1712, it came to mean what it does today, a female teacher or instructress, chiefly one employed in a private house.

Underlying these changes which reflect the declining power of women from positions of high rank and status to the relatively lowly position of paid employee in the private schoolroom is the enforced domestication of women in society. In contrast the masculine *governor* has retained its C14th meaning of one who governs or exercises authoritative control over subjects or inferiors. Because *governess* has connotations of powerlessness, the masculine term is bestowed upon any woman who is appointed to govern a state.

Joan Kelly argues that at the start of the historical transition from feudal to bourgeois society, ideas about woman's incapacity to govern both reflected and reinforced the systematic transfer of power and authority to men. (*Women, History and Theory*) There was some resistance to this essentially Aristotelian view that the female was a mutilated, therefore inferior, version of the male from women such as the French writer Christine de Pisan (1364–c1430). The Salic Law which prevented women from inheriting the French crown had been introduced in 1328, but during de Pisan's lifetime women in Europe were still governing and defending their own domains. She argued forcefully against the patriarchal notion that denied women the right to govern and reduced them to the subjection of their husbands on grounds of 'natural' incapacity.

As the European states consolidated, women were steadily excluded from positions of governance. De Pisan, like other women who engaged in polemical debate against the MISOGYNIST publications of the day, used history to find precedents of female governance. Following the death of Queen Elizabeth I (1533–1601) several English male writers inveighed against the right and ability of women to govern. Although probably the most notorious example, John Knox's First Blast of the Trumpet Against the Monstrous Regiment of Women, was written in 1558, some years before Queen Elizabeth I's death. Ester Sowernam demolished the argument set forth in the scurrilous pamphlet *The Arraignment of Lewde, Idle, Froward and Unconstant Women* (1611), by citing Queen Boadicea who had taught the Romans "that a woman could conquer them who had conquered almost all the men of the then known world".

These early feminist arguments, rather like Boadicea, may have won battles but they didn't win the war. In the C15th and C16th the effects of a bourgeois construction of gender combined with male state control to push women into the domestic sphere. Teaching or governessing was one of the few respectable occupations open to an educated, single, middle-class woman. Like being a 'lady's companion', "it was located in a private home and could be regarded as a pseudo-familiar position with either very little or even no cash reward to degrade her femininity". (Leonore Davidoff, *Rights and Wrongs of Women*) The devalued nature of the job may explain why, by

1885, the title 'governess' was no longer applied to the wife of a governor. The same negative associations may also explain why, after 1788, a man who taught young pupils privately came to be called a tutor rather than a governor.

The low social and economic status of the governess was as fragile and delicate as she was supposed to be. The Annual Register of 1759 suggests that the word was used to protect middle-class sensibilities: "The MISTRESS of the school is called governess for the word mistress has a vulgar sound with it." The deportment, even the appearance, of the governess was all important – especially since an educated woman was regarded as a BLUESTOCKING, which in the early C19th denoted a COQUETTE, eg: " 'For my part' said Mrs Merrington. . . 'I think good looks are rather out of place in a governess.' " (Mary Elizabeth Hawker, *Mademoiselle*, 1890)

The term *governessy* (since 1893) is today used uncharitably of women considered prim and sexually repressed – *bluestocking* acquired exactly the same connotations of asexuality. When applied to a woman prime-minister, *governessy* – like NANNY – diminishes her powerful position and suggests that there is something 'unwomanly' about her for having spurned domesticity in favour of a world of politics and power which is considered to belong 'naturally' to men.

Hack

Hackney possibly derives from the Old French *haquenee*, meaning an ambling horse. It was standard English in the C14th for a medium-sized type of horse used for riding and driving, as distinguished from a war horse. *Hackney* was then applied to a hired horse, from which developed the C19th term *hackney carriage*, originally a hired horse and carriage. Another theory proposes that the word derives from the Middle English *hackenei*, an area in London now called Hackney, where a particular breed of horse was bred. And indeed this second theory is now the one which is generally accepted.

In the C16th *hackney* became a term for a common drudge, presumably from the notion of a tired out, frequently ridden, hired horse. The sexual imagery of riding extended the meaning of the word to a HARLOT or BAWD. Samuel Johnson gives: "To hack, to hackney: to turn hackney or PROSTITUTE." (1755) In the abbreviated form *hack*, this sense was then extended to fee-for-service writers and low-level political time-servers. The 1811 edition of the *Dictionary of the Vulgar Tongue* defined *Hackney Writer* as "One who writes for attornies or booksellers." The expression *hackneyed phrase* originally meant words for hire; today it means one that is well-worn or over-used.

In the C20th *hack* lost its earlier negative female sexual connotations and came to denote a taxicab (since 1912) or its driver, a white person (US Black prison slang) and, in the UK, a bad journalist or, used opprobriously, any journalist. The British satirical magazine *Private Eye* trivialises (see TRIVIA) women journalists by referring to them as *hackettes*. (For significance of the *-ette* suffix, see SUFFRAGETTE.)

Hag

If there be in here any bit of iron,
The work of a haegtesse, it must melt.
If you were pierced in skin or pierced in flesh
Or pierced in blood or pierced in limb
May your life not be torn away

. . . .

This is to cure you from the shooting of haegtessan.
I will help you. Be whole now. May the Lord help you.

C10th charm against haegtesse-shot

The Old English *haegtesse*, from which the C13th *hegge* or *hagge*, was probably shortened, denoted a terrifying evil spirit, demon or infernal being in female form. Anglo-Saxon scribes used both *haegtesse* and *wicce* (WITCH) to translate *pythonissa*, the mortal spirit of divination believed to be skilled in the mysteries of death and hell, as well as *parcae*, the immortal FATES or Furies, who controlled human destiny. The Indo-European root word meant to seize or catch and, by extension, to fence (in). The sense of seize may have led to the meaning of *haegtesse* as one who seized her (usually male) victims.

By the end of the C14th, Christianity having triumphed over pagan religions, *hag* meant an evil female spirit (less terrifying or dangerous than a witch), as well as the debased sense of an ugly, repulsive OLD WOMAN, with the implication of maliciousness or viciousness, eg, "Oppression. . . makes handsome women Hags ante diem." (Sir Richard Steele, *The Englishman*, 1713)

By the end of the C16th when both Church and State fanned popular fear of witchcraft, *hag* once again came to mean witch. The women who were persecuted, tortured and killed were usually old women and thus, by very definition, ugly. *Hag-knots* were the tangles in the manes of horses supposedly used by witches for stirrups.

Today *hag* is a contemptuous term for an ugly woman or for any disliked woman. It is especially used of the stereotype fat, ugly, domineering mother-in-law figure (see BATTLE-AXE). The term is largely reserved for women deemed by men to be no longer of any sexual or reproductive value.

Haggard

Adopted from the Old French *hagard*, *haggard* may come from the same root as HAG or it may be formed on a German word for hedge or bush, or haw (ie, the fruit of the hawthorne). This, in turn, may have some connexion with the possible root of *hag* in the sense of to fence (in).

When it entered the English language in the mid-C16th, a *haggard* was a wild female hawk caught when in her adult plumage. From 1579–1680 the word was used figuratively, first for a wild and intractable woman and later for a person of either sex who was not to be captured. In 1605 *haggard* acquired the sense of a wild-looking person, referring especially to a wild expression of the eyes. This developed into the word being used for "the injurious effect upon the countenance of privation, want of rest, fatigue, anxiety, terror or worry". (OED) A woman being persecuted, tortured and condemned to death for being a hag, or WITCH, would fit this description exactly. Indeed, from 1658–1715 *haggard* become a synonym for a witch, probably as a result of the mistaken belief that the word was derived from hag, meaning witch, with the *-ard* suffix which by then had become well established as a pejorative ending for words (eg, *bastard, drunkard, laggard*, etc.)

Samuel Johnson defined *haggard* as "anything wild or irreclaimable", presumably from the sense of a wild hawk, and *haggardly* as "deformed, ugly" (1755). These two senses seem to have combined to lead to the development of the word to mean WANTON and unchaste (see CHASTE). Contrarily, *haggard* also came to mean a woman reluctant to yield to wooing. A wanton woman, of course, epitomised a male dilemma; she was 'captured' by every man who paid to have sex with her, but at the same time she had escaped from woman's rightful place in the home subject to a husband's dominance.

In the early C19th, strongly influenced by *hag* in the sense of an ugly OLD WOMAN, *haggard* acquired its current sense of gaunt or scraggy-looking from the loss of flesh with advancing years.

Harlot

The origins of *harlot* are thought to lie in the medieval Latin *arlotus, erlotus*, meaning glutton. For reasons that puzzle etymologists when *(h)arlot, herlot* entered Old French it meant young fellow, knave or vagabond – hardly the class of person with the means to indulge in gluttony. The Normans introduced *harlot* into English in the C13th with the meaning of vagabond, beggar, rascal, rogue, low fellow or knave. Other senses were also male-specific: an itinerant jester, buffoon or juggler (1340–1483); a male servant (C14th to 1536); fellow, or, playfully, good fellow (1386–1634).

In the C14th both sexes could be accused of *harlotry* in the sense of buffoonery, jesting, scurrilous or obscene talk or behaviour. By the end of the C14th *harlotry* was also applied specifically to females with the sense of profligacy or vice in sexual relations, one who was not CHASTE and the practice or trade of a (female) PROSTITUTE. In the late C15th, perhaps indicating something of the contempt men felt towards the women they had to pay in order to satisfy their sexual desire, *harlotry* briefly denoted filth or trash.

By 1485 *harlot* was applied to a woman as a general term of execration. And by the C16th the word was firmly established to mean a female prostitute. In C16th translations of the Bible, *harlot* was used in preference to the 'whore' of Wycliffe's 1382 translation, probably because it was regarded as being less offensive. When applied to males, *harlot* also degenerated from its earlier senses: it was applied to a LOOSE-living man or fornicator (see FORNICATE) – but it was little more than a mild insult.

Although the term continued to be applied to men in this sense for another century, so strong was the negative female association that a folk-etymology emerged which derived the word from *Arlette*, mother of William the

Conqueror, previously known as William the Bastard. In the mid-C18th Samuel Johnson offered two more etymological theories: *herlodes*, Welsh for a GIRL and *horelet*, meaning a little WHORE. In the C20th Joseph T Shipley suggested that *harlot* first meant a camp-follower (see BAGGAGE) of either sex, from the Old High German HARI, meaning army, plus the Anglo-Saxon *loddere* meaning beggar, and explained the development of the word thus: "since the camp-followers were mainly women, the sex and meaning grew limited accordingly". (*Dictionary of Word Origins*)

The English language contains many different words for a prostitute and the dictionaries all tend to treat them as synonyms: thus a whore is defined as a harlot or a prostitute, a prostitute is defined as a whore or a harlot, and so on. But there are shades of difference in all of these terms which are sometimes difficult to discern. *Harlot* is rarely used in the C20th except archaically and it perhaps still has connotations of 'rascal', which make it less opprobrious than either *whore* or *prostitute*.

Harpy

The *Harpy* of Greek and Roman mythology entered English in the C16th from the Old French *harpie*, from the Latin *harpyia*. This was adopted from the Greek word meaning snatchers, which is related to *harpazein*, to seize. (*HAG* has a similar etymological history.)

In the mythology of the ancient Aegeans, the living were snatched away by the death-goddess who appeared in the aspect of a sea BIRD. Later Greek myth transformed her into the *harpuiai*, beautiful winged monsters with the pale faces of beautiful starving women, the bodies of vultures, sharp claws and bears' ears. Homer, who mentioned only one, personified whirlwinds and hurricanes as *harpuiai*. Later writers name three Harpies: Aello ('storm'), Celeno ('blackness') and Ocypete ('rapid'). The tradition of naming hurricanes after women, the bad aspect of MOTHER-nature, continued into the second half of the C20th, when male names also began to be adopted.

Towards the end of the C16th *harpy* was used in English in a transferred, figurative sense and applied to rapacious, plundering or grasping persons who preyed upon others. Aggrieved clients were particularly prone to refer to their lawyers as harpies.

It was not until the late C19th that *harpy* acquired its current sense of a shrewish (see SHREW) or depraved woman. This may be connected to an erroneous belief that *to harp on*, meaning to dwell on a subject to a wearisome or tedious length, was etymologically connected to *harpy*. In fact, this phrase, shortened from "to harp forever on the same string" is a musical metaphor and is totally unconnected.

The association of the original awesome female death aspect of a Greek goddess may have combined with what sounds suspiciously like a masculist attitude towards a stereotyped nagging woman figure to produce the present-day sense of *harpy* as a greedy shrewish woman.

Harridan

The origins of *harridan* may lie in the French *haridelle*, meaning an old JADE, or tired old horse, and, figuratively, a gaunt, ill-favoured woman. It is with this second sense that *harridan* entered English in the early 1700s. Samuel Johnson defined the word as "a decayed STRUMPET" (1755), which suggests that an elderly PROSTITUTE was regarded as no better than rotting vegetable matter. The 1811 edition of the *Dictionary of the Vulgar Tongue* defined *harridan* as "a miserable, scraggy, worn out HARLOT, fit to take her BAWD'S degree". All the connotations of the contempt and vituperation reserved for elderly women whom men have to pay to satisfy their desires for illicit sex are found in this C18th and C19th sense of the word – it's as if their own self-disgust and fear of ageing were dealt with by projecting it onto the OTHER, the female object. This was not new to the C18th, eg: "More than anything I despise the old bawd who is flirtatious when her breasts are withered. Who ever takes her for a friend is a fool if he pays up." (C14th English poet John Gower, *Le Mirour de l'Omne*. Translation by Marina Warner)

In the C20th *harridan* ameliorated slightly. Today it has lost all negative sexual connotations and means a SHREW, or a HAGGARD and ill-tempered OLD WOMAN, and is often applied approbriously to a mother-in-law.

Hen

It is a sad house where the hen crows louder than the cock.

C16th–C18th proverb

Hen derives from the Indo-European root *kan-* meaning to sing, (see CHARM). According to Heller, Humez and Dror, hen was originally "a male domestic fowl noted for his singing". The word first generalised to a fowl of either sex and then specialised to denote a female fowl, probably upon the introduction of another term, cockerel, for the male of the species. (*The Private Lives of English Words*). The OED however, records the first use of hen word as being "The female of the common domestic or barn door fowl. . ." from the mid-C10th, later coming to mean a fowl of either sex "as in the domestic state the females greatly exceed in number the cocks kept, and their economic importance is more prominent. . ."

To judge by the figurative uses of various 'hen'-related words over the centuries, these female animals have not been held in high esteem. By 1522 *hen-hearted* meant timorous, cowardly, faint-hearted or pusillanimous.

These have never been qualities which any self-respecting male would admit to. In the C17th *hen* become a jocular but insulting term for a woman. This sense has persisted in Scottish dialect where it is used as a term of endearment for a woman. Another C17th sense of *hen* reduced women to a function of their sexual usefulness (to men); it was used vulgarly to mean a MISTRESS. Since 1680 *hen-pecked* has been applied derisively to males domineered over by, or subject to the rule of, a WIFE (see UXORIOUS).

The imagery of the domestic fowl has provided a rich source of expressions and words in the English language, all of which are negative about women. A CHICK is a sexually attractive but probably BIRD-brained young woman; *hen-party*, which is used dismissively of a gathering of women, totally lacks any of the connotations of strength and power of the male equivalent term, *stag-party*. Today *hen* is applied to a woman, especially an older one, regarded as fussy and officious. A man who displays these qualities has a better chance of being considered in a positive light as someone attentive to detail, and as a result will become 'cock of the walk'. It is, however, more likely that he will be considered EFFEMINATE and called an 'OLD-WOMAN'.

The obedient quality of hens is something that some men appreciate in their women, eg: "My destiny has been cast among cocksure women. Perhaps when a man begins to doubt himself, women, who should be NICE and peacefully hen-sure, becomes instead inostensibly cocksure. She develops convictions, and she catches men. And then woe betide everybody!" (D H Lawrence (1885–1930), *Phoenus: Art and Morality*)

Hermaphrodite

In Greek mythology Hermaphroditos was the son of Aphrodite (see APRIL) and Hermes. This child grew together with the NYMPH Salmacis while bathing in her fountain; 'he' grew long hair and female breasts, thus combining both female and male characteristics.

In *Greek Myths* Robert Graves interpreted Hermaphroditos, like the ANDROGYNE or bearded woman, as a religious concept referring to an early stage in the transition from what he believed was once a matriarchal society (see MATRIARCHY) to the sacred kingship of patriarchal society when the king, as the QUEEN's consort, was privileged to deputise for her in ceremonies and sacrifices – but only if he wore her robes: "this was the system in early [matriarchal] Sumerian times, and in several Cretan works of art men are shown wearing female garments".

Since the late C14th when hermaphrodite was adopted in the English language it has denoted an abnormal individual among the higher vertebrates, having both female and male reproductive organs, synonymous with the word *androgyne*.

Suggesting a male fear of the feminine in themselves, since the late C16th the word has connoted feminine weakness in a man, ie, an EFFEMINATE man. But whereas a male is weakened by femininity, male power when transferred to a woman is not diminished; the word can also connote a virile female. At around the same time *hermaphrodite* came to be used of a catamite or "a boy kept for unnatural purposes" as the OED puts it. In the C17th *hermaphrodite* came to denote a male homosexual.

Herstory

The rewriting or respeaking of *history* as *herstory* – coined by some FEMINISTS in the early 1970s – is guaranteed to annoy most men, many women and almost all linguists. The feminists who use it do so, not to annoy, but to make the political point that history almost inevitably means *his* story, so herstory becomes the female equivalent. Linguists point out that the word comes from the Latin *historia*, meaning history, inquiry or story, and has absolutely no connexion with the English word *his*. The same argument rages around the preference of some feminists for *wimmin* instead of *women*, in order to lose the *men* element. Deborah Cameron explains that the reason linguists find this kind of thing so irritating is that it is inconsistent – sometimes etymological history is counted as relevant, sometimes not – and in any case they tend to dislike the un-Saussurean view that linguistic history is at all salient for speakers of current English.

To get so intensely annoyed by feminist neologisms (*chairperson* can have the same effect) can only be regarded as an over-reaction for, as Cameron calmly points out: "Herstory is an excellent word in many contexts pointing out with wit and elegance that most history is precisely the story of men's lives; while wimmin might be universally applauded as a clever piece of spelling reform, had it not become associated with the unpopular 'extremism' of the women's movement." (*Feminism and Linguistic Theory*, 1985)

Hole

Akin to the Old High German adjective *hol*, meaning hollow, *hole* entered Old English in the C10th with the meaning of a hollow place or cavity. By the C16th, having acquired several other meanings, including that of the orifice of any part of the body (1340), a secret or hiding place (C14th), and a secret room in which an unlawful occupation is pursued (1483), *hole* became slang for VAGINA. Could it have been this sense which caused the development of the word, by the early C17th, to mean a small dingy lodging, an unpleasant place; a term of contempt or depreciation of any place?

Like *CUNT* and several other words and expressions signifying the vagina, *hole* also came to mean sexual intercourse, eg, 'He likes a bit of hole', as well as a woman viewed solely in terms of sex-object, eg, ' a BIT, or piece, of hole'. Although the connotations of one sense of a word may not necessarily carry over to other senses, the use of *hole* given in Webster's as "an area where there is something missing", may suggest that to call a vagina a 'hole' implies a contemptuous devaluing of the female genitalia as a nothing or an absence.

Honey

By the C9th the word *hunig* (related to the Old High German *honag*) had entered English to denote the sweet, viscid, yellow fluid from the nectar of flowers, collected and treated by bees. By the C14th it was a term of endearment for a sweetheart applied to both sexes but mostly to a female loved one or WIFE. It was also used in the sense of fond talk, which subsequently pejorated to mean a sneaking and ingratiating manner, hence the expression *honeyed tones*.

In the C18th *honey* was male-specific slang for a harmless, foolish, good-natured fellow, but *honey-pot* was a decidedly female-specific slang term for VAGINA, eg: "'Tis as hard a matter for a pretty Woman to keep herself honest in a Theatre [see ACTRESS] as 'tis for an Apothecary to keep his Treacle from the Flies in Hot Weather; for every Libertine in the Audience will be Buzzing about her Honey-Pot . . ." (Aphra Behn. c1640–88) In the C19th *honey-pot* came to be used to denote a woman – yet another term which describes a woman as a container or VESSEL. There can be no doubting the function of woman: *honey* became slang for semen. In the same century *honey-fucking*, or the more euphemistic *honey-fuggling*, meant sexual inter-course in a romantic, idyllic sense, used by the writer P Wylie in the following passage from his book *Finnley Wren* (1934): "Doris was only seven and sexual exposure might have damaged her. He was keenly aware of mysterious pains and penalties attached to 'honey-fuggling'." Honey-fuggling would have been a lot less romantically idyllic to the pre-pubescent female (for whom the word NYMPHETTE was coined) than it was to the male adult paedophile.

Hooker

There is no general agreement among etymologists about the origins of *hooker*. Eric Partridge suggests the word is based on the C16th *huckster*, meaning peddlar, hawker or mercenary person, from the Middle English verb *huck*, meaning to bargain. He traces its development through thief, card-sharper and pickpocket before it eventually arrived in the USA in the C19th as a slang term for a PROSTITUTE. Another theory proposes that *hooker* was the name given to the female camp-followers (see BAGGAGE) of General

Joseph Hooker's division during the American Civil War. Yet another suggestion is that the source was the C19th red-light district in New York called Corleon's Hook. Webster's believes that it probably derives from the verb *to hook* in the sense of entrapping someone into improper, undesirable or foolish activity (see CIRCEAN).

There are several words and expressions in the English language which suggest a male fear of women who allegedly use devious, possibly even devilish means to entrap, ensnare, seize, or SNATCH them against their will. Both HAG and HARPY derive from words meaning to seize. The very word *snatch* has been a euphemism for the VAGINA since the late C19th. This usage derives from *snatch* meaning a hasty, illicit or mercenary copulation (C17th–C20th). In the 1930s *snatch* became a term for "girls viewed collectively as 'fun' " (*A Dictionary of Slang and Unconventional English*).

To be hooked, meaning to be caught, is used usually of a man to imply that he has been trapped by a woman into marriage. One sense of the phrase *to be let off the hook* is used of a married man let out on his own (ie, by or from his wife) for a night with convivial companions – with the implication that extra-marital sex may take place.

As a term for prostitute, *hooker* suggests a means by which men absolve their guilt for seeking to satisfy their desire for illicit sex: a hook, like a talon or a magical CHARM is difficult to escape from. Such an attitude is entirely reminiscent of a refusal to accept responsibility for one's own actions expressed in the childhood cry, 'But (s)he made me do it'.

Housewife

A house does not need a wife any more than it does a husband.
Charlotte Perkins Gilman (1860–1935)

In the C13th and C14th the housewife was the female coordinator, organiser or head of a household. As households at this time, before the emergence of centralised nation states, were centres of legal, political and economic activity, the housewife wielded significant power. Four hundred years later the role of housewife had degenerated to that of a married woman who occupies herself with the menial domestic affairs of her household and who engages in no employment for pay or profit. The often used phrase "I'm just a housewife. . ." reveals the extent to which both the housewife and her role have become under-valued: "housework is not socially counted as work – the implication of this image being that of the housewife herself as an uninteresting, worthless person; a cabbage". (Ann Oakley, *Housewife*)

Joan Kelly (*Women, History and Theory*) traces the origins of this process of devaluation to Renaissance distinctions between public and private life which were reinforced and perpetuated by attitudes which sought to contain women in the domestic sphere. By the mid-C15th the housewife was "one who manages her household with skill and thrift, a domestic economist". (OED) This definition suggests that although she was perhaps more highly valued than today, her sphere of influence was severely reduced from that of her housewifely predecessors. A sign, perhaps, of just how inconsequential a housewife was coming to be regarded was the pejoration of *huswif* to mean a light, worthless or pert woman or GIRL (1546–1705). In this sense the word was superseded by its derivative, *HUSSY*.

The now obsolete word *cotquean*, from *cot*, meaning small house, and *QUEAN*, meaning wife, also followed a path of pejoration. Originally synonymous with *housewife*, it became next a term of abuse for a vulgar, scolding woman (see SCOLD) and finally, from the C16th–C19th: "a man who fusses over and meddles in affairs that should be the housewife's". (*Dictionary of Early English*) This rigid notion of a gender division of labour plus the devaluing of the role of housewife is well illustrated in *Romeo and Juliet* (1592): when Capulet says "Look to the bakt meats, good Angelica, spare not for cost", the Nurse replies scornfully, "Go you cotqueane, to, Get you to bed."

The etymology of the word *menial* provides yet further evidence of this devaluation. Adopted from the Old French *mesnie*, meaning household, by the C16th it had degenerated to mean (of servants) lowly, degrading, humble or servile: the menial work of the housewife was one lacking in interest or dignity.

Ideas about housework and the status of the housewife were also affected by the establishment of industrial capitalism which accelerated the transition of housework from the realm of manufacture to that of service. The menial aspects of housework – once performed by the young, unmarried servant, usually the MAID-servant – and supervised by the married woman (ie, the housewife) increasingly became the work of the wife herself. The unmarried female began to be employed in paid labour outside the home. By the C19th *housewife* had acquired negative connotations attached to women whose husbands were unable to afford servants.

Another consequence of the industrial revolution was the emergence of the modern housewife as the dominant mature female role. This was reinforced by notions of FEMININITY as expressed by the English writer and art critic John Ruskin: "The woman's power is not for rule. . .and her intellect is not for invention or creation, but for the sweet ordering, management and decision. She sees the qualities of things, their class, their places". (*The Queen's Garden*. 1868) The equation of housewife with a woman's 'natural' role was succinctly expressed in the male slang use of the word *housewife* for VAGINA (C19th–early C20th).

Marx and Engels analysed the emergence of the modern housewife some-what differently from Ruskin, seeing it as one of the underpinnings of capitalism: women, as an unpaid labour force, function to maintain the paid labour force and thus keep wages down and profits up, since otherwise, society would have to provide, and pay for, these services.

Placing the housewife in the context of patriarchal society, Kate Millett pointed out that although women in the C20th might have more economic rights than previously, "Yet 'woman's work' in which some two thirds of the female population in most developed countries are engaged, is work that is not paid for. In a money economy where autonomy and prestige depend upon currency, this is a fact of great importance." (*Sexual Politics*)

The diminishing of the status of the housewife has led to a folk etymology which proposes that the word means a woman who is "married to a house rather than to the man she once thought it was all about". (*Banshee*, Journal of Irishwomen United. 1980) Many women have pointed out that *housewife* is inadequate to describe the many roles that it embraces: "I'm not married to a house. I hate the word 'housewife'. They say 'What are you?' And you say 'I've got a baby. . .I'm a mother and a wife', and they say 'Oh just a housewife'. Just a housewife! You're never just a housewife. Into that category goes everything. . ." (Ex-shop assistant married to a lorry driver, quoted in Ann Oakley, *Housewife*)

The difference is enormous between the medieval housewife who directed the affairs of the household and the C20th one who "is not considered much except by those who want to make sure she stays put". (Sheila Rowbotham, *Dreams and Dilemmas*)

Hoyden

Probably an adoption of the Dutch *heiden*, meaning heathen or gypsy, *hoyden* was originally a male-specific term applied to a rude, ignorant or awkward fellow and later to a clown or a boor (1593–1708). From 1676, while losing its male application, *hoyden* acquired the sense of a rude or ill-bred girl or woman, and later a boisterous or noisy girl, sometimes called a *romp*. Such behaviour, of course, was considered totally inappropriate in a woman and ran counter to societal concepts of FEMININITY. Hence, in the C20th, *hoyden* became synonymous with TOMBOY.

Hussy

An abbreviation of *huswif* (HOUSEWIFE), *hussy* originally denoted the MISTRESS or female manager of a household (1530–1800). Pejoration accompanied the diminishing status of a housewife as political matters and affairs passed from the individual family household to centralised governments of nation states and, later, as paid productive labour passed out of the household and into the factory. Domestic labour became identified with female labour and, in a developing bourgeoisie, with peasant, and then working-class women. By the mid-C17th, *hussy* denoted a rustic woman. In some rural districts it was used as a friendly synonym for WOMAN or LASS. It degenerated to mean a woman of low or improper behaviour or of light character. It also acquired negative sexual connotations, coming to be used of a pert or mischievous young woman, a synonym for MINX. At first used jocularly, *hussy* later became a more opprobrious way of addressing a woman. In 1755 Samuel Johnson defined *hussy* as "a sorry or bad woman; a worthless WENCH". Although it retained its earlier connotations of sauciness, by the late C19th the degeneration of *hussy* reached its nadir: it denoted a lewd, or brazen woman, a PROSTITUTE or JADE.

Muriel Schulz has pointed out that many of the terms in the English language which refer to domestic working women degenerated and acquired negative sexual connotations, eg, *laundress*, *needlewoman*, SPINSTER, and nurse have all, at some time, been euphemisms for a mistress (in the sexual sense) or prostitute.

Hysteria

Heller, Humez and Dror state that "The Greek word *husteros* meant 'latter, lower'. In its feminine form *hustera*, it came to be applied specifically to 'the lower part of a woman's anatomy, the WOMB'." (*The Private Lives of English Words*). The OED, however, gives no connexion between *hustero* and *hustera*. *Hustera*, it states, is the Greek for womb and probably related to UTERUS whereas *husteros* is from the Indo-European *ud-* and related to out. *Husterikos* meaning of, or pertaining to the womb, was the name given to both the malady and the associated behaviour of what in English came to be called hysteria.

According to Ilza Veith in her study, *Hysteria: The History of a Disease*, observations in ancient Egypt of a prolapsed womb may have given credibility to a belief that this organ wandered around the body. Hence the notion of the womb as an uncontrolled animal which, according to Plato "longs to generate children. When it remains barren too long after puberty, it is distressed and sorely disturbed and straying about the body and cutting off passages of the breath, it impedes respiration and provokes all manner of diseases besides." The Greeks concluded that this disturbance continued until appeased by the passion and by love: "Such is the nature of women and all that is female." (Plato, c429–347 BC)

That the disease got its name from the Greek word for the womb, Veith writes: "Inherent in this is the meaning of the earliest views on the nature and cause. It was perceived to be solely a disorder of women caused by alterations of the womb. The association of hysteria with the female generative system was in essence an expression of awareness of the malign effect of disordered sexual activity on emotional stability. But these concepts go back to man's earliest speculations about health and disease, long before the term 'hysteria' had been coined and they indicate the prominent role that sexual life played in general well-being even in remote antiquity."

In the Middle Ages, much influenced by St Augustine, social attitudes towards hysteria changed. The Church held sexual abstinence to be a virtue (see CHASTE, VIRGIN) and to associate it with adverse effects was unthinkable. The official explanation of the manifestations of hysteria was that they were caused by a woman's alliance with the devil. Hysteria ceased to be a disease: it became the visible token of bewitchment and as such fell into the domain of the Church and later the temporal powers of the emerging nation states which endorsed the WITCH-hunt of the Inquisition. "A careful study of the Malleus Maleficarum," notes Veith of the witch-hunters' handbook of the late C15th, "reveals beyond doubt that many, if not most of the witches as well as a great number of their victims described were simply hysterics who suffered from partial anaesthesia, mutism, blindness and convulsions and, above all, from a variety of sexual delusions".

In the C16th, however, as men began to wrest the business of healing from the traditional women-healers (the prime victims of the witch-hunters), those afflicted with hysteria were once again seen to require medical rather than religious attention.

When the Latin term *Hysteria passio*, ('hysterical passion') was first adopted into the English language in the early C17th this affliction, thought to be peculiar to women, was already termed the *mother* (since the C14th), eg: "Oh how this Mother swells up towards my heart! Historica passio, downe thou climbing sorrow". (Shakespeare, *King Lear*, 1605) In the mid-C17th the term *Mother-fits* was used to denote the choking symptoms of hysteria. A medical treatise of the time provides other names: "This disease is called by diverse names amongst our authors: passio hysterica, suffocatio, praefocatio, strangulatus utri, cadicus matricis etc., in English, the mother or the suffocation of the mother, because most commonly it takes them with choking in the throat: it is an effect of the Mother or womb wherein the principal parts of the bodie by consent do suffer diversely according to the diversitie of the causes and diseases wherewith the MATRIX is offended."

Robert Burton in *The Anatomy of Melancholy* (1628) referred to hysteria as 'MAID'S, NUN'S or WIDOW'S melancholy', reflecting the ancient view of the cause as sexual abstinence and something which, as Germain Greer writes in *The Female Eunuch* "a good husband could fix".

Yet another C17th term for hysteria was *the vapours*. This had been in use since the C15th for "Exhalations supposed to be developed within the organs of the body (especially the stomach) and to have an injurious effect upon the health." (OED) From 1665–1750 *the vapours* denoted "A morbid condition supposed to be caused by the presence of such exhalations; depression of spirits, hypochondria, hysteria, or other nervous disorders." (OED)

It is generally believed that not until the C19th was it discovered that those without a womb could suffer from hysteria. In fact the English physician Edward Jorden (1578–1632) who provided a major turning point in the history of the disease, had already seen the brain, not the womb, as the source, and was the first to detect hysteria in men.

In the C18th the original uterine theory returned. The English physician William Cullen (1712–90) introduced the word *neurosis* which became synonymous with *hysteria*; he was also the first to use the word NYMPHOMANIA as a form of hysteria from which only women suffered. Barbara Ehrenreich and Deidre English write of a variety of diagnostic labels used for "the wave of invalidism gripping the female population" (*For Her Own Good*) during this period: neurasthenia, nervous prostration, hyperaesthesia, dyspepsia, rheumatism and hysteria were all more or less interchangeable to a medical profession which greatly profited from diagnosing and treating the disease among their middle-class female patients.

In the C19th hysteria was adopted by the relatively new profession of psychiatry. It became a sign of madness and the numbers of female inmates in lunatic asylums swelled. Elaine Showalter explains: "In a society that not only perceived women as childlike, irrational and sexually unstable, but also rendered them legally powerless and economically marginal, it is not surprising that they should have formed the greater part of the residual categories of deviance from which doctors drew a lucrative practice and the asylums much of their population. Moreover, the medical belief that the instability of the female nervous and reproductive systems made women more vulnerable to derangement than men, had extreme consequences for social policy. It was used as a reason to keep women out of the professions, to deny them political rights, and to keep them under male control in the family and the state. Thus medical and political policies were mutually reinforcing. As women's demands became increasingly problematic for Victorian society as a whole, the achievements of the psychiatric profession in managing women's minds would offer both a mirror of cultural attitudes and a model for other institutions." (*The Female Malady*)

For some members of the medical profession, however, there was a growing awareness that hysteria could not be defined by recourse to ancient uterine theories. The French pathologist Jean Charcot (1825–93) among whose students was the young Sigmund Freud, wrote eloquently: "Keep it well in mind and this should not require a great effort, that the word 'hysteria' means nothing, and little by little you will acquire the habit of speaking of hysteria in man without thinking in any way of the uterus."

Veith writes that towards the end of the C19th "The word had become etymologically meaningless: J. Babinski coined the term 'pithiatisme' which to him expressed its most important features since it combined the Greek word *peitho* meaning 'I persuade', and *iatos* meaning 'curable', believing that amenability to cure by persuasion was not only the most important characteristic of hysteria but also of diagnostic importance. Although the term still lingers in medical dictionaries, it failed to become part of the general medical vocabulary." But the medical profession, while redefining hysteria, proved reluctant to renounce the word itself, eg: "The word 'hysteria' should be preserved. Although its primitive meaning has much changed. It would be very difficult to modify it nowadays, and truly it has so great and beautiful a history that it would be difficult to give it up." (Pierre Janet, 1859–1947)

Examining the prevalence of hysteria among middle-class women in the C19th, Ehrenreich and English suggest that "the hysterical fit for many women, must have been the only acceptable outburst – of rage, or despair, or simply of energy – possible". Showalter supports this theory: "Hysterics also expressed 'unnatural' desires for privacy and independence. . .During an era when patriarchal culture felt itself to be under attack by its rebellious daughters, one obvious defence was to label women campaigning for access to the universities, the professions, the vote, as mentally disturbed. And of all the nervous disorders of the fin de siècle, hysteria was the most strongly identified with the FEMINIST movement. But. . .if we see the hysterical woman as one end of the spectrum struggling to redefine women's place in the social order, then we can also see feminism as the other end of the spectrum, the alternative to hysterical silence and the determination to speak and act for women in the public world."

But, as Ehrenreich and English point out, "As a form of revolt it [hysteria] was very limited." By the end of the C19th *hysterical* had become almost synonymous with FEMININE in literature, where it represented all extremes of emotionality: " 'Hysteria' was linked with the essence of 'feminine' in a number of ways. Its vast unstable repertoire of emotional and physical symptoms – fits, fainting, vomiting, choking, sobbing, laughing, paralysis – and the rapid passage from one to another suggested the lability and capriciousness traditionally associated with the feminine nature." (Showalter) Mutability was a characterstic of hysteria because it was seen to be a characteristic of women; in other words, *'la donna e mobile'*.

Freud, student of Charcot and admirer of Janet, was to have a huge influence on the redefinition of hysteria in the C20th; his studies divested it of much of the mystical importance it had held for more than two millennia. And as Showalter writes, "Psychoanalysis was not moralistic; it did not judge the hysteric as weak or bad, but saw hysterical symptoms as the product of unconscious conflicts beyond the person's control." Freud found hysteria a 'feminine' neurosis but as Juliet Mitchell explains, to Freud, "women are supposed to be feminine, but this gives them no more exclusive rights over hysteria than it does over femininity". (*Psychoanalysis and Feminism*) The classical Freudian theory of hysteria "distinguishes between two forms of hysteria: conversion-hysteria which corresponds to the traditional medical concept, and anxiety-hysteria which is now more commonly known as phobia". (Charles Rycroft, *A Critical Dictionary of Psychoanalysis*) Rycroft notes: "A curious fact. . .is that Freud never wrote a definitive formulation of his views on hysteria and. . .it is extremely difficult to discover what the classical theory of hysteria is." But Mitchell suggests that "In the body of the hysteric, male and female, lies the feminine protest against the law of the father", and that some aspects of hysteria "can clearly come from pre-oedipal days. . .which Freud connected with the mother-attachment".

Mitchell, Veith and Showalter all comment on the extent to which hysteria – now termed 'conversion syndrome' by psychoanalysts – is no longer a major female malady. Mitchell, commenting on the reduced emphasis psychoanalysts place on ego-development today notes, "If. . .hysteria is primarily a means of achieving ego-satisfaction, this lack of attention could easily account for the nearly total disappearance of the illness." Veith claims that it is an almost extinct disease which only occurs among the "uneducated of the lower social strata", although Rycroft comments drily, "Psychoanalysts who work in private practice are none the less quite familiar with hysterical phenomena."

But in popular usage, the tag 'hysterical' continues to be levelled at women, especially feminists or women who express anger; men displaying similar symptoms are more likely to be described as 'obsessional', a term which, although invariably derogatory, can connote highly valued characteristics such as attention to detail and rationality.

Of this Casey Miller and Kate Swift write: "In contrast to descriptives like VIRAGO and TOMBOY, the word hysteria is usually used to describe a woman as though she were simply behaving according to expectations. . .Hysteria now refers to a specific psychoneurosis that may affect anyone, male or female. In popular usage it is a state of excessive fear or other emotion in individuals or masses of people, but in this sense men – whether individually or in groups – are seldom said to be hysterical. After a series of rapes at a large state college in 1974, news stories repeatedly described a 'mood of hysteria' among women students on the campus. The description, according to the dean of women, was totally false. 'The mood of the women is one of concern and anger' she told reporters. 'When men feel concern and anger, it is called concern and anger, never hysteria.' No comment was required on the power of the label to evoke images of hysterical women as potential victims of RAPE." (*Words and Women*)

To the definition of *hysterical* in Webster's as "exhibiting unrestrained emotionalism", the response of Juli Loesch, an organiser for the United Farm Workers, was to coin the word 'testeria', which she defined as "The condition of having puny, inadequate emotional responses."

Jade

Of unkown origin, the now obsolete word *jade* entered English in the C14th to denote a poor or worn-out old horse. It came to be applied to a vicious and worthless horse and, by the C16th, it came to be "A term of approbation applied to a woman" (OED). It was applied both to an old woman (see ANILE) and to what *The Oxford Dictionary of Etymology* calls a "reprehensible girl or woman" and Brewer's defines as a "young woman (often in the sense of HUSSY but not necessarily contemptuously)".

In 1755 Samuel Johnson defined a *jade* as "A sorry woman. A word of contempt noting sometimes age, but generally vice", and "A young woman: in irony and slight contempt". As an example of usage he quoted Addison: "You see now and then some handsome young jades among them: the SLUTS have very often white teeth and black eyes." The 1811 *Dictionary of the Vulgar Tongue* gives merely, "A term of reproach to women." Towards the end of the C19th the early sense of tiredness and that of the sexual excesses of a slut were fused into the verb *to jade*; used mostly in the past tense this came to mean to wear out with hard work or surfeit.

Jane

Jane has been one of the most popular female first names since the C14th when it was adopted from the French *Jean*, or its feminine, *Jehanne*.

In the mid-C19th a *Jane Shore* was rhyming slang in the UK for a WHORE, derived from Jane Shore who was a celebrated MISTRESS of King Edward IV. A LADY Jane, possibly a working class joke on the amorous habits of royalty, became low slang for the VAGINA at about the same time. *Jane* fared better in J Redding Ware's *Passing English* (1909) which recorded the use of the term among the upper classes since 1882 for a short, handsome, cheery woman.

From 1916 *Jane* became Australian (see SHEILA) and US slang for a WOMAN – yet another example of the practice of calling a woman from a name given to her genitalia. In the US from 1922 Jane was also the name given to a man's sweetheart.

As the female counterpart to the male name *John*, in the USA *Jane* is used in several corresponding terms: *Jane Doe* (from *John Doe*) is used in legal proceedings for any female party whose name is unknown; in 1968 *Jane*

Crow was used by FEMINISTS to mean discrimination against women formed on the analogy with *Jim Crow*, meaning discrimination against Blacks. *Jane* is also used to denote a restroom, bathroom or public toilet for women. (A *john* is the corresponding male term).

Jane, along with *dame* and *doll*, is one of the most popular slang terms for a woman in the US today.

Jezebel

In 1558 the Protestant Reformer John Knox wrote his infamous *First Blast of the Trumpet against the Monstrous Regiment of Women*. In it he inveighed against Catholic practices: "He [ie, the devil] hath raised up these Jesabelles (our mischievous Maryes) to be the uttermoste of his plagues." Knox was alluding to the biblical Queen Jezebel, wife of King Ahab: "And when Jehu was come to Jezreel, Jezebel heard of it: and she painted her face, and tired [adorned] her head, and looked out at the window." (2 Kings 9:30)

Hence *Jezebel*, and the expression *a painted Jezebel*, came to mean a flaunting or shameless woman of bold spirit but LOOSE morals, and subsequently an objectionable or shrewish woman (see SHREW). In 1669 Henry More described Jezebel's taste in 'pranking herself up' as MERETRICIOUS, ie, characteristic of a PROSTITUTE. Susan Brownmiller writes: "From its beginnings, Christianity stood opposed to the BROTHEL, the theatre and cosmetics, often treating the three as if they were one composite evil. Preachings by Saints Ambrose and Cyprian and the writings of Tertullian exhorted against cosmetics, jewellery and bright clothing as a sign of a WHORE: a virtuous, submissive woman did not call attention to the lures of her sex. A similar theme was expounded by Puritan moralisers in Elizabethan England: painted women were shameful, dishonest Jezebels and the cause of worldly sin. In fashionable Paris or in decadent Venice where the Renaissance inspired cosmetic decoration, worldly Catholics might be immune to the idea that makeup was akin to moral looseness, but in stodgy Protestant England and its American outpost the suspicion prevailed." (*Femininity*)

To C16th Protestants all attempts to improve upon God's handiwork were the work of the devil. Another objection was rooted in the notion that cosmetics were designed by deceiving females to disguise their real (ie, bad or evil) natures, in order to attract men: indeed, according to Jewish mythology Azazal invented face paints for precisely this reason. The idea lives on: " 'War paint' is a snide term for cosmetics that women dislike, for it brings to mind one version of the battle of the sexes in which the conniving female prepares her trap to ensnare and capture the unwitting male." (Susan Brownmiller, *Femininity*)

In the C19th to early C20th *Jezebel* came to be used as low-slang for the penis. Partridge suggests that this is perhaps an allusion to Kings 9:33: "And he said, throw her down, So they threw her down."

Jilt

The English personal names *Gillian* and *Julian* derive from *Julius*, a Roman family name. Both were very popular names in the Middle Ages in England; their derivatives, *Gillet, Gillot, Jillet, Gill* and *Jill* were especially popular among the serving and labouring classes. In the C16th *Gillot*, or *Jillet*, became a designation for a flighty young woman, and sometimes a contemptuous or familiar term for a young woman or WENCH. Other diminutives of female names, such as MOLLY, DOLLY, and BIDDY, underwent the same path of semantic derogation acquiring negative connotations of sexual incontinence. By the late C16th *Jill* and *Gill* had become synonyms for flirt. (Samuel Johnson defined *flirt* as "A woman of LOOSE, giddy or flighty character; a pert young HUSSY.") Shakespeare coined *flirtgill* (later *Gillflirt*) to mean the more pejorative, WANTON woman.

Jilt appears to be the result of a process of syncopation whereby the last vowel sound from *Gillot* or *Jillet* was dropped. As a noun, *jilt* first appeared in 1672 with the now obsolete sense of a woman who has lost her CHASTITY, a HARLOT or STRUMPET. In 1674 the English lexicographer Thomas Blount defined JILT as "a new canting word signifying to deceive and defeat ones expectation, more especially in the point of amours". (*Glossographia, or A Dictionary Interpreting Such Hard Words as Are Now Used*) Johnson made it quite clear that the term was female-specific: "A woman who gives her lover hopes and deceives him." (1755)

Although the verb *to jilt* eventually came to be applied to men as well it has always had strong female associations. The OED's definition of the noun's modern sense (now rarely used) makes this point somewhat obliquely: "one who capriciously casts off a lover after giving him [sic] encouragement". (It can be safely assumed that the OED is not suggesting the word is applied to male homosexuals.) In a widened sense *jilt* also came to mean a deception or, as a verb (now obsolete), to deceive, cheat, trick or delude. Was it, perhaps, these connotations that prompted Samuel Johnson to say of *Gill*, "the ludicrous name for a woman"?

According to some feminist linguists, the etymological history of a word such as *jilt* demonstrates a "systematic semantic derogation of women". Muriel Schulz, writing of the repeated contamination of terms designating women argues that "we cannot accept the belief that there is a quality inherent in the concept of woman which taints any word associated with it. Indeed, the facts are against this interpretation. Women are generally acknowledged to be – for whatever reason – the more continent of the two sexes, the least promiscuous, and the more monogamous." ('The Semantic Derogation of Women').

Why, then, should there be so few male equivalents for words like *jilt, flirt,* COCKTEASE and *COQUETTE*. Historically, men have proved themselves to be easily as capable – if not more so – of deception and of making false promises. Ever the more mobile and economically independent of the two sexes, men have not only found it easier to jilt but also, in doing so, have enhanced their reputation as virile conquerors by leaving behind them a list of capriciously spurned lovers. A term like *Don Juan* – the archetypal male jilter – has positive connotations of manliness.

As the jilted party women have been the greater losers. A rejected woman is regarded as second-hand, 'used' goods who is of diminished value as a marriageable commodity. She loses not only her love-object but also her potential protector and economic supporter – and possibly also her VIRGINITY. The jilted man, however, has lost only his love-object. But the amount of rage underlying the definitions of *jilt, flirt,* etc indicate that he has suffered a huge blow to his ego. Dorothy Dinnerstein suggests that the experience of rejection for an adult male echoes his early experiences as a baby when abandoned or rejected by his first female love object, his MOTHER. Thus a man's sense of loss when jilted reminds him of his early dependency upon the woman who provided nurturance and protection which, if he is to prove himself truly masculine in adult life, he is no longer prepared to admit to needing: "Woman's is the first outside centre of awareness and will that we meet, the first proof, to the nursling who still in some sense lives on in each of us, that its own is not the solitary omnipotent, all-embracing subjectivity. . . This early maternal subjectivity seemed both alien and rampant; it belonged to an ill-defined, boundless external presence, not a clearly delineated creature. This is why the rules define strongly marked female individuality as unseemly (why female caprice, charming so long as it carries a haphazard, mystifying aura, must not appear to issue from a formed, firm centre: why, although 'a LADY has a right to change her mind', an overtly strong-minded woman is no lady)." (*The Mermaid and the Minotaur: the rocking of the cradle and the ruling of the world*)

June

The origins of the name of the month June have been disputed since Roman times. Some have claimed it was named in honour of the goddess Juno, others that it refers to the Roman *gens* (family) of Junius, and yet others believe it to be the month of the *juniores*, or youths, who at this time of the year were paraded in front of the elders, or *majores* – hence *maius* for the month of MAY – before being accepted as soldiers.

In support of the first theory a vestige of the worship of Juno, goddess of marriage and the reproductive life of women, remains in contemporary Western society: "BRIDES still choose to marry in the month of June, thus assuring themselves of the beneficence of the goddess after whom the month is named". (Patricia Monaghan, *Women in Myth and Legend*)

Juno had many different aspects, sometimes erroneously thought to be different goddesses. As Pronubia she was an arranger of appropriate matches, as Cinxia she ruled over the first undressing by the husband, as Populonia she was the goddess of conception, as Ossipago she strengthened the bones of the foetus, and as Lucina she was the birth goddess. According to Barbara G Walker "Every Roman woman embodied a bit of the Goddess's spirit, her own soul a *juno*, corresponding to the *genius* of a man." (*The Woman's Encyclopedia of Myths and Secrets*) Monaghan describes *juno* as "not so much a guardian spirit as an enlivening inner force of femaleness." The word *juno* in this sense dropped from later vocabularies which Walker suggests is because "church councils of the early Middle Ages sometimes maintained that women are soulless".

Lady

Lady derives from the Old English *hlaefdige*, from *hlaf*, meaning loaf, and the root *dig*, meaning to knead. The masculine equivalent *lord*, also derives from *loaf* plus the word for ward or warden. When *lady* entered English c825, it first denoted a MISTRESS in relation to servants or slaves, a synonym for HOUSEWIFE, ie, the female head of a household. The lady of the household was the person upon whom the servants were dependent for their daily bread. In this sense the word was obsolete by the mid-C18th. *Lady* was also originally a title which signified very high status: one which since 900 has been applied to the VIRGIN Mary, as in 'Our Lady'.

By 1000 *lady* was the feminine designation, corresponding to *lord*, for a woman who ruled over subjects or to whom obedience or feudal homage was due. But by the C15th it was no more than a mere courtesy title. Muriel R Schulz has pointed out that this mild form of debasement, a process of democratic levelling, occurs more frequently to women's titles than to men's: "Lord, for example is still reserved as a title for deities and certain [ennobled] Englishmen, but any woman may call herself a lady. Only a few are entitled to be called Baronet and only a few wish to be called DAME, since as a general term, dame is opprobrious. Although governor degenerated briefly in C19th cockney slang, the term still refers to one who 'exercises a sovereign authority in a colony, territory or state'. A GOVERNESS, on the other hand is chiefly 'a nursemaid' operating in a realm much diminished from that of Queen Elizabeth 1 who was acknowledged to be the 'Supreme Majesty and Governess of all persons' (OED). We might conceivably, and without affront, call the Queen's equerry a courtier, but would we dare to refer to her lady-in-waiting as a COURTESAN? Sir and master seem to have come down through time as titles of courtesy without taint. However, MADAM, MISS and mistress have all derogated, becoming euphemisms respectively for 'a mistress of a BROTHEL', 'a PROSTITUTE' and 'a woman with whom a man habitually FORNICATES'." ('The Semantic Derogation of Women')

Like *madam*, *miss*, *mistress* and countless other woman-related words, *lady* travelled the path so often followed by pejorated terms designating a woman. As they degenerate they slip past respectable women and finally settle upon those involved in illicit sex. In the late C14th *lady* was used as the title of a woman who was the object of chivalrous devotion. From this, the next step down to a 'lady-love' or mistress in the sexual sense was but a short one. By the C16th *ladybird*, *lady of the evening* and *lady of pleasure* were all euphemisms for WHORE. The 1811 edition of the *Dictionary of the Vulgar*

Tongue defined *Lady of Easy Virtue* as "A woman of the town, an impure, a prostitute." And, somewhat mysteriously, it defined *lady* itself as "A crooked or hump-backed woman." In the C19th the process of pejoration was complete when the word, like *housewife*, became a low slang synonym for VAGINA. Since this time *lady* has also been used as the less derogatory, but still disrespectful, term for a WIFE or MOTHER, as in the phrase *the* OLD LADY.

The terms *young lady*, and *young woman* to denote a young, usually unmarried, woman of superior position, were first used towards the end of the C18th "to connote the artificiality, primness, sentimentality, etc, attributed to young ladies". (OED) According to the same source these terms are "now avoided in polite use, except among old-fashioned speakers and jocularly. Various particular applications formerly existed: from the C17th–early C19th, a young woman or girl waited upon by a MAID was called 'her young lady'; until late C19th, girls at boarding school were spoken of and addressed as young ladies. Nowadays, [young lady] is frequently applied, with the intention of avoiding the supposed derogatory implication of young woman, to female shop assistants or clerks of good appearance and manners."

Lady did, however, retain some of its earlier connotations of high status as the analogue of *gentleman*, although the OED makes the point that this use is now "not very elevated" since a gentleman is of lower status than a lord. The term was – and still is – used as a form of flattery intended to exalt a woman's position.

Lady also become synonymous with FEMININE; the adjective *ladylike* denoted femininity. But whereas a man can indulge in highly ungentlemanly behaviour and preserve – even enhance – his masculinity, a woman who challenges the norms of what is considered ladylike runs the risk of being thought less than feminine. This is illustrated by the C19th private boarding schools for girls whose aims, according to the British educationalist R L Archer, were to inculcate femininity: "to produce a robust physique is thought undesirable, rude health and abundant vigour are considered somewhat plebian. . .a certain delicacy, a strength not competent to walk more than a mile, an appetite fastidious and easily satisfied joined with that timidity which commonly accompanies feebleness. . . all are held more ladylike". (*Secondary Education in the Nineteenth Century,* 1921)

At the beginning of the C20th no woman with the strength to challenge this masculist ordering of things was considered a lady, especially not "Those who go in for 'women's rights' and general topsy turveyism. Some smoke cigars in the streets, some wear knickerbockers (see BLOOMER), some stump the country as 'screaming orators'. All try to be as much like men as possible." (cited in Brewer's) Eighty years later little had changed: "Mr Williams told the court he did not consider it ladylike for women to drink pints in his lounge, and said if they wanted to drink like men they should go into the public bar or skittle alley." (*The Times,* 1980)

Patriarchal class attitudes have constructed a concept of femininity which can be seen by comparing modern uses of *lady* and *woman*. The implications of the word *lady* clearly exasperated the US poet, Ella Wheeler Wilcox (1855–1919):

Woman
Give us that grand word 'woman' once again,
And let's have done with lady; one's a term
Full of fine force, strong, beautiful and firm,
Fit for the noblest use of tongue or pen;
And one's a word for lackeys.

Negative attitudes towards the working class are revealed in various uses of *lady* as explained by Casey Miller and Kate Swift: "The (non-existent) terms 'First woman' or 'leading woman' lack the esteem that lady as an honorary epithet bestows. Incorporated into a job title such as cleaning lady, a strong sense of condescension is conveyed for the title lady sits uncomfortably on a working class woman." (*The Handbook of Non-Sexist Writing*) Working women are seldom 'ladies' in the sense that a woman who works is never considered truly feminine.

That our concept of femininity is strongly influenced by masculist attitudes was succinctly expressed by the English novelist Dorothy Sayers who in 1947 invited comparison of the implications of the two expressions "The ladies, God bless them!" and "The women, God help us!" Miller and Swift sum up this issue as follows: "A lady who makes men uncomfortable about themselves is no longer a lady, as by definition, a lady is a woman bred to please. Both a lady and a whore are supposed to give men what they think they want in the way they want it."

The word *lady* can have a weakening effect: a lady's razor, computer, car, etc. implies a flimsy version of a standard robust commodity. But concepts of femininity are changing: like *dame*, *lady* can imply a somewhat unladylike but nevertheless admired quality of gutsy determination as in the phrase "She's one helluva lady".

Lass

Lass had entered English by 1300 to denote a GIRL. Like *girl* itself (as well as *boy* and *lad*), its etymology is 'difficult', as the OED puts it. *Lass* may be a northern dialect development of *lask*, possibly from the Old Norse *laswa*, the feminine of *laswar*, meaning unmarried. This is represented in Old Swedish by *losk kona*, meaning unmarried woman, a specific use of the sense unoccupied, or having no fixed abode, originally 'free from ties'.

Developing some sexual connotations *lass* was used in the late C16th for a 'LADY-love' or a (female) sweetheart, thus infantilising an adult woman. In the late C18th in Scottish and northern dialect lass came to denote a MAID-servant, suggesting virginity (see VIRGIN) or an unmarried state in a female domestic servant of any age. In the C19th *lass* was applied playfully to a MARE or a BITCH.

In modern usage *lass* is the ordinary word for a girl or young woman in northern and north-Midland dialects of England; in the southern counties it has little or no currency.

Leman See WOMAN

Lesbian

Beautiful women,
my feelings for you
will never falter

Sappho, c600 BC

The poet Sappho lived on the Aegean island of Lesbos; her reputation was such that Plato called her 'the tenth muse'. Today, both Sappho and Lesbos are best known for providing the English language with two words for female homosexuality, *lesbian* and the obsolescent *sapphism*.

Before *lesbian* came to be the generally accepted term to denote a female homosexual in the 1890s, the words *fricatrice* (1605), from, the Latin *fricare*, meaning to rub, and *tribade* (1602), from the Greek verb for to rub, were occasionally used to denote a lesbian. The OED fails to make this very clear in the case of *fricatrice* which it defines as "a lewd woman". (*Lewd* denotes lascivious, unchaste, indecent and obscene.) Little imagination is required to grasp the implications behind its definition of *tribade*: "a woman who practices unnatural vice with another woman".

Writers (especially lexicographers) have tended to indulge in much circum-locution when it came to describing what is now called lesbianism or lesbian practices, revealing attitudes which range from the homophobic to the romantic. It was generally assumed that St Paul's letter to the Romans concerning pagans who rejected the 'one true god' probably referred to sexual relations between women: "God gave them up unto vile affections: for even their women did change the natural use into that which is against nature." (Romans 1:26). In 423 St Augustine, whose theories about sex were fundamental in shaping Christian attitudes, warned his SISTER who governed (see GOVERNESS) a convent: "That love which you bear one another ought not to be carnal, but spiritual: for those things which are practised by immodest women, even with other females, in shameful jesting and playing, ought not to be done even by married women or by GIRLS who are about to marry, much less by WIDOWS or CHASTE VIRGINS dedicated by a holy vow to be handmaidens of Christ."

The French writer Pierre de Bourdeille, Seigneur de Brantome, (1540–1614) may have been the first to use *lesbian* in its modern sense but he preferred the euphemistic '*donna con donna*' in *Lives of Fair and Gallant Ladies* in which he devoted many pages to describing lovemaking between women in the court of Henry II. He viewed it as some sort of harmless sexual training for young women before they married – infinitely preferable to heterosexual fornication (see FORNICATE) which could result in illegitimacy: "there is a great difference betwixt throwing water in a VESSEL and merely watering about it and around the rim".

This attitude towards lesbianism was widely shared in the C16th: it presumably assuaged male fears of being unnecessary to women. This fear may lie behind the myth manufactured by Ovid who insisted that Sappho became heterosexual: "No more the lesbian DAMES my passion move, All other loves are lost in only thine, Ah youth ungrateful to a flame like mine" (*Epistle of Sappho to Phaon*. 1710 English translation of the 1697 French *Dictionary Historical and Critical*)

Other descriptions for lesbian practices over the years include: mutual masturbation; corruption or vice; unnatural sexual acts; pollution; defilement or impurity; fornication; sodomy; buggery; coitus; copulation; lewdness; and unchastity. The fear or hatred of lesbians which these terms suggest was, however, seldom acted upon. At worst, sexual contact between women was treated as a female form of sodomy when at times it was treated especially harshly if the use of a DILDO was suspected. Mostly, however, it was seen as a petty sin on a par with masturbation.

In the C19th homosexuality began to be defined as a medical problem associated with criminality. The German psychiatrist Carl von Westphal, referred to homosexuals (a term coined in the 1860s) as 'congenital inverts'. His theory influenced the sexologist Richard von Krafft-Ebing who, in turn, influenced the English sexologist Havelock Ellis who considered lesbianism a 'cerebral anomaly'. Ellis was convinced that the growing demand for female emancipation had "involved an increase in feminine criminality and in feminine insanity. . . In connexion with these we can scarcely be surprised to find an increase in female homosexuality, which has always been regarded as belonging to an allied, if not the same, group of phenomena."

Feminists today will recognise a familiar masculist accusation levelled at women who challenge the traditional patriarchal ordering of society: women who refuse to stay in their 'natural' place (the home), must be bad, mad, abnormal and overly masculine – ie, lesbian.

The late C19th sexologists defined love between women purely in terms of lesbian genital sex. Lillian Faderman argues that this definition would have mystified many women from the previous three centuries, during which period non-genital but nonetheless passionate love relationships between women had been something of a fashion. The term *Boston marriage* had been coined in New England in the late C18th for long-term monogamous relationships between two women who were independent of men. At the same time, "To the very end of the C19th, the sexual potential of love between decent, healthy women was still unacknowledged by many seemingly sophisticated authors: sound women were asexual. It was doubtful enough that they would concern themselves with any form of sexual satisfaction, but that they would seek sexual expression without a male initiator was as credible as claiming to hear the thunder play 'God save the King'." (Faderman, *Surpassing the Love of Men*)

But the influence of the sexologists and, above all, of Freud, meant that love necessarily meant sex, and that sex between women was a sickness. "Generally, male authors", writes Faderman, "looked at lesbian love with a compassion such as one might feel for a famished, whimpering creature, knowing it was in one's power to provide it with food and thus cure it of its sorrows." To the less compassionate it was a dangerous sickness since it was something that removed women from the sphere of male control.

In the 1930s the word GAY began to be used in the USA by both female and male homosexuals in a self-confident attempt to reject definitions which connoted perversion. In the 1970s lesbians both sides of the Atlantic preferred the term *lesbian* and, no longer content with the limited definitions of the medical and psychoanalytical experts, began to define the term for themselves, eg: "We do not become lesbians by leaping into bed with another women but rather, lesbianism is the result of a woman's discovery that she can and does love women coupled with her refusal to be exploited in a heterosexist way." (Sally Gearheart, *Loving Women*, 1974) Lesbians who rejected all the trappings of masculist or heterosexist society called themselves lesbian separatists or radical lesbians.

Adrienne Rich has pointed out that *lesbian* is a highly charged word, the meaning of which depends upon the personal convictions and/or the prejudices of the individual. "For some it continues to carry a range of negative connotations from 'sick' to 'man-hater' and 'pervert' ". (*On Lies, Secrets and Silence*)

Nothing could prove Rich's point more clearly than a comparison of the definitions provided by the OED and Webster's. The OED defines *tribade*, *lesbian* and *sapphism* as "unnatural sexual relations between women" and states sternly that *sapphism* derives from the name of Sappho "who was accused of this vice". *Vice* is defined as "Depravity or corruption of morals; evil; immoral or wicked habits or conduct; indulgence in degrading pleasures or practices." A further point: far from being 'accused' of anything, even the most superficial reading of the surviving fragments of Sappho's poetry makes it quite clear that she publicly and proudly proclaimed her love for other women. Those who prefer their dictionary definitions without indignant moralising will find greater tolerance in Webster's where *lesbian* is defined as "of or relating to homosexual relations between females. . .so-called from the reputed sensuality of the Lesbian people (ie those from the island of Lesbos) and literature". *Lesbianism* gets the value-free definition of "lesbian love", and *sapphism*, derived "from the belief that Sappho was homosexual", is defined as "sensual desire of a woman for other women".

C20th slang terms for lesbian include: *les-be-friends*; *lesbo*; *lezzy*; *les girls*; *Leslie*; *less-than-a-mans*; BUTCH and DYKE. They are mostly used by those for whom lesbianism has negative connotations of sickness or abnormality. In Britain the pejorative word *bent* is applied to homosexuals. *Bent* in this sense probably derives from its earlier slang use for criminal and has no etymological connection with the term *lesbian rule*, the name given since 1605 to a mason's ruler made of lead which can be bent to fit the curves of a moulding; hence, used figuratively, a principle of judgement that is pliant and accommodating.

Loose

Loose comes from Old Norse *lauss*, which is related to the Old English *leas*, meaning lying or untrue. In Old English *leasung* the meaning was first extended to false witness, deceit, hypocrisy or artifice; then to empty talk, from which developed the sense of frivolity or laxity. In 1300 when *loose* first appeared in written English the connotations of freedom in the word *laxity* led to the extension of the meaning of *loose* to denote free from bonds or fetters or physical restraint, used of persons or their limbs.

The original connexion with speech in the sense of untruth produced the term (since 1390) *loose talk* – *loose* in this sense meaning wanting in retentiveness or power of restraint. The early sense of frivolity and laxity combined with that of freedom may have developed the use of *loose* in the sense of loosely clad or naked (1423–1709). This in turn may have influenced another sense, that of free from moral restraint, lax in principle, conduct or speech. This was used chiefly in the narrower sense of unchaste (see CHASTE) WANTON, dissolute or immoral (since 1470). The connexion between loose clothing and loose conduct was preserved in several, now obsolete, phrases of the C16th, C17th and C18th: *loose-bodied* (of a dress), *loose-gowned*, *loose-hilted* and *loose-legged* were all used, mostly of women, to mean lewd, incontinent, wanton and unchaste.

Loose has been used of both women and men to denote immorality since the C15th. But various expressions demonstrate that the connotations for each gender have been different. A man 'on the loose' was on a spree, suggesting a short period of dissolute behaviour. A woman on the loose, however, was considered to have completely broken all ties with conventional behaviour, as the term denoted a PROSTITUTE. Similarly, a male *loose* FISH was no more than a rascal with some dissipated habits (since 1827); when applied to a woman it meant a common prostitute (since 1895).

The OED explains that in the sense of free from physical restraint, *loose* is now used only in implied contrast with a previous, usual or desirable state of confinement. Presumably the state of confinement desired of woman is the home where she will be subject to male domination.

In the C20th *loose* is seldom applied to men. Because the concept of FEMININITY requires women to be the very opposite of lewd, unchaste or wanton, *loose* has acquired connotations of moral condemnation which seem inappropriate for a man whose masculinity requires no moral constraints.

Madam

In Anglo-French and Middle English *ma dame* was used by children to address their mother. (*DAME* at this period denoted MOTHER.) But since the mother in the surviving examples of the use of this term is a QUEEN or LADY of very high rank, it is not known whether or not *ma dame* was used further down the social scale. Other uses include, since 1297, the spoken address for a MISTRESS by servants and, until the Reformation, a title for NUNS – who were mostly the daughters of the upper classes. The lowest social grade in which the title could be claimed is provided in Chaucer's *Canterbury Tales* where he indicates it was an advantage gained by a citizen's wife when her husband was made an alderman: "It is ful fair to been y-clept 'Ma dame', And goon to vigilyes al bifore, And have a mantel Royalliche y-bore." Echoes of this lampooning of a woman who assumes a title above her station exist in the C19th–C20th phrase *a proper (little) madam* for a WOMAN or GIRL with an imperious or bossy manner.

By the C16th married women of all social levels were addressed as 'madam(e)' to distinguish them from SPINSTERS who were called 'mistress'. This may reflect higher esteem bestowed upon married rather than single women or it may simply have been borrowed from the French title for a married women. This French connexion has stayed with *madam* lending an often spurious tone of chicness: "It is also frequently assumed (instead of 'MRS') by English or American professional singers or musicians, and by women engaged in businesses such as dress-making, in which native taste or skill is reputed to be inferior to that of French women." (OED)

Madam proved to be no more resistant to derogation than most other titles for women, (eg, *mistress*, QUEEN, *dame*, HOUSEWIFE, etc) and it acquired negative sexual connotations. In the chivalrous poetry of the C14th and C15th the (male) lover addressed his mistress (literally his employer, but also the object of his courtly love) as 'madam'. In the C18th *madam* became a term for a kept mistress, a COURTESAN, or a PROSTITUTE. By the beginning of the C19th it had specialised to a term of contempt for a female considered a HUSSY or a MINX. The OED suggests that the reason for this "may perhaps, so far as the origin is concerned, belong partly to Madame, as being more or less due to prejudice against foreign women". In the C19th, in keeping with early associations of high rank, *madam* became the term for a female proprietor or manager of a BROTHEL.

Madam stays there today, in brothels, as well as being applied to female customers by ingratiating salespersons and to female addressees as the feminine equivalent of 'sir' in a written address.

Madeleine See MAUDLIN

Madrigal

Madrigal, a lyrical love poem set to music, entered English in 1588 via the French, from the Italian *madrigale*. Its most likely origin is the medieval Latin term *carmen matricalis* meaning song of the WOMB. *Matricalis* derives from Latin *matrix*, formed on *mater*, meaning MOTHER, first denoting a pregnant woman and later extended to mean womb. *Carmen* derives from the same root as that of HEN, CHARM and *chant*.

The Private Lives of English Words by Heller, Humez and Dror offers four other possible woman-related explanations for the extended use of the adjective *matricalis* to describe this poetical–musical form. Some etymologists claim the secular nature of the madrigal meant they were written in the vernacular or 'mother tongue' rather than in Church Latin. Others point to the ecclesiastical musical form of the madrigal and suggest that the 'Mother Church' was the influence. Another hypothesis is that the lyrics of the madrigal expressed the love of a mother for her children. The fourth theory is that the simple construction of the madrigal form could be performed by someone straight from the womb.

Maid/Maiden

Maiden, from which *maid* is shortened, entered English c1000, first to denote a GIRL or young unmarried WOMAN and, a few years later, a female VIRGIN (1035). Both *maid* and *maiden* connoted sufficient rank and dignity to be applied to the Virgin Mary (1035–1834). But by the end of the C14th *maid* had degenerated and was applied to young unmarried female domestic servants.

Over the centuries, virginity has been demanded of most young women employed as maids in domestic service. While frequently sexually abused by the males of the household, in return for a bed, clothing, food and 'protection', they were paid only nominal wages. Unlike the conditions laid down for young male domestic servants, to be a maid meant she had to hang on to her maidenhead: pregnancy would result in dismissal in a cloud of moral opprobrium. In reality her dismissal was due to the refusal of the householder to pay her a family wage. Feminism, more efficient contraception and cheaper, safer, abortion methods in the C20th have contributed to a relaxation in rules concerning the virginity of female domestic labour – although they remain among the most exploited workers. The wages of barmaids, chambermaids, nursemaids, housemaids and any "girl or woman employed to do domestic work in a home, motel, hotel or institution" (Webster's), are generally well below family wage rates and those who 'live in' often have to obey the rule 'no visitors of the opposite sex in the bedrooms'.

The qualities of a maid or maiden, other than the primary one of chastity and virginity, were once sufficiently highly valued for them to be acceptably applied to men. King Malcolm 4 of Scotland (1141–65), as well as being young and possibly CHASTE, was reputably so kind and generous that he earned the title 'Malcolm the Maiden'. From 1300–1497 a man who had always abstained from sexual intercourse was known as a maid, with apparently no derogation. But, like virginity, maidenly qualities of gentleness, coyness, modesty, timidity, kindness, etc. have never been compatible with the gender construction of masculinity. The C19th expression *maiden-meek* suggests that a good young woman is one who submits to male control. That she is also feeble is suggested by the phrase *maiden's water*, a reference to urine, meaning weak tea or beer.

Most dictionary definitions of *maid* or *maiden* include words such as 'unconquered' or 'unviolated'. Male violence, competitiveness and the fight to win the right to go where no man has gone before, are all implied in the language of 'taking' a woman's maidenhead. The imagery of war is further implicit in the late C16th use of *maiden* to apply to any town, castle or fortress which had not (yet) been conquered. The violent ravaging (see RAPE) effect of blades and hammers are further evoked by the use of *maiden*, since the early C17th, to describe soil, snow or metal which has never been ploughed, disturbed or worked. (See also MOTHER (nature))

John Leland's eponymous heroine of *Fanny Hill* (1749) refers to her maidenhead as "That darling treasure of mine, so eagerly sought after by the men, and which they never dig for but to destroy." Was it MISOGYNY or MISANDRY (a word not coined until the mid-C20th) which influenced the development of *maid* and *maiden* to acquire the sense of unspotted, unsullied, unpolluted or uncontaminated? Samuel Johnson's definition of *maidenhead* captures a male ambivalence of desire and self-revulsion: "Newness; freshness; uncontaminated-state. This is now becoming a low word." (1755) By this time *maiden* had already sunk to the lowest point in its etymological history: from 1670–1850 it was a slang term for a WHORE.

In this last sense a maiden was, presumably, recognised to have at least some usefulness. Other terms and expressions have strong implications of uselessness. The OED gives several examples of the figurative use of *maiden* to mean "That [which] has yielded no results." In sporting jargon *maiden* is used of a game in which there has been no score (since 1598). A *maiden horse* is one which has never won a race (since 1760).

The height of female 'uselessness' (to men) is the woman who herself has apparently no 'use' for men. The stereotype figure of the 'old maid' is a cruel one with a long history. The term has been used pejoratively since the late C17th, eg: "An old maid is now thought such a curse". (*The Ladies Calling*. 1673) Dictionaries give uniformly negative definitions of OLD WOMAN or *old maid*, ie SPINSTER, HAG, CRONE, etc. An *old maid* is defined as a prim, conservative, nervous, woman, one who frets over inconsequential or trivial details (see TRIVIA); a fussbudget or a PRUDE.

Although a maiden might be polluted or contaminated by heterosexual genital contact, crucial to the concept of the old maid is the notion that sexual intercourse is vital to the good health of a woman (see HYSTERIA). Without it she is at best useless (ie, not a mother), and at worst hysterical and even dangerous because untamed.

The C19th woman's rights reformer Frances Power Cobbe put up a spirited defence of the old maid – also pointing out the prevailing double standard: "Nor does the 'old maid' contemplate a solitary age as the bachelor must usually do. It will go hard but she will find a *woman* ready to share it. . . She thinks to *die*, if without having given or shared some of the highest joys of human nature, yet at least without having caused one fellow-being to regret she was born to tempt to sin and shame. We ask it in all solemn sadness – Do the *men* who resolve on an unmarried life, fixedly propose to die with as spotless a conscience?" (*Celibacy vs. Marriage. Essays on the Pursuits of Women*, 1863)

Her question went largely ignored. By the beginning of the C20th old maids were, to many, indistinguishable from FEMINISTS, SUFFRAGETTES and LESBIANS: all were sick or mad and, like the women – mostly old spinsters or widows – persecuted as WITCHES in earlier centuries, they were dangerous. In 1911 an anonymous letter to *The Free Woman* warned against the old maid: "In the auditorium of every theatre she sits, the pale guardian. . .she haunts every library. . . In our schools she takes the little children, and day by day they breathe in the atmosphere of her violated spirit." Here is the rub: a woman's maidenhead has to be violated by a man to prevent her soul from being violated.

But, of course, times change. In England in the 1920s when male teachers felt threatened by the increasing number of women in 'their' profession (encouraged both during and immediately after World War 1) married women were legally disbarred from teaching. The argument that 'old maids' polluted the minds and souls of little children was no longer considered valid. Of paramount importance was that married women got on with the 'real' job for women – breeding and nurturing their own children rather than presenting competition to males in the labour market.

Since 1591 the term *maiden name* has been used for a woman's last name (ie, that of her father) until she married and acquired the family name of her husband. Implicit in *maiden* is the notion of a woman's virginal or chaste status before her marriage. The absence of a male equivalent term – or custom – reinforces the view that, unlike a single woman, a single man is not expected to be sexually inexperienced before marriage.

The use of patronymic last names emerged in the C14th. These names reveal the relationship between the child and her or his father. Ignoring the existence of women, the authors of *The Story of English* wrote: "In Anglo-Saxon peasant society it was enough for a man to be identified as Egbert or Heoragar. Later, a second stage would produce the 'son of' (or the Celtic Mac or Mc) prefix or suffix – Johnson, Thomson, Jobson." (There have never been any surnames with a 'daughter of' suffix or prefix although this does occur in Iceland.)

After gender-neutral geographical names such as Brooks, Rivers, Hill, etc. "The second most common form of identification was [male] occupation: Driver, Butcher, Hunter, Glover, Saddler, Miller, Copper, Weaver, Porter, Carpenter, Mason, Thatcher, Salter, Waxman, Barber, Bowman, Priest, Abbott, Piper, Harper, Constable." It is true that male-specific names dominate, but the authors might have been a little less androcentric, for names such as Nun, Queen, Maggs, Babbs, Sisson, etc (the last three derive from the first names of women rather than from female occupations) also exist.

In the C18th, married women began to lose their first names as well. Suggesting a total loss of identity the wife of a doctor, for example, might be known as Mrs John Smith or Mrs Doctor Smith. Elizabeth Cady Stanton (1815–1902), a founder of the women's movement in C19th America who insisted on retaining both her maiden and her personal name when she married Henry Stanton, protested; "I have very strong objections. . .to being called Henry. There is a great deal in a name. It often signifies much and involves a great principle. Ask our colored brethren if there is nothing in a name. Why are the slaves nameless unless they take that of their master? Simply because they have no independent existence. . .The custom of calling women Mrs John This and Mrs Tom That, and colored men Sambo and Zip Coon, is founded on the principle that white men are lords of all. I cannot acknowledge this principle is just; therefore, I cannot bear the name of another."

Lucy Stone, another American C19th woman's-rights campaigner also refused to adopt her husband's family name, even though this meant she lost the right to vote in the Massachusetts school elections in 1879 – something she had long fought for. "My name is the symbol of my identity," wrote Stone, "and must not be lost." For a short period the term *Lucy Stoner* was applied to any woman who refused to relinquish her maiden name when she married, and who campaigned to change the law which made this a legal requirement. It was a term of contempt used by those who opposed women's rights, but it was proudly adopted in 1921 by the founders of the Lucy Stone League to help women with the legal and bureaucratic difficulties involved in keeping their own names.

It is no longer illegal for married women to retain their maiden name, but strong social pressures persuade the majority to conform to tradition. Many feminists continue to campaign against the patronymic system of naming in which "only males are assured permanent surnames they can pass on to their children. Women are said to 'marry into' families, and families are said to 'die out' if an all-female generation occurs. The word family, which comes from the Latin *famulus*, meaning servant or slave, is itself a reminder that wives and children, along with servants, were historically part of a man's property." (Miller and Swift, *Words and Women*)

Historians Jill Liddington and Jill Norris pointed out the particular problem this presents to those recuperating women's history (see HERSTORY) from obscurity: " . . . one of the most active women, Helen Silcock, a weaver's union leader from Wigan, seemed to disappear after 1902. We couldn't think why until we came across a notice of 'congratulations to Miss Silcock on her marriage to Mr Fairhurst". (*One Hand Tied Behind Us*)

In the 1970s many feminists – especially in the USA – adopted various strategies to combat the symbolic loss of self-identity implicit in *maiden name* and *surname*: "A handful of women have even exchanged their patriarchal names for matriarchal ones ('Mary Ruthchild') or followed the black movement tradition of replacing former owner's names with place names or letters (for instance 'Judy Chicago' or 'Laura X'). Many tried to solve the dilemma of naming with the reformist step of just adding their husband's name ('Mary Smith Jones') but that remained an unequal mark of marriage unless their husbands took both names too." (Gloria Steinem, *Outrageous Acts and Everyday Rebellions*) In response to the sexual double standard implicit in the term *maiden name*, some feminists today prefer to use *birth-name*.

Mammy

In the southern states of the USA, Black women slaves who nursed the children of their white slave-owners were called *mammy*, a nursery term for MOTHER, from the early days of slavery in the late C18th. White writers in the C19th appear to have seen this title as a mark of affection, eg: "These too were greeted always by the kind appelatives of 'daddy' and 'mammy' " (*Southern Literary Messenger,* 1837); "Mammy, the term of endearment used by white children to their negro nurses and to old family servants" (*Dictionary of Americanisms,* 1859); "The old mammies and uncles who were our companions and comrades" (*Ole Virginia,* 1887).

By the C20th *mammy* was used of any Black woman. The mammy figure was a racist stereotype of a fat, jolly and, above all, docile Black woman. To Black Nationalists the term became the female equivalent of the 'Uncle Tom' stereotype: a mammy was a Black woman subservient to the white establishment. Seemingly only dimly aware of the negative connotations of the term, Webster's states that its use is "often taken to be offensive".

Mammy serves as a reminder that, as slaves, Black African women were brought to the New World for only one reason – to breed more slaves. After performing this function their value was enhanced as wet nurses to the babies of the slave-owners. The use of a child's nursery word infantilised the women of whom it was used; GIRL was another C19th term for a Black woman. When used of a white woman *girl* can be a form of flattery, when used of a Black woman it reinforces the belief – and hope – that a Black person never grows up.

Mare See NIGHTMARE

Mascot

Today, a mascot is no more than an innocuous superstitious object which supposedly brings good luck. The origins of the word reveal an altogether more powerful and malevolent aspect of superstition: its source is the medieval Latin *masca*, meaning WITCH.

The word entered English as a result of the opera *La Mascotte* by Edmond Audran which opened on 29 December 1880. This *mascotte* was infinitely more acceptable than any witch had been, eg: "*Les envoyes du paradis / Sont des Mascottes, mes amis, / Heureux celui que ciel dote d'une Mascotte.*" ('Those sent from paradise are mascots, my friends, happy is he to whom heaven gives a mascot.')

Thus *mascot* came to mean a person or thing supposed to bring good luck, synonymous with CHARM or *amulet* which the OED defines as "an ornament, gem or relic often inscribed with a spell, magic incantation or symbol believed by the wearer to protect against evil such as disease or witchcraft, or to aid him [sic] in love or war".

Mascot then became the term applied to something, usually a young woman or an animal, adopted by a team or regiment or other group as a cherished symbolic figure of good fortune. Mascots are often attractive young women whose FEMININE, DOLL-like qualities are in stark contrast to the supposedly manly qualities of strength, maturity and bellicosity of the sports teams and regiments which adopt them.

Maternal

From the Latin *mater*, meaning MOTHER, *maternal* entered English in 1492 with the sense "of, or pertaining to, a mother, characteristic of mothers or motherhood, ie motherly". (OED) The male corresponding term, *paternal*, did not enter English until 1605.

Unlike paternity, maternity has always been regarded as an instinct, ie, something that is "a natural or inherent aptitude, impulse or capacity; a large inheritable and unalterable tendency of an organism to make a complex and specific response to environmental stimuli without involving reason; behaviour that is mediated by reactions below the conscious level". (OED)

From the dictionaries a picture emerges of women unconsciously compelled to become mothers and, once they are, to feel and display 'natural' emotions of love, warmth and desire to breed and to nurture. Any woman who lacks this instinct is not 'natural' – she is less than a woman, she is certainly not FEMININE. The OED, for example, gives one definition of maternal as "having the instincts of motherhood" and gives the following example: "She is not maternal. . . I never saw a baby held so awkwardly (Gertrude Atherton, *Doomswoman*, 1892)"

The picture of paternity is of a male whose conscious feelings are governed by his intellect. Whereas maternalism is defined as "the quality or state of having or showing maternal instinct", paternalism is "The principle and practice of paternal administration; government as by a father; the claim or attempt to supply the needs or to regulate the life of a nation or community in the same way as a father does those of his children." (OED)

The use of *maternal* is further evidence of a widespread belief that women are closer to nature than men, and are ruled by instinct rather than by reason. In *The Second Sex*, Simone de Beauvoir catalogues numerous cases of women with no wish to become mothers (like herself) or who found motherhood irksome or unfulfilling. She concludes: "These examples all show that no maternal 'instinct' exists: the word hardly applies, in any case, to the human species. The mother's attitude depends on her total situation and her reaction to it. . .this is highly variable."

Matriarchy

Matriarch, from the Latin *mater*, meaning MOTHER, and the Greek *arkhos*, meaning ruler, entered English in 1606. The OED defines it as "A woman having the status corresponding to that of a patriarch", and states that its present day use is "now usually jocular". There is a noticeable disparity between this definition and that of *patriarch* (since c1175): "The father and ruler of a family or tribe", which presumably could – but doesn't – read "A man having the status corresponding to that of a matriarch." The OED's definition of *matriarchy*, which entered English in 1885, stresses that patriarchy is the norm: "The form of social organisation in which the mother, and not the father, is the head of the family, and in which descent and relationship are reckoned through mothers and not fathers." *Patriarchy* (since 1632) is defined as: "Social organisation marked by the supremacy of the father in the clan or family both in domestic and religious functions, the legal dependence of wife or wives and children, and reckoning of descent and inheritance in the male line."

Matriarchal, meaning of or pertaining to a matriarch or to maternal rule, entered English in 1863, two years after the Swiss jurist and classical scholar Johann Jakob Bachofen published *Das Mutterrecht* ('Mother Right'). This was an investigation of the religious and juridicial character of matriarchy in the ancient world. He posited an Arcadian matriarchal world in which dominion of the mother over family and state had been generated by woman's profound dissatisfaction with the unregulated sexuality that men had forced upon her. He believed that its roots lay in the moral and historical fact of the primacy of 'mother right' which sprang from the natural and biological association of mother and child – a role for woman which he termed a "natural vocation". He supported his theory with countless passages from ancient classical literature. But his theory was not acceptable to Victorian sensibilities and had little impact at the time.

Friedrich Engels, however, was influenced by Bachofen; *The Origin of the Family, Private Property, and the State* (1884) identified father-right and the end of the matrilineal clan with the beginnings of private ownership and slavery. To Marxists ever since, matriarchy has been defined as an egalitarian, pre-class society in which women and men shared equally in production and power.

Another major theorist was Robert Briffault whose three-volume work *The Mothers* (1927) defined matriarchal society as a historical period in which the real social bonds of society grew out of "the natural and biological dominance of the primitive mother over the group which she created, the awe attaching to her magical nature and powers".

Others who have accepted the existence of an ancient matriarchal society include Helen Diner (*Mothers and AMAZONS*. 1929), Robert Graves (*The White Goddess*, 1961), Elizabeth Gould David (*The First Sex*, 1971), and Merlin Stone (*The Paradise Papers*, 1976).

Cheris Kramarae and Paula A Treichler in *A Femininst Dictionary* provide sixteen quotations on the subject of matriarchy, all with slightly different shades of meaning. From these there appears to be a confusion between *matriarchy*, *matrilineality*, *matrilocality* and *matrifocality*. The dictionary definition of *matriarchy* has been given above; *matrilineal* is used for a society in which kinship and inheritance passes through the mother's line; *matrilocal* was defined in 1906 by the anthropologist N W Thomas as a community in which, upon marriage, the husband removes to the wife's local group or family; *matrifocal*, literally 'mother-focused' (see FOCUS), was coined by another anthropologist, Raymond T Smith, in 1956, to refer to societies in which the mother is highly valued, giving her some economic and political power within the kin group, and in which the balance of power between the two sexes is relatively egalitarian.

Undoubtedly matrilineal and matrifocal societies have existed – and in some remaining primitive tribes, still do. But, as Adrienne Rich writes, "The question. 'Was there ever true universal matriarchy?' seems to blot out, in its inconclusiveness, other and perhaps more catalytic questions about the past." Rich evades the problem by using the term *gynocentric* "in speaking of periods of human culture which have shared certain kinds of woman-centred social organisations. Throughout most of the world, there is archeological evidence of a period when Woman was venerated in several aspects, the primal one being maternal; when Goddess-worship prevailed, and when myths depicted strong and revered female figures. In the earliest artifacts we know, we encounter the female as primal power."

In her essay 'The Myth of Matriarchy: Why Men Rule in Primitive Society', Joan Bamberger points out that in order to posit and define matriarchy, most sociologists and linguists have accepted mythological accounts as a reliable reservoir of actual history. But, " . . . rather than replacing a historical reality, myth more accurately recounts a fragment of collective experience that necessarily exists outside time and space. Composed of a vast and complex series of actions, myth may become through repeated recitation a moral history of action while not in itself a detailed chronology of recorded events. Myth may be part of cultural history in providing justification for a present and perhaps permanent reality by giving an invented 'historical' explanation of how this reality was created. . . Myths are rarely, if ever, verbatim histories, although they probably can be demonstrated to reinterpret certain crucial events in the growth and development of individual life cycles.

"The final version of woman that emerges from these myths is that she represents chaos and misrule through trickery and unbridled sexuality. This is the inverse of Bachofen's view of pre-Hellenic womanhood, which he symbolised as a mystical, pure and uncorrupted Mother-Goddess. The contrast between mid-Victorian notions of the ideal woman (they are not those of ancient Greece as Bachofen supposed) and the primitive view, which places woman on the social and cultural level of child is not as great as it appears. The elevation of woman to deity on the one hand, and the downgrading of her to child/chattel on the other produce the same result. Such visions will not bring her any closer to attaining male socio-economic and political status, for as long as she is content to remain either goddess or child, she cannot be expected to shoulder her share of community burdens as the co-equal of man. The myth of matriarchy is but the tool used to keep her to her place. To free her, we need to destroy the myth."

Matriculate

It is often assumed that *matriculation*, the enrolment of students at universities after they have fulfilled certain entrance requirements, is connected to the use of the term *Alma Mater* (gracious MOTHER), which since the C19th has been applied to universities. There is no direct connexion, although *matriculate* has its roots in the late Latin *matricula*, the diminutive of MATRIX meaning womb, from *mater*, meaning mother. But *matriculate* probably developed from *matricula* in the sense of roll or register made of parchment from the uterine membrane of a gravid animal, called *matrix*, in classical Latin. Hence *matricula*, meaning a list or register of persons belonging to an order, society or such like, which entered English in the mid-C16th although by this time paper, not parchment, was used.

At first *matriculate* meant to insert a name in a register or official list or, in military terminology, to enrol (1577–1715). Occasionally it was also used to mean to adopt a child, to adopt or naturalise an alien, foreign custom or book etc; and to consign to MATERNAL care (1579–1768). The specific meaning of *matriculate* connecting it to having one's name officially registered at a university or college has proved to be the most enduring.

Matrix

In Latin *matrix*, formed on *mater*, meaning MOTHER, originally meant a pregnant animal, a female used for breeding, the parent stem, and later came to denote WOMB.

When the word first entered English in 1526 there seems to have been some confusion about the female reproductive organs as *matrix* was used for the womb and, occasionally, for the ovaries and the uterine tubes, eg: "The partes of the Female are the wombe and the rest which by a general name are called matrices." (*The Body of Man*, 1615) *Ovary* did not enter English until the mid-C17th; *fallopian tubes*, named after the Italian anatomist Gabriel Fallopius (1523–62) entered English in the early C18th.

By the mid-C16th the meaning of *matrix* had extended to a place or medium in which something is bred, produced or developed. By 1605 it was used for a place or point of origin or growth, which led to it being used to mean a cradle. By 1626 *matrix* meant a mould in which something is cast or shaped, as in the 'bed' used for striking coins (see MONEY). It was also used figuratively for the source or origin, eg, the authorship of a work. But in this sense *matrix* began to be replaced by *paternity* (see MATERNITY) in the early C19th.

Matron

When compared with *patron*, *matron* is sometimes cited as etymological evidence of a historical process of diminishing female power. But the two words have never possessed strictly equivalent meanings. *Matron* entered English c1375 from the Old French, originally from the Latin *mater*, meaning MOTHER, to denote a married woman, usually with the connotation of moral or social rank or dignity. *Patron* was first used in the late C13th to denote a man who held the right of presentation to an ecclesiastical benefice or the holder of an advowson – so called from the Roman *patronus*, a protector of clients, an advocate or defender.

By the C15th the meaning of *matron* had specialised to denote a married woman who was an expert in matters of pregnancy and childbirth but who was not a professional MIDWIFE. The C18th–C19th term *jury of matrons* was a jury of discreet women impanelled to inquire into cases of alleged pregnancy or loss of VIRGINITY, eg: "A jury of matrons is resorted to. . .when a feminine prisoner condemned to death pleads pregnancy in stay of execution." (*Encyclopaedia Britannica*, 1845)

While *matron* has always been female-specific, *patron* gradually extended to include women. At first, in the C15th and C16th, *patroness* was used for a female patron (formerly 'matron') saint, as well as a woman who was a pattern or model to her sex. It later denoted a female holder of an advowson (since 1538) and finally a female patron, ie, a woman who sponsors a social or charitable function or one who financially supports an artistic venture, sometimes called a *benefactor* or *benefactress*. She still may be called a *patroness*, but this word has been superseded by *patron*. A female benefactor is today usually called a *patron*. A woman who adopts an air of superiority and condescension is described as *patronising*, and female intercessing saints are known as *patron saints*. *Matron* as the title for a married female saint (since 1519) is now seldom used.

Since the mid-C16th the female-specific term *matron* has, on occasions, lost its original sense of a married woman, but has kept some connotations of high social standing. By the beginning of the C18th *matron* denoted "one of the grave women that have oversight of children in a hospital". (*The New World of English Words*, 1706) Such women were usually upper-class, often unmarried, whose charitable work did not defy conventional attitudes towards a woman's role. Today *matron*, as the term for the head nurse of a hospital, has largely been replaced by *superintendent*. This is probably because an increasing number of men have been appointed to this job: a woman may be called a *patron* but it is never acceptable for a man to have a woman's title.

Matron has degenerated from its early sense and is now mostly applied to a somewhat stolid woman, "taken jocularly as the representative of certain social prejudices and rigorous notions of conventional propriety supposed to be characteristic of the English upper middle class". (OED) In the USA *matron* is applied to women a little lower down the social scale. It is used for women who supervise the maintenance of order and discipline among women and children in a school, police centre or reformatory and to the female attendant in women's rest rooms, one "who assists the patrons [sic] and keeps the room clean". (Webster's)

Maudlin

A woman who was living an immoral life in the town had learned that Jesus was dining in the Pharisee's house. . . She took her place behind him, by his feet, weeping. His feet were wetted with her tears. . .he said to the woman 'Your faith has saved you, go in peace.'

St Luke 7 (New English Bible)

Both the woman's personal name *Madeleine* (since 1320) and the adjective *maudlin* (since 1607), meaning tearfully, weakly emotional or effusively sentimental, derive from *Mary Magdalene*, the name of the penitent one-time HARLOT of the New Testament. Little is known about her. She may have been a common streetwalker, an important *hetaira* (a pagan harlot-priestess), or a part-time PROSTITUTE, since her name may come not from the town of Magdala on the Sea of Galilee, but from the Greek word for hairdresser.

After Mary, the mother of Jesus, Mary Magdalene is the most significant woman in Christian legend. Together the two Marys represent the VIRGIN/WHORE dichotomy which permeates Christian theology and western patriarchal society.

The tears of Mary Magdalene have had an important influence upon the meaning of *maudlin*, and upon the gender construction of FEMININITY. From 1616 the meaning of the word extended to denote that stage of drunkenness characterised by the shedding of tears and effusive displays of affection – in sobriety regarded as 'natural' feminine characteristics. The tendency to cry or cry easily has always been perceived as a sign of effeminacy in a male (see EFFEMINATE).

In the mid-C18th the notion of Mary Magdalene's immorality was revived in the use of *magdalene* for homes for the refuge and reformation of prostitutes, after the Magdalene Hospital in the City of London. Mary Wollstonecraft (1759–97), the English woman's-rights theorist, was scornful of such institutions which she believed did nothing to prevent the conditions which forced women into prostitution in the first place: "Many innocent GIRLS. . .are 'ruined' before they know the difference between virtue and vice. . . Asylums and magdalenes are not the proper remedies for these abuses." (*A Vindication of the Rights of Women*). From c1840–90 a *magdalene marm* was colloquial English for an unsatisfactory female servant. This was defined as "A servant from the magdalene, a refuge for fallen women in the Blackfriars Road [London] which existed there until about the middle of the C19th. The women who went out as servants had been too often pampered there." (*Passing English*, 1909)

A French shell-shaped cake (shell-FISH have had a long association with women and have been used as a symbol of the VAGINA) called a *madeleine* originated in the small town of Commercy in Lorraine. It was named after their creator, a C19th pastry chef, Madeleine Paulmier. Of the English cake also called a *madeleine*, cookery writer Elizabeth David notes: "How the English madeleine, a sort of castle pudding covered with jam and coconut, with a cherry on the top, came by the same name is something of a mystery." (*French Provincial Cooking*)

May

May first appeared in English in the C10th. The word was probably a Middle English coalescence of the Old Norse word for boy or son with the Old English poetical word *maeg*, which often occurred with the meaning of WOMAN and sometimes of MAID or VIRGIN. In the C14th, *may* was used briefly to denote a male relative or kinsman.

As the name for the fifth month of the year in the Julian and Gregorian calendar (c1050), *May* derives from a totally different source. It was adopted from the Old French *mai*, possibly a development from the Latin *maius*, the neuter of *maior* meaning greater or larger. *Maius* may be connected to the name of the ancient goddess Maia, of both Roman and Greek mythology. The Greek Maia, whose name meant grandmother, MIDWIFE or wise one, was the eldest and most lovely of the seven daughters of Pleione and Atlas. Along with her sisters, Maia, originally the goddess of night and sky, was transformed into the constellation known as the Pleiades. To the Romans, Maia was the mother of the phallic god Hermes; she was the fire goddess who ruled the forces of growth and warmth including sexual heat.

A more pedestrian etymological theory about the origins of *May* is that it derives from the Latin word *majores*, meaning elders, those who examined the *junores* (see JUNE) or youths who wished to enter the military.

May replaced the Anglo Saxon name for the fifth month, *trimilchi,* which, according to the Benedictine scholar Bede (c673–735) derived its name from the Saxon practice of milking cows three times a day during this month.

The expression *January and May* used to describe the marriage of a very young woman to an old man was first used by Chaucer (C1345–1400). In the *Merchant's Tale*, May is a sexually promiscuous beautiful young woman who marries an easily deceived man of sixty: "And Januarie hath faste in armes take, His fresshe May, his paradys, his make." (c1386)

Meat

Originally meaning an article of food or DISH, (c897–1726), the connotations of *meat* were once totally positive ones of nourishment and pleasure. By 900 *meat* denoted food (as distinct from drink), and by 1200 it was used figuratively, as in the phrase *to be meat and drink to a person*, to mean a source of intense enjoyment. In the C14th *meat* referred to the flesh of animals used for food, later narrowing to denote the flesh of animals other than fish and poultry.

Perhaps because of the association with the word *flesh* (since 1000 *one flesh* has been used of WIFE and husband to express the closeness of the relation created by marriage hence, by 1300 its euphemistic use in reference to sexual intercourse), by the late C16th *meat* was a low colloquial generic term for the human body – only rarely the male – as an instrument for sexual pleasure. It also became slang for the VAGINA and, very occasionally, for the penis too.

The Dictionary of Historical Slang lists several phrases colloquially popular since the C15th, some still in use, which evoke an image of woman as dead flesh, bloodily carved up, hacked at, minced by a butcher or cook, and eventually served up for male consumption. A BIT *of meat* meant firstly sexual intercourse (from the male standpoint) and later a PROSTITUTE. *Fresh meat* was a prostitute new to the trade. *Hot meat*, sometimes *hot* MUTTON or *beef*, was used of a fast or LOOSE woman, a prostitute, and for the vagina. *Raw meat* referred either to a prostitute naked in the sexual act or was a general term for any woman. A *meat house* was a BROTHEL. A *meat market* was a term for a rendezvous of prostitutes, the female BREASTS and the vagina; it is used today by FEMINISTS to disparage beauty QUEEN contests in which young women are encouraged to parade their bodies like cattle for sale. A *meat merchant* was a procuress. A *meat-monger* denoted 'a woman given to wrenching' (see WENCH). A *sweetmeat* has meant both a penis and a very young woman who is a kept *mistress*. In the C20th the expression *a cut or slice off the joint* is a UK slang term used by men meaning to have intercourse with a woman.

Menopause/Menstruation

Oh! Menstruating woman, thou'st a fiend
From whom all nature should be screened.
C15th (?) anonymous English poet cited in Simone de Beauvoir,
The Second Sex

It is an undoubted fact that meat spoils when touched by menstruating women.
British Medical Journal, 1878

Menstruum, the earliest word for the menstrual discharge, was the neuter form of the Latin *menstruus*, meaning monthly from *mensis*, meaning month. It entered English in 1398: "That superfluyte hythe menstruum for it flowyth in the cours in the mone lyght." (John de Trevisa) Another use of *menstruum*, to denote a solvent, is explained by the OED: "in alchemy the base metal undergoing transmutation into gold was compared to the seed within the womb, undergoing development by the agency of the menstrual blood. The medical writers spoke of the human foetus as consisting of a 'spermatic' and a 'menstrual' part, derived from the two parents respectively; the alchemists employed this language in a transferred sense, the 'menstruum' with them being the solvent liquid."

From 1400 to the late C19th the term *flowers* was used for the menstrual discharge. This was based on the French word *fleurs*, literally meaning flowers, but probably really a corruption of the Old French *flueurs*, from the Latin *fluor*, meaning flow or flowing. (See FLOWER)

The term *monthly period*, later shortened to *period*, appeared in 1822. In the sense of a course or extent of time, *period* originates in the Greek word denoting going round, or cycle. Echoing John de Trevisa's words, *period* also has strong connections with the moon. The OED gives the following definition for *period*: "a round of time or series of years marked by the recurrence of astronomical coincidences (eg the changes of the moon falling on the same days of the solar year) used as a unit of chronology".

The adjective *menstrual* first entered English in the C14th meaning pertaining to the menses. Its subsequent history shows alchemical, lunar and floral connections and, in the late C16th, it acquired the sense of monthly, happening once in the month. The 'menstrual' element in alchemy referred to that which was supposed to be added to metal in the process of its conversion to gold. In 1665 the English mathematician John Wallis wrote: "There is no other connexion between the Moon's motion and the Tydes Menstrual period, than a casual Synchronism." In the sense of lasting or extending over a month it has been a botanical term since 1866, used of a plant in bloom or foliage for over a month.

In the mid-C18th *catamenia*, from the Greek word for monthly, began to be used, but never as widely as *menses* (the plural of Latin *mensis*, month) which entered English in 1597. The Greek words for month and cessation, however, gave the word *menopause* which has been in use since 1872.

Menstruation is a subject which has long been surrounded by taboos. In *Female Cycles*, Paula Weideger points out that the supposedly technical terms *menstruation*, *catamenia* and *menopause* are themselves euphemisms. Penelope Shuttle and Peter Redgrove reveal how the various slang terms reflect social usage and individual experience. "Frequently terms used by the men express disgust: 'blood and sand'; 'dirt red'; 'gal's at the stockyards'; 'ketchup'; 'the rat'; or sexual unavailability: 'ice-box'; 'Mickey Mouse is Kaput'; 'manhole covers'; 'she's covering the waterfront'; or sexual ambiguity: 'her CHERRY is in sherry'; 'she's out of this world'. Only occasionally have any of the slang terms reflected sexual availability: 'she's in season' or 'really slick'. (*The Wise Wound*)

The most common euphemism employed by women since the late C19th is *the curse* probably shortened from the C19th expression *the curse of Eve*. Of this Weideger writes: "The most damning euphemism attached to menstruation reflects the belief that the monthly flow of blood is the curse God laid upon woman for her sin in Eden." This was spelled out by the writers

Michael Ross and Bernie West in the popular US situation comedy *All in the Family* (1973): Archie Bunker, the lead male character, says: "Read your Bible. Read about Adam and Eve. . . Going against direct orders, she makes poor Adam take a bite of that apple. So God got sore and told them to get their clothes on and get outta there. So, it was Eve's fault God cursed women with this trouble. That's why they call it, what do you call it, the curse."

Shuttle and Redgrove suggest that the negative term *curse* might originally have been *course* or *courses*. Also denoting a flow of liquid, *courses* was first used in this sense in the C16th: "Beware that they which haue their monthly courses, doe not then. . .come neare." (Thomas Hyll, *The profitable Arte of Gardening*, 1568) In 1839 "The. . .expressions of 'the illness' or 'the courses' are those in most common use among the vulgar" (*The Cyclopadia of Anatomy and Physiology*, ed. Robert B Todd)

In the C20th *courses* became obsolescent. The term *curse* reflects Simone de Beauvoir's view that menstruation is at best an "untidy event" and at worst "a burden, and a useless one from the point of view of the individual". "It is not easy," she continues, "to play the idol, the fairy, the faraway princess, when one feels a bloody cloth between one's legs; and more generally, when one is conscious of the primitive misery of being a body." (*The Second Sex*) Despite the advent of tampons which would have diminished some of de Beauvoir's misery, the menstrual flow, as Susan Brownmiller writes, "its testament to female fertility and to gender, runs diametrically counter to the prized FEMININE virtues of neatness, order and a dainty, sweet and clean appearance". (*Femininity*)

Mary Daly claims that "the history of attitudes towards menstruation from ancient times. . .demonstrates male fear, envy, and hatred of women. The menstruating woman is called filthy, sick, imbalanced, ritually impure. In patriarchy her bloodshed is made into a badge of shame, a sign of her ontological impurity." (*Gyn/Ecology*) Pliny's C1st definition of menstrual blood made this explicit: "A fatal poison corrupting and decomposing urine, depriving seeds of their fecundity, blasting garden flowers and grasses, causing fruits to fall from branches, dulling razors. . . if the menstrual discharge coincides with an eclipse of the moon or sun, the evils resulting from it are irremediable. . .congress with a woman at such a period being noxious and attended with fatal effects to man." (*Natural History*)

In early Judaeo-Christianity a similar notion is enshrined in Leviticus: "When a woman has a discharge of blood which is her regular discharge from her body, she shall be in her impurity for seven days and whoever touches her shall be unclean until the evening. . .And if any man lie with her at all, and her flowers be upon him, he shall be unclean seven days; and all the bed whereon he lieth shall be unclean." *Flowers* was subsequently translated as impurity. In *The Mothers* (1927), Robert Briffault pointed out that in Arabic the words for 'pure' and 'impure' originally referred to menstruation, which was the source of the concept. "By the same token," explain Shuttle and Redgrove, " 'Taboo' or 'sacred' in Polynesian and Siouan is the same word as 'menstruating'." (The very word *taboo* was adopted from the Tongan word *tabu*.)

Judy Grahn argues that "Women's oldest magical-science powers revolved around menstruation and birth, and the blood of both these states of being was considered sacred. In fact, I believe *sacred* itself meant the menstrual state. To ritually shed blood, meant the ability to take on women's ancient powers. The transfer of the rites and paraphernalia of blood power from secret all-female covens and temple ceremonies into male hands and into the hands of the people as a whole was pivotal in the transition from woman-based to man-based society." (*Another Mother Tongue*)

Examining the various taboos surrounding menstruation, Reay Tannahill suggests that all blood was once considered magical but menstrual blood contravened the dimly recognised rules. Losing it did not mean death, it flowed for no apparent reason and was characteristic only of women. Thus it was feared because it was inexplicable. "Blood magic and simple bafflement could have been enough to make man wary of woman during her periods. Isolating her may have appeared as sensible insurance against the unknown. And woman may not have objected. . .The recurring theme is one of uncleanness, which need not be taken only in the magical or religious sense. . . Some anthropologists argue that prehistoric man experienced a sense of wonder at the miracle of procreation. . .and deduce that the menstrual taboos that grew and fossilized as the human race developed were actually a reflection of woman's exalted state as the propagator of man . . .(But) there was no reason to exalt women for doing what came naturally. Modern feminists may come nearer the truth in believing that the taboos, once established, were deliberately transformed into a weapon against woman's self-assertion.

"No-one knows when or how a man discovered that women could not produce children unaided, but it seems probable that this occurred during the early part of the neolithic era and that the discovery hardened his attitude towards menstruation. If his semen was the mystical catalyst of the process that ended in childbirth, then menstruation which demonstrated woman's failure to conceive, must have appeared as an insult and a rejection, a blood-letting that brutally denied his new role as childmaker." (*Sex in History*)

As Weideger states, it seems likely that menstruation taboos are the result of the fears of one sex about the other. Citing numerous women who responded to her questionnaire, she does not accept the totally negative attitude of women such as Simone de Beauvoir: "For a woman, the taboo acts as a constant confirmation of a negative self-image. It represents the source of the shame she feels about her body and her sexuality. The moment she refuses to abide by the rules of the taboo, she will no longer be defined by its laws." (*Female Cycles*)

Meretricious

The origins of *meretricious* lie in the Indo-European root *smer-* or *mer-*, meaning portion, part or share. The Latin word *mereri*, meaning to deserve (a portion or share), is cognate with the Greek *meros* meaning part or share. From this the Latin *merere* meaning to earn money, or serve, from hire, developed. From the same stem with a feminising diminutive the word *meretrix* developed. This probably originally denoted a female who worked for hire. Etymologists suggest that "since the number of gainful trades open to women in ancient Rome, where the law decreed that they could neither own property nor MONEY as long as there was a single extant male relative, was limited, *meretrix* came to mean PROSTITUTE". (Heller, Humez and Dror, *The Private Lives of English Words*)

Meretrix entered English in this last sense in 1564. Since 1626 *meretricious* has meant of or pertaining to, characteristic of or befitting a HARLOT. In the same century the word came to connote one particular characteristic of which prostitutes were allegedly especially guilty: deception. In 1611 the now obsolete word *meretriculate* – a parody on MATRICULATE and possibly also a pun on *trick* – was used in the sense of to deceive as a harlot. Since 1633 *meretricious* has had the meaning of alluring by false show of beauty, richness or attractiveness.

The brazenness with which male guilt was transferred onto the objects of their desire for illicit sex is breathtaking. The deception presumably practised by men who had sex with prostitutes on their wives is repressed; instead, it is the prostitutes who are condemned for using their deceiving CHARM to lure men from the straight and narrow. The connotations of falseness associated with *meretricious* also suggests male disappointment with their experiences of paid-for impersonal sex.

In the C20th *meretricious* is rarely used in a direct reference to prostitution. With the sense of "exhibiting synthetic or spurious attractions: based on presence or insincerity: cheaply ornamental" (Webster's) it is often applied to a showily attractive style of painting or writing, perhaps with the suggestion that the artist or author has prostituted themself.

Midwife

Midwyf first appeared in the C14th based on the Old English *med* or *mid*, meaning with, and WIFE in the older sense of WOMAN. Thus the obsolete C13th word *midwoman*. *Midwife* either originally meant a woman by whose means the delivery is effected, or a woman who is *with* the mother at birth.

The traditional role of the midwife was that of the 'wise woman' who was skilled in herbal healing, nursing the sick and attending to the pregnant, and the newly born. In her article 'Wisewoman and Medicine Man', Ann Oakley states that "Etymologically and historically, four words or roles have been closely related. These are WOMAN, WITCH, midwife and healer. The medieval church viewed healing women, or witches, as their implacable enemies." As Barbara Ehrenreich and Deidre English have pointed out, again and again, the 'crimes' that witches allegedly committed "included what would now be recognized as legitimate medical acts – providing contraceptive measures, performing abortions, offering drugs to ease the pain of labor". (*For Her Own Good*) The Inquisitors who wrote the *Malleus Maleficarum* ('Witches Hammer'), reserved their greatest wrath for the midwife, asserting: "The greatest injuries to the Faith as regards the heresy of witches are done by midwives; and this is made clearer than daylight itself by the confessions of some who were afterwards burned."

Oakley connects the witch-hunting era from the C14th–C17th as the period in Europe in which "medicine emerged as a predominantly male professional discipline, and the traditional female lay healer was suppressed". Obstetrics, however, survived this particular onslaught and remained the province of female midwives even among the upper classes for another three centuries. But in the C19th and C20th the female control of reproduction was eroded by the inclusion of obstetrics in the curricula of professional medical training. By 1930, at the instigation of the American Medical Association, US Congress outlawed midwives and the new overwhelmingly male 'obstetricians' replaced them.

In England the scientising and professionalising of obstetrics was dealt with in a way that did not totally exlude the female midwife. The term *man-midwife* entered English in the 1600s. Unlike the female midwife the man-midwife – or *acoucheur* as he became known in the C18th – was usually a member of the Barber-Surgeon Company. "In the processes of definition and specialization which occurred over the eighteenth and nineteenth centuries, female midwifery became the area of non-surgical obstetrics dealing with 'normal' labour. The man-midwife turned into the obstetrician trained in the use of surgical techniques for the management of difficult childbirth." (Oakley) In the early C20th midwives were integrated into the male-dominated medical profession by a system of training and licensing. The 1975 Sex Discrimination Act in the UK made male midwives a legal possibility.

Minge

From the Latin *mingere*, meaning to void urine, *minge* entered English in the early C17th, meaning to urinate. It was used only rarely but reappeared in the late C19th as slang for the VAGINA. Its origins in this sense are East

Anglian dialect, possibly from the Romany. During World War 1 *minge* became UK military slang for a group or collection of women, possibly also influenced by the word *binge*, denoting a spree that soldiers on leave might indulge in which included (ideally) 'wine, women and song'.

Mingy, meaning miserly, mean and disappointingly small, does not, as is often supposed, have any connection with male attitudes towards female genitalia, but is probably formed on a combination of *stingy* and *mangy*. *Minge* in the sense of vagina is now largely UK working-class slang only.

Minx

The source of *minx* is unknown, although it may be a corruption of *minikin* which was adopted from the Dutch *minneken*, formed on *minne*, meaning love, plus a diminutive-forming suffix. The now obsolescent *minikin* first appeared in English in the mid-C15th as a playful or endearing term for a woman. By 1761, in a transferred sense, it meant a small or insignificant thing, and by 1879 had degenerated to denote a "slight, delicate, affected, GIRL". (*Shropshire Word Book*) While *minikin* has retained this sense it has also acquired the ameliorated sense of "darling: one dearly beloved: the object of one's affection". (Webster's)

Minx travelled a slightly different path of pejoration and amelioration. During the second half of the C16th it denoted a pet DOG and was also a proper name.

By the 1590s *minx* had degenerated to denote a pert girl or HUSSY. For a woman to be described as pert was far from complimentary. From the Latin *aperire*, meaning to open, in Middle English *pert* meant open or bold and developed the senses of lively, vivacious, saucily free, forward or assured. Such characteristics were not acceptable in a society where women were expected to be anything other than forward or free. Thus, by the beginning of the C17th *minx* was applied to lewd or WANTON women and to HARLOTS. In the C20th *minx* is applied to a young woman who is considered pert and sly. Both these character traits have been traditionally associated with prostitutes – and indeed, with women in general.

Misandry/Misogyny

Misogynist, meaning a woman-hater, is formed on the Greek *misogunes*, from *misein*, meaning hate, *misos*, meaning hatred, and *gune*, meaning WOMAN. It first appeared in written English in 1620 (spelled misogenyst).

In 1980 Sheila Ruth defined *misogyny* as a word which "Includes the beliefs that women are stupid, petty, manipulative, dishonest, silly, gossipy, irrational, incompetent, undependable, narcissistic, castrating, dirty, over-emotional, unable to make altruistic judgements, oversexed, undersexed. . . Such beliefs culminate in attitudes that demean our bodies, our abilities, our characters, and our efforts, and imply that we must be controlled, domin-ated, subdued, abused, and used, not only for male benefit but for our own." (*Issues in Feminism: A First Course in Women's Studies*)

It was not until 1946 that *misandry*, meaning hatred of men, from the Greek *aner*, *andr-*, meaning a man, entered the vocabulary.

Miss/Mrs/Ms

When you call me Miss or Mrs
You invade my private life,
For it's not the public's business
If I am, or was, a wife.
        Anon, quoted in Miller and Swift *The Handbook of Non-Sexist Writing*

In the C16th and C17th *Miss*, *Mis* and *Mrs* were the written abbreviations of MISTRESS which, in its earliest sense, denoted a woman, married or unmar-ried, who ruled or was head of a household also called HOUSEWIFE. Like *master*, it conveyed high prestige and, when prefixed to a woman's name, was a title of respect.

By the mid-C17th *Mistress* and its abbreviations had pejorated and acquired negative sexual connotations: *Mistress* had the sense of CONCUBINE; *Miss* denoted a kept mistress; and all the terms were occasionally used for a common PROSTITUTE.

During this period the distinction between *Mrs* and *Miss* was one of age: *Mrs* was applied to all adult women, *Miss* was defined by Samuel Johnson (1755) as "an infantine" term applied to female children and to schoolgirls who had only recently left school.

By the C19th *Miss* and *Mrs* had become labels identifying marital status. Casey Miller and Kate Swift propose the following theory to explain this development: "The timing suggests a connection with women's increasing participation in the industrial revolution. The period was one of social ferment. Up to the time that large numbers of women left their homes to work in the new industries, the ordinary woman's primary identity had been that of a daughter, a WIFE or mother. She lived and worked under the roof of the man who ruled her person – her father or husband – and her relationship to him was apparent or easily learned. Once women gained a measure of independence as paid labourers, these ties were obscured and loosened. A man could not tell by looking at a woman spinning cotton in a textile mill to whom she 'belonged' or whether she was 'available'." (*Words and Women*)

Another reason for the change may have been the desire of married women

– a more powerful group than single women – and their husbands, to dissociate the female marital status from the word *Miss*, which Samuel Johnson defined in 1755 as "a STRUMPET, a concubine; a WHORE, a prostitute".

Around 1800 a new convention arose: the suspended existence of the married woman came to be symbolised by the total submersion of a wife's identity in her husband's name, preceded by the title 'Mrs'. (See MAIDEN)

In the C20th there have been several attempts to abolish the use of *Mrs* and *Miss* as a distinction between married and unmarried women. In 1906 the US writer Ambrose Pierce defined *Miss* as "A title with which we brand unmarried women to indicate that they are in the market. . . In the general abolition of social titles in this our country, they miraculously escaped to plague us. If we must have them let us be consistent and give one to the unmarried men." In 1914 the US feminist Fola la Follette urged a return to the use of *Miss* as the general title for women both before and after marriage. By the 1940s many secretarial, etiquette and word-usage handbooks for women endorsed her proposal. The title *Ms* was another suggestion made by such books – and, indeed, was occasionally used.

But *Ms* went largely unused until two factors forced it upon the US public. First, the growth of direct mail order selling made the abbreviation acceptable as an effective saver of both time and money. Secondly, a large number of women in the late 60s made political objection to the use of the *Mrs/Miss* distinction, believing that their elimination in favour of *Ms* allowed the person to be seen as a woman in her own right rather than in relation to (a male) someone else. In 1972 the US Women's Liberation Movement magazine, entitled *Ms* appeared. The success of the magazine probably led to the more widespread acceptance of the title. *The American Heritage Dictionary* became the first dictionary to include the term.

The OED included *Ms* in its 1976 supplement, defining its as "a compromise between Mrs and Miss". For all their supposed love of compromise, Ms met more opposition among the British than among other Anglophones. The objections to its use have been largely emotional and frequently very silly. Who is to say whether the sound of *Ms* is any better or worse than that of *Miss* as some have claimed? (The unspelled vowel sound of *Ms* appears in no other word in the English language; this may explain the reluctance of many to adopt it.) Another objection is that its spelling bears no relationship to its pronunciation – an argument which could be made against *Mr*, but is not.

There must be deeper reasons for the intensity of feeling behind the objections to the use of *Ms* apart from the ignorant belief that language either does not (or should not) change. Robin Lakoff suggests that patriarchal order requires women to be labelled into the available and the non-available. But the increasing number of single-mother families and lesbian and heterosexual cohabitees makes the *Miss/Mrs* distinction no longer a very reliable indication. For many women, brought up to believe that a husband is the acme of successful womanhood, the title *Mrs* confers an attractive status. It continues to be a subtle form of social pressure on women, encouraging them to marry by lumping together single women with the young and inexperienced. The unspoken assumption underlying *Miss* is that these women are unwanted (by males). *Miss* has long had the negative connotations of old MAID, SPINSTER and that 'unfeminine' of female states, barren. *Ms*, used mostly by women who choose not to marry, has these same connotations plus the often negative associations of the liberated woman, ie, strident, bitchy (see BITCH), HARPY, VIRAGO, etc. Lakoff concludes that "the attempt to do away with Miss and Mrs is doomed to failure if it is not accompanied by a change in society's attitude to what the titles describe". (*Language and Woman's Place*)

Mistress

Both *mistress* and *master* originate in the Indo-European root meaning great or much. *Master* developed from the Old English *magister*, a common Germanic adoption from Latin reinforced by the Old French *maistre*. The Old French *maistresse* was adopted into Late Middle English in the early C14th, some five centuries later than *master*.

Master originally meant a teacher (c888), and *mistress* first entered English with the sense of a woman who has charge of a child or young person (c1320–c1400). By the C11th the meaning of *master* had extended to a man having control or authority, generally over the actions of others, ie, a director, leader, chief, commander, ruler or governor (c1000–1596). Adopting this sense, *mistress* came to denote a female governor (see GOVERNESS) of a territory, state or people (c1366–1785). By 1362 a *master* was a man who employed another in his service; *mistress* acquired this sense in 1462. In one sense only did *master* lag behind *mistress*: by the beginning of the C15th *mistress* was used to denote the female head of a household or family; *master* did not acquire this meaning until 1536.

A divergence in the spheres of power between the sexes which developed during the Middle Ages is revealed by the different realms over which a mistress or master ruled. *Master* denoted a victor (since c1290) and one who has the power to control, use or dispose of something at will (since 1340). *Mistress* began to be used of a woman who illicitly occupied the place of a wife (c1430). By the early C16th *mistress* in this sense developed the meaning of "a woman who has command over a man's heart; one who is loved and courted by a man; a sweetheart or lady love". (OED) This amelioration may have been due to the fact that many marriages took place not for love, but for purposes of consolidating power and patrilineal succession – although this was nothing new to the C16th.

In some contexts, as Casey Miller and Kate Swift have pointed out, both *mistress* and *master* retain a sense of authority over another; "In their most common uses, however, master now denotes excellence in performance, and mistress labels the so-called kept woman." (*Words and Women*) Another major difference is that whereas *mistress* is gender-specific, its masculine form is not. *Masterpiece*, for example, was C18th–early C20th slang for the VAGINA, and a *Masterpiece of Nightwork* emerged as an elaborate early C20th expression for a very pretty HARLOT. Publishing houses in the C20th have no difficulty in including women writers in a list called 'Modern Masters'; but so contaminated is *mistress* that in the mid-1980s the British feminist publishers VIRAGO, opted for the title 'Pioneers' for books about the lives and ideas of women to avoid labelling Simone de Beauvoir, Teresa of Avila, Queen Victoria, etc as kept women. Use of *mistress* to denote a female schoolteacher has only just escaped contamination; could this be because a woman of learning is considered to be something of a BLUESTOCKING which has connotations of asexuality?

The mid-C17th *mistress-piece*, the equivalent of *masterpiece* is, according to the OED, now used only rarely. This is not surprising: in the C19th *mistress* connoted the exact opposite of mastery in, for example the nautical term *Mistress Roper*. This was the name given to inexperienced sailors from "their alleged handling of the ropes in a womanly or unseamanlike fashion". (Brewer's)

Mistress has often been seized upon by feminist linguists as an example of what Muriel R Schulz calls a rule of semantic derogation of women, meaning the devaluation of woman-related words through the pejoration and acquisition of negative sexual connotations, a process which is seldom discernable in the male-equivalent words or in man-related words. Maria Black and Rosalind Coward inject a necessary note of caution about adopting what amounts to a male-conspiracy theory of language: "Etymological data is clearly vital. . .but taken in isolation from other changes and uses in the language it can produce a very distorted picture, eg *Mistress* had been in use quite early as a specifically sexual term meaning 'sweetheart'. In addition, the disappearance of *mistress* as head of the household surely could not be separated from the appearance of another term, that of HOUSEWIFE bearing witness to very definite transformations of households and conceptions of women's place in them. Language does not simply reflect its past history nor its current function. Linguistic value has to be understood in relation to other aspects of overall structure of language. We have to understand not just histories of words, but the relationship of terms to other terms, the relationship between terms in statements, the relationship between statements." (*Screen Education* No 39, 1981)

Moll/Molly

Moll and *Molly* are the familiar pet forms of the personal name Mary. Like many pet forms they were especially popular among the labouring class and travelled the same path of degeneration as did many such names, eg, Kitty, DOLLY, BIDDY, etc. Since the C17th *moll* has been applied contemptuously to a WENCH, LASS, HARLOT and a PROSTITUTE. Hence the mid-C19th term *moll-shop* for a BROTHEL and the late C19th slang use of *moll* for VAGINA. In the early C19th *moll* showed some signs of amelioration: it was first a slang term for 'a girl' (one can assume from this definition in *A Dictionary of Slang and Unconventional English* that the lexicographer meant a young woman). And, from c1890, it was a slang term for a sweetheart. Godfrey Irwin's *American Tramp and Underworld Slang* (1931) defined *moll* as "any woman regardless of character or condition".

Since c1820 *moll* has also been used to denote an unmarried female companion of a criminal or a tramp. This usage combines the sexual connotations of *moll* and of an earlier term, *Moll Cutpurse*. The latter denotes a female criminal, so called after Mary Frith, a notorious pickpocket and the heroine of Dekker and Middleton's play *The Roaring Girl* (1611) who also made an appearance in Nathan Field's play *Amends For Ladies* (1618). In the US a *gun-moll* became slang for a woman who carried a revolver for her 'man'. A gangster's moll became stereotyped in many of the popular Hollywood crime movies of the '40s and '50s.

Molly also pejorated, but totally differently. In the C18th *to molly* meant to bugger (someone) and the adjective *mollying* was used of a man 'addicted' to buggery (1744). Since 1754 a *molly* or a *Miss Molly* has denoted an EFFEMINATE man or boy, eg: "It would be sad. . .if John Bull were to be EMASCULATED by Miss Mollyism." (*Blackwood's Magazine*, 1834) By 1829 a *molly-mop* meant an effeminate man, and a *molly-head* became slang for a 'soft-head' or a simpleton in 1902. It has been suggested that this sense may have been influenced by the Latin *mollis*, meaning soft.

Other women's names have also been borrowed for terms of contempt for homosexual and effeminate men: *Miss Nancy* (1824) from which developed the C20th *nancy-boy*, meaning a sodomite: *Pansy* denoted a sodomite from c1895–1914 and has been a derisive heterosexual slang term for a male homosexual since the 1920s; *Gussie* has been Australian slang for an affected and/or effeminate man since c1890. Similarly, *Sissy*, or *Sissie* (occasionally spelled with a C), from SISTER, was originally a polite society term for an effeminate man in the 1890s and subsequently came to mean a passive male homosexual. The C20th gay term *molly* DYKE denotes a passive lesbian.

Since 1833 a *molly-coddle* has been "one who coddles himself or is coddled; one who takes excessive care of his health" (OED) *Coddle* entered English first to mean to treat as an invalid in need of nursing, and later to nurse overmuch. The OED explains that "it differs from pamper in that it is those who are supposed to be weakly that are coddled". Weakness has never been a part of the gender construction of masculinity, hence *molly-coddle* came to denote an effeminate man. This effeminacy expressed itself in that most despised of creatures, "A man who does household work; one who interferes with women's business", which is how the *English Dialect Dictionary* defined *molly-coddle* in 1903.

Molly-coddle may be based on *Molly-cot* (1826), which meant one who fusses about domestic concerns or a man who performs a woman's domestic duties. *Cot* was shortened from COTQUEAN, which was based on *cot* (originally a small house or hut) and QUEAN (originally a woman). Thus *cotquean* meant a HOUSEWIFE of a labourer's cot. The word later pejorated acquiring the senses of one who has the manners of a labourer's wife, ie, a rude, ill-mannered woman, synonymous with coarse, a BELDAM, and a SCOLD, and also a man who acts the housewife, one who busies himself unduly or meddles with matters belonging to the housewife's province (1592–1825). The OED provides the following illuminating example of usage: "A Stateswoman is as ridiculous a creature as a cotquean; each of the sexes should keep within its bounds." (Joseph Addison, 1719).

In the USA another female personal name was borrowed to form the contemptuous compound term *cot-betty* (1700), meaning a man who does the housework. One hundred and fifty years later, *betty* (from Elizabeth) emerged in the UK as a verb with the sense of to fuss about like a man who busies himself with a woman's duties. In 1869 the *Lonsdale Glosssary* defined *cot* as "a man who interferes in the kitchen, a molly-coddle". Webster's leaves us in no doubt of how such a man has been perceived to transgress the bounds of acceptable masculine behaviour in its definition of *molly-coddle*: "a spineless weakling".

Money

The words *money*, *monetary*, *mint*, *admonish* and *monitor* all have links with the Roman goddess of marriage and the reproductive life of women, Juno Moneta, from whom the month JUNE may have got its name. The Romans translated the name of the Greek goddess Mnemosyne, whose name meant remembrance or memory, as *moneta*. Originally, the verb *monere* meant to call to mind, but it later came to mean to call to mind with the intent of instruction or admonition. *Moneta* was added to the name of the goddess Juno in her aspect as monitress, warner or admonisher, since she warned her worshippers of encroaching danger, especially the women of potentially bad husbands.

In 344 BC a temple was built to Juno Moneta to which was attached the first Roman mint. Thus *moneta*, first the name given to the place where coins were stamped out, was later used of the money itself. The Old French *moneie* was a development from this, and was adopted into the English language by 1330.

The 1798 edition of the *Dictionary of the Vulgar Tongue* defined *money* as: "A girl's private parts, commonly applied to little children: as, Take care, Miss, or you will show your money." If the VAGINA of a young girl was a precious commodity, the C19th–early C20th term *money-box* suggests that the older women's vagina was only a receptacle for something much more precious (to some): "The Victorians. . .revealed themselves in their slang expression for the orgasm – 'to spend' – a term freighted with economic insecurity and limited resources, perhaps a reflection of capitalist thrift implying that if semen is money. . .it should be preciously hoarded." (Kate Millett, *Sexual Politics*) *Purse* (a small container for money) has been a low colloquialism for the female pudendum since the C17th.

Mother

If women get tired and die of bearing, there is no harm in that; let them die as long as they bear; they were made for that.

Martin Luther (1438–1546)

According to Barbara G Walker, quoting from *Hindu Myths* by Wendy Doniger O'Flaherty in *The Woman's Encyclopedia of Myths and Secrets*, "Sanskrit *matra*, like the Greek *meter*, meant both 'mother' and 'measurement'. Mathematics is, by derivation, 'mother-wisdom'. Root words for motherhood produced many words for calculation: metric, mensuration, mete, mens, mark, mentality; geo-metry, trigono-metry, hydro-metry, etc. Women did temporal and spatial calculations for so long that. . .men once thought women were able to give birth because they had superior skill in measuring and figuring. Men imagined that if they could master these feminine skills, they could give birth, too. Male ancestors told one another that if they could only learn to measure the earth, they would 'happily create progeny'."

The Oxford Dictionary of Etymology gives no indication of this theory, merely tracing *mother*, which, when it first entered English in the mid-C11th denoted a female parent, back to Old English *modor*, meaning WOMB. *Modor* ultimately originated in the Indo-European *mater*, meaning mother. For the source of *metric* it gives the Indo-European *me*, meaning measure.

In ancient mythology the universe was thought to be created by the Great Mother Goddess or Divine Ancestress variously named Isis, Arinna, Ishtar, Nana, Innin, Inanna, Nut, Anahita, etc. In the mid-C11th, in an extended sense, *mother* also meant a female ancestress. Since 1000 the word has been used of the earth, considered as the mother of its inhabitants and productions. Hence the terms *Mother Earth* (since 1586) and *Motherland* (since 1711).

Brewer's gives the following account of the source of *Mother Earth*: "When Junius Brutus (after the death of Lucretia) formed one of the deputations to Delphi [see DELPHIC] to ask the oracle which of the three would succeed Tarquin, the response was 'He who should first kiss his mother'. Junius instantly threw himself on the ground exclaiming 'Thus, then, I kiss thee, Mother Earth', and he was elected consul." Walker points out that "Thousands of feminine names have been given to the earth. Continents – Asia, Africa, EUROPE were named after manifestations of the [Mother]

Goddess. Countries bear the names of female ancestors or of other manifestations of the Goddess: Libya, Lycia, Russia, Anatolia, Holland, China, Chaldea, Scotia, etc. Every nation gave its own territory the name of its own Mother Earth." In his essay 'The History of Nature', Mick Gold notes that this concept was not restricted to ancient Mediterranean cultures: "The American Indians regarded the earth as a great mother and found the white man's way of exploiting the earth abhorrent. 'You ask me to plow the ground! Shall I take a knife and tear my mother's breast? You ask me to dig for stones! Shall I dig under her skin for her bones? Then when I die, I cannot enter her body to be born again.'"

A related term is *Mother Nature* (since 1601); the mother in this sense is represented as both good and bad – a protecting and a controlling power – of which Dorothy Dinnerstein writes: "The mother, then – like nature, which sends blizzards and locusts as well as sunshine and strawberries – is perceived as capricious, sometimes actively malevolent. Her body is the first important piece of the physical world that we encounter, and the events for which she seems responsible the first instances of FATE. Hence Mother Nature, with her hurricane daughters Alice, Betty, Clara, Debbie, Edna. Hence the fickle female Lady Luck." (*The Mermaid and the Minotaur*, Sherry B Ortner argues that by personifying and feminising nature woman becomes identified with, or seems to be the symbol of "something that every culture devalues, something that every culture defines as being of a lower order of existence than itself. We may. . .broadly equate culture with the notion of human consciousness (ie systems of thought and technology), by means of which humanity attempts to assert control over nature." ('Is Female to Male as Nature is to Culture?') Margaret Walters explains the significance this had for Simone de Beauvoir: "Woman is always and archetypally OTHER, seen by and for men, always the object, never the subject. (So she came to stand for nature, mystery, the non-human; what she represents is more important than what she experiences.)" ('The Rights and Wrongs of Women') Dinnerstein concludes that "Our over-personification of nature, then, is inseparable from our under-personification of woman. . . If we could outgrow our feeling that the first parent was semi-human, a force of nature, we might also be able to outgrow the idea that nature is semi-human, and our parent."

Since 1000 *mother* has been applied figuratively to things more or less personified, with reference either to a metaphorical giving birth, to the protecting care exercised by a mother, or to the affectionate reverence due to a mother, eg, the Church, state, earth, etc. But different applications of *mother* in the history of the word reveal an ambivalent attitude towards the primary love object. For just as the good mother is cherished and venerated as the one who creates, loves and nurtures, so also is she feared and hated as the bad mother, the one who thwarts the desires of the young infant, who rejects and abandons her child when she withdraws the breast. Ultimately, she is associated with death; she is the despised CRONE, for each child she gives birth to is destined to die.

This ambivalence is reflected in the terms given to membranes of the brain: (since 1400) the dense, tough outer membranes of the brain have been known as the *dura mater*, or 'hard mother', and the delicate innermost membrane the *pia mater*, the godly, meek, mild or 'soft mother'. Since 1593 *motherhood* has been used to imply the feeling or love of a mother and, in a transferred sense, it has come to be applied attributively in North America of an issue or report, to mean protective or withholding the worst aspects. On the other hand motherly love and tenderness could be smothering: since 1880 *a mother's boy* has denoted a sissy (see SISTER) or a boy or man who resembles, or is dominated by, or excessively attached to, his mother, and the phrase *tied to one's mother's apron strings* means completely under one's mother's thumb, used particularly of a young man dominated by his mother.

It has not only been sons who have suffered at the hands of their mothers: from C15th–C17th *mother*, later *mother fits*, denoted HYSTERIA, which derives from the Greek word for WOMB – an affliction then believed to be peculiar to females. The phrase *like mother makes it* (late C19th–C20th) means very well cooked and extremely tasty, "Probably with allusion to many married men's stock complaint 'Umph! Not like (my) mother makes it.' " (*The Penguin Dictionary of Historical Slang*); but *mother's milk* and *mother's ruin* in the C19th denoted gin, with reference to the harmful effects of alcohol.

With allusion to the incest taboo, *mother-fucker* has been coarse slang for a base, despicable person since the mid-C20th (originating in the US). But the taboo did not prevent the term *mother* from denoting a BAWD. Both *Mother Abbess* (adopted from French) and *mother of* MAIDS also meant the same thing. (This last term derived from, and was in derision of, the c1570–1800 title of the head of the maids of honour in the Royal Household.) *Mother, Mother Damnable* and *Mother Abbess* later came to mean the female keeper of a BROTHEL. According to the 1811 edition of the *Dictionary of the Vulgar Tongue, Mother of all Saints* was slang for "The monosyllable" (see CUNT); *Mother of All Souls* and *Mother of St Patrick* were equivalent Irish terms.

Another sense of *mother* found in several applications since 1384 is that of the source or prototype, the parent stock on which anything grows and the main stem or channel from which others branch off (see also MATRIX). Hence the use of the word of a country or city in relation to its natives; of a city, country or institution from which another originates. Psychoanalyst Carl Jung remarked that cities have always been likened to the Mother, because they contain citizens in their BOSOM. Since c1380 the Church as an institution or corporation has often been personified and spoken of poetically and rhetorically as 'she', and *Mother Church* has been a favourite appellation of the Catholic Church since the same period. The principal church of a country, city or region is called the *mother*, of which another church is said to be the DAUGHTER or offshoot.

This sense of *mother* as the source may also have influenced the use of the word in the C16th–C18th to denote dregs or scum. This originally referred to the mucilaginous waste substance of oil, and later to the scum rising to the surface of fermenting vinegar and corresponded to the French *mere de vinaigre*. According to the OED the "original notion may have been that the substance was a portion of the 'mother' or original crude substance which remained mixed at first with the refined product". Webster's notes that its etymological source was akin to Middle Dutch *modder* and *moeder*, meaning mud or swamp, or dregs, Middle Low German *moder* or *modder*, meaning putrid body or swampland, and *mudde*, meaning thick mud.

The reverence owed to a mother is implicit in the application of the word to the Virgin Mary (since 1366); on the other hand since 1386 it has also been a term of address for an elderly woman of the lower class. The expression *mother's meeting* has no connotations of respect as it is used facetiously to refer to a group of people, men as well as women, who meet to GOSSIP. More respect and love, however, is paid to one's *Mother Tongue* (since c1380), the first language learned as a child. Webster's tells us that the use of *mother* in the terms *mother-in-law* and *stepmother* suggest the filial affection and respect due to such a woman by the adoptive child; but since the late C18th the term *Mother-in-law's bit* has meant a small PIECE, "mothers-in-law being supposed not apt to overload the stomachs of their husband's children". (*Dictionary of the Vulgar Tongue*) Likewise, there is little hint of affection or respect in *Old and Bitter* (ie, ale) which is Cockney slang for mother-in-law.

For every definition of *mother* or a mother-combination term which contains connotations of love, respect and reverence there seems to be another connoting fear, hatred or disrespect. Of this ambivalence Simone de Beauvoir wrote: "The respect that haloes the Mother, the prohibitions that surround her, suppress the hostile disgust that is mingled spontaneously with the carnal tenderness she inspires. A certain masked horror of maternity survives, however. It is of especial interest to note that since the Middle Ages a secondary myth has been in existence, permitting free expression of this repugnance: it is the myth of the Mother-in-Law. From fable to vaudeville, man flouts maternity in general through his wife's mother, whom no taboo protects. He loathes the thought that the woman he loves should have been engendered: his mother-in-law is the visible image of the decrepitude to which she has doomed her daughter in bringing her forth. . . But if his laugh is full of rancour, it is because he knows well enough that his wife's lot is the lot of all: it is his. In every country tales and legends have similarly incarnated the cruel aspect of maternity in the stepmother. It is her stepmother who would have Snow White perish. In the figure of the wicked stepmother. . .survives the antique Kali with her necklace of severed heads." (*The Second Sex*)

But perhaps the last laugh belongs to the mother-in-law. Chuck Barris, a Hollywood producer known for inventing television game-shows in which the contestants agree to submit to humiliation, failed to launch a series of programmes which made mothers-in-law the butt of the joke. Ruefully he explained it had failed because every mother-in-law turned out to be somebody's mother.

Mount

There are many horse-related metaphors in the English language which originated as mild or contemptuous designations for women and subsequently derogated to become terms of abuse with negative sexual meaning. HARRIDAN, originally a worn-out horse, was first used of a gaunt woman and came to mean a decayed STRUMPET or a 'half-WHORE, half-BAWD'. JADE, once denoting a broken down or vicious horse ended up as a synonym for a whore. A *hackney* or HACK, first a common riding horse for hire, pejorated to mean a bawd or PROSTITUTE. TIT, denoting a small horse was used first of a small girl and later a HARLOT.

Since 1509 the verb *to mount* has meant to get upon the back of a horse or other animal (occasionally upon a person's back) for the purpose of riding. By 1592 it was used in a transferred sense to mean "To get upon, for the purposes of copulation" (OED), eg: "Instead of backing the brave Steed, o'mornings, to mount the Chambermaid". (Ben Johnson, 1630) In the mid-C19th a *mount* was a pejorative term for a WIFE or a MISTRESS.

Like the Middle English use of the verb *to ride*, meaning to mount a woman in copulation, *mount* refers to sexual intercourse specifically from the male standpoint. The notion behind all these metaphors is that of woman as a horse to be broken in, tamed, domesticated and kept on tight reins, to be put to work and/or give pleasure to the male rider. Since the C18th–C20th a *rider* has been a colloquialism for a frequently amorous male.

Since the 1920s *stud*, an anglo-Irish word shortened from the standard English term *studstallion*, has been applied with little or no opprobrium to "a virile man" (*A Dictionary of Slang and Unconventional English*) or, according to *Webster's Ninth New Collegiate Dictionary*, any "young man, esp. one who is virile and promiscuous". In Australian slang *stud*, shortened from *studmare*, denotes a mistress, especially one who is available whenever required. In current usage *stud*, when used of a man, has some negative connotations. This pejoration is, perhaps, a result of feminism: a man noted mainly for his ability to perform sexually is no longer as widely appreciated as he once was.

A couple of expressions refer to the more adventurous sexual position with the woman on top – but although they do not have the connotations of a woman as a passive dumb animal they employ the imagery of the man as a beatified victor in shining armour, eg, *Riding St George* or *the Dragon upon St George* (late C17th–mid-19th). This position was once considered to be efficacious if the couple wanted their child to be a bishop.

Mouse

Mouse entered English c828 as the name for an animal of any of the smaller species of the genus *Mus* of rodents. By the early C16th it was a playful term of endearment, chiefly addressed to a woman (c1520–1798). By the late C18th *mouse* had pejorated and was London police slang for a woman, especially a HARLOT arrested for brawling and assault (c1780–1800). At about this time it was used in the phrase *a parson's mouse-trap* to connote a male victim; The 1811 edition of the *Dictionary of the Vulgar Tongue* defined this term as "The state of matrimony." From c1850 the former term of endearment had degenerated to become a vulgarism for the VAGINA. It was also UK slang for a flaccid penis (was this the result of being caught in the matrimonial trap?).

In the C20th *mouse* ameliorated and, presumably with connotations of a small, CUTE, timid pet rather than of a germ-ridden, disease-spreading rodent, became a slang term for a girl-friend, sweetheart, fiancée or wife. A *little white mouse* is current UK slang, mostly used by women, for a tampon.

Mrs/Ms See MISS

Muff

Muff was adopted from the Dutch *mof*, a shortening of Middle Dutch *moffel*, *muffel*, from the medieval Latin *muffula*, a thick glove. It entered English in 1599 with the sense of a cylindrical covering, usually of fur, into which both hands may be thrust to keep them warm.

Given the shape, texture and warmth of a muff perhaps the only surprising aspect of the later development of the word to mean VAGINA is the length of time it took to emerge. In 1699 *The New Dictionary of Canting Crew*, circumscribed by a legal prohibition on the printing of the word '*CUNT*', defined *muff* as "A woman's secrets" and provided the following example of usage: "To the well wearing of your muff, mort" which translates as "To the happy consummation of your marriage, WENCH". In the C20th someone who practises cunnilingus came to be called a *muff-diver* (since 1935), and in Dublin slang *muffing* denotes the practice of sniffing women's bicycle seats (also known as *schnarfing* and *snurging*).

From the part (see BIT) to the whole: according to the OED, in 1914 *muff* became US slang for a woman or young woman, especially one of low morals or a PROSTITUTE. Webster's maintains a silence on the word. The

Dictionary of American Slang makes amends with a graphic definition of *muff*: "the vulva, especially when covered with much pubic hair".

The use of muff as a verb meaning to mishandle, to make a mess of, appeared in the mid-C19th. This was formed on the slightly earlier use of *muff* as a designation for someone bad at sport or, in a wider sense, for someone without skill or aptitude or generally deficient in a practical sense. The OED suggests that this may convey "the scoffing accusation of keeping one's hands in a muff".

Muliebrity

From the Latin *muliebris*, meaning of a woman, formed on *mulier*, meaning woman, *muliebrity* entered English in the late C16th with the sense of womanhood, or possessing full womanly powers.

Webster's invites us to compare *muliebrity* with its masculine equivalent, *virility* (from the Latin *vir*, meaning man). Since the late C15th when *virility* entered English it has connoted vigour, force, energy and power, including that of procreation. The OED states specifically that *virile* is used "of persons" who are "not weak or effeminate". (Could a woman–person possibly be effeminate?) The powers of womanhood connoted by *muliebrity* are a little more nebulous – something which many women feel to be the actual case. The OED gives "the state or condition of being a woman"; "the state of being a grown woman"; and "womanliness". *Womanly* it defines as "Possessing the attributes proper to a woman; having the qualities (as of gentleness, devotion, fearfulness, etc) characteristic of women,"; and, "in derogatory use, in reference to the bad qualities attributed to women". *Virility* has never had any derogatory uses.

From examples of usage quoted in the OED one can deduce that the so-called power of womanliness turns out to be weakness, madness, feebleness, a weakness for the latest fashion, malice, moral incontinence, contrariness, and deceitfulness. Another definition of *womanliness* is that of having the character of a woman as contrasted with a girl. This is a power which patriarchal society attempts to diminish by its infantilisation of women as demonstrated by the application of words such as DOLL, BABE, CHICK, GIRL, etc to a woman of any age.

Mutton

Moto(u)n, meaning the flesh of sheep used as food (since 1290) was a Middle English term adopted from the Old French *moton*, which developed from the medieval Latin *multo(n)*, probably of Gaulish origin.

Since the early C16th *mutton* has been applied, in a transferred sense, most often to women and usually pejoratively. The earliest example of this is the Scottish use of the word as a term of contempt for a woman (1508–c1560). In 1518 the English Tudor poet John Skelton used *mutton* in the sense of 'food for lust' for a PROSTITUTE: "And from thens to the halfe strete, To get us some freshe mete. Why, is there any store of rawe mutton?" (*Magnyfycence*) The term *laced mutton* (1578–1694) at first meant nothing more derogatory than a STRUMPET. But by the end of the C16th it denoted a diseased prostitute: "You may. . .eat of a little warm mutton, but take heede it be not Laced, for that is ill for a sicke body." (Nicholas Breton). *Laced* in this sense may be a reference to the lacing on women's underwear (see STRAIT-LACED), possibly punning on the culinary use of the verb *to lace*, meaning to make a number of incisions in the BREAST of a BIRD. *Laced*, from the Latin *laquere*, meaning to ensnare, is also used in the sense of administering poison. Which is doubtless how a man with syphilis or gonorrhoea feels.

From c1670 *mutton* acquired the meaning of sexual pleasure and the sexual act, "almost solely from the man's stand point" as *The Dictionary of Historical Slang* helpfully explains. Its meaning also narrowed, coming to denote VAGINA like so many other female-specific slang words which degenerated to indicate the part as distinguished from the whole. Until it became largely obsolete in the C20th, *mutton* was used in several compound terms and expressions which expressed contempt for women. From the late C17th to the C20th a *leg of mutton in a silk stocking* was low slang for a woman's calf or leg. A *mutton in long skirts* (C17th–C19th) was a vulgarity for a woman. *Mutton Walk* (c1820–80) referred to the saloon at the Drury Lane Theatre in London where men could meet women considered 'easy' or 'LOOSE', and became a general term for London fast life. *Mutton-shunters* (1883–c1915) were policemen with the duty of keeping street prostitutes moving along.

Male contempt for an OLD WOMAN is contained in the C19th–early C20th slang term *ewe-mutton*, which denoted an elderly or amateur prostitute, and in the still extant phrase *mutton dressed (up) as lamb*, meaning a middle-aged or old woman who dresses in a manner considered more befitting to a younger woman.

Applied to a woman, *mutton* – like MEAT which is still used in a similar way – connotes dead, fleshy, inhumanity. Both words further suggest that a woman is no more than a DISH to be served up for male consumption. And *mutton* also draws upon a sheep image: sheep are not known for their intelligence.

Nag

Nag appeared in English c1400, first to denote a small riding horse or pony, and later an inferior or unsound horse. The word may be formed from a combination of the Dutch *negge* meaning a small horse, and the Old English *(h)naegan*, to neigh.

In the c16th *nag* became a term of abuse applied mostly to women, eg: "You ribaudred nagge of Egypt / Whom leprosy o'ertake", (Shakespeare, *Antony and Cleopatra*. 1606) Using Shakespeare as his source, Samuel Johnson (1755) defined *nag* as a contemptuous term for a paramour, but in his quotation from Shakespeare, "You ribauld nag of Egypt / Hoists sails, and flies", he may have been missing the point of the playwriter's sexual imagery.

Nag is yet another example of the horse metaphor which suggests a woman is a MOUNT to be 'ridden' by a male rider. Like JADE, HACK, and other horse-related words, *nag* underwent a process of sexual derogation. The connotations of a tired old horse was used to denigrate all women, not just old and tired ones. By the early C19th *naggy/ie* was UK slang for VAGINA, presumably from an earlier sense of the word as WHORE. By the late C19th *naggie* was a slang term for any woman.

In the C19th *nag* was first used in the totally different sense to mean someone who persistently engages in petty-fault finding or scolding. In this sense *nag* may derive from the Norwegian and Swedish *nagga*, meaning to gnaw, nibble or irritate, or from the Low German *(g)naggen*, meaning to irritate or provoke. A nag, like a SCOLD, is generally perceived to be female, eg: "Man was formed to BULLY as woman was formed to nag." (*The Saturday Review*. 1863) In *Feminism and Linguistic Theory*, Deborah Cameron points out that within folk linguistics – the name given to a collection of etymological beliefs which are accepted as common sense within a society – it is possible to isolate 'stereotypes', popular pictures of the speech of particular groups. "Folklinguistics inculcates an important set of value judgments on the speech and writing of the two sexes. A whole vocabulary exists denigrating the talk of women who do not conform to male ideas of femininity: nag, BITCH, strident." Nagging is an important ingredient in the negative stereotype image of the HOUSEWIFE, the mother-in-law and the MOTHER; but then nagging is, perhaps, one of the few ways open to the powerless to make their presence felt and get their voice heard.

Nan/Nanny

The origins of *nanny* are unknown although it is thought that, like *nan*, *nanna* (or *nana*) and NUN, it comes from an Indo-European child's word for an adult woman other than the mother.

In the C16th and C17th the phrase *nice as a nanne's, nanny's* or *nun's* HEN meant very affected, delicate, prim or fastidious (see PRUDE). In the C17th *nanny* became a low colloquialism for a WHORE (who was, presumably, considered to be none of these things). In the same century a *nanny-house* or *nanny-shop* was slang for a BROTHEL. It has been conjectured that in this sense *nanny* derives from the female personal name *Nan*, a pet form of Ann(e) which was popular among the British serving class at a time when female servants, or MAIDS, were often regarded as the personal sexual property of their male employers. For a brief period in the early C18th, *nan* was a synonym for a serving maid. Another explanation for the sexual pejoration of the word is that, like NICE – which also meant both fastidious and WANTON in the C17th – a whore might affect or adopt the behaviour of a delicate, prim woman. It was yet further 'proof' of female wile and deceit.

The OED dates the first use of *nanny* in the sense of a child's form of address to a nurse (hence a word denoting a children's nurse) in 1795. Jonathan Gathorne-Hardy, author of *The Rise and Fall of the British Nanny*, found an earlier date: in 1711, Lady Mary Wortley Montague wrote a letter to her old nurse, starting, "Dear Nanny".

But *nanny* in this sense did not gain widespread acceptance until the 1920s. Prior to World War 1, the term was used mainly by children. Adults during the C19th applied the titles *Nurse* or MRS to these usually unmarried and childless women who looked after the young offspring of the middle and upper or monied classes. *Mrs*, also applied to the cook in such households, was a mark of respect, but the status of nannies remained suspended halfway between the mother and the rest of the servants. *Nanny*, or *nan*, was also a child's name for a grandmother in Welsh, Midlands and Northern England dialect since the C19th which is slowly gaining wider use in the C20th.

In the C20th *nanny* became used in a transferred sense of a person or institution perceived to be unduly protective or apprehensive, eg: "He was so calm and soothing and nanny-like that she wanted to hit him." (A Wilson, *The Middle Age of Mrs Eliot*, 1958). This has been analysed by some psycholinguists as a reflection of ambivalence towards the early nurturing love-object. Thus Britain under the rule of Prime Minister Margaret Thatcher is called a *Nanny-State* by those who dislike her aura of calm, unrelenting, lack of compassion.

Nice

Nice derives from the Latin *nescius*, meaning ignorant. The Old French *nice*, meaning silly or stupid, was adopted into English in the late C13th with the sense of foolish, stupid or senseless. By the C14th its meaning extended to WANTON or lascivious and was chiefly applied to women, perhaps because "a silly woman [was] assumed to be a wanton one, a person whose favours might be easily obtained". (Heller, Humez, Dror, *The Private Lives of English Words*) Fortunately for the men who wished to satisfy their desire for illicit sex there is evidence to suggest there were plenty of 'nice' women around. In the C15th *nice* acquired a whole range of senses, some apparently contradictory. Used of dress it meant either extravagant and flaunting or very trim, elegant and smart. Other senses included; strange, rare, or uncommon; slothful, lazy or indolent; and COY, shy, or affectedly modest, "possibly because a 'wanton' might be coy while another woman, whose behaviour the 'wanton' woman aped or caricatured, might be shy". (Heller, Humez, Dror) In the early C16th *nice* became strongly related to perceived characteristics of femininity with the senses of unable to endure much, tender and delicate (1502–1710), and by the end of the C16th it was sometimes used to mean EFFEMINATE or unmanly. In the same century, with an extension of the earlier sense of shy, *nice* developed to denote fastidious, dainty or difficult to please. *Nice* in the sense of fastidious, as in *a nice distinction*, survives today.

By the C17th in complete reversal of wanton, *nice* developed the sense of precise or strict in matters of reputation, punctilious, scrupulous or sensitive. By the end of the C18th it had become a general epithet of approval for an agreeable person or something from which one derives pleasure or satisfaction. A century later a slight derogation was discernible: 'a nice GIRL', used of a woman, tended to be used with some derision. The American novelist Edith Wharton explained this use of the word in this way: "He had never wanted to marry a 'nice girl': the adjective connoting. . .certain utilitarian qualities. . .apt to preclude the luxury of CHARM." (*House of Mirth*, 1905) By the late 1960s *nice* had reverted to its C14th meaning: the University of Dakota survey of current slang defined *nice girl* as "a sexually permissive girl".

With understandable exasperation, the OED notes, "In many examples [of usage] from the 16th and 17th centuries it is difficult to say in what particular sense the writer intended it to be taken." Some linguists claim that *nice*, along with other words such as *pretty*, *darling*, *charming* (see CHARM), *sweet*, *lovely*, CUTE, *precious*, etc, is typical of a vocabulary of imprecise and trivial words (see TRIVIA) used more frequently by women, perhaps as a way of avoiding stating opinions directly as men are thought to do. Jane Austen (1775–1817) was well aware of the 'unmanly' implications behind the use of the word. In *Northanger Abbey*, Henry Tilney explodes in an expanse of masculinity: "this is a very nice day, and we are taking a very nice walk, and you are two very nice ladies. Oh, it is a very nice word indeed – it does for everything. . .now every commendation on every subject is comprised in that one word."

But one person's virile explosion is another person's petty petulance. To conclude that the use of an imprecise term such as *nice*, is an example of female use of deficient, trivial or weak euphemistic language is to beg the question. Dale Spender points out, "it requires a patriarchal frame of values to interpret this as evidence of the triviality of women's vocabulary". (*Man Made Language*) To characterise women's language as an indication of their inherent stupidity or foolishness is to isolate a female stereotype which reinforces the idea of male superiority.

Nightmare

In Anglo-Saxon England an oppressive bad dream was believed to be caused by a *mare* or *maere*, an evil demon which sat on the chests of sleepers. *The Latin and English Epinal Glossary* (700) defined *mare* as an incubus, the word *incubus* being adopted from the Latin, formed on *incubare*, meaning to lie upon (from which *incubate* and *incumbent* derive). An incubus was a demon in male form which was believed to have sexual intercourse with women while they slept. In female form this demon was called a *succubus* or *succuba*, formed on the medieval Latin word *succubare*, meaning to lie under (from which *succumb* derives). Wet dreams were attributed to the nocturnal attentions of succubi who were believed to suck out the essence of men's souls. In the mid-C15th *mare* was another name for spectre, HAG or WITCH. By 1622 *succubus* had become a synonym for a STRUMPET or WHORE and was a term of abuse for a 'low' woman.

In the late C13th *nightmare* entered English as another word for both succubus and incubus. By the mid-C16th its meaning had extended to "a feeling of suffocation or great distress felt during sleep from which sleepers vainly endeavour to free themselves". (OED) The early association with witches continued into the C17th when a bad dream was also known as the *night-hag* or *the riding of the witch*.

Mare in the sense of an evil demon was obsolete by the mid-C18th since when it has been popularly believed that the 'mare' in *nightmare* refers to a female horse and has often been depicted as such in the arts. But in this sense *mare* derives from the Old English *mere*, meaning horse. Drawing upon the sexual imagery of a woman as a MOUNT to be 'ridden' by a male rider, *mare* has been applied contemptuously to a woman since 1303.

Nooky

Nook, meaning a secluded or sheltered place among natural scenery (since 1555), is probably the origin of *nooky* (also *nookie* and *nookey*) which, since the late 1920s has meant variously, "sexual activity; a woman considered solely as a sexual object; the VAGINA, coitus; a PIECE". (*Dictionary of American Slang*) Alternatively, it may derive from *nug*, a late C17th–mid-C19th verb meaning to fondle, and once a term of endearment, but which, by the mid-C18th, produced the cant terms *nugging-dress*, meaning an odd or exotic dress especially a LOOSE dress affected by and characteristic of HARLOTS, and *nugging-houses* or *nugging-ken*, meaning a BROTHEL. Use of *nooky* was at first offensive, eg: "Still, nooky was nooky he told himself, and who cared what the woman was like if the lay was good." (A West, *The Trend is Up*, 1960) As a euphemism for sexual intercourse *nooky* is no longer gender-specific nor as offensive as it once was.

Nubile

Nubile is an adoption of the Latin *nubilis*, formed on *nubere* meaning to take a husband, from which *connubial* (of marriage or husband or WIFE) and *nuptial* (of marriage or wedding) also derive. Also related to *nubere* is the Greek *numphe* meaning BRIDE or NYMPH; one of the names of Hera, goddess of women and their sexuality, was Nympheuomene whose name means 'seeking a mate'.

Nubile entered English in the mid-C17th, referring to women with the sense of marriageable or of an age or condition suitable for marriage. In the 1970s the word came to be used to describe women, especially young ones, in terms of their sexual attractiveness (to men) with a strong connotation of virginity (see VIRGIN). The notion behind this modern sense of the word is that an OLD WOMAN is not considered suitable for marriage because she is no longer sexually attractive or reproductively active.

Nun

The Old English word *nunne*, meaning child's nurse, derives from the Late Latin *nonna*, meaning child's nurse or nun. Like NANNY, it probably originated from baby-talk as did the Greek *nanna*, or *nenna*, meaning a female relative or aunt. Since c900 *nun* has denoted a woman devoted to a religious life, especially one living in a convent under the vows of poverty, CHASTITY and obedience.

Although chastity for females has always been one of the major tenets of the Christian Church, a woman who consciously chooses to live independently of men fuels male fantasy and fear. Thus nuns have been the butt of crude sexual jokes for centuries. In the late C16th a *nunnery* (ie, a convent) became a euphemism for a BROTHEL. This piece of irreverence may also have been influenced by Protestant opposition towards the disestablished Roman Catholic Church. And there was probably some reality to the notion: it was the custom during the Middle Ages for daughters to be placed in nunneries simply because they were unmarried and therefore costly to keep at home or because the family could not afford to pay a dowry. Lapses from the vow of chastity on the part of these unwilling nuns were not uncommon.

In the late C18th COURTESANS and HARLOTS were called *nuns; abbess* became another word for a procuress. These slang terms were obsolete by the C20th but the unchaste nun – a symbol of the VIRGIN-WHORE dichotomy – has continued to excite the male imagination. She has featured, for example, in the films of Buñuel as well as in many cheap blue movies, pornographic magazines and strip clubs.

Nymph/Nymphet

Nymph was adopted, via the Old French *nimphe*, from the Latin *nympha*, an adoption of the Greek *numphe*, meaning BRIDE. One of the aspects of Hera, the Greek QUEEN of the gods who was worshipped as the goddess of women and their sexuality, was Nympheuomene whose name means 'seeking a mate'. The Latin word is related to *nubere*, meaning to take in marriage, from which the word NUBILE derives. Mythologically, a nymph was one of the many classes of semi-divine creatures, imagined as beautiful MAIDENS or VIRGINS, who lived in the sea (Nereids or Oceanids), in rivers and fountains (Naiads), in woods or trees (Dryads or Hamadryads) and in mountains and rocks (Oreads).

Since the late C16th *nymph* has been used poetically, first for a young and beautiful woman, and later as a synonym for a maiden or DAMSEL. It was borrowed in the C17th by anatomists as the name for the labia minora, eg: "Nymph: little pieces of Flesh in a Woman's Secrets". (*Blancard's Physical Dictionary*, 1693) (See CLITORIS.) Hence the C18th use of *nymphish* to mean bewitching, in the sense of a sexually alluring woman.

This may have influenced the C20th use of *nymphet*, which originally denoted a young or little nymph. In 1955 the Russian-born American novelist Vladimir Nabokov reintroduced the word into the English language in his novel *Lolita*. He defined *nymphet* as follows: "Between the age limits of nine and fourteen there occur maidens who, to certain bewitched travellers twice or many times older than they, reveal their true nature which is not human, but nymphic (that is, demoniac); and these chosen creatures I propose to designate as 'nymphets'."

From a non-masculist perspective the novel is about the kidnap, coercion and RAPE of a child under the age of consent. But the words *Lolita, nymph* and *nymphet* (occasionally spelled *nymphette*) have become interchangeable for a sexually precocious young woman or GIRL, ie, a SIREN who lures supposedly mature men to their doom, reflecting very common male fantasies of illicit sex with female child virgins.

Nymphomania

Medical treatises dating back to ancient Egypt reveal that women have long been considered to be constitutionally the more disorderly and innately lustful of the two sexes. Women have been perceived to be closer to nature (see MOTHER) and ruled by emotion and intuition, unlike men who are ruled by reason and intellect. The source of woman's labile nature was thought to be her WOMB. This was likened by the ancient physicians to a wandering wild animal which could only be controlled by frequent intercourse or pregnancy. Untamed, the uterus (the term was adopted in the C17th from the Latin for belly or womb) caused symptoms of a disease known to the Greeks as *husterikos*, formed on *hustera*, meaning womb. The word *nymphomania*, to describe a form of HYSTERIA, was first used by the Scottish physician William Cullen (1712–90). It was formed from the Greek *numphe*, meaning bride (from which NYMPH derives), and *mania*, which is related to *mainesthai* meaning be mad.

Cullen classified *hysteria libidinosa* as an illness of mainly physical origin, connected to menstruation, to young widowhood and to the passions of a sensitive mind: "It occurs especially in those females who are liable to the Nymphomania." (*First Lines of the Practice of Physic,* 1796)

The medical definition of nymphomania had changed by the C19th largely as a result of French psychiatrist Philippe Pinel (born 1745) who perceived hysteria as part of what he called 'mental alienation': "Nymphomania is most frequently caused by lascivious reading, by severe restraint and secluded life, by the habit of masturbation, an extreme sensitivity of the uterus, and a skin eruption upon the genital organs." (This last symptom may, in fact, have been a sign of venereal disease which many PROSTITUTES suffered from; prostitutes were generally considered to be highly libidinous and particularly disorderly.) Based on two case studies, one in which he believed nymphomania had been triggered by marriage to an impotent husband and the other as a result of enforced separation from a lover, Pinel described the nymphomaniac in the following graphic terms: "she abandons herself to her voluptuous leanings, she stops fighting them, she forgets all rules of modesty and propriety; her looks and actions are provocative, her gestures indecent; she begins to solicit at the moment of the approach of the first man, she makes efforts to throw herself in his arms. She threatens and flares up if the man tries to resist her. . ."

One of Pinel's major contributions to medical science was to influence the growing number of psychiatrists that men suffered from hysteria and from nymphomania (or *furor uterinus*, as he called it) which was "for the woman what satyriasis is for the man". But satyriasis (from the mythological satyr, a male nymph) never received the same degree of medical attention that nymphomania did in the C19th. Presumably most males who displayed the symptoms outlined by Pinel were acclaimed as sexual athletes; nymphomaniacs found themselves consigned to mental asylums.

In *The Female Malady*, Elaine Showalter argues that medical insistence upon the sexual instability of women was used as one of the reasons to keep them "out of the professions, to deny them political rights, and to keep them under male control in the family and the State". Any manifestation of female sexuality was abhorrent to the physicians and psychiatrists who imposed upon the female inmates of Victorian asylums the "ladylike [see LADY] values of silence, decorum, taste, service, piety and gratitude". The apotheosis of this moral management of women was the surgical practice of clitoridectomy performed by Dr Isaac Baker Brown in the mid-C19th as the certain cure for nymphomania. "Clitoridectomy," writes Showalter, "is the surgical enforcement of an ideology that restricts female sexuality to reproduction. With their sexuality excised his patients gave up their independent desires and protests, and became docile childbearers."

With the advent of psychoanalysis in the late C19th came yet another definition of *nymphomania* which finally ended the association of hysteria with the womb. Clearly influenced by Freudian theory, Webster's defines *nymphomania* as "Excessive desire by a female for sexual activity, usually based on feelings of personal inadequacy". In its definition of *satyriasis* no mention is made of inadequacy but it is, at least, referred to as "abnormal".

The definitions provided by the OED reflect the 'He's a sexual athlete; she's a raving nympho' double standard. *Nymphomania* is "A feminine disease characterised by morbid and uncontrollable sexual desire". *Satyriasis*, on the other hand, is not an abnormal pathological affliction, but only "Excessively great venereal desire" – a definition the OED borrows from the *Sydenham Society Lexicon* of 1897. As Gloria Steinem points out: "Nymphomania. . .was mainly used to condemn any woman who made more sexual demands than one man could handle. . .The sexually aggressive woman [of the post 1960s] is a SLUT or a nymphomaniac, but the sexually aggressive man is just normal." (*Outrageous Acts and Everyday Rebellions*).

Old Woman See ANILE

Other

Judith Okely describes Simone de Beauvoir's *Second Sex* as "a devastating account of the conditions of women's subordination which arises mainly from being treated as 'the Other' by man". (*Simone de Beauvoir*)

Tracing the origins of this idea of alterity, or otherness, back to Aristotle who wrote, "The female is a female by virtue of a certain lack of qualities; we should regard the female nature as afflicted with a natural defectiveness", de Beauvoir explains her essentially Hegelian and existentialist view as follows: "humanity is male and man defines woman not in herself but as relative to him; she is not regarded as an autonomous being. . .she is simply what man decrees; thus she is called 'the SEX' by which she appears essentially to the male as a sexual being. For him she is sex – absolute sex, no less. She is defined and differentiated with reference to man and not he with reference to her; she is incidental, the inessential as opposed to the essential. He is the Subject, he is the Absolute – she is the Other."

De Beauvoir explains why it is so difficult for women to shake off the otherness which defines them: "To decline to be the Other, to refuse to be a party to the deal – this would be for women to renounce all the advantages conferred upon them by their alliance with the superior caste. Man-the-sovereign will provide woman-the-liege with material protection and will undertake the moral justification of her existence; thus she can evade at once both economic risk and the metaphysical risk of a liberty in which ends and aims must be contrived without assistance."

De Beauvoir's notion of woman as other has been challenged by the French feminist and linguist Luce Irigaray who "has pointed out the reductive inaccuracy of this concept which posits women as whatever men are not (ie if man is active, woman is passive; if he has a phallus, she lacks it) when applied to female sexuality. Women are different from men, but not opposite to them, and the binary oppositions which locate them at one end of a male/female polarity are artificial, reflecting both the exclusion of women from the making of what counts as knowledge (philosophy and science, for instance) and the dominance of one particular sort of science." (Deborah Cameron, *Feminism and Linguistic Theory*)

Cameron explores the special status the concept of binary opposition has in linguistics: "Since Saussure, many other linguists have found the two-way contrast useful in their analyses of linguistic systems. . .and it has become institutionalised. Students learn early to look for binary oppositions rather than, say, three-term contrasts, in language, and may even be told what some theorists maintain, that to do so is a universal property of the human mind. . . It is possible to adduce a good deal of evidence in support of this claim. . . But we are on shakier ground if we claim it is a rule of language itself that female terms have a negative meaning. . .To say that the language embodies value judgements based on these plus and minus categories is a theoretical vulgarity even the most chauvinist linguist would re-pudiate. . .The male/female opposition itself, of course, remains of cultural and political interest to feminists. As Helene Cixous points out, it is felt in many societies to be the fundamental dichotomy: but the explanation lies mostly outside linguistics, electing a very general and conscious patriarchal policy of constructing a sexual dichotomy in every area of human experi-ence."

Paraphernalia

Paraphernalia derives from the Greek word *parapherna*, formed on *para*, meaning beside, and *pherne*, meaning dowry, which was related to *pherein*, meaning to bear or carry with you. Roman jurists used the word *parapherna* for all property which a married woman *sui juris* held apart from her *dos*, or dower, over which her husband could exercise no rights without her consent.

The word was adopted directly from the Latin and first appeared in written English in the 1478–79 Year-book of King Edward IV which stated: "As to her apparel, which is called in our law paraphernalia, of this by agreement with her husband she can make a will" (translated from the official court French). By the mid-C17th English jurists used the word to refer to those articles of personal property which a married woman was legally allowed to keep and, to a limited extent, deal with as her own. *The New World of English Words* (1706) defined *parapherna*, or *Parapherna Bona*, as "Those goods that a Wife brings her Husband over and above her Dower, as Furniture for her Chamber, Wearing Apparel, Jewels, etc." Under English and Scottish common law *paraphernalia* came to refer only to her purely personal belongings – mainly her clothing and her 'odds and ends' – and not articles of household furniture even though these had been wedding presents to the WIFE and were once included as paraphernalia.

One of the effects of the English Married Woman's Property Acts of the 1870s and '80s, in which the doctrine of separate property was extended to certain kinds of property to which a married woman might become entitled whether living with her husband or not, was to denude the word *paraphernalia* of all legal significance. As a result it acquired first the sense of "articles that compose an apparatus, outfit or equipment", and later "the mechanical accessories of any function or complex scheme". (OED) This notion of complexity affected its current informal use to denote any complicated procedure or rigmarole, eg, 'I can't bear the paraphernalia of getting planning permission.'

Petticoat

Originally, *petticoat*, literally, a little coat, from the French *petit*, meaning little, denoted a short coat worn by a man beneath his doublet (1412–1542).

It was also used for a type of tunic or chemise worn by women, girls and young children. By the C16th *petticoat* was the name given to a woman's underskirts. By the end of the century it was used symbolically to signify the female sex in the phrase *to wear* or *be in petticoats*, meaning to be a woman or to behave in a manner befitting to a woman. By 1600 *petticoat*, like SKIRT, was a synonym for a WOMAN.

Lurking behind *petticoat* is a notion of FEMININITY which connoted female weakness. In 1625 the British anatomist James Hart used the word to undermine the role of women healers, whom he called "The ignorant Empiricke, the peticoate or woman-physician." An anonymous, but presumably male, C18th writer who styled himself 'Chagrin the Critick' clearly feeling threatened by the growing number of women writers, or AUTHORESSES, whined "I hate these Petticoat-Authors; 'tis false grammar, there's no feminine for the Latin word, 'tis entirely the masculine Gender, and the language won't bear such a thing as a She-author."

The phrase *petticoat government* has generally meant undue rule or predominance of women in the home or in politics, although when John Dunton wrote *The Prerogative of the Breeches: an answer to petticoat Government written by a true-born Englishman* at the time of the accession to the throne by QUEEN Anne he defined it a little more diplomatically: "By [this], I mean when Good Women Ascend the Throne, and Rule according to Law, as is the case of the present Queen. Again, by Petticoat Government I mean the discreet and HOUSEWIFELY Ruling of a House and Family." When a man is ruled, governed or influenced by petticoats he is considered a weak, HEN-pecked, EMASCULATED object of pity or derision. Petticoats bestow no power to men. But breeches can bestow power to a woman. A woman who controls the household or husband is said to 'wear the trousers'.

In *The Mermaid and the Minotaur*, Dorothy Dinnerstein argues that the difficulty of accepting female authority as totally legitimate results from the way in which children are initially both nurtured and controlled by the mother: "Female will is embedded in female power which is. . .the earliest and profoundest prototype of absolute power. . . So the essential fact about paternal authority, the fact that makes both sexes accept it as a model for the ruling of the world is that it is. . .a sanctuary from maternal authority." She detected evidence of Freud's inability to tolerate the thought of female power once infancy is over, "in a petulant reference to that hateful American novelty, female suffrage". In his essay *The Future of an Illusion* (1927), Freud blamed the US prohibition of alcohol in the 1920s on "the influence of petticoat government". Dinnerstein concludes: "The phrase simultaneously derides the notion of female participation in politics and exaggerates the power that females can thereby exert: if the petticoats have a voice at all, it implies, their voice is bound to take over altogether."

Piece

Piece, originating in the Old French *piece*, entered English in 1225 to denote a separate or detached portion, part, BIT or fragment of anything. Used of a person, usually disparagingly, it was first applied at the end of the C13th to an individual, as in one of a multitude, army or company. It became applied chiefly to women in the C14th and later was used mostly with a deprecatory attribute, eg: "A washpish, cholerick SLUT, a crazed piece". (Robert Burton, *The Anatomy of Melancholy*, 1621)

Piece was standard English for a woman or young woman until the late C18th when it became a low colloquialism, generally used with negative sexual overtones. The 1811 edition of the *Dictionary of the Vulgar Tongue* provides a vivid definition: "A WENCH. A damned good or bad piece; a GIRL who is more or less active and skillful in the amorous congress. Hence the (Cambridge) toast, May we never have a piece (peace) that will injure the constitution." (The Cambridge University professors would have been relieved to know that although Queen Victoria proved herself to be skilled at amorous congress – she bore nine children – the British constitution survived the accession of this wench to the throne.)

In the C19th *piece* (or BIT) *of SKIRT, stuff, muslin* and MUTTON were all slang terms for a woman as a sexual object. The OED notes that *piece of goods* was applied either contemptuously or humorously: it is not known whether the females to whom the expression was applied ever appreciated the humour of being referred to as less than a complete person.

In the C20th *piece* has continued to be used in this derogatory sense in the compound terms *piece of TAIL, ass, flesh,* CRUMPET, etc. Just how derogatory a word it is is made starkly clear by Jackie Collins in her novel *Hollywood Wives* (1983): "sometimes he felt the need to have a woman underneath him who wasn't his equal. A full-breasted piece – who was just that – a piece. No conversation. No intellectual meeting of the minds. Just a lay."

Pig

Middle English *pigge* is of obscure origin, but may come from a root represented in the Old English word *picbred*, meaning swine-food or acorn.

By the mid-C16th *pig* was applied, usually opprobriously, to another animal or a person of either gender, presumably because of the characteristics thought typical of pigs, ie, stubborn, greedy, mean, dirty and shit-revelling.

In England and several European countries from C17th–C19th there was a widespread popular myth about a woman of rank or wealth who reputedly had the face of a pig and for whom a husband was being sought. From this legend the term *pig-faced* entered English in the early C19th, for an extremely ugly woman.

The 1811 edition of the *Dictionary of the Vulgar Tongue* provides several definitions which all suggest how unloved this animal was. *Pig* it defines as a police officer – a term which was to re-emerge in the C20th; *Cold Pig* was a "jocular punishment inflicted by the MAID servants, or other females of the house, on persons lying over long in bed: it consists in pulling off all the bed clothes, and leaving them to pig or lie in the cold"; *Pigsnyes* it defines as "small eyes. . .a vulgar term of endearment to a woman".

In the C20th when applied to women and to GAYS, *pig* acquired negative sexual connotations, eg: "A woman, sottish, surly, disgruntled, stinking – who has sunk to the lowest level of prostitution. The bum who keeps a pig rents her out to others." (*Dialect Notes*, 1927); "A girl who is both promiscuous and drunken" (University of South Dakota, *Current Slang* 1968–70); "A woman considered by gay men to be sexual competition" (*Dictionary of American Slang*). *Pig-suck* is a contemptuous gay term for a heterosexual male, *pig pile* and *pig party* are both terms for a gay sexual orgy. In the late 1960s *male chauvinist pig* became a widespread term of abuse among feminists which was applied to sexist men.

Pin Money

Pins were once costly items often made of silver used to secure a woman's hair, hat, shawl, scarf and so on, or worn merely for ornament. So expensive were they that C14th and C15th wills often contained special bequests for the express purpose of buying pins. Hence, the term *pin* MONEY which entered English in the late C17th to denote an annual sum allotted to a woman by her husband for her personal expenses, especially her clothes. In C18th England, although the law gave husbands almost total power over the household income, including most of the money brought by the bride to the marriage, marriage settlements among the wealthy often assured a wife of up to £500 per year spending, known as *pin money*.

By the late C19th the value of pin money declined: pins themselves were by now mass-produced and therefore cheap, and the Married Women's Property Acts of the 1870s and '80s took away much of the power of husbands over their wives' own incomes. *Pin money* came to mean a woman's pocket expenses, a trifling sum of money. The term was also slang – now seldom used – for the income earned by women from adultery or occasional prostitution (see PROSTITUTE). In this sense *pin* was an allusion to the penis.

Pin-up

As an adjective, *pin-up* was first used in 1677 for anything that was pinned up. In the C20th *pin-up* acquired a whole new meaning which the US magazine-writer Hartzell Spence believes he invented. In the spring of 1942, during World War 2, Spence listed what he thought the new GI's magazine *Yank* should contain: "Every issue should have a pin-up picture for soldiers to pin up on the barrack's wall to remind them of the girls back home. . .we took to calling it 'the pin-up' and sent photographers out to shoot pin-up pictures. I had never heard the expression before. It was a spontaneous coinage to meet the need and it sort of passed into the language." (*The Story of English*) In fact, in this sense, the term had already been 'invented'. In *Life* magazine of 7 July 1941 an anonymous journalist had written: "Dorothy Lamour is No. 1 pin-up girl of the US Army."

In what can only be seen as a laudable attempt to use non-sexist language the OED 1982 supplement merely obscures the generally accepted gender of a pin-up: "Applied to a favourite or sexually attractive young person, the typical subject of such a photograph (designed to be fixed to a wall). . .pertaining to or characteristic of such a picture or person." But pictures of male persons designed to be fixed to a wall are very seldom referred to as pin-ups. The original female gender of such pictures continues to be firmly attached to the meaning of the term – and the original pin-ups were photos of women portrayed as sex objects specifically designed for the male gaze. The definition in Webster's is both more and less accurate, as it defines *pin-up* as: "a photograph of a pin-up GIRL" and "a girl whose physical CHARMS, attractive personality or other glamorous [see GLAMOUR] qualities make her suitable subject of a photograph pinned on an admirer's wall". The term *pin-up girl* was – and indeed, still is – used, but the models, film stars, ACTRESSES or sweethearts usually were, and are, women, not girls.

The original function of the pin-up was to improve male morale by confirming the macho essence of the soldier. It has been reported that in August 1945 a photo of the film star Rita Heyworth, a favourite forces pin-up 'girl' (she was then aged 27), was taped to the undeniably phallus-shaped atomic bomb which was dropped on the citizens of Hiroshima in 1945.

Pin-ups continue to be mass-produced for male consumption. They are standard decoration for servicemen's billets, the cabs of lorries or trucks, and the walls of males whose masculinity is reinforced by the images of female sex objects. The term *pin-up boy* entered US English in 1969 but is not widespread: perhaps because a sexually attractive male has to be a man.

Porcelain

Porcelain, which entered English in c1530, denotes a fine kind of white earthenware with a transluscent body and a transparent glaze, another term for china-ware (1634) or china (1653). With allusion to the fineness, beauty and fragility of this ware, *porcelain* has been used figuratively, especially of a woman or her complexion, since the first half of the C17th, eg: "She is herself the purest PIECE of Purslane. . .that 'ere had liquid sweetmeats lick'd out of it." (Richard Brome, *The Sparagus Garden,* 1640)

Porcelain is also the name given to the *Cypraea Moneta* or Cowry shell (since 1601): "In many places shells are current for coins; particularly a small white kind. . .called in the Indies cowries. . .in America, porcelaines." (*Encyclopaedia Britannica.* 1797)

The origins of *porcelain* reveal an extraordinary web of female associations and allusions. It was the C13th explorer Marco Polo who first adopted the Italian word *porcellana* for the cowry (also called the VENUS shell) because of its fine white translucent shell. *Porcellana* derives from *porcella*, meaning little sow, from the Latin *porca*, the feminine of *porcus*, meaning swine. *Brewer's Dictionary of Phrase and Fable* maintains that this was because the shape of the cowry shell, "is not unlike a PIG's back". Had Ebenezer Cobham Brewer who first compiled this dictionary in 1870 turned a cowry shell over he would have found an even more likely reason; its ventral side closely resembles the vulva of both a SOW and a human female. *Vulva* derives from the Latin *volva*, or *vulva*, meaning womb, as well as a culinary term for a sow's womb. *Porcus* was used in Latin for the female pudendum as well as for swine. A further link between the sow and the female human is the hymen which is possessed by no other animal.

Pornography

Pornography is derived from the Greek *porne* and *graphos*, giving, according to *The Oxford Dictionary of Etymology*, "writing about PROSTITUTES". In fact, PORNE is best translated by the more derogatory word WHORE, since *pornoi* was the term for the lowest class of prostitutes, or a term of denigration when applied to others. The Greeks had a hierarchy of prostitutes at the top of which were the COURTESANS, euphemistically called *hetairae*, literally meaning comrade or companion. Next, there were the female entertainers – flute-players, dancers, acrobats, etc – who supplemented their incomes with prostitution. Beneath them came the streetwalkers. The *pornoi* were slaves who worked in BROTHELS; they were considered the lowest of the low and lacked status even among other prostitutes. The Greeks had many words and expressions for prostitute including the *chopper-up*, *bridge woman*, *parish worker*, *public woman*, *shut-in*, *she-wolf*, *dice*, *foal*, *kneading trough*, *ground thumper*, and *bedroom article*.

Until *pornography* was coined in the mid-C19th the adjective *bawdy* (see BAWD) ie, pertaining to prostitutes, or *bawdy stuff* was applied to any material considered "full of all filthiness, scurrility, bawdy, dissoluteness, cosinage, conycatching and the like". (1593) At first, most of the books written or translated into English that fitted this description were about whores and brothel life. *Cosinage* and *conycatching* both denoted cheating, deceiving and playing confidence tricks, all of which were perceived to be tricks of the prostitute's trade. But by the time *pornography* entered the English, the word was technically already something of an anachronism. The development of cheap mass-production printing, the increase in literacy and the development of the novel all had their effect on this type of literature. Of the vast number of pornographic books published in Victorian England, many were no longer specifically about prostitution: the subject matter had passed into the private house and was increasingly related to the realities of family life and tied to romantic love as against the conventions of society. The choice of the word *pornography* was perhaps the result of the previous use of *bawdy* and of Victorian double standards which polarised all women into MOTHER/VIRGIN or whore. By the turn of the C19th *pornographic* was applied to anything considered impure, obscene or erotic.

An early definition of *pornography* is found in a medical dictionary of 1857 which gave "a description of prostitutes, or of prostitution, as a matter of public hygiene". This is presumably a reference to mid-C19th medical attempts to codify madness, which often used photographs of prostitutes and other so-called degenerates as 'scientific' evidence. A legal definition of obscenity in 1868 provided a definition of pornography that survives today: "whether the tendency of the matter charged as obscenity is to deprave and corrupt those whose minds are open to such immoral influences, and into whose hands a publication of this sort may fall". The minds that Victorian sensibilities were most concerned about were those of children, women and the working class. Since then this definition has given the moral censors of society the ability to prosecute the writings of Zola and de Maupassant and other literary works considered by many to be literary works of erotic art, as well as books about contraception, female sexuality, abortion, and lesbianism (see LESBIAN), etc.

One of the main problems concerning pornography has revolved around the issue of definition and how to distinguish between the erotic and the pornographic. Dictionary definitions of *pornography* often confuse the two: "explicit description or exhibition of sexual activity in literature, films, etc., intended to stimulate erotic rather than aesthetic feelings". (*Concise Oxford Dictionary*) The conservative approach has been to define anything that exposed the human body as obscene and therefore capable of depraving and corrupting. The liberal approach has defined pornography as just one more aspect of our ever-expanding knowledge of human sexuality and therefore acceptable.

A third perspective has been provided by FEMINISTS, some of whom have argued that pornography is the theory and RAPE the practice. Susan Brownmiller defines it as "A male invention, designed to dehumanize women, to reduce the female to an object of sexual access, not to free sensuality from moralistic or parental inhibition." (*Femininity*) Looking back to the slave status of the Greek *pornoi*, Gloria Steinem maintains that "Pornography is not about sex. It's about an imbalance of male–female power that allows and even requires sex to be used as a form of aggression." (*Outrageous Acts and Everyday Rebellions*)

In her study *Pornography: Men possessing Women*, Andrea Dworkin stresses that pornographic images are not only symbols of men's desire to objectify and humiliate women, but that the images are themselves violence against women, with effects similar to those of physical violence on women's self-image and attitude: "In the male system, women are sex; sex is the whore. The whore is *porne*, the lowest whore, the whore who belongs to *all* male citizens: the SLUT, the CUNT. Buying her is buying pornography. Seeing her is seeing pornography. Seeing her in sex is seeing the whore in sex. Using her is using pornography. Wanting her means wanting pornography. Being her means being pornography."

To Dworkin, the very existence of the word has a significance over and above what it says about cultural beliefs. It is in itself a form of social control. To see degrading images and know men seek them out for pleasure teaches that women are despicable, expendable objects. It teaches women that men want to hurt them, and that women had better be afraid.

To Lynne Segal, the main problem of defining pornography and distinguishing it from erotica may not simply be one of definition: "I suspect that some of the emotional horror feminists and other women feel towards sexist pornography (which I share) is not simply that they think it encourages men to rape and objectify women (there is no evidence they need pornography for that), but that it is obnoxious because it both degrades and titillates us. And that is *not* a connection which we like. It feels as though the connection is thrust upon us from outside, by pornography itself, which if removed would sever the connection. But it is not unusual for feelings we dislike to seem to come from somewhere else, when in fact they are buried inside us as well as reflected in the social world which shaped them to begin with." (*Sex and Love, New Thoughts on Old Contradictions*)

Pretty

The word *pretty* falls into a category of words which, like *darling*, CHARMING, *sweet*, *lovely*, CUTE, NICE, *precious*, etc "have become the property of women and children alone". (*The Daily Chronicle,* 1907)

In Old English, *praettig* meant tricky, sly, cunning, wily or astute, and was usually used to express appreciation. The word was obsolete for about five centuries, re-emerging in the C15th in various senses, none identical with *praettig* but derivable from it. The sense development from deceitful through tricky, cunning, clever, skilful, admirable, pleasing and nice, to *pretty* in its current sense has close parallels in the words *canny*, *cunning*, *clever*, *fine* and *nice*. And, like *nice*, *pretty* is often used ironically to mean the exact opposite, ie, *a pretty kettle of fish* means a situation which is far from pretty.

Samuel Johnson defined *prettiness* as "Beauty without dignity; neat elegance without elevation," (1755), since then *pretty* has become even more devalued. The OED reveals the derogatory and infantilising connotations of *prettiness* in its current sense: "Beauty of a slight, diminutive, dainty or childish kind." The term *pretty-boy*, meaning, since 1885, an EFFEMINATE male or a male homosexual (see GAY), makes it clear that our societal construction of masculinity does not admit prettiness as any part of it. The *Longman Dictionary of the English Language* makes this abundantly clear, defining pretty as "appearing or sounding pleasant or nice but lacking strength, force, manliness, purpose, or intensity".

Pricktease See COCKTEASE

Prostitute

The Latin *prostitutus*, *prostituta*, the past participle of *prostituere*, meaning to expose publicly or to offer for sale, is formed on *pro*, in the sense of for or on behalf of, and *statuere*, meaning set up or place (hence also *statute*).

Prostitute, denoting "a woman who is devoted, or (usually) who offers her body to indiscriminate sexual intercourse, especially for hire; a common HARLOT (OED)", entered English in 1613. The word itself was already in use (since 1530) as a verb meaning "To offer (oneself, or another) to unlawful, especially indiscriminate, sexual intercourse, usually for hire and to devote or expose to lewdness. (Chiefly reflexive of a woman.)" (OED) In 1553 the noun *prostitution* entered English for the action of prostituting or condition of being prostituted, ie: "Of women: The offering of the body to indiscriminate lewdness for hire (especially as a practice or institution); whoredom, harlotry." (OED) From c1540–1677 *prostitute* was used in the sense of to offer with complete devotion or self-negation or, simply, as a synonym for to devote. In 1563 it began to be used figuratively to mean debased or debasing, and subsequently developed the senses of abandoned, basely venal, devoted to infamous gain and, finally, corrupt. As an adjective it was also used to mean offered or exposed to lust (as a woman) and, more generally, abandoned to sensual indulgence or licentiousness. From 1603–

1708, construed as a past participle, it denoted given over or devoted, and, later, exposed or subjected to something evil. By the mid-C17th *prostitute* was well established as the generally accepted word for what, in Old English, had been termed *miltestre*, from the Latin *meretrix* from which MERETRICIOUS derives, and for various other words, such as BAWD, HARLOT, WHORE, STRUMPET, etc, which over the years had acquired subtle shades of different meaning. *Prostitute* also replaced *prostibule*, only ever very rarely used in the early C17th, adopted from the Latin word *prostibulum*, which meant both a prostitute and a BROTHEL formed on the Latin *prostare*, meaning to stand forth publicly as for sale.

The mingling of the sense of devotion with moral opprobrium evident in the C16th and C17th meanings of the word may reflect Christian, especially Protestant, attitudes towards ancient sexual customs. In her study of the suppression of women's rites in pre-Judaeo-Christian society, Merlin Stone writes: "The women who followed the ancient sexual customs of the Goddess faith, were repeatedly referred to as 'ritual prostitutes'. This choice of words. . .reveals a rather ethnocentric ethic, probably based on biblical attitudes. Yet, using the term 'prostitute' for women whose title was actually *quadesh*, meaning holy, suggests a lack of comprehension of the very theological and social structure the [ancient] writers were attempting to describe and explain." The *quadishtu* were priestesses who devoted their lives to the goddess and who made love to various male worshippers during religious festivals: the money they received was a votive offering to the goddess: "Where you stand obviously determines what you see. From the point of view of those who followed the religion of the Goddess, they were simply carrying out the ancient ways. From the point of view of the invading Hebrew tribes, the older religion was now perceived as an orgiastic, evil, lustful, shameful, disgraceful, sinful, base fertility cult. But we may suspect that underlying this moral stance was the political manoeuvring for power over land and property accessible to them only upon the institution of a patrilineal system. . .Was it perhaps for these reasons that the Levite laws declared that any sexual activities of women that did not take place within the confines of the marriage bed were to be considered sinful, ie against the laws of Yahweh?" (*Paradise Papers*)

To Christian theologians then, the prostitute was a contemptible creature not simply because she posed as a loving woman and had sexual relations with men in return for financial reward, but because her entire life was devoted to the lusts of the flesh (*luxuria*), which was the prime sin. Some early Christians, however, were notably pragmatic in their attitude towards prostitution. St Augustine commented: "Rid society of prostitutes and licentiousness will run riot throughout. . . Prostitutes in a city are like a sewer in a palace. If you get rid of the sewer, the whole palace becomes filthy and foul". (*De Ordine*) Thomas of Chobham wrote a manual for confessors in the C12th in which he remarked sagely: "Prostitutes should be counted among the wage-earners. They hire out their bodies and supply labour. It is wrong for a woman to be a prostitute but if she is such, it is not wrong for her to receive a wage. But if she prostitutes herself for pleasure and hires out her body for this purpose, then the wage is as evil as the act itself."

Since prostitution was not considered sinful in the sense of fornication (see FORNICATE) or adultery, it became the concern of civic tribunals, not of the ecclesiastical courts. In the C14th, for example, a series of regulations were issued in London insisting that all prostitutes should be housed either in Lock Lane, near the Smithfield meat market or in the 'stews' of Southwark on land owned by the Bishop of Winchester who collected rent from these tenants, gave them their hours of work (ie, not at the same time as Church services nor at night when Parliament was sitting), and fined them if they had a paramour, wore an apron or did not wear unlined hoods of striped cloth to distinguish them from other women. According to Shulamith Shahar, "In general the attitude to prostitutes in the Middle Ages was undoubtedly better than in the C16th and C17th when royal absolutism, the Reformation and the Counter Reformation, and the fear of venereal disease, combined to intensify oppression of prostitutes and render attitudes towards them increasingly hypocritical." (*The Fourth Estate*)

In Protestant England prostitutes were flogged, branded and even, on occasions, put to death. But this puritanical tightening up of morals did nothing to prevent the increase of prostitution which, like venereal disease, was rampant during the C17th and C18th. Obviously this was not a trade for a respectable woman, although those at the upper end of the social scale, usually termed COURTESAN or MISTRESS, were openly tolerated and, to a point, admired. The plays of Aphra Behn (c1640–89), for instance, many of which were presented to the Royal Court, made more overt reference to prostitution than the plays of earlier puritan times: even Shakespeare tended to rely upon punning innuendo. The common prostitute, however, earned the reprobation of society; she was despised, punished and treated as scum. In short she was a SLUT. From 1630–1761 *prostitute* developed the meaning of debased by being made common or cheap, or hackneyed – from the word HACK which also came to mean a prostitute.

By the end of the C18th prostitution had become defined as a major social problem. Mary Wollstonecraft (1759–97) was one of the first women reformers to make the point that "prostitutes were ignorant and underprivileged rather than WICKED", and made a classic attack on the attitude of well-intentioned reformers: "Asylums and Magdalenes [see MAUDLIN] are not the proper remedies for these abuses. It is justice, not charity, that is wanting in the world!" Concerned about the total dependency of women on men which, for her, robbed both sexes of dignity and made it virtually impossible for women to act as free moral agents, she did not endear herself to patriarchal society by referring to marriage as 'legal prostitution'.

In the C19th, "Definitions of the prostitute and attitudes towards prostitution were multiple, fragmented and frequently contradictory." (Lynda Nead, *Myths of Sexuality*) On the one hand, prostitution was "defined as the most threatening manifestation of moral degeneration and was regarded as a meta-system which could erode and destroy the nation" (Nead), and on the other, the prostitute was, as the historian W E H Lecky (1838–1903) claimed "ultimately the most efficient guardian of virtue. But for her, the unchallenged purity of countless happy homes would be polluted, and not a few who, in the pride of their untempted CHASTITY, think of her with an indignant shudder would have known the agony of remorse and despair." (*History of European Morals*) Virtue and chastity, essential elements of the feminine ideal, were middle- and upper-class luxuries which the poor could simply not afford, "Thus the working class provided a kind of sexual sewer for the wealthy." (Eva Figes, *Patriarchal Attitudes*)

The notion of the repeated hiring out of her body also became a factor in C19th definitions of prostitution – more important than the loss of virtue, eg: "A prostitute is a designation of character. . .to form the character, and to justify the designation, there must be the voluntary repetition of the act." (Ralph Wardlaw, *Lectures*, 1842)

The Contagious Diseases Acts of 1864, '66 and '69 were introduced as a means of checking the spread of venereal disease among soldiers and sailors in various towns in Ireland and southern England. Women accused of being 'common prostitutes' were registered, subjected to a periodical examination and, if found to be diseased, incarcerated in a certified lock-hospital for a period of up to nine months.

But the definition of a 'common prostitute' was vague, eg: " 'What is your definition of a prostitute?' 'Any woman whom there is fair and reasonable grounds to believe is, first of all, going to places which are the resorts of prostitutes alone and at times when immoral persons only are usually out. It is more a question as to mannerism than anything else.' " (Report of the Select Committee on the Contagious Diseases Act, July 1869)

Nead identifies two dominant images of the prostitute in the C19th: "The first representation defined [her] as a figure of contagion, disease and death; a sign of social disorder and ruin to be feared and controlled. This construction shifted the focus away from the question of the effects of prostitution on the woman herself and emphasised its effects on respectable society; the prostitute stood as a symbol of dangerous forces which could bring about anarchy and social disintegration.

"The second displaced these connotations of power and destruction and defined the prostitute as a suffering and tragic figure – the passive victim of a cruel and relentless world."

Nead concludes that both these images resulted in the definition of prostitution as deviant and abnormal, which sought to separate the prostitute from respectable society through claims concerning her appearance (shades of aprons and striped hoods of the C13th), her habits and lifestyle (like the C16th WANTON she spurned the home in favour of gadding about abroad), and her moral and sexual behaviour (which was not CHASTE and therefore unfeminine).

Contemporary sources generally agree that a decline in the use of prostitutes took place in the first two decades of the C20th. This may be attributable to the growth of the amateur prostitute: "This seems to have meant many young women engaging in sexual intercourse before or outside marriage or in some cases the latter practice combined with the acceptance of minor favours or presents from men." (Sheila Jeffries, *The Spinster and her Enemies*) Another factor may have been a change in attitude towards prostitution largely due to women's-rights reformers, notably Josephine Butler (1828–1906) who campaigned against the Contagious Diseases Acts, which were eventually repealed after much agitation in 1886, and who rebelled against the notion that woman was either madonna or whore, exemplified by the following couplet of Lord Byron: "Man's love is of man's life a thing apart, 'Tis woman's whole existence." (1819–24)

Current legislation surrounding the institution of prostitution continues to define the prostitute as the criminal but not her male clients. In the 1970s, prostitutes hitherto silent (or silenced) began to organise and speak for themselves. A group of prostitutes in San Francisco in 1973 formed an organisation determined to decriminalise prostitution; they called themselves COYOTE, which stands for 'Call Off Your Old Tired Ethics'. With a little more irony a collective of prostitutes with similar aims in the UK called themselves PUSSY.

In *Paradigmatic Woman: The Prostitute* (1972), Julia P Stanley "compiled and analyzed 220 terms for sexually promiscuous women (she stopped at that number because she'd 'reached the point of diminishing returns'; she notes 'the very size of the set and the impossibility of collecting *all* the terms for prostitutes is a comment on our culture. As linguists we assume that the existence of a new lexical item indicates a cultural need for a term that expresses a new concept. Isn't it strange that the set of terms that refer to prostitutes is one that's constantly expanding?'). In contrast, there are relatively few terms for promiscuous men; Stanley lists 22, and notes 'there's no linguistic reason why the set is so small'. Stanley sets out the semantic features that define the categories represented by the terms for prostitutes: A. Denotive: i. cost (cheap, expensive); ii. method of payment (direct, indirect); iii. positive. B. Dysphemistic or euphemistic (whether the term exposes male disdain for the sexuality of women or conceals his disdain). C. Metonymic (whether the term refers to women through reference to a specific portion of their bodies). D. Metaphoric (whether the term refers to women through comparison to another object or animal). This semantic set provides 'a paradigm of the definition of women in our culture'. 'The names that men have given to women who make themselves sexually available to them reveal the underlying metaphors by which men conceive of their relationships with women, and through which women learn to perceive and define themselves. The metaphors that underlie the terms for sexually promiscuous women define and perpetuate the ambivalent sex-role stereotypes that a male-dominated culture sets forth for women.' " (Barrie Thorne and Nancy Henley, *Language and Sex*)

The word *prostitute* invariably means a female. Very occasionally in the mid-C17th it was used to denote a catamite, and since 1948 it has been applied to a man who undertakes male homosexual acts for payment, but he is usually referred to as a *male prostitute*. Thus *prostitute* is one of the few words in the English language where the norm is female rather than male. Thorne and Henley make the point that "Sex and marriage is the only semantic area in which the masculine word is not the base or more powerful word." As well as *prostitute/male prostitute*, they also cite BRIDE/*bridegroom* and WIDOW/*widower*.

Prude

The French word *prude* was probably a back formation from *prudefemme*, meaning excellent woman, one worthy of esteem. This was the feminine equivalent of *prud'homme*, meaning good man and true, based on *prud*, an Old French word which developed along the lines of brave, good, virtuous, modest and, finally, respectable. Like the English word *proud*, it originated in the Latin *prodesse*, meaning to be of value or to be good.

When *prude* first entered English in 1704, a direct adoption from the French, it was applied adversely, with strong implications of affectation, to denote a woman who maintains or affects excessive modesty or propriety in conduct or speech. It was also used, again adversely, to describe a person of either gender who maintained or affected extreme propriety of speech or behaviour, especially in regard to relations between the sexes. Although its connotations of modesty, decorum and demureness were considered essential characteristics of FEMININITY in the C18th, *prude* denoted a sense of formality and primness considered extreme and unattractive in a woman.

In *The Spinster and her Enemies*, Sheila Jeffreys argues that the concept of the female prude was an important weapon in attacks on late C19th feminists and their opinions. It was used to undermine female reformers who offered any critique of men's sexual behaviour. One such reformer was the English woman's rights campaigner Elizabeth Wolstenholme-Elmy (1834–1919) who was deeply concerned about the sexual abuse of women and angered by the way in which women were reduced to a merely sexual function by men's obsession with physical love. Her solution was to promote the ideal of sexual self-control and a notion of celibate 'psychic love' between heterosexuals.

This was not an appealing proposition to most men who became increasingly alarmed by the growing number of women who asserted their right to live independently of them. Labelling Wolstenholme-Elmy and women who shared her views 'prudes' was an attempt to dismiss their radical FEMINIST ideology.

In the 1920s the concept of the female prude was refined with the aid of psychoanalytic theory of sexual repression, which was used to 'explain' the psyche of the allegedly prudish feminist. Walter Gallichen, the influential author of *Modern Woman and How to Manage Her* (1909), *Sexual Antipathy and Coldness in Women* (1927) and *The Poison of Prudery* (1929) was one of the many sexologists of the early C20th alarmed by women who took to the streets to demand the vote, many of whom spurned marriage and heterosexual relationships: the SPINSTER, the SUFFRAGETTE, the BLUESTOCKING, the LESBIAN – all challenged the C19th stereotype of the angel in the house. All were condemned as prudes, afflicted with what Gallichen and others like him perceived as a mental sickness, a sign of HYSTERIA: "prudery," he argued, "arises as reinforcement of resistance against forbidden thoughts, and the resistance may be so heightened that it becomes a pathological symptom".

With the re-emergence of the women's movement in the late 1960s, the abusive appellation *prude* was again wheeled out to attack women who opposed patriarchal ideology. Those women who weren't prudish ran the risk of being considered LOOSE.

Pussy

Since the early C16th *puss*, probably from the Middle Low German *pus*, and *puskatte*, of unknown origin, has been a conventional proper name for a CAT. By 1605 it had become a nursery synonym for *cat*, now mostly superseded by *pussy* – the -*y* suffix commonly forms pet names or familiar diminutives.

In the late C16th *puss* began to be applied as a term of endearment for a loved one, especially a woman. This may have been used in preference to *cat* since these animals were strongly associated with WITCHES. In 1664 *pusse* emerged as coarse slang for the VAGINA, and in this sense *puss* is akin to the Old Norse *puss*, meaning pocket or pouch; Icelandic and Low German words for vulva; Old English *pusa* or *posa*, meaning BAG; and the Greek *byein*, meaning to stuff or plug. By extension, *puss* became a slang term for sexual intercourse and was applied to any woman considered sexually from the male point of view. Around 1880 the coarse slang term *to eat pussy*, first meaning to engage in sexual intercourse, and later (in the C20th) denoting cunnilingus, began to be used. This perhaps led to the term *cat-house* (since 1931) for a BROTHEL, or it may simply derive from the use of cat to refer to a woman.

Cats are perceived to possess the supposedly FEMININE characteristics of slyness, maliciousness and spitefulness (hence *catty* since 1903), and at the same time they are also considered to be compliant, weak, submissive and passive which probably influenced the pejorative use of *pussy* since the 1920s for "a finicky, old maidish [see MAID] or EFFEMINATE boy or man; a homosexual". (OED) In US military slang a *pussy-cat* is a decidedly 'unmanly' pilot who is overcautious, fearful or reluctant. In the late 1930s *pussy-talk* appeared as a negative term for female talk dismissed as GOSSIP. In *The Female Eunuch*, Germaine Greer recorded that "Women in

America are reported to be manipulating their menfolk by pussy-power, which is wheedling and caressing, instead of challenging." This term both exaggerates the power of women and undermines them and their speech at the same time.

Quaint

In the C13th *cointe*, or *queinte*, denoted knowing, skilled, clever and ingenious or, in a bad sense, cunning, crafty, given to scheming and plotting. It was adopted from Old French, ultimately from the Latin *cognitus*, meaning known, the past participle of *cognoscere*, meaning to ascertain.

From its positive senses *quaint*, as it came to be spelled, developed to mean elegant (especially in speech), clever or cleverly wrought, and hence beautiful, fine and dainty. This development was possibly influenced by the french *comtus*, from the Latin *comere*, *comptus*, meaning to arrange or adorn. At the same time, perhaps because elegant speech was considered something of a rarity, *quaint* developed the sense of strange, unusual, odd or curious. The early negative sense of cunning influenced the use of the word to mean a CHARM or incantation of a WITCH, eg: "'DAME' seyd the bysshop, 'do thy queyntse, And late us se how hit shall ryse'. Thys wycche here charme began to say, The slop [a magic bag, used especially to steal milk from cows] ros up, and yede the weye [whey]". (*Handling Synne*. C14th) Hence, a clever trick.

By the C18th these various senses merged, resulting in the meaning "unusual or uncommon in character or appearance, but at the same time having some attractive or agreeable [ie, charming] quality, especially having an old-fashioned daintiness, fastidiousness or prettiness". (OED)

As a noun, the word denoted CUNT from the C14th–early C20th, (since the late C16th only surviving in North Country dialect), eg: "Pryvely he caught her by the queynte." (Chaucer, *The Miller's Tale*. 1386) Eric Partridge's annotated reprint of the third edition of the *Dictionary of the Vulgar Tongue* suggests that "Chaucer may have combined Old French *coing* with Middle English *cunte* or he may have been influenced by the Old French *cointe* meaning neat, dainty and pleasant." Chaucer was very likely also punning on both the clever and cunning senses of *quaint*: the owner of the *queynte* in *The Miller's Tale* was a skilled adulteress.

Quean/Queen

Both these words originate in the Indo-European root *gwen*, meaning woman. From this root the Greek for woman, *gune*, *gunaikos*, gave the English language the words *gynaecology*, ANDROGYNE, MISOGYNY, etc. Another word derived from this root is the Old Irish *ben*, also meaning woman, from which BANSHEE derives. Two Old English words, *cwen* (c825), meaning both a female ruler and the wife or female consort of a king, and *cwene* (c1000), meaning WOMAN, provide one of the earliest examples of what linguists call radiation, ie, the development of more than one distinct sense from a common historical source.

Originally, *queen* and its male counterpart, *king*, denoted high status, pre-eminence and a sphere of power, with connotations of regal and majestic. But a king has always been recognised as being more powerful than a queen, both in terms of inheritance, which is patrilineal, and as evidenced by the fact that whereas a king's wife is called 'Queen', a queen's husband is only ever a prince. A difference in meaning emerged in 1612, only nine years after the death of Queen Elizabeth 1, when *queenlike* or *queenly*, unlike *kinglike*, acquired the negative connotations of haughty. There is no evidence to suggest that Queen Elizabeth was any more proud, arrogant and supercilious than many of her kingly predecessors; perhaps the notion of a woman with power fitted uncomfortably into the patriarchal concept of FEMININITY.

The sexual derogation of *queen* began during the reign of Queen Victoria (1819–1901) when the word was used as slang for an attractive woman, a 'girlfriend' or female partner. This use may have been influenced by the slang phrase *Queen's woman*, used to denote a "PROSTITUTE who received medical attention under the terms of the Contagious Diseases Acts of the 1860s". To the women's-rights reformers who campaigned against these acts, this phrase "received medical attention" of the OED would have seemed highly euphemistic for the legal and medical harassment to which the police were empowered to subject any woman suspected of prostitution – there were no legal provisions to arrest or examine the male pimps, clients or procurers of prostitutes.

In 1924 *queen* was defined in the Australian paper *Truth* as "an EFFEMINATE person". This was probably a euphemism for a male homosexual or, more specifically, "the effeminate partner in a homosexual relationship". (OED) *The Penguin Dictionary of Historical Slang* states that this is an incorrect spelling of *quean* which probably derived from the sense of HARLOT, influenced by the woman's personal name *Queenie*, which was popular among the working class in the C19th. *Queen* in this sense was at first a derogatory epithet used by heterosexuals, but in the 1960s gays co-opted the word using it often in combination form, such as *drag queen*, *rubber queen*, etc as "a designation of appearance, preference and character". (Bruce Rodgers, *The Queen's Vernacular – A Gay Lexicon*)

Queen is one of several examples of feminine designations which have degenerated while their corresponding masculine terms have remained untainted. *King*, as well as *prince*, *governor*, *father*, *uncle*, *Mister*, *Sir*, *monk*, etc, have all retained their original positive senses. However, *queen*, as well as *princess*, GOVERNESS, MOTHER, *aunt*, MISTRESS, MADAM, and NUN have all degenerated and/or become sexually abusive terms at some time. Alleen Pace Nilsen has also pointed out that the *queen/king* pairing reveals a tendency in the English language for man-related words to travel into compounds while the feminine word is a dead end: "a queen may rule a kingdom but never a queendom". ('Sexism in English: A Feminist View' in *Female Studies*, 1972)

The now almost obsolete *quean* took less time to pejorate and acquire derogatory sexual connotations. Originally, simply a woman, it then narrowed in meaning to refer specifically to a female serf. Like many words applied to the labouring or serving classes, in early Middle English or pejorated to become "a term of disparagement or abuse, hence: a bold, impudent or ill-behaved woman, a JADE, a HUSSY, and specifically a HARLOT or STRUMPET (especially in the 16th and 17th centuries)". (OED)

Apart from the above mentioned Australian example, in the C20th *quean* survives only in Scottish dialect where it retains its original meaning of woman. Since it usually refers to a young or unmarried woman, some linguists suggest that because of the connotations of desirability (to men) and thus sexual availability it may be beginning to undergo a process of pejoration common to so many similar woman-related words.

Rape

What men or gods are these? What maiden's loth?
What mad pursuit? What struggle to escape?
John Keats (1795–1821), *Ode on a Grecian Urn*

Rape, rapt, rapture, ravage, ravish and *ravishing* all originate in the Latin verb *rapere*, meaning to seize, SNATCH or take by force. At some time in their etymological histories all these words have had the sense and/or connotations of carrying away by force, of sexual violation and that of transportation to a state of ecstasy and delight.

Some of the earliest definitions of *rape* are embedded in patriarchal concepts of woman as male property: "It seems eminently sensible to hypothesize that man's violent capture and rape of the female led first to the establishment of a rudimentary male-protectorate and then sometime later to the full-blown male solidification of power, the patriarchy." (Susan Brownmiller, *Against Our Will*) Merlin Stone points out in *The Paradise Papers*, that under Levite law the death penalty existed for married or betrothed women who were raped. This, she argues, exhibits not only patriarchal insistence upon knowledge of paternity but also the belief that rape meant the theft of a father's daughter's VIRGINITY or a husband's wife's CHASTITY, rape was a crime that either damaged a man's goods before a woman could reach the matrimonial market or that damaged a man's honour and status.

When *rape* first entered English c1400, it denoted the violent seizure of goods or property as well as the act of carrying away a person, especially a woman, by force. By 1481 this last sense became wholly female-specific and *rape* meant the sexual violation of ravishing of a woman. Towards the end of the C16th *rape* was used in a transferred and figurative sense in the context of robbing or despoiling a written text or the countryside – the land was personified and feminised either as a MAIDEN (eg, VIRGIN soil, snow, etc) or as a MOTHER, ie Mother Nature.

Borrowed from the Old French *ravir*, the word *ravish* entered English in the C13th. It was used either non-gender-specifically, to mean the seizing or carrying off of a person violently or, female-specifically, to mean the carrying away of a woman by force, sometimes with the implication of subsequent violation. By 1436 *ravish* was used synonymously with *rape* for the sexual violation of a woman.

Influenced by the notion of being carried away, from 1382–c1622, *ravish* acquired the sense of transportation to a state of ecstasy of joy or delight. By the late C16th this developed to the use of *ravishing* as an adjective to mean

ENCHANTING. In 1623 this sense of *ravishing* influenced the meaning of *rape*, so that it, too, was also occasionally used to imply transport or delight. In the C20th, *rape* in this sense is used only rarely, although for some the word continues to have positive connotations, eg: "A little bit of rape is good for a man's soul." (Norman Mailer, 1972) *Ravishing*, meanwhile, has lost its connotations of sexual violence and has come to mean outstandingly attractive, delightful or pleasing to the eye, usually the male roving eye, as the word is almost only ever used of a woman or a feminised object.

Historically, *rapt* and *rapture* have also combined the concept of violent abduction and forced sexual violation with the seemingly opposite concept of being transported to a state of ecstasy. In 1400 *rapt* meant to be taken up and carried to heaven – a sense it retains today. Briefly, in the C15th, it became the past participle of *rape* in the sense of the forced abduction and sexual violation of women. From 1609–1709 *raptor* was a synonym for a ravisher, or rapist. Similarly, *rapture*, which entered English in 1600, first denoted the act of carrying off and raping a woman (obsolete by 1728) and then, since 1629, the state of mental transport, exaltation or ecstasy.

The inability to distinguish women from the property of their fathers and husbands has resulted in legal definitions of rape which excluded the forced sexual violation of Black women by white men in the USA during slavery: "rape meant, by definition, rape of white women, for no such crime as rape of a black woman existed in law. Even when a black man sexually attacked a black woman, he could only be punished by his master; no way existed to bring him to trial or to convict him . . .." (Eugene Genovese; cited in bell hooks, *Ain't I a Woman*, 1981) Yet another result has been the widespread exclusion (apart from some states in the US, most Scandinavian countries and Scotland) of the rape of wives by husbands in the legal definition of the word. For how can you 'rape' what you already 'own'?

The inability to distinguish between female rape fantasy and the violent, degrading, traumatic reality of rape continues to pervade legal definitions; although legal statutes ostensibly exist to protect women from the criminal aspects of male sexuality, in practice the law tends to put women on trial and interrogate them about their degree of responsibility and complicity for the rape.

In her article 'Rape is a Four-letter Word', Muriel R Schulz asks why it is "we have no four letter word for the act of taking women sexually by force"? She points out that although, "The organs and processes of sex and elimination provide us with a set of terms in English which we designate 'dirty words', it is ironic that the most vicious sexual act of all is not among them." She suggests that the answer lies in the difference between female and male experience of the act of rape: "A man who believes that the only women who get raped are those who ask for it, or who thinks that women probably secretly enjoy being raped, or who holds that rape would be impossible if the woman really resisted. . .must invariably have a different set of images associated with the term rape than does a woman. Women can easily imagine the helpless paralysed fear of an innocent victim of an attack, the pain of forcible entry, and the trauma necessarily associated with a violent assault. To a man, rape may possibly be considered a myth, or else an insidious lie, dreamt up to entrap him, or both of these; to a woman it is neither myth nor lie, it is a frightening reality."

Which is not to say that women are incapable of rape fantasies. Juliann C Fleener defines female rape fantasy as something which enables a woman to maintain power and control. She defines the rape myth as something which "suggests the erect penis is the source of ecstasy for a struggling yet willing female victim". (*Rape Fantasies as Initiation Rites: Female Imagination in the Lives of Girls and Women,* 1979).

Dale Spender, Muriel R Schulz and others point out that *rape* is a remarkably innocuous term about which there is a form of neutrality which they consider surprising for such a violent act. They believe that the word itself describes the experience of rape solely from a male perspective, ie, from that of the rapist: "A woman who has been attacked in this way has no other name except *rape* to describe the event, but with the inbuilt neutrality of meaning, *rape* is precisely what she does *not* mean. . .Women need a word which renames male violence and MISOGYNY and which asserts their blameless nature, a word which places the responsibility where it belongs – on the dominant group." (Spender, *Man Made Language*)

But, as Deborah Cameron argues, although languages and their history are invaluable resources for feminists in their analysis of society, reform on a wide scale is problematic, and is especially unhelpful when it proceeds from simplistic theories about the workings of language in general: "Words cannot be brought before some linguistic United Nations for definitive judgement; this one is sexist, that is neutral, the other is feminist. Words exist, the theories of linguists notwithstanding, only when they are used. Their meanings are created (within limits, certainly, but pretty elastic limits) by a speaker and hearer in each uniquely defined situation. . .in the mouths of sexists, language can always be sexist."

Relict See WIDOW

Rib

And the Lord God caused a deep sleep to fall upon Adam, and he slept: And he took one of his ribs, and closed up the flesh instead therof; And the rib, which the Lord God had taken from man, made he a woman, and brought her unto the man. And Adam said, This is now bone of my bones, and flesh of my flesh: she shall be called Woman, because she was taken out of man.

Genesis 2:22–23

The Old English *ribb,* akin to Old High German *rippi,* meaning rib and the

Greek *erephein* meaning roof over, was used allusively to mean a WIFE or WOMAN from the late C16th to the late C19th. When *De Humani Corpori Fabrica* ('On the Structure of the Human Body') by Andreas Vesalius was published in the C16th, it caused a sensation as it claimed, on the evidence of human dissections, that women and men had an equal number of ribs.

In the late C18th–C20th the term *crooked rib* was a colloquialism for a cross-grained wife. In US slang, during World War 2, *rib-joint* was used to mean a BROTHEL. This was perhaps a pun on *rib* as woman, *joint* as slang for both a place and for VAGINA, and *spare rib*, the cut of MEAT, especially pork (see PIG), which was also slang for both woman and vagina.

In the UK a feminist magazine (since the early 1970s) is entitled *Spare Rib*. A similar taste for irony is expressed in the names of other feminist publications, eg, SHREW, VIRAGO, BITCH, *Manifesto* and *Red Rag* (ie, to a bull, and sanitary towel).

Sapphism See LESBIAN

Scold

Scold is probably an adoption of the Old Norse *skald*, meaning poet; in modern usage it denotes a habitual or persistent fault-finder. Heller, Huez and Dror, the authors of *The Private Lives of English Words*, think that if this is so "the history of the word constitutes one of the more dramatic examples of linguistic pejoration in our language". The reason for this pejoration can be traced to the Old Norse poets who specialised in satirical verse; *skaldskapr*, mentioned in Icelandic lawbooks, refers to versified libel. Hence, when *scold* entered English in 1200, it denoted a person, especially a woman, of ribald speech and later almost only ever a woman addicted to abusive language. The term soon came to refer to an abusive woman and this sense was extended to mean a quarrelsome, vituperative, generally female, person. By the C15th this type of woman, also referred to as a HARPY, was perceived to be such a widespread nuisance that legislation was introduced to protect those plagued by a 'common scold', ie "a woman who disturbs the peace of the neighbourhood by her constant scolding". (OED)

In the C20th *scold* denotes a habitual or persistent fault-finder of either sex, but it remains primarily associated with women. Barbara G Walker finds this not at all surprising, offering the following theory about the etymological history of the word: "One of the three Norns (Scandinavian FATES) was Skuld, the death-Norn. Skuld was a variant of Skadi, an eponymous MOTHER [goddess] of Scandinavia and a typical destroyer. Norse poet-shamans were servants of Skuld and called themselves *skalds*; Christians said they indulged in witchcraft or 'skulduggery'. Skuld would lay the death curse on the whole universe at doomsday. Her name gave rise to 'scold', ie a woman gifted with the power of cursing. She cut the thread of every life." (*The Woman's Encylopedia of Myths and Secrets*)

The crime of scolding was a serious one of which many women persecuted for being WITCHES were accused, eg: "I have bene a scoulder and a slanderouse person, and a source of strife amongst my neighbours." (Katharine Oliver, *Confessions*, 1595, recorded in the *Transactions of the Royal Historical Society*) A woman convicted of the offence might get away with a mere fine. More horrendously, she might be confined in a brank, a Scottish term for a padlocked bridle, also called a scold's bridle, which consisted of a kind of iron framework to enclose the head, and a sharp metal gag or bit which entered the mouth and restrained the tongue. A brank dated 1633 still exists in a church at Walton-on-Thames near London, inscribed: "Chester presents Walton with a bridle, To curb women's tongues that talk too idle". Even more potentially dangerous to the victim was the cucking-stool which Brewer's describes this instrument of torture as "A kind of stool often used for ducking scolds, disorderly women, dishonest apprentices etc, in a pond." The word may have been a corruption of the French *coquine* for a HUSSY or, more likely, from the old verb *cuck*, to void excrement. Persistent offenders had their tongues cut out.

That the scold was greatly feared there can be no doubt: "A frank scold is a devil of the feminine gender; a serpent perpetually hissing and spitting of venom; a composition of ill-nature and clamor. You may call her animated gun-powder, a walking Mount Etna that is always belching forth flames of sulphur, or a real Purgatory, more to be dreaded in this world than the pope's imaginary hothouse in the next." (Anon, *Poor Robin's True Character of a Scold,* 1678)

But C16th and C17th legislators considered cursing a more serious crime for a female to commit, one against which Parliament legislated in 1624. By the Restoration in 1660, when the king was returned to the throne, the term FISHWIFE was synonymous with a swearing woman; in the early C18th a *Billingsgate* – after the London fish market – was defined as a scolding, impudent SLUT. In 1755 Samuel Johnson defined a *scold* as "A clamourous, rude, mean, low, foul-mouthed woman." In 1811 the *Dictionary of the Vulgar Tongue* offered the term *A scold's cure* for a coffin, translating the phrase, "The blowen [see BLOWZY] has napped the scold's cure" as "the BITCH is in her coffin".

In the C19th the struggle to control unruly women continued. No longer tortured with bridles, ducking chairs, mutilation, nonetheless the almost exclusively male medical profession discovered the mental asylum as the perfect institution by which to rid society of the evil influence of the scold. Furneaux Jordan, a surgeon at Queen's College, Birmingham, England, in an analysis of battered wives (1886), stated that a woman's sharp tongue was one of her hereditary characteristics which predisposed her to madness and empowered her to drive men mad making them unable to resist hitting her. Elaine Showalter writes that silence was one of the 'ladylike' (see LADY) values which psychiatrists "successfully imposed on even the wildest and most recalcitrant female maniacs", making it "an integral part of the program of moral management of women in Victorian asylums". (*The Female Malady*) Generally, the scold was not perceived to be as dangerous as she had been hitherto, and the word *scold* began to ameliorate, eg: "All women love to be married, were it only for the sake of having somebody to scold at." (A Cunningham, *Traditional Tales,* 1887)

Screw

Screw entered English in the C15th for a cylinder with a spiral ridge or thread running round it, either on the inside, known as a *female*, or *interior*, *screw*, or on the outside, known as a *male*, or *exterior*, *screw*. The word was adopted from the feminine Old French noun *escroue*, which probably originated in the Latin *scrofa*, meaning breeding SOW. This development will be immediately understandable to anyone who has seen the spirally ridged appearance of a hog's erect penis.

In the early C17th *screw* became used as a verb, meaning to penetrate with a winding course. By the C18th *to screw* was coarse slang for to copulate with a woman. From this sense *screw* also became a vulgar term for "A STRUMPET, a common PROSTITUTE". (*New Canting Dictionary*, 1725) It later became used for any woman considered in sexual terms (from a male perspective).

In the C20th the phrase *to screw around* first meant to be sexually promiscuous and later, in a transferred sense in the USA during World War 2, was slang for to mess or fool about. According to the 1966 *ABZ of Scouse* (ie, Liverpool slang) " 'A bloody good screw' might refer to an attractive girl." Since the late 1960s feminists have asserted that sexual intercourse was not something men did *to* women but *with* them; the verb is now used by either sex for sexual intercourse (SEE BALL).

Scrubber

In current usage *scrubber* is a term of abuse for a woman who is considered coarse, shabbily-dressed, dirty-looking and promiscuous; another word for a SLATTERN. This sense derives from a merging of two quite different meanings of *scrub* each with its own history.

Scrub, meaning a low stunted tree, entered English in 1398 from Middle English *shrobbe*, from the Old English *scrubb* or *scrybb*, meaning a rough plant or bush. Two hundred years later *scrub* had developed the sense of a mean insignificant fellow, a person (usually male) of little importance or of poor appearance, ie, a runt or a nobody. By 1710 *scrub* denoted insignificant, mean and contemptible.

In the sense of to rub hard, *scrub* entered English in the late C16th derived from Middle English *scrobbe*, probably from Middle Low German or Scandinavian *schrobben*, meaning to rub hard. By the end of the C16th *to scrub* meant to clean or scour by rubbing with water and a brush (which would once have been made from the twigs of a shrub or scrub). At around this same time, *scrub* appeared briefly as a verb meaning to wear mean attire; a sense presumably influenced by the type of clothes worn by those (usually women) employed to scrub floors. From 1603–22 *scrubbing* denoted squalid and beggarly. By 1782 *scrubby* came to mean insignificant, shabby, paltry or of poor appearance. Since the late C19th, as a verb, *scrub* has been used colloquially, meaning to drudge, influenced by the arduous and poorly paid nature of scrubbing floors, steps, etc.

When *scrubber* first appeared in the mid-C19th it had none of its present connotations of sexual promiscuity and referred merely to someone who cleaned with a vigorous action, eg: "Her floor is scoured everynight, after all are in bed but the unlucky scrubber, Betsey, the MAID of all work." (Mrs Kirkland, *Griswold*, 1839) Betsey and her sister scrubbers in Victorian households were more than just unlucky. Not only were many of them subjected to the sexual harassment of their male employers, many were also forced into prostitution to supplement their paltry incomes. Hence, presumably, the figurative use of *scrubber* for an ill-bred or degenerate animal or an ill-favoured despicable person (since 1876). In 1900 a *scrub* was defined in *Dialect Notes* as "A disreputable person who frequents the streets."

In the mid-C20th *scrubber* was incorporated into Jazztalk to become a derogatory term for a female groupie, ie, "very young girls who follow jazz bands around the country". (*Encounter*, 1959) In 1964 the British political weekly journal *The New Statesman* noted " 'Scrub' is a Rocker girl; that is, some one not fond of washing, according to the Mods and a bit of a TART." (Rockers and Mods were followers of either rock or pop music.) The nuances of *scrubber* greatly depended upon the musical taste – and gender – of the user: "The word 'scrubber' has cropped up quite frequently in this story, and perhaps the time has come to attempt a precise definition of what it means, or rather meant, for I understand that in the beat world it has become debased and now means a PROSTITUTE. In our day this was not the case. A scrubber was a girl who slept with a jazzman but for her own satisfaction as much as for his." (George Melly, *Owning Up*, 1965) Perhaps unaware of its history, but fully cognisant with a male vocabulary of terms of abuse for working women who could not afford the luxury of middle-class standards of cleanliness and tidiness, Germaine Greer wrote: "The most recent case in which contempt for menial labour has devised a new term of abuse for women is the usage of scrubber for a girl of easy virtue." (*The Female Eunuch*)

In Australia, *scrubber* had a different history. In 1859 the word appeared as a colloquialism, first for an animal and later for a person who lives in the bush or scrub. By the early 1970s a female scrubber was a woman who was like "a MARE that runs wild in the scrub country, copulating indiscriminately with stray stallions". (B Mather, *Snowline*, 1973)

Seamstress

The Old English *seamestre* was the feminine formation corresponding to *seamere* meaning tailor. From the late C16th this was written as *sempster* and from the early C17th as *seamster*. The word was based on the Old English *seam*, which probably derives from the common Germanic *sau* or *su*, meaning sew. *Seamster* was therefore originally a feminine designation, although in Old English it was occasionally applied to a man but it later became only applicable to male tailors. In the early C17th *sempstress*, later *seamstress*, became the commonly used word for a female who sewed. *Tailor*, derived from the Latin *talea*, meaning twig or cutting, entered English in the C13th and became the commonly accepted term for a male who sewed.

Alleen Pace Nilsen cites the difference between *seamstress* and *tailor* as an example of sexism in the English language: "the concept of the masculine usually has positive connotations (compare chef with cook; tailor with seamstress; major with majorette)." But it is the users of English who are sexist, not the language itself: whereas *tailor* suggests a male who is highly valued for his professional skill and expertise, *seamstress* implies an undervaluing of a female who sews.

Sex

Adopted from the Old French *sexe*, from the Latin *sexus* (masculine) and *secus* (neuter), *sex* entered the English language in 1382 to denote either of the two divisions of organic beings distinguished as female or male. The word was rarely used before the C16th when it passed into common usage and adjectives began to be linked to it reflecting societal concepts of FEMININITY and masculinity. Thus, men have been called, on occasion, *the better* or *sterner sex*; and women, *the gentle(r)*, (since 1583), *weaker* (since 1613), *fairer* (since 1665), *softer* (since 1753), *devout* (since the mid-C17th), and *the second* (since 1820) *sex*. In the C20th *sex-kitten*, *sex-boat*, *sex-bomb* and *sex-pot* have been applied mostly to women regarded as objects of (male) sexual desire.

Since the end of the C16th women have also been reduced simply to *the sex*, eg: "The sex would certainly gain by showing a little more of their legs." (Alexander Jardine, 1789) Maria Black and Rosalind Coward cite this usage as an example of "The discursive formation which allows men to represent themselves as non-gendered and to define women constantly according to their sexual status." They argue that "The women's movement takes its existence from the fact that however differently we are constituted in different practices and discourses, women are constantly and inescapably constructed as *women*. There is a discourse available to men which allows them to represent themselves as people, humanity, mankind. This discourse, by its existence excludes and marginalises women by making women the sex." (*Screen Education*, 1981)

Sexism/Sexist

A sexist is one who proclaims or justifies or assumes the supremacy of one sex (guess which) over the other.
                     S Vanauken, *Freedom for Movement Girls – Now,* 1968

Although sexism has existed for thousands of years, the words *sexist* and *sexism* didn't enter English until the 1960s in the USA. They were modelled on the parallel notions of *racist* white chauvinism and *racism* from the Black Liberation Movement. The OED traces the first use of *sexist* to 1965: "When you argue that since fewer women write good poetry this justifies their total exclusion, you are taking a position analogous to that of the racist – I might call you in this case a 'sexist' – who says that since so few negroes have held positions of importance. . .their exclusion from history books is a matter of good judgement than discrimination." (D M Leet, *Speech*) *Sexism* followed a couple of years later: "Sexism is judging people by their sex where sex doesn't matter." (C Bird, *Vital Speeches*, 1968)

Although both words are not, as all the major dictionaries point out, gender-specific, they have generally replaced the term *male chauvinist/ism* for attitudes and behaviour expressing male superiority and have become widely accepted as a feminist term for: "The behaviour, policy, language, or other action of men or women which expresses the institutionalized, systematic, comprehensive view that women are inferior." (Cheris Kramerae and Paula A Treichler, *A Feminist Dictionary*) (*Chauvinist* was adopted from the French in the mid-C19th, formed on the name of Nicolas *Chauvin*, a veteran of the 1st Republic and Empire noted for his demonstrative patriotism, and popularised as the name of a character in *La Concorde Tricolore* (1831) by the brothers Cogniard.)

Sheila

The female personal name *Sheila* is a phonetic rendering of *Sile*, the Irish form of *Celia*, from *Cecilia*, which is from the Latin *Caecilia*, the feminine of *Caecilius*, the name of a Roman plebeian *gens*, from the root *caecus*, meaning blind. St Cecilia was a mythical saint whose bones were 'discovered' by Pope Paschal 1 in the C9th in a catacomb with the name 'Calliste' – probably

Artemis Calliste, the muse of music. The Pope declared that Cecilia was a VIRGIN martyr of the C2nd or C3rd who had been tortured to death for refusing to marry her pagan bridegroom on her wedding day. Her name meant 'Lily of Heaven', a title of the ancient mother-goddess. The lily, once a yonic symbol, became a Christian symbol of virginity and CHASTITY. St Cecilia became the patron saint of music.

The name was introduced into England in 1066 by Cecilia, Abbess of Caen, the daughter of William the Conqueror. The usual English form was *Cicely* or *Sisley* with the pet diminutives *Ciss* and *Siss*. According to *The Oxford Dictionary of English Christian Names*, the Latin form *Cecilia* was adopted in the late C18th "probably in part on account of Mme D'Arblay's novel of that name (1782)".

In Ireland, Sheila na Gig, or Sile na Gciocg, was an ancient goddess of life and death – her name originally meant 'Sheila of the breasts'. Surviving rock carvings reveal her with a grinning, often skeletal face, huge buttocks, full breasts, bent knees and with both hands holding open her VAGINA.

Sheila was very popular in Ireland, where the word *sile* came to mean an EFFEMINATE man synonymous with sissy (see SISTER). In the C19th the name (also spelled *Shelah, Sheelagh, Sheelah, Shela* and *Shaler*), travelled to Australia with the Irish: firstly the convicts, then in the mid-century, with those seeking their fortune in the goldrush, and also with the peasantry who were forced to emigrate to escape the famine and adverse economic conditions of their homeland.

In *The Australian Slanguage*, Bill Hornadge maintains that the most common nicknames for women in the C19th were *Donah* and *Clinah*, but these were superseded around the turn of the century by *Sheila*, which may have been derived from an Irish generic name of *Sheela* or *Shela*, applied to any young woman. He appears to have his dates wrong: *Sheila* first appeared as a generic name for young Irish women, the counterpart of *Paddy* in 1828 in a journal entitled *The Monitor*. It soon became a term of disrespect applied to all women. An old bush ballad of the late colonial period tells us just how disrespectful:

> And he bit that rookin' sheila on the stern.
> Then the sheila raced off squealin'
> And her clothes she was un-peelin';
> To hear her yells would make you feel forlorn.

From this it can be deduced that *Sheila* was a derogatory epithet applied to a sexually promiscuous woman – a common development for women's personal names favoured by the working or serving class. A school-yard rhyme of the 1970s cited in *Cinderella Dressed in Yella* supports this theory. In reference to the London sex and spy scandal of the 1960s which involved John Profumo, a Member of Parliament, and two women, Mandy Rice Davies and Christine Keeler, children in Melbourne sang the following:

> Half a pound o' Mandy Rice,

Half a pound o' Keeler,
Put 'em together and what have you got?
A pound of sexy Sheila.

The disparaging term *sheila talk* is still occcasionally used to denote GOSSIP, or trivial conversation (see TRIVIA) revolving around topics primarily of interest to women, eg: "beats me how any bloke can enjoy himself talking with women. Sheila talk has always driven me up the wall." (Henry Williams, *My Love had a Black Speed Stripe*. 1973)

Shiksa

Mostly used by Jews in the USA, *shiksa* (also *shicksa, shiksah* and *shikse(h)*) is usually a disparaging term for a gentile young woman. It is also used of "a Jewish girl who does not observe Jewish precepts". (Webster's) *Shiksa* entered English in 1892 from the Yiddish *shikse*, adopted from the Hebrew *sigsa*, formed on *sheges*, meaning a blemish or aberration, plus the feminine suffix.

Shickster, which entered English a little earlier, in the mid-C19th, was a slang term for the same thing, ie, "Any gentile woman or girl. . .a none too respectable girl or woman." (*Dictionary of Slang*, 1937) Or, put less euphemistically: "The way for shyster in American English is paved by shickster. . .of Yiddish origin; in criminal's cant it designated a respectable girl or lady. . .but it soon deteriorated to PROSTITUTE." (*English Studies, a Journal of English Letters and Philology*, 1965) *Shickster* may derive from *shice*, meaning no good, possibly from the German *scheisse*, meaning excrement.

There is no masculine word corresponding to *shickster: shegetz*, the male equivalent of *shiksa*, is seldom used.

Shrew

Every man can rule a shrew save he that hath her.

John Heywood, *Proverbs*, 1546

Shrew, the name for the small, insectivorous, MOUSE-like animal with a long, sharp snout, entered English c725. The Old English word *screawa* or *scraewa* is related to Old High German *scrawaz*, meaning dwarf, Middle High German *schrawaz, schrat* and *schrouwe*, meaning devil, Norwegian *skrogg*, meaning wolf, Swedish dialect *skrugge*, meaning devil, and Icelandic *skroggr*, meaning old man.

Early superstitions surrounding the shrew maintained it was a venomous animal empowered to cause paralysis, eg: "*Mus Arancus*, a kynde of myse called a shrew, whyche yf it goo ouer a beastes backe, he shal be lame in the chyne [foot]." (Sir Thomas Elyot, *Dictionarie*, 1545) In the early C17th the term *shrew-run* denoted paralysis caused, it was believed, by being overrun by a shrew-mouse.

From c1250–1650 *shrew*, sometimes emphasised by the adjectives *cursed* or *false*, was used of a wicked, evilly-disposed or malignant man, a mischievous or vexatious person, a rascal or a villain. In this sense *shrew* is generally believed to be a figurative use of its earlier meaning, brought about by the superstitions.

In the C14th one sense of *shrew* was strongly influenced by its association with evil. From 1362 until the C16th the word was applied to the Devil, and to a person, especially a woman, given to railing (ie, a SCOLD) or other behaviour considered perverse or malignant. In this latter sense, by the end of the C16th, *shrew* had become female-specific and was frequently used of a scolding, cursing or turbulent WIFE who, if convicted of scolding was punished by such tortures as the scold's bridle or the cucking, or ducking, chair. Between 1573 and 1661 *shrews* and *sheep* were contrasted as types of wives of opposing character, eg: "They noted, that although the VIRGIN were somewhat shrewishe at the first, yet in time she myght become a sheepe." (John Lyly, *Euphues*. 1580) The cursing aspect of a shrewish wife resulted in the now obsolete verb *to beshrew*, meaning to make wicked or evil or to deprave, pervert or corrupt (c1325–1556), and to invoke evil upon, to wish (one) all that is bad, to invoke a curse upon, and to curse, objurgate or blame greatly as the cause of misfortune (1377–1682).

In *Women and the Devil in Sixteenth-Century Literature*, Lucy de Bruyn traces the history of the shrewish woman back to ancient legend: "Ever since strife came into the world by sin, the question of equality of the sexes has been a serious problem. For woman, who had disobeyed god himself, surrender to her husband became at times most difficult. A world literature sprang up in which her 'wayward, shrew-shaken' disposition was emphasised. Rabbinical, cabbalistic, heathen and Christian legends vied in the portrayal of this quality." De Bruyn detects three stereotypes of the 'unnatural' woman in the C16th: the WITCH, the WANTON and the shrew. Of the three the shrew was the most feared. The wanton, "though untrue to her nature, possessed a peculiar CHARM which enticed men to follow her. The witch, wicked and revengeful, tempted him to persecute her, in which he often succeeded and from which he received a certain satisfaction. . . But the shrew, unkinder and more unnatural than any of her sex, held no attraction for mankind. On her account, men sank into servility and was degraded contrary to his nature."

The devil was believed to be directly involved in female shrewishness. But whereas he was master of the witch and the wanton, in the shrew he had a MISTRESS. And an unruly, disobedient mistress at that: "A shrew strikes terror into a demon even". (*Bihars Proverbs*) With her BESOM the shrew threatened devils (the Dutch word for a shrew in this sense was *helleveeg*, meaning hell-sweep), many of whom preferred to return to hell rather than face their mortal shrewish wives on earth. De Bruyn concludes: "At times the devil was compared so favourably with this specimen of womankind and was depicted as so good-natured [in comparison], that it seemed as if man had lost faith in him as well as in woman."

Like the witch and the wanton, the shrew contradicted a patriarchal concept of the submissive, biddable woman. She personified self-asssertion – a direct antithesis of the ideal woman. The shrew sapped a man's very manhood: "To be ruled by a woman showed his own weakness, it meant loss of freedom, and this may well have been the reason why a shrew, considered the most unnatural of her kind, was depicted as a devilish creature, the worst evil on earth." (De Bruyn) A psychoanalytic explanation suggests that male fear of female sexuality, which is extended to a fear of women in general, is responsible for a perception of woman as inherently evil. Karen Horney described this process in the following terms: "Everywhere the man strives to rid himself of his dread of woman by objectifying it. 'It is not', he says, 'that I dread her; it is that she herself is malignant . . . She is the very personification of what is sinister.'"

As the belief in witches waned, and women were no longer persecuted for alleged associations with the devil, *shrew* began to lose its connotations of evil. *Shrewd* in its original sense of malignant, depraved and wicked (1303) became obsolete and developed the weaker sense of malicious or merely mischievous. From this it developed the favourable sense of cunning or artful which later led to its current sense of clever, keen-witted, astute or sagacious, applied to both sexes.

As a term of abuse, *shrew* re-emerged in the late 1960s when it was applied to women's liberationists. The irony was not lost by the London Women's Liberation Workshop which used *Shrew* for the title of their militant publication (cost: 6 pence for women and 9 pence for men until equal pay).

In the mid-C17th one James Howell wrote: "It is better to marry a shrew than a sheep; for though silence be the dumb orator of beauty. . .yet a phlegmatic dull wife is fulsome and fastidious." (*Familiar Letters,* 1645); in 1982 the feminist perspective was suitably shrewlike: "I'd rather be a shrew than a piece of dough." (Janice Mirikitani, quoted in *Asian American Literature*).

Siren

In classical mythology the sirens were three fabulous monsters, Parthenope, Ligea and Leucosia, who were part-woman, part-bird. According to Homer (c850–800 BC), they lived on the coast of Cyrene and lured sailors to destruction by their ENCHANTING songs. Ulysses escaped their enticing CHARMS by filling his crews' ears with wax and lashing himself to the mast of his ship. Parthenope, a town in southern Italy gets its name from the siren who, falling in love with Ulysses, threw herself into the sea and was cast up in the Bay of Naples.

Since 1558 *siren* has been applied figuratively to someone (almost always a woman) who sings sweetly, charms and allures or deceives, especially a dangerously fascinating woman, eg: "Deceyving syrens, whose eyes are Adamants, whose wordes are witchcrafts [see WITCH]". (*Greene's Groatsworth of Witte*, 1592)

In 1819 Cagniard de la Tour invented an acoustic instrument for producing musical tones used in numbering the vibrations in any note, and called it a *sirene*. In 1879 the same name was given to the instrument used on steamships for giving fog-signals or warnings. Thus the siren, once the very cause of a watery death which must under no circumstances be listened to or heeded, became associated with survival: man had finally tamed her.

In 1907 the horns of motor cars were called *sirens*, and the word was later applied to the wailing and screaming warning devices of police cars, ambulances, fire engines and, during World War 2 in the UK, to the air-raid warning machines. The word was borrowed for one-piece garments resembling overalls (or the BLOOMERS of the C19th), designed to be worn by women in air-raid shelters. These, termed *siren-suits*, were subsequently worn by both sexes and, after the war, by women as a fashionable article of clothing. The choice of name may also have been influenced by the 'enticing' sense of *siren* as they revealed the shape and outline of a woman's body.

Sister

Old English forms of *sister* are thought to have derived from the Indo-European *swesr* or *suesor*, formed from the suffix meaning 'one who' and the same root from which the modern English word *sew* is derived. Etymologists believe that kinship names for family members reflect a semantic fading of terms which once specified the functions performed by each member of the family rather than simple genetic relationships. Thus *sister* originally signified the family sewer or SEAMSTRESS. The Latin *soror*, which derives from the same Indo-European compound root, was later adopted by English in *sorority*, originally meaning a body or company of women united for some common cause, especially for devotional purposes; it was later largely replaced by *sisterhood*.

Several uses of *sister* suggest positive associations with the supposedly inherently FEMININE traits of caring, warmth, affection and sympathy. Since the C10th nuns have been called *sisters* – specific orders, such as the Sisters of Mercy, Charity, etc, make this connotation even clearer. In the C19th *sister* became the title for a nurse, later, specifically the head nurse of a ward.

Unlike *brotherhood* which has always connoted positive values of strength and comradeship, *sisterhood*, when used loosely to denote a number of females with some common aim, has, according to the OED, often been used in a negative sense. It gives as an example: "Those members of the female sex. . .who agitate questions they know nothing about. The *Saturday Review* calls the latter 'Shrieking Sisterhood' (G C Davies, *Mountain Meadow and Mere,* 1873)." This term, used in the C19th of women reformers, degenerated to mean female busybodies until it became obsolete in 1910, by which time the subtly undermining words FEMINIST and SUFFRAGETTE were in vogue. *Sisters of the Bank,* a C19th term for PROSTITUTES, provides yet another example of a word denoting a woman which acquired negative sexual meaning. Perhaps both terms reveal a male fear of female-bonding.

When women joined together to serve others they represented no threat to partiarchal society. It was a different matter when they joined together for their own purposes. In the C17th women began to form female-only groups largely for self-educational purposes. They did not consciously congregate as a political movement but they did want to develop 'friendship' among women and were widely ridiculed (see BLUESTOCKING). By the C19th this movement had become more overtly political. English novelist Sarah Ellis, one of the more conservative writers of the first Victorian generation, sheds some light on why the idea of female-bonding should have been so feared. Advocating what was by now called sisterhood she asked: "What should we think of a community of slaves who betrayed each others' interests? of a little band of shipwrecked mariners upon a friendless shore who were false to each other? of the inhabitants of a defenceless nation who would not unite together in earnestness and good faith against a common enemy:" (*The Daughters of England,* 1844).

At a time when an increasing number of women were challenging male hegemony, the term *weak sister* came to be used (mid-C19th) to denote someone of either sex who was considered ineffective or unreliable. In the C20th the term has come to denote a member (female or male) of a group who needs aid: an element or factor that is weak and ineffective as compared with others in the group. An interesting pejoration also occurred to the word *sissy* (or *cissy*). Originally a mid-C19th colloquialism in the US, denoting a (little) sister or young girl, by 1887 *sissy* acquired the sense of an EFFEMINATE, cowardly man or boy (see SHEILA). Any positive qualities of sisterliness desirable in females were unacceptable in males.

By the beginning of the C20th *sister* was beginning to be used by Blacks, prostitutes and, later, by feminists, who felt themselves united by white male exploitation. In 1968 the slogan (some would say battle-cry) 'Sister-hood is Powerful', which first appeared in the feminist book *Notes from First Year*, was adopted by the Women's Liberation Movement on both sides of the Atlantic. In 1932 the US feminist theologian Mary Daly declared that "The word sisterhood no longer means a subordinate mini-brotherhood but an authentic bonding of women on a wide scale for our own liberation." The desire for sisterhood echoed the urge for friendship as expressed by the earlier 'feminists'. But this notion of sisterhood was something very different, it "embodied an attack on the principle of hierarchy: in a patriarchal society, male domination is assured through a structural policy of divide and rule. Women are separated from each other and from a collective awareness of their oppression as women by an enclosure within the sexist nuclear family, and by a subjection to the general principle of hierarchical (male) structure. To overcome this they must assert their identification with one another and also their dissent from the male practice of hierarchical order. The 'slogan' 'sisterhood is powerful' encapsulates both these statements." (Introduction, Mitchell and Oakley, *The Rights and Wrongs of Women*, 1976).

In the early 1980s feminists in Australia coined the term *stick-sisters* for women who refused to be divided and ruled by the experience of having had sex with the same man; far from viewing each other as rivals, stick-sisters are supportive of each other.

Skirt

Old English *scyrte*, meaning shirt, was adopted from the Old Norse *skyrta*. It is not known how, by 1300, the word had changed its meaning to denote the lower part of a woman's gown and, especially in modern use, the separate lower outer garment which starts at the waist.

In the C15th the meaning of *skirt* extended to mean the border, boundary or outlying part of a territory, country, etc, hence the term *outskirts* (of a city), meaning the suburbs. The imagery employed in this use is that of the VAGINA as the citadel whose outskirts have to be traversed before access can be gained. By 1560 *skirt*, like PETTICOAT, had become standard English for a woman, and *the skirt* was the generic noun for women referred to collectively.

By the late C19th *skirt* had acquired negative and overtly sexual connotations: a *light skirt* was slang for a LOOSE woman; *to skirt* was used to mean to be a HARLOT; *to do a bit of skirt* meant to copulate with a woman; *skirt-hunting* referrred to a male pastime of searching out women for purposes of sexual intercourse; *a* BIT *or* PIECE *of skirt* was both a woman and her VAGINA.

During World War 1, *skirt* ameliorated and passed into US slang to denote an attractive woman – but then, a woman's attractiveness may well have been determined by her degree of sexual availability. According to the *Dictionary of American Slang*, by World War 2 *skirt* had become the third most popular slang term for a woman after DAME and JANE and could be used in (fairly) polite conversation.

A man who 'hides behind skirts' is a derided weakling in need of protection. Someone who 'skirts' a topic of conversation does so because of the decidedly unmanly fear of or inability to, confront difficulty, complexity, danger or controversy.

Slag

Slag entered English in the mid-C16th to denote a piece of refuse matter separated from a metal in the process of smelting. It was adopted from the Middle Low German *slagge*, perhaps formed on *slagen*, meaning to strike or slay, from the fragments or dross resulting from hammering.

By the end of the C18th this sense of waste in *slag* became combined, or possibly confused, with the word *slack*, which developed from the Old English word denoting indolent, careless or remiss to mean loose in the C13th, and dull and inactive in the C14th. Since the C15th *slack* has also denoted small or refuse coals, probably from Middle Dutch *slak*, meaning dross. This resulted in the use of *slag* as a term of contempt for a worthless or insignificant person, especially a coward, eg: "Slag: a slack-mettled fellow, one not ready to resent an affront". (1788 edition of the *Dictionary of the Vulgar Tongue*) By the beginning of the C20th *slagger*, (possibly a corruption of *slacker*, meaning a shirker or a very lazy person) became slang for a BROTHEL-keeper. This presumably influenced the development of the word in the UK to mean a rough or brutal person (1934), any objectionable or contemptible person (1943), worthless matter, rubbish or nonsense (1948), a vagrant or petty criminal (1955), and a PROSTITUTE or promiscuous woman, a synonym for a SLATTERN (1958). In 1983 the British weekly journal *New Society*, commenting on a survey of British teenagers, noted: "The commonest insult, used by both sexes, is 'slag'. But all the insults [the survey] came across seemed to relate to a girl's reputation – although they might bear *no* relation at all to a girl's sexual behaviour. One problem for girls is that there aren't equivalent terms they can use against boys. . .that amount to an attack on their whole personality or social identity." (quoted in *The Slanguage of Sex*).

In the Antipodes, *slag* pejorated differently; in 1958 *The New Zealand Listener* recorded that a *slag* was "a white girl who lives with or is friendly with coloured people of either sex". In the US *slag* meaning to criticise severely entered slang vocabulary in 1974, as a result of an article in *Rolling Stone*: "I think it was good copy at the time to slag everything. Everybody was getting slagged, the Beatles were getting slagged." (Paul Gambaccini quoting Paul McCartney)

Slattern

Slattern may be formed on the northern English dialect verb *slatter*, meaning to spill or splash awkwardly, to slop or to waste, eg: "a dirty slattering woman" (*Northern Country Words*, 1674). According to *The Oxford Diction-*

ary of English Etymology, it was formed on the Middle English *sleate*, meaning dash, perhaps originating in a Scandinavian word meaning to slap. *Slattern* is first recorded in the *Gloucester Glossary* of 1639: "A slaterne, ie a rude ill bred woman". From this developed its modern sense of an untidy, slovenly woman, a SLUT or PROSTITUTE. Only rarely has the word ever been applied to a man.

Webster's suggests a different etymology; one which indicates the sheer horror provoked by a woman who does not conform to a clean, orderly ideal: "Probably a modification of German *schlottern*, to hang loosely, waddle, slouch. . .from Middle High German *slottern*, *slattern*, *sluttern*; akin to Dutch *slodderen* to hang loosely, *slodder* a slovenly person, slut; Icelandic *sludda* clod of spittle, *slydda* sleet, slush; Middle High German *slote* mud, slime, *sloten* to stagger, shake; Old Norse *slothra* to drag oneself forward; Gothic *slauthjan*, to be anguished, shaken and probably Middle English *sloor* mud."

Muriel R Schulz points to many words in the English language which demonstrate that "To be fat and sloppy is. . .unforgivable in a woman." She lists the following words in evidence: "COW, a clumsy, obese, coarse, or otherwise unpleasant person which specialized to refer mainly to women and later to a degraded woman and then a PROSTITUTE; DRAB, originally a dirty, untidy woman, later a HARLOT or prostitute; TROLLOP originally an unkempt woman extended to mean a LOOSE woman and eventually a hedge WHORE; mab (see DOWDY), first a slattern and then a woman of loose character and now in the US a prostitute; and slut and slattern both first used to designate a person, especially a woman, who is negligent of his [sic] appearance which acquired meanings of a sloppy woman or prostitute." ('The Semantic Derogation of Women').

These terms, as Schulz notes, all originally designated fat or sloppy women and they all underwent pejoration and acquired negative sexual overtones at one time or another. "Are there," she asks rhetorically, "any [terms] designating slovenly men?"

Slut

The origins of *slut* are unknown: "contact with Continental words similarly used and having the same consonant framework sl..t, cannot be proved". (*The Oxford Dictionary of English Etymology*) Its development followed a path very similar to that of SLATTERN. *Sluttish* entered English in the late C14th as an adjective used of both women and men to mean dirty and untidy in dress and habits, especially to an extent thought repulsive and disgusting. By the late C16th the word was female-specific. To denote a dirty, slovenly or untidy woman, *slut* is first recorded in 1402. Within fifty years it had degenerated and acquired the negative sexual sense of a promiscuous woman, or HUSSY.

An untidy, promiscuous woman was not one who could be controlled, hence, presumably, the development of the word in the C15th to mean a troublesome or awkward creature; a "bold or impudent girl" (OED); "a saucy or brazen girl" (Webster's).

In the 1450s *slut* also denoted a kitchen-MAID or a drudge, probably influenced by the understandably unkempt appearance of lowly serving women who were also considered to be the personal sexual property of their masters. In the C17th *sluttery* denoted drudgery or "work appropriate to a slut" (OED). Briefly in the C17th, according to the OED, *slut* came to be used playfully, or without any serious imputation, of bad qualities, eg: "Our little girl Susan is a most admirable slut, and pleases us mightily." (Samuel Pepys, *Diary*, 1664) There is no record as to whether Susan actually enjoyed the playfulness of her employer, a self-avowed lecher.

In the C20th in the UK, *slut* has come to be a widespread term of abuse, synonymous with SCRUBBER and SLAG, applied to any woman who does not accept the sexual double standards of society.

Snatch

The origins of *snatch* are obscure. It may be related to *snack*, at first meaning bite (especially of a dog), which developed into a morsel of food or a quick 'bite' to eat, and also to C14th Northern dialect *sneck*, meaning door-latch. These words, etymologists suggest, imply a possible base of *snak*, represented by the Middle Dutch *snakken*, meaning to gasp and, perhaps originally, to open the jaws suddenly. When *snatch* first entered English it denoted a trap, snare or entanglement (C14th–1655). Since 1577 it has meant a hasty catch or grasp, or a sudden grab or snap at something. By the end of the C16th *snatch* was used allusively to refer to hasty or illicit or mercenary sexual intercourse (with a woman), eg: "I could not abide marriage, but as a rambler I took a snatch when I could get it." (Robert Burton, *Anatomy of Melancholy*, 1621) Hence, since the end of the C19th, *snatch* came to be used as slang for the VAGINA. This sense was probably also influenced by the Yorkshire dialect use of *snatch* as a collective noun for women.

The association of the vagina with a snapping jaw – the *vagina dentata* – is a symbol of male castration fear which has appeared in primitive legend the world over. In psychoanalytic terms this is explained by H R Hays as follows: "The sucking infant, which had a cannibalistic desire to consume the mother, projects an instinctive memory of its own sadism into the female vagina and transforms it into a biting mouth." (*The Dangerous Sex*, 1966) This memory is one which can be revived in the male by heterosexual intercourse after which the once erect penis goes limp and thus seems to 'die', or is perhaps 'killed' by the snatching vagina of a woman, viewed as a SORCERESS.

Sorceress See CIRCEAN

Sow

Sow, the name for an adult or full-grown female PIG, entered English c725. It derives from the Indo-European root *su*. By 1508 it was a term of abuse, applied to both genders, but especially to a fat, clumsy or slovenly woman, eg; "a term of Reproach given many times to a fat, lazy, rank, big-breasted Woman". (*The New World of English Words*, 1696); "A fat woman" (1785 edition of the *Dictionary of the Vulgar Tongue*); "An inelegant female, a dirty WENCH" (*A Glossary of North Country Words*, 1825)

In US slang, *sow* has followed the path of many words which once designated a fat or untidy woman; like BLOWZY, SLATTERN, TROLLOP, COW, and SLUT, *sow* acquired pejorative and negative sexual connotations. It is defined in the *Dictionary of American Slang* as "Any young, unkempt female, especially if promiscuous. *Some Student Use*."

Spare Rib See RIB

Spinster

Spinster is based on the Old English root *spinnan*, to spin, and the suffix -*estre*, giving spinner or one who spins. This suffix was originally applied to female occupations and the women who did them, but as men began to take over women's traditional jobs it came to be applied to men as well. It finally came to be used mainly of male or neutral agents, often with a pejorative sense, as in *gangster*, *huckster*, *trickster*, etc. The feminine suffix -*ess*, introduced from the Norman in 1066 later took over, giving words such as SEAMSTRESS, GOVERNESS, MISTRESS, ACTRESS, etc; the word *spinster* remains an exception in the English language.

When it first entered English in Langland's *Piers Plowman* in 1362, *spinster* denoted a woman. According to Brewer's: "It was reckoned by our forefathers that no young woman was fit to be a WIFE till she had spun for herself a set of body, table and bed linen. Hence the MAIDEN was termed a spinner or spinster." The word was, however, also used of any male spinner.

In the C14th *spinster* became appended to the names of women spinners to denote their occupation. During the Middle Ages it seems likely that spinsters enjoyed a higher status than was to become the lot of working women in the clothing industry of subsequent generations. In her study on Joan of Arc, Marina Warner notes that at one point in her trial Joan insisted stoutly on her feminine skills: "She did not shepherd animals in the fields, she retorted, and she challenged any woman in Rouen to better her at sewing or spinning. Spinning is the quintessential sex-stereotyped activity. . . Joan was claiming higher social status through an activity where, for once, women took precedence over men. A seamstress or spinster, the female, ranked higher than a male cowherd."

In the C17th *spinster* became the English legal designation for an unmarried woman. This appears to have been the result of several factors. Spinning had long been a symbol of women; since the C14th DISTAFF (an implement used in spinning) had been used figuratively of the female sex. In heraldry the armorial bearings of a woman were originally represented by a spindle. By the end of the C16th, until they married, young women of the labouring class (that is, the vast majority of the population) worked at home to support themselves from an early age, and a considerable number of these were spinsters (in the sense of spinners). So *spinster* became synonymous with an unmarried woman and hence a VIRGIN. Further, the word MAID, which was in general use for an unmarried female, had connotations of youth and may have seemed inappropriate in a society where women outnumbered men and a large number of women never married. Another factor determining the choice of *spinster* to denote a single woman may have been the negative associations of an OLD WOMAN and the pejorative connotations of *old maid*. In *The Ladies Calling* (1673), a best-selling etiquette book, Richard Allestree wrote: "An old Maid is now. . .look'd on as the most Calamitous creature in nature."

There is a hint of resistance to the new term – perhaps because of its class origins and perhaps because *spinster* became a colloquial term for a HARLOT between c1620 and 1720. *A Glossographia* published in 1656 insisted that *spinster* was "the onely addition for all unmarried women, from the Viscount's Daughter downward". And there is a suggestion of bafflement about the new use to which the word was put in *The Spinster: a Defence of the Woollen Manufacture* (1719): "I write myself spinster, because the laws of my country call me so."

In her study of women in the C17th, Antonia Fraser writes: "The concept of an unmarried female beyond a certain age and not demonstrably in the care of a male, tended to bring about a kind of bewilderment at best." (*The Weaker Vessel*) This may explain the OED definition of *spinster* as "A woman still unmarried; esp one beyond the usual age for marriage", whereas BACHELOR is merely "an unmarried man (of marriageable age)". A bachelor of course is never too old to marry – an unmarried woman once past childbearing age becomes an old maid, defined in Webster's as "a prim, nervous person of either sex who frets about inconsequential details: FUSS-BUDGET".

Mary Daly points out that if one looks up *bachelor* in a dictionary there is no reference to old maid or old maidish qualities. She suggests that the dictionary definitions of *spinster* and *bachelor* reflect a double standard, the effect of which has been "a powerful weapon of intimidation and deception, driving women into the 'respectable' alternative of marriage, forcing them to believe, against all the evidence to the contrary, that wedlock will be salvation from a fate worse than death, that it will inevitably mean fulfillment. The alternatives, traditionally, have been the roles of PROSTITUTE, NUN, mistress. In more recent times, another alternative has been the life-style of 'swinging single', euphemistically called 'bachelor girls'." (*Gyn/Ecology*)

In one sense *spinster* has enjoyed some amelioration since the C17th when *spinning-house* and *spin-house*, derived from the Dutch *spinhuis*, were terms for a house of labour and correction for women, especially for harlots, and a work-house, respectively. (This is presumably why *spinster* became used colloquially for a HARLOT.) But the term has never really recovered from the spinster-baiting of the late C19th and early C20th when the issue of what was known as 'surplus' or 'excess' women was exacerbated by an increasing number of women choosing celibacy voluntarily. Such women were invariably considered dangerous and were lumped together with other breeds of dangerous women – SUFFRAGETTES, FEMINISTS and LESBIANS.

In her study on feminism and sexuality between 1880 and 1930, Sheila Jeffries writes: "The development of a class of spinsters proud to proclaim that they were happy, fulfilled, had made a deliberate choice and were vital to the political struggle to women, met with serious opposition. It was not just men who wanted to deride and undermine the position of these women. Some feminists went into the attack." (*The Spinster and Her Enemies*)
In 1911 the magazine *Freewoman* carried an article entitled 'The Spinster' written 'By One' in its first issue which, while arguing for the removal of the savage restrictions which condemned unmarried women to celibacy, was also a vicious onslaught upon the spinster: "I write of the High priestess of Society. Not of the MOTHER of sons, but of her barren SISTER, the withered tree, the acidulous vessel under whose pale shadow we chill and whiten, of the Spinster I write. Because of her power and dominion. She, unobtrusive, meek, soft-footed, silent, shamefaced, bloodless and boneless, thinned to spirit, enters the secret recesses of the mind, sits at the secret springs of action, and moulds and fashions our emasculate society. She is our social nemesis."

But what was so wrong with a society in which there is an abundance of women? "Who, or what," asks the historian Charlotte M Macdonald "are they surplus to? The notion of 'surplus' of women seems to imply that women are only valid so long as they can be attached to a man. If there are more women than men then there are women 'left over', who are redundant in the coupling of members of society." The so-called 'problem' of what to do with surplus women was perceived as a major social problem by Victorians and Edwardians from which survives the image of the prim, prudish (see PRUDE), pining spinster. Perhaps behind the attacks on spinsters and the negative connotations of the word lies the patriarchal fear that women, or at least some women, can actually do very well without men.

Squaw

Squaw, meaning a North American Indian woman or WIFE, entered English in 1634 via the white settlers. According to *The Oxford Dictionary of English Etymology*, the word was adopted from the Narragansett term for a woman. Webster's, however, maintains that it is of Algonquian origin, akin to both the Narragansett word and to the Natick word *squa*, meaning female creature.

The settlers noted that the North American aboriginals used the word disparagingly of white women: "And when they see any of our English women with their needles, or working quoites, or such things, they will cry out 'Lazie Squaes'!" (Lechford, *Plan Dealing*, 1642) Thus *squaw* came to be used, on occasions, by whites as a synonym, also opprobrious, for a wife or spouse (since 1822), or as an adjective meaning female, eg, a *squaw-horse*. In a transferred sense, both SEXIST and racist, *squaw* was applied to a weak or EFFEMINATE man, eg: "By way of expressing their utter contempt for him they called him a squaw" (A Welcker, *Tales of the 'Wild and Woolly West'*, c1890). White racist hatred of miscegenation is resonant in another late C19th use, ie, "The squaw-man – the miserable wretch of European blood who marries a Crow or a Blackfoot." (*The Pall Mall Gazette*, 1884) In the USA this term degenerated even further in the C20th as a heterosexual term of abuse for an effeminate GAY.

Strait-Laced

In the mid-C16th *strait-laced* came to mean excessively rigid or scrupulous in manners of conduct, narrow or over-precise in one's rules of practice or moral judgment, in short, unpleasantly prudish (see PRUDE). It was used of both sexes but its origins are female-specific. *Strait* was used as an adverb in the C12th to mean tightly, originating in the Latin *strictus*, meaning strict. This sense of constriction (also surviving in the narrows, or *straits*, of a sea) was originally employed to refer to a fashion for women of wearing stays or a tightly laced bodice.

The corset, from the Old French *corset*, literally, a 'little body', has long been considered a necessary device to improve the 'inadequate' shape of the female body in Western society: "We know from the art and documents of the sixteenth century that two powerful queens, Catherine de Medici of

France and Elizabeth of England, were among the first to wear the compressing cage, taking on, as it were, the armour of their noble knights to push the soft flesh and rib cage inward. How fascinating that history's first tight-lacers should have been the Medici and the Virgin Queen, two bold, ambitious women who were called 'unnatural' in their thirst for power. Why did they do it? What made them want to subject their chest and stomach to such discomfort, they who negotiated treaties and plotted murder with such competent skill? Could it have been that the singular quality their enemies whispered they did not have – a womanly weakness, a soft, yielding nature – might best be proved and ceremoniously displayed by that excessively small and breathlessly feminine bodice? The slender waist was not exclusively a feminine vanity. Elizabeth's father, Henry the Eighth, compressed his middle in order to give his chest that extra-burly look – but King Henry and other men stopped short of physical pain. . .The truth is, men have barely tampered with their bodies at all, historically, to make themselves more appealing to women. . . A woman, on the other hand, is expected to depend on tricks and suffering to prove her feminine nature, for beauty, as men have defined it for women, is an end in itself." (Susan Brownmiller, *Femininity*)

Over the years fashions have changed; a slender waist has not always epitomised the ideal female. Yet the etymologies of words such as BLOWZY, COW, SLATTERN, SLUT and SOW, all suggest that fatness in a woman has usually been associated with disorderliness, uncontrollability, promiscuity and general disparagement.

Simone de Beauvoir understood well the consequences of being strait-laced. In her autobiographical volume about her mother, she uses the image of corsetry as both metaphor and fact to describe her mother's upbringing, part of which was passed on to her: "Thinking against oneself often bears fruit; but with my mother it was another question again – she *lived* against herself. She had appetites in plenty: and she underwent this denial in anger. In her childhood her body, her heart and her mind had been squeezed into an armour of principles and prohibitions. She had been taught to pull the laces hard and tight herself. A full-blooded, spirited woman lived on inside her, but a stranger to herself, deformed and mutilated." (*A Very Easy Death*, 1966)

When the term is spelled *straight* rather than *strait*, this is no more than a spelling variant, but the etymology of *straight* reveals an interesting insight into patriarchal double standards. Since 1868 *straight*, when used non-gender-specifically, has meant well-conducted and steady. Used only of a woman, however, it has implied virtuous and CHASTE – long seen to be synonymous with FEMININITY. Not to be strait-laced makes a woman lascivious and sexually immoral (and therefore unfeminine); to be strait-laced makes her a narrow-minded prude and sexually undesirable (to a man). She's damned if she does and damned if she doesn't.

Street-Walker

If a woman's place was in the home, it was equally apparent that any female who walked the streets (on her own) was no LADY. *Street-walker* entered English in 1592 to mean a common PROSTITUTE, ie, one whose field of operations was not in a BROTHEL but in the streets, the urban equivalent of a hedge-WHORE. *Street-girl* (1907) was a euphemism for a prostitute. It also denoted a homeless or neglected girl (or young woman) who lived chiefly in the streets, suggesting that attitudes had become a little more humane towards the poor and homeless by the beginning of the C20th than hitherto. From this it may be inferred that the campaigns of woman's-rights reformers to expose the plight and defend the rights of prostitutes during the C19th had achieved some positive results.

Strumpet

In 1327 *strumpet*, of unknown origins, entered English meaning a debauched or unchaste (see CHASTE) woman, a HARLOT or PROSTITUTE. The word has been the source of several other words and expressions (now mostly obsolete): *to strump it* (1553) meant to play the strumpet; *strumpery* (c1470–1573) referred to the practice of harlotry; a *strumpeteer* (1663) was a whoremonger (see WHORE); *strumpetocracy* (since 1818) was a jocular term for the notion of (PETTICOAT) rule or government by strumpets; *strum* and *rum-strum* were defined as "a handsome WENCH or strumpet" in the *Dictionary of the Canting Crew* (1700) and as "a battered prostitute" in *The Vocabulary of East Anglia* (1825). The slang verb *to strum*, meaning to have sexual intercourse with a woman (c1780–early C20th) was probably influenced both by *strumpet* and by *strum* in the sense of idly playing a string instrument; the expression *to play a rough tune* (on her) also meant to copulate with a woman. The *Stram*, referring to harlots' street-walking (see STREET-WALKER) (c1900) may have been formed on a combination of *strumpet* and the US slang use of *stram* meaning to walk some distance. In the US today the verb *to strump*, from an early sense of 'to brand as a strumpet', has come to mean to belie or slander.

Stuff

Since the early C19th the phrase *a* BIT *of stuff* has referred to a woman, sometimes an overdressed woman. *Stuff* probably puns on several meanings of the word which has its origins in Late Latin *stuppare*, a verb meaning to plug or stop up, formed on *stuppa*, meaning tow or cork. In late Middle English *stof(fe)*, or *stuff(e)* was adopted from the Old French *estoffe*, meaning material, furniture or provision. Hence, by 1438 *stuff* meant property, especially moveable property, household goods or utensils, as well as material in the sense of that of which something is made. By the late C16th *stuff* was used figuratively to mean what a person (or another animal) is made of, or their essence (especially used of persons and horses), while retaining an earlier meaning of material, especially woven textile, for making clothing.

By 1668 *stuff* had begun to pejorate and was used to denote what was worthless or rubbish. In *Tom Jones*, Henry Fielding used *stuff* to refer to indecent matter: "A grave matron told the master [of a puppet show] she would bring her daughters the next night, as he did not show any stuff." (1749) Such stuff might presumably have had the unfortunate effect of turning young women into *hot stuff*, a phrase that has been used to refer to a lustful person since the late C16th.

The reduction of a woman to an article of clothing or some sort of textile can be found in several words, such as SKIRT, PETTICOAT, PIECE and *muslin* – the last being used to refer to a young woman, especially if a *prostitute*, around the beginning of the C19th.

In the expression *a bit of stuff* can be seen the reduction of a woman to part object – also found in terms like *a piece* or *bit of* FLUFF, etc. It is possible, too, that with its connotations of household property the expression would have seemed particularly appropriate to apply to a woman within patriarchal society.

The use of *stuff* as a verb – to ram or press into a receptable or VESSEL, which originates in the Latin meaning of *stuppare* – clearly influenced a mid-C19th slang use of *stuff* meaning to copulate with (a woman), which may derive from an upholstery term. Hence the expression (*go and*) *get stuffed*. Women, like sausage skins and mattresses, are for stuffing.

Succubus See NIGHTMARE

Suffragette/Suffragist

The Oxford Dictionary of Etymology traces the word *suffrage*, on which *suffragette* and *suffragist* are based, via C13th French to the Latin word *suffragium*, meaning voting tablet, and preceded by *suffragies*, meaning prayers. Another theory is that its origins lie in the Latin *suffrago*, meaning the hock or ankle-bone of a horse, which may have been used by the Romans for balloting.

In the C13th *suffrage* meant a vote in favour of a proposition or election of a person. By the mid-C16th its sense had been extended to mean any vote, for or against, a controverted question or nomination. By 1665 it denoted simply voting or the exercise of a right to vote. This novel concept of a right to vote may have been influenced by the Cromwellian revolution of the 1640s.

The next landmark in the etymological history of the word was the French Revolution (1729–98). In 1798 the term *universal suffrage* first appeared. To most, however, 'universal' meant adult male. Due to the campaigns of women reformers during the early C19th *woman-suffrage* and *woman-suffragist* entered written English in 1867 and 1888 respectively.

On 10 January 1906 the English newspaper the *Daily Mail* reported that Prime Minister A J Balfour had received a deputation of 'suffragettes'. This new word denoted not just an advocate of extending the political franchise to women – the English language already possessed the word *suffragist* (since 1888) for this. Rather, it was used to refer to those women who, as members of the Women's Social and Political Union (WSPU), attracted much public attention by their increasingly militant actions.

The coining of *suffragette* did not merely provide what may seem, superficially, simply a happy fusion of the notions of female suffrage and the female advocates of it. The essential significance of the French suffix *-et* or *-ette* is diminutive: a clarinet is a little clarion; a cigarette is a little cigar, etc. By extension this suffix also connotes something that is synthetic or of less value than the real thing, as in *flannelette* and *leatherette*. Thus *suffragette* was not neutral but, subtly, it was intended to undermine the aims and methods of the women who worked to extend the franchise.

Nonetheless, members of the militant WSPU embraced the name, calling their newspaper, edited by Christabel Pankhurst, *The Suffragette*. Their attitude was explained in a novel by Elibabeth Robbins in 1907: "Very well. . . Suffragettes if you like. To get abuse listened to is the first thing: to get it understood is the next. Rather than not have our cause stand out clear and unmistakable before a preoccupied, careless world, we accept the clumsy label: we wear it proudly. And it won't be the first time in history that a name given in derision has become a badge of honour!" (See BLUESTOCKING).

Today, *suffragette* is the label usually applied to those mainly middle-class women members of the London-based WSPU. *Suffragist* is applied to the mainly working-class women in the Midlands and northern England who, while advocating the right to vote for women be obtained by legal means, saw the whole issue in class terms and as a means to a far greater end.

Surname See MAID/MAIDEN

Suttee

The Hindu custom of the self-immolation of a woman on the funeral pyre of her dead husband is known as *suttee*. If the WIDOW showed reluctance, her family forced immolation upon her. The Urdu word derives from the Sanskrit *sati*, meaning faithful or virtuous WIFE, formed on *sat*, meaning good, wise or true, literally meaning being, the present participle of the verb *as*, to be.

The practice (the word did not appear in English until 1786) can be traced to ancient Greece, eg: "The patriarchal practice of suttee, attested here [by the myth of Alcestis who poisoned herself after the death of her lover Admetus] and in the myths of Evadne [self-immolation] and Polyxene [who was either sacrificed on the tomb of Achilles or threw herself on the point of a sword after his death], grew from the Indo-European custom which forbade widows to remarry; once this ban was relaxed, suttee became less attractive." (Robert Graves, *Greek Myths*)

The Hindu religion, however, continued to forbid re-marriage and insisted upon suttee for childless widows to spare them from the temptations of impurity, teaching that the husband's death was the fault of the widow – because of her sins in a previous incarnation if not in her present one.

In 1829 the practice was outlawed in British Imperial India by Lord Bentinck, whose determination to anglicise India had once resulted in a massacre at Vellone when he attempted to ban Sepoy beards and turbans. In 1885 *The Times* noted: "A ceremony called 'cold suttee' is described in books on Hindu customs. When the relatives had a very NICE sense of honour, and a widow's proclivities outraged it, they made a feast at which she was the principal guest. She was sumptuously regaled and at the end drugged to death."

In some parts of the Indian continent today, suttee continues illegally. A widow is thought to be an expensive liability to the family of the dead husband and, often with the tacit sanction of the authorities, is disposed of by invoking the ancient Hindu religious custom. There is no evidence that the widows themselves willingly submit to suttee.

Tail

Since the C9th *tail* has denoted the distinct flexible appendage to the posterior extremity of an animal. It seems totally understandable why the penis should be called a *tail*, but less clear why the vulva should have earned this name. The OED assures us that since 1362 *tail* has been used more often to refer to the female pudendum than to the male sexual member. This sense may have been influenced by the use of *tail* (since 1297) to refer to the train or tail-like portion of a woman's dress; SKIRT and PETTICOAT also came to be used to denote both a woman and her VAGINA.

By the late C18th *tail* was slang for sexual intercourse and for a PROSTITUTE. The 1785 edition of the *Dictionary of the Vulgar Tongue* translates "Mother, how many tails do you have in your cab?" as "How many GIRLS have you in your NANNY house [BROTHEL]?"

Slang and Its Analogues (1890–1904) provides a long list of imaginative 'tail'-compound terms culled from, among others, Langland, Chaucer, Shakespeare, Rochester and Tom Brown. A penis has been called a *tail-pike, -pin, -pipe, -tackle, -trimmer* and *tenant-in-tail.* This last also meant a WHORE and "constitutes an indelicate pun on legal Standard English *tail* (derived from French *taille*, assessment), limitation as to freehold or inheritance. (OED) The vulva has been known variously as a *tail-gap, -gate* and *-hole. Tail-feathers* were a woman's pubic hair. The hymen was once known as *tail-fence. Tail-*FLOWERS denoted the menses. *Tail-fruit* referred to children. *Tail-trading* meant harlotry (see HARLOT). WANTON women have been called *hot, light* or *warm in the tail. Hot-tailed* or *with tail on fire* denoted a venereally infected wanton woman. In the USA, *tail*, after PIECE, is "the most common word for the combined woman-vagina-coitus concept in vulgar use by males," according to the *Dictionary of American Slang.*

Tart

The origins of *tart* may lie in an Indo-European root meaning twist, from which developed such Latinate forms as *torque* and *contort. Tart* entered English c1400 from the Old French *tarte*, the name of a type of pastry or pie with a sweet filling. The round or twisted shape of a small pastry seems to be the connexion with its root.

In the mid-C19th *tart* was applied to a young woman as a term of endearment. It may have been a contraction of, or rhyming slang for, 'sweetheart'. Like HONEY-*bun*, *sweetie-pie*, *cupcake* and other terms employing a similar image, *tart* presumably derives from the notion of the supposed – and required – sweetness in a woman, and perhaps from a male view that women are small, quick-to-consume, edible morsels.

At first, *tart* was used of any loved woman, but by 1904 it had degenerated and was used of a fast, LOOSE, immoral or unchaste (see CHASTE) one. This shift in meaning is not surprising in a society which evaluates women as sexual objects. (Little girls, after all, are made of spice as well as sugar.) The word pejorated to a term of abuse to denote a PROSTITUTE. During World War 2 *tart* became slang for a catamite or a male PROSTITUTE.

Since the 1930s the verb *to tart* (*up*) has meant to dress up or adorn, usually in a showy, gaudy or TAWDRY manner. This clearly reflects a view that prostitutes – and possibly all women – deceive by dressing to give the impression of quality which does not underlie an attractive exterior.

Tawdry

Aethelthryth, or Etheldreda (Audrey in Old French), was a C7th princess, the daughter of King Anna of East Anglia. She married King Ecgfrith of Northumbria but later deserted him and sought sanctuary from King Wulfare of Mercia, where she founded an abbey in the city of Ely and lived piously until she died of throat cancer in 679. She convinced herself that her disease was God's just punishment for her youthful vanity, manifested by a penchant for beautiful bejewelled necklaces. The citizens of Ely adopted Audrey (a corruption of her name) as their patron (or MATRON) saint, celebrating her memory annually with a fair on 17 October. *Tawdry* is a contraction of *saint* and *Audrey*.

Until the 1670s *Tawdry laces*, or *tawdry* as they became known, were highly fashionable ornaments. But as the quality of tawdry deteriorated – they were cheaply made for the peasant and serving women of the region – the word came to denote gaudy and shoddy value, eg: "Taudry or Tawdry. . .tricked up with such tinsel STUFF, or Lace as is usually sold at Audrey-fair in Cambridgeshire." (*The New World of English Words*. 1706) Influenced by the country WENCHES who purchased their tawdry at the fair, the word acquired negative connotations and came to mean untidy, slovenly and ungraceful (1671–c1820). Today *tawdry* denotes anything that is cheap and nasty.

Termagant

The origins of *termagant* lie in the Latin *tri-*, meaning three or triply, plus *vagant*, the present participle of the verb *vagari*, meaning to wander, so designating the moon wandering under the triple-goddess names of Selene (Luna), Artemis (Diana), and Persephone (Proserpina). Selene's sphere of wandering was the heavens; she was the early Greek full-moon MOTHER goddess who, winged and crowned with a crescent, drove her lunar chariot across the sky at night. Artemis was the VIRGIN moon-goddess who roamed the earth with a band of NYMPHS, avoiding men and killing any male who looked on her. Persephone was the CRONE aspect of the triple-goddess whose sphere was death and the underworld.

When *Termagant* first entered English (c1205), in the form *Tervagent*, it was the name given to an imaginary god supposedly worshipped by Mohamme-dans. This male deity was a regular character in the mystery plays popular in England in the C15th and C16th. He was always represented as a violent and turbulent person – as befitting an infidel. Hence the use of *termagant* in the C16th for a savage, violent, boisterous or quarrelsome person of either gender. By the mid-C17th *termagant* had become female-specific, used only of a woman whose overbearing and quick-tempered nature defied conven-tional notions of FEMININITY. Brewer's suggests that this gender change occurred because the Termagants of the mystery plays wore long flowing Eastern gowns which must have seemed feminine to Tudor audiences.

Today, *termagant* has come to mean that most disliked – and possibly feared – of women: the SHREW, VIRAGO or VIXEN who cannot be controlled (by men); one who refuses to accept that women, like children, should be seen but not heard. In the Victorian poem *Kate Carnegie and those ministers*, by J Watson a *termagant* is defined as a woman "who would call her husband an idiot aloud before a dinner table". (1896)

Testify

To *testify*, meaning to bear witness to or give proof of, originates in the Latin word *testis*, meaning witness.

It has been posited that *testicle* also derives from this root. According to this hypothesis the Latin *testis* originates in the Indo-European word for three. This was either because in Roman law three witnesses were generally required to convict a criminal or because a witness is a 'third person' observing a transaction between two people. And as a man's testicles are a fundamental witness to his virility, the specialised sense of 'witness(es) to manhood' allegedly derives from the general sense of 'witness'. In support of this theory it has been pointed out that the ancient patriarchal Semites once swore oaths by placing their hand on their own or each others' testicles. This custom of swearing had the effect of making a witness legal.

In *Gyn/Ecology*, with more sense of fun than a serious grasp of etymological theory, Mary Daly explores why a woman's own words are so often discredited in patriarchal society: "Since women do not have testicles, they cannot really be qualified to testify – give evidence – in patriarchal courts. Moreover, the christian bible appropriately comprised two divisions called *testaments*. This term, of course, is also derived from *testis*. Clearly, the idea of a woman swearing on the bible is incongruous. Her testimony (also from *testis*) does not count." (Daly might have gone further in her word play: in scriptural language *testimony* signifies the Mosaic Law, or decalogue, as inscribed on the two tablets of stone: *stones* has been slang for testicles since the C12th.) Testament, in fact derives from testamentum meaning will, an early Christian Latin rendering of the Greek *diatheke* meaning covenant.

Daly teases out some further implications of her theory: "The words of the women who had 'seen' the risen Christ were at first discredited, but the error of those who disbelieved the women was rectified when the reports were confirmed by male witnesses. The women's perseverence in perpetuating a patriarchal fantasy was finally rewarded. So also in post-christian secular society, where beliefs are managed by the mass media, women are still rewarded for perserverence in promoting male propaganda. It is when women speak our own truth that incredulity comes from all sides. Thus, in an accused rapist's trial, the raped woman's word is usually the chief evidence for the prosecution, and this is commonly evaluated as worthless."

Tit

Over the centuries *tit* has denoted a BREAST or nipple, a small animal, a horse, a silly person, a GIRL, a WOMAN and a WHORE.

Tit has been used to denote a small animal since c1325 – surviving in *titmouse*. As a name for a small horse, *tit* entered English in the late C16th. According to Webster's, it later came to be used of an inferior or weedy horse, which led to its figurative use by the C20th for a fool, a stupid or ineffectual person, a nincompoop. (This last is defined in the 1811 edition of the *Dictionary of the Vulgar Tongue* as "a foolish fellow; also one who has never seen his wife's ****". (see CUNT)

Towards the end of the C16th *tit* denoted a young woman. This was presumably influenced both by *tit* in the sense of a small animal and by the equine connexion – other words denoting a type of horse (especially a weak or stunted horse) which also transferred their sense to mean a woman include HARRIDEN, HACK, and JADE. Until the C18th *tit* had positive connotations and was used of a young woman who was considered admirable in some respect. But by the C19th it had pejorated and was used usually opprobriously, especially for a woman of LOOSE character, a HUSSY, a MINX or a HARLOT. At around the same time *tit* became another word for the VULVA, or VAGINA, perhaps an abbreviation of *tit-BIT* – yet another word which suggests a woman is little more than a small, quick-to-consume, edible morsel for a man. Like *TAIL*, *tit-bit* was also used occasionally for a penis. Perhaps this joke use of *tit-bit* did not seem so very funny to those who need to infantilise and diminish women in order to confirm their own powerful strength and size, and may explain why *tit-bit* did not survive very long as a term for the virile member.

The word *titter*, denoting a suppressed laugh, probably derived from its sense of a giggle, or perhaps from the Scots use of *titty* for a SISTER (since 1725). It may also have been influenced by the use of *tit* and *titty* for both a female and her BREAST. Around the beginning of the C19th *titter* appeared as a criminals' and tramps' cant term for a GIRL or young WOMAN. *Titty-oggy* (or *tittie-oggie*) entered English slang in the late C19th as low slang for fellatio.

The use of *tit* meaning breast is an unrelated word, being a by-form of *teat*, from the C17th or earlier. The use of *titty* in this sense dates from c1740.

Tomboy

Short for *Thomas, Tom* has often been used as a generic name for any male representative of the common people, eg, the phrase *Tom, Dick and Harry* is used for any men taken at random from the common run; *Tom Tyler* was used to mean any ordinary man (c1580–1640); *Tommy Dodd* has been rhyming slang for a sodomite since c1870; a British soldier in World War 1 was known as a *Tommy* or *Tommy Atkins*. In the late C18th *Tom* began to be applied to the male of various beasts and birds, *tom cat* (originating in *The Life and Adventures of a Cat*, 1760, in which the male hero was called Tom the cat) being the most obvious survivor. The verb *to tom*, meaning to copulate, probably derived from this in the late C19th. From about the same date *Tommy* became slang for a penis, the menses (see MENSTRUATION) and a female PROSTITUTE – now obsolescent.

When *tomboy* first entered English in the mid-C15th it meant a rude, boisterous or forward boy. By the time this usage became obsolete, towards the end of the century, it had became female-specific to denote a bold or immodest woman (1579–1700). The Protestant reformer John Calvin (1509–64) used *tomboy* in this sense in 1579: "Sainte Paule meaneth that women must not be impudent, they must not be tomboyes, to be shorte, they must not bee unchast." Casey Miller and Kate Swift point out that "This quotation illustrates the first thing that customarily happens to a low-value word when it is switched from males to females: it acquires a sense of sexual promiscuity." (*Words and Women*) This pejorative sense persisted for some centuries. In 1700 the *Dictionary of the Canting Crew* defined *Tom-boy* as "a

Ramp or Tom rig". *Rig* entered English in 1575 to mean a WANTON young woman – possibly derived from *wriggle*; *ramp* meant a bold, vulgar, ill-behaved woman or girl (1450–1728).

But a more positive sense of *tomboy* began to assert itself. By 1876 the English novelist Charlotte Yonge defined tomboyism as "a wholesome delight in rushing around at full speed, playing at active games, climbing trees, rowing boats, making dirt-pies, and the like" – clearly not 'FEMININE' behaviour, but nonetheless increasingly perceived as acceptable behaviour in very young females. Miller and Swift suggest the following reasons for this amelioration: "Perhaps the aura of full-blown female sexuality was incompatible with the sense of sexual inexperience or innocence brought to mind by the word boy. In any case, as the male meaning of tomboy disappeared and the female meaning dropped in age level, the word began to acquire some of the attractive qualities of *boy*."

Modern definitions of *tomboy*, eg: "a wild romping girl who behaves like a boy" (*The Concise Oxford Dictionary*) – raise some pertinent questions asked by Miller and Swift: "But why must a girl be defined in terms of something she is not – namely, a boy? Where is the word that would bring to mind a lively spirited girl without the subliminal implication of imitation or penis envy? Most girls who like sports and the out-of-doors or who have intellectual or mechanical abilities are not trying to be boys. They are trying to be themselves. To call them tomboys, even with the intention of being complimentary, cannot help but confuse their self-perception and undermine their sense of female identity."

And what word would one use to describe a boy who supposedly behaves like a girl? No boy enjoys being called a *sissy* (derived from SISTER), which denotes an EFFEMINATE man or boy or a cowardly person. As Sara Stein remarks in *Girls and Boys*: "A girl's feminine identity is not threatened by a dose of masculinity as a boy's is by a dose of femininity, because the implications for loss of self are not the same. The words 'sissy' and 'tomboy' do not have equivalent pejorative value."

Tramp

The verb *to tramp*, entered English in the C14th, probably from the Low German *trampen* meaning to tread or walk with a firm, heavy, resonant step. By 1664 the negative connotations of someone who could not afford any means of transport other than foot influenced the development of *tramp* as a noun to mean a woman or man who travels from place to place on foot in search of employment; a worthless, begging or thieving vagrant. In the 1920s the word joined the long list of words which assumed negative and sexual connotations when applied specifically to women. The *Dictionary of American Slang* defines *tramp* as: "a promiscuous GIRL or WOMAN, regardless of social class, marital status, or intelligence. Thus a tramp can be the cheapest PROSTITUTE or a refined married society woman who can't resist men." There are notably few words in the English language which express anything other than approval for a man who cannot resist women – provided, of course, he is not dominated by them. (See HEN; UXORIOUS)

Tribade

Originating in the Greek word *tribein* meaning to rub, *tribade* was the earliest (1601) of words to enter the English language for what is now called a LESBIAN. The heterosexism of the OED's definition of *tribade* makes shocking reading today: "A woman who practices unnatural vice with other women."

Webster's perpetuates a common myth in its definition of *tribadism*: "A homosexual practice among women which attempts to simulate heterosexual intercourse." Tribadism consists of one woman lying on top of another and stimulating the clitoris of each with rubbing movements: there is no attempt to simulate the penile penetration of heterosexual intercourse. As Germaine Greer points out in *The Female Eunuch*: "The prevalence of tribadism as the principle lesbian mode of lovemaking argues the relative unimportance of the masculine fantasy."

Trivia

From the Latin *tres*, meaning three, and *via*, meaning way, *trivia* originally referred to the place where three roads met, ie, a crossroads. In ancient Greece, crossroads were sacred to the trinitarian goddess, Hecate Trevia ('Hecate of the Three Ways'). Her three-faced image guarded three-way crossroads where travellers made offerings of cake and MONEY at her shrines. Today, money is still thrown into the Trevi fountain in Rome named after this goddess.

The modern sense of *trivial* – commonplace, ordinary, of small account, trifling, inconsiderable – may have been influenced by crossroads being a place where women met to exchange news. *The Women's Encyclopedia of Myths and Secrets* suggests that it may also be connected to early attempts to belittle the cult of the trinity goddess and diminish the importance of the pagan custom of offering gifts to her image for protection on journeys.

The subject matter of women's conversation has long been dismissed as trivial GOSSIP – a device which has the effect of silencing women. In *Toward a New Psychology of Women*, Jean Baker Miller suggests that men allocate to women that which is outside their control and which they fear, precisely because it is outside their control: "When women have raised questions that reflect their concerns, the issues have been pushed aside and labelled trivial matters. In fact, now as in the past, they are anything but trivial; rather they are the highly charged, unsolved problems of the dominant culture as a whole and they are loaded with dreaded associations. The charge of triviality is more likely massively defensive, for the questions threaten the return of what has been warded off, denied and sealed away – under the label 'female'."

Trollop/Trull

Trollop entered English in the early C17th to mean an untidy or slovenly woman, a SLATTERN or SLUT, and, sometimes, a morally LOOSE woman or trull. It may derive from the Old French *troller*, once a hunting term meaning to quest or to go in quest of game without purpose. From this, the word *troll* entered English in the late C14th, meaning to move or walk about, to ramble, saunter or stroll. By the C16th this gave rise to a figurative use of the word with the senses of draw on, as with a moving bait, and to entice or allure. (See SIREN.) In the 1960s *troll* re-emerged as homosexual slang meaning to walk the streets or cruise in search of a sexual encounter. *Trull*, an archaic C16th term for a PROSTITUTE may be related to the German *trulle* meaning a slattern.

Many words in English with connotations of female untidiness and/or a lack of sense of direction or purpose have resulted in their being used to describe a PROSTITUTE. A woman who does not seem to know that her place is in the home becomes a threat to the need for order: a disorderly woman can only be a WANTON, a slattern, etc. It was presumably the connotation of disorderliness which resulted in the use of *trollop* in the C19th for "a large piece of rag, especially wet rag" (*The Oxford Dictionary of English Etymology*) and, in Scotland "a large, unseemly, straggling mass of anything". (*Etymological Dictionary of the Scottish Language*)

One definition of *trollop* found in Webster's – "a dissatisfied restless woman" –persuaded some feminists in the 1970s to reclaim the word with pride.

Twat

The origins of *twat*, which entered English in the mid-C17th as a low term for the VULVA, are obscure. It may be connected to *twachylle* or *twitchel*, a C15th term for a passage or path between hedges, eg: "She. . .wyth her twachylle will encrece ánd multeply". (*Reliquiae Antiquae*, c1460) In the C18th a surgeon or doctor was occasionally called a *twat-scourer*.

In what *The Penguin Dictionary of Historical Slang* calls "the literary world's worst 'brick' ", the English poet Robert Browning suffered from the misapprehension that *twat* denoted a NUN's headdress – probably the result of reading "They talk'd of his having a Cardinall's Hat, They'd send him as soon an old Nun's Twat." (*Vanity of Vanities*, 1660) Hence, in his play *Pippa Passes* (1841): "The owls and bats, Cowls and twats, Monks and nuns, in a cloister's moods, Adjourn to the oak-stump pantry!"

In the USA in the C20th *twat* became slang for both the VAGINA and a woman, herself, when considered (by men) as a sexual object. According to the *Dictionary of American Slang* this particular reduction of a woman to a mere part of her anatomy is "usually used in a gentler, more relaxed, more humorous way than 'CUNT', 'ass' or 'PIECE' ". *Twat* is also occasionally used for the buttocks of either a woman or a man.

Uxorious

Formed on the Latin *uxor*, meaning wife, *uxorious* entered English by the end of the C16th to mean dotingly or submissively fond of a WIFE. Examples in the OED reveal a male neurotic fear of wifely domination: "Whose mannish housewives. . .make a drudge of their uxorious mate" (Joseph Hall, *Satires*, 1598); "EFFEMINATE and Uxorious Magistrates, governed and over-swaid at home under a FEMININE usurpation" (Milton, *Eikonoklastes* 1649); "A prince whose manhood was all gone, And molten down in mere uxoriousness". (Tennyson, *Marriage of Geraint*, 1859)

No word exists which suggests that loving a wife could be even faintly pleasant. Nor does any word exist which describes a submissive love for a husband. There is, perhaps, no need for such a word in a society whose very marriage service has enjoined the BRIDE, but not the groom, to obey her spouse.

Vagina

The Latin for a sheath or scabbard is *vagina*. In his comedy *Pseudolus*, the Roman playwright Plautus (c250–184 BC) makes joking euphemistic use of the word *vagina*, "Did the soldier's sword fit your sheath?" As a result, the word *vagina* was directly adopted into English in the late C17th as the anatomical term for the female organ.

In *The Second Sex*, Simone de Beauvoir makes the following observation about the bellicose connotations of so much of language connected with sex: "The erotic vocabulary of males is drawn from military terminology: the lover has the mettle of a soldier, his organ is tense like a bow, to ejaculate is to 'go off'; he speaks of attack, assault, victory. In his sex excitement there is a certain flavour of heroism. 'The generative act', writes Benda in *Le Rapport d'Uriel*, 'consisting in the occupation of one being by another, imposes on the one hand the idea of the conqueror, on the other of something conquered. Indeed, when referring to their love relations, the most civilized speak of conquest, attack, assault, seige, and of defence, defeat, surrender, clearly shaping the idea of love upon that of war. . ." (SEE RAPE.)

Vamp

A fool there was and he made his prayer
(Even as you and I!)
To a rag and a bone and a hank of hair
(We called her the woman who did not care)
But the fool he called her his lady fair –
(Even as you and I!)

Rudyard Kipling, *The Vampire*, 1897

The ultimate origin of *vamp*, a shortening of *vampire*, may be the Turkish word *uber*, meaning witch. This also appeared in various forms in several Slavonic and Uralic languages such as Russian, *upyr*, Bulgarian, *vapir*, and Magyar, *vampir*. Adopted from the French *vampire* or German *vampir*, *vampire* entered English in the C18th for the preternatural being of Slavonic myth who returned from the grave in the guise of a monstrous BAT to suck the blood of sleeping persons who usually became vampires themselves. Since 1741 the word has been used in a transferred sense for a person of either gender of malignant and loathsome character, especially one who preys ruthlessly upon others; a vile and cruel exactor or extortioner.

Vamp, meaning a woman who uses her CHARM or wiles to seduce and exploit men, owes its existence to the Hollywood publicity machine which packaged the silent movie ACTRESS Theda Bara. In 1915 she starred as a *femme fatale* in the sensational film *A Fool There Was* based on a Kipling poem, *The Vampire*, which was written to accompany a painting of the same name by Philip Burne-Jones. Hollywood claimed that Bara's name was an anagram of 'Death Arab' (her real name was Theodosia Goodman). She was made to wear indigo makeup to emphasise her pallor and was surrounded by death symbols such as human skulls and ravens. Served by Nubian slaves and stroking a serpent, she received journalists hungry for hype who named her 'The Vamp'. Further roles as Carmen, Madame Du Barry, Salome and Cleopatra served to reinforce her vamp image.

The vamp is the woman whose charms both attract and destroy the men who seek her. She is the SIREN, the feared blood-sucking ADVENTURESS who cannot be controlled or dominated by male adventurers. (And how much better to be an adventurer – one who seeks adventures, who lives by his wits, than an adventuress – a woman who seeks position or livelihood by questionable means.) In *The Second Sex*, Simone de Beauvoir traces the vamp, or 'bad woman of Hollywood films', back to Circe, the Homeric WITCH who gained the rulership of Colchis near the Black Sea by first marrying its prince and then killing him, and who seduced Odysseus's crew before turning them into swine.

Venereal

Venereal, meaning of, or pertaining to, or associated with sexual desire or intercourse, entered English in the mid-C15th. It was an adoption of medieval Latin *veneria*, formed on the Latin *venus, veneris,* meaning love. Venus was personified by the ancient Romans as the goddess of love and sexuality although originally she was a spirit of charm and beauty, goddess of wild strawberries and herbs, of pine cones and of cypress trees.

Patricia Monaghan maintains that, "We use her name, or words related to it, often: in vain, and winsome, fain, and win – and in that particular form of adoration, veneration. (She was the goddess of venereal as well.)" (*Women in Myth and Legend*).

The etymological histories of these words are complicated, but there do appear to be some connexions. At first the verb *to win* meant to struggle; the Old English *winnan* meaning to strive after, can be traced back to the Indo-European *wen-,* meaning to strive for or desire. From this root the Latin *venus* developed. To *wish*, meaning to have a desire for, was *wyscan* in Old English, related to Old High German *wunsken*. This developed from the Common Germanic *wukskjan*, probably ultimately formed on *wun, wen* and *wan*, from which the words *wean, winsome, wont* and *ween* all derive.

It is difficult to sustain the theory that *fain*, meaning glad or happy, is in any way connected to *Venus*: *The Oxford Dictionary of Etymology* traces the word back to the Gothic *faheps*, meaning joy, but says that ultimately its origins are unknown. Likewise *vain* is probably unconnected: when it entered English in the C14th it denoted senseless or silly, and it derives from the Latin *vanos*, meaning empty or without substance, related to *vacuus*, meaning vacant and *vastus*, meaning waste.

Barbara G Walker associates her name with the city of Venice and with "Venery [which] used to mean hunting; for, like her eastern counterpart Artemis, Venus was once a Lady of Animals, and her Horned God – Adonis, both the hunter and the sacrificial stag – became venison, which meant 'Venus's son'." (*The Woman's Encyclopedia of Myths and Secrets*)

Venery means both sexual indulgence and, now only in archaic use, hunting. The two meanings, however, have different derivations. In the former sense, *venery* is related to *venus*, being an adoption of medieval Latin *veneria*, formed on *vener-, venus* love. The latter sense is from the Old French *vener* from the Latin *venari* meaning to hunt.

Venison, originally the flesh of an animal killed in the chase (C13th), derives from the Latin noun *venatio* meaning hunting, hunt and game. It seems highly unlikely that venison ever meant 'venus' son'.

The Italian city of Venice certainly has strong connections with Venus: she was the mother-goddess of the Venetian tribes of the Adriatic who named their city after her. Venus also gave her name to Venusberg, the mountain in central Germany containing a cavern where in medieval legend Venus held court. The ancient astrological sign for Venus – a circle with a cross joined to it underneath – is another inheritance from the goddess: it became the female symbol and was adopted by the women's movement in the late 1960s.

Barbara G Walker makes an imaginative association between the planet Venus, which appears as the first star of the evening, and the etymological connexions with desire; an age-old children's response to seeing the evening star, is to chant: "Star light, star bright, first star I see tonight, I wish I may, I wish I might, have the wish I wish tonight."

Venus See VENEREAL

Vessel

The term *weaker vessel* owes its origins to William Tyndale's English translation of the New Testament of 1526. In the first letter of St Peter, having enjoined wives to "be in subjection to your own husbands", he urges

these husbands to give "honoure unto the wyfe as unto the weaker vessel."
(1 Peter 3:7)

In her study of women in England in the C17th, Antonia Fraser observes:
"By 1600 the phrase was freely employed – by Shakespeare amongst others
– to denote either a particular female or the female sex as a whole.
Throughout the century following, the words of St Peter, founded on those
of St Paul, might form part of the marriage service as an alternative to a
sermon: so that there was a fair chance that most women would listen to
them at least once – on the most important day of their life, their wedding
day. . . Man then was the stronger, woman the weaker vessel. That was the
way God had arranged Creation, sanctified in the words of the Apostle."
(*The Weaker Vessel*)

Weak entered English in the C13th from the Old Norse word *veikr*, meaning
not strong, or feeble. A century later it acquired a further meaning of pliant,
flexible, readily bending – a masculist view of FEMININITY also discernible in
the etymological histories of such woman-related words as BUXOM and
LESBIAN. In the C16th *weak* was also used to denote a deficiency in power to
control emotion and in bodily or muscular strength, especially of a child or
woman, ie, one who is inferior in respect of physical strength.

Vessel, originating in the Late Latin *vascellum*, meaning a small vase or urn,
and a ship, is yet another example of a word which describes a woman as a
container. Although when it was first used figuratively in the early C14th it
was non gender-specific, definitions of *vessel* in the OED show that it had
some obvious female connotions – of a woman's sphere of power, the house
and especially the kitchen. *Vessel* denoted: a household utensil, especially
one usually of a size suitable for carrying by hand; any article designed to
serve as a receptacle for a liquid; and a WOMB.

Fraser argues that during the C17th the notion of women as inherently
weaker gave way to a more paternalistic notion of women as the 'softer SEX'
or the 'gentler sex' whose weakness entitled her to the special tenderness
and protection of the male. She might still be weaker than a man but at least
her soul was "of the same innate worth and dignity". (Cornelius Agrippa,
Female Pre-eminence or the Dignity and Excellency of that Sex, above the Male,
English translation, 1670) Crucial to this reappraisal of women was the
Civil War (1642–51) in which women proved themselves of equal valour
and strength: "To most 'tis known The weaker vessels are the stronger
grown. The vine which on the pole still lean'd his arms Must now bear up
and save the pole from harms." (James Strong, *Joanereidos: or, Feminine
Valour Eminently discovered in Westerne Women*, 1645) "An uneasy impression," writes Fraser, "that women were 'stronger grown' was one of the many
disquieting feelings produced in the masculine breast by the course of the
Civil Wars."

In her study of the allegory of the female form, Marina Warner suggests that
the metaphor of the body as vessel, although used for both sexes, is more
closely associated with women, as wombs: "It is the underlying metaphor of

the container that inspires the use of feminine gender for ships and cars, and perhaps even the Bank of England's nickname, 'The Old Lady of Threadneedle Street'." (*Monuments and Maidens*)

Vestal

The Roman goddess Vesta derived her name from her Greek counterpart Hestia, whose name meant hearth, house or household. Virginal, CHASTE and abhorring war, Hestia was the most sacred of the twelve Olympian deities who, as goddess of the hearth, dwelled in every private house. There were never any statues to Hestia: she was seen only in the fire of the hearth, living in the centre of every home, symbolising family unity, and by extension, as goddess of the public hearth, she embodied the social contract.

In Rome, Vesta was served by priestesses (at first four, later six) known as Vestal VIRGINS. It was their job to ensure that the sacred fire in the Forum at Rome never went out. They were chosen by lot from girls between the ages of six and ten to serve for thirty years, during which time they swore to remain virgins. The punishment for losing their virginity was burial alive. This insistence upon virginity was not an ascetic statement about morality and the corruption of the flesh, which was a later Christian concept, but originated from the idea that continence was a magical state of power. "Temple virgins like the vestals were forbidden intercourse during their period of office largely because their exalted position gave them political power that might be abused by a lover." (Marina Warner, *Alone of All Her Sex*) The early Christians were particularly virulent in their opposition to the worship of this pagan goddess, although some details of the habits and lifestyles of the Vestal Virgins can be detected in Christian convent rules for NUNS.

In the 1590s *vestal* was applied figuratively to a virgin, a chaste woman or a nun. Thus Shakespeare bestowed the title upon QUEEN Elizabeth I: "A fair vestal enthroned by the west." (*A Midsummer Night's Dream,* 1596) In 1918 *The London Guide* recorded the slang use of *vestal*: "Ironical for an incontinent person" (c1810–50). Recalling the sacred fire of the Roman goddess, a wax match was called a *vesta* (1839) – this name continues in a brand-name of a British match, 'Swan Vestas'. In 1843 a particular brand of household stove also acquired the name 'Vesta'.

Virago

Man should be trained for war, and woman for the recreation of the warrior.
                                                            Nietzsche (1844–1900)

Like *virtue*, *virago* originates from the Latin *vir* meaning male person. The word first appeared in English as a direct adoption from the Latin Vulgate version of the Bible where it was the name given by Adam to Eve in Genesis 2:23: "*Haec vocabitur virago, quoniam de viro sumpta est.*" ["And Adam gaf here a name lyke as her Lord and said, she shal be called Virago, whiche is as moche to saye as made of a man and is a name taken of a man"]. (Caxton's *The Golden Legende,* 1483) This meaning became obsolete as later translations replaced 'Virago' with 'WOMAN'.

This version of the creation of woman influenced a late C14th meaning of *virago*, applied to a woman, as the other face of Eve: "a man-like, vigorous, and heroic woman: a female warrior; an AMAZON". (OED) Another late C14th meaning of *virago*, at first a WICKED woman and later a TERMAGANT, SCOLD, or SHREW, demonstrates the extent to which a female warrior was seen as inherently unsettling to the social order in which war is defined as a male activity and highly valued masculine characteristics are closely associated with war.

Very briefly, around the beginning of the C17th, *virago* was occasionally applied to a man: "Why man, hee's a verie divell, I have not seen such a firago. . .They say he has bin a Fencer to the Sophy." (Shakespeare, *Twelfth Night,* 1601). But by this time the concept of the virago was too closely associated negatively with female aggression, rather than with positive male qualities of bellicosity, for it to become an acceptable term for a man. Casey Miller and Kate Swift believe that because the word designated exceptional strength and vigour "it ceased to be used of men, perhaps because it signified no more than was expected of them". (*Words and Women*)

Today, *virago* is used to designate a noisy, domineering woman, often used opprobriously of hated female stereotypes like the mother-in-law. The founders of the British feminist publishing house in the early 1970s named their company Virago, not without a little irony.

Virgin

When *Virgin* entered English c1200 it was chiefly used as the title for the Virgin Mary or, with reference to early Christian times, of a MAIDEN or CHASTE woman who was distinguished for her piety or steadfastness in religion and regarded as having a special place among the members of the Christian Church because of these qualities. The word was adopted from the Anglo-Norman *virgine* which was itself adopted from the Latin *virgo, virginis* meaning maiden. Etymologists suspect that – unlike the words VIRAGO, *virility,* etc – *virgin* is not based on the root *vir,* meaning man (male). Two specialised senses of *virtue,* which does derive from *vir,* suggest that a link with this root may have been presumed. *Virtue,* from the Latin *virtus,* originally meant the state or quality of manliness which included such qualities as courage, strength, fortitude, power and moral rectitude. In the C13th one specialisation of *virtue* from which the male element had faded gave the meaning of power or efficacy, present in such phrases as *the virtue of medicine*; and – very much a part of the Christian ascetic belief – virginity was thought to bestow a power. Another sense found in the same century and applied to both sexes was that of moral rectitude. In ancient Greece and Rome virginity itself had rarely been represented as a virtue on its own and was omitted from the early canonical lists and tables of virtues. However a specialisation of the sense of moral rectitude, well established by the late C16th, applied it to the sexual purity or chastity of women but never the chastity of men.

Presumably because of the association with the mother of Christ, by the early C14th *virgin* was synonymous with chaste, denoting a woman, especially a young woman, who had never experienced sexual intercourse – a sense which it retains. By the C14th its meaning was extended to include men and boys. But the association with FEMININITY has always been strong: the *virginal*, the musical instrument, was so named possibly because it was used in convents to lead the virginals (hymns to the Virgin Mary), or because it was intended for the young women of Parenthia, or because the title of the first music published for it in England in the C16th was *Maiden's Songs,* or simply because it was mostly played by young women. In the C16th, influenced by the ancient pagan concept of the MOTHER Earth goddess whom it was believed should not be violated by man, the word began to be used in a transferred sense to describe things, such as mountains, countryside, earth, metal, etc which had not yet been touched, handled, cultivated or employed for any purpose. The name of *Virginia*, given to that part of North America in which the first English settlement was made in 1607, was chosen in honour of Elizabeth 1 who was known as the 'Virgin QUEEN' and also, perhaps unconsciously, because the land was presumed to be hitherto unviolated by man (ignoring, of course, the existence of the indigenous Indian population). (See RAPE)

Until the mid-C18th, the term when applied to persons almost always connoted youth, but in 1759 it began to be applied to an unmarried or OLD WOMAN, ie, an old maid or SPINSTER – perhaps bestowing some dignity, if not power, upon a group of women usually reviled. In the late C18th *virgin* was applied to a city, fortress, etc to mean "That which has never been taken or subdued" (OED), an image which reflects a male desire to control woman by sexual conquest. In the mid-C20th the meaning of *virgin* widened and lost its strictly sexual and usually feminine connotations: in a transferred sense it came to be used of anyone who was considered naive, innocent or inexperienced, eg: "He had no strong political ideas. . .He described himself as a 'political virgin'." (Len Deighton, *Funeral In Berlin,* 1964)

As the title given to many of the ancient love goddesses, such as Artemis, Parthenos, Diana, Venus, etc, *virgin* may seem an odd choice since they clearly did not abstain from sexual intercourse and, indeed, had offspring to prove it. It would seem that *virgin*, when used of these goddesses, did not have the meaning which we attach to it today; it was used of a woman who had much sexual experience, and was even used of PROSTITUTES.

A clue to understanding how the word came to mean the opposite of what it once meant can be found in the original meanings of the words *maiden* and *chaste*. *Maiden* initially denoted an unmarried woman – it was not until the C9th that the Christian elders decreed that sexual intercourse should only take place within marriage – a decree widely ignored then as now. *Chaste* derives from the Latin *casta*, meaning morally pure or holy, and did not necessarily denote total abstinence from all sexual relations. But when *chaste* entered English in the C13th it meant pure from unlawful sexual intercourse, continent, virtuous. A virtuous woman was, of course, modelled on the Virgin Mary (also given the title 'Maiden') who was sexually innocent. Henceforth chastity became synonymous with virginity.

The correct Latin expression for the untouched virgin is not *virgo* but *virgo intacta*. The real significance of *virgin* is to be found in its use as contrasted with 'married'. As J G Frazer pointed out: "The Greek word *parthenos*. . . which we commonly translate Virgin, means no more than an unmarried woman, and in the early days the two things were by no means the same. . ." (*The Golden Bough*, 1917)

In her study of the cult of Mariolatry, Marina Warner explains how this shift in meaning came about: "Christianity also parted company with paganism and the cultures of most tribes who believed in parthenogenesis [reproduction without fertilization] in its use of the symbol of virginity. By insisting on the chastity of the mother goddess, the matriarchal image [see MATRIARCHY] could be utterly transformed as to content, although to all outward appearances it remained unchanged. For in the case of pagan goddesses, the sign of the virgin rarely endorses chastity as a virtue. Venus, Ishtar, Astarte, and Anat, the love goddesses of the near east and classical mythology, are entitled virgin despite their lovers. . . Diana, the virgin huntress, goddess of the moon, who imposed a vow of chastity on her NYMPHS, appears at first glance to be an exception. To our eyes, however, her very prominence is a cultural distortion: her cult in Roman times was negligible. Christianity fastened on her and added such typical Christian virtues as modesty and shame to her personality so that the chthonic myth of Diana and Actaeon, in which a goddess sacrifices a man to the underworld, has become a feeble story of a PRUDE's moral indignation. Artemis. . .Hippolyte. . .Athene. . . Parthenos. . .their sacred virginity symbolized their autonomy and had little or no moral connotation. They spurned men because they were pre-eminent, independent. Which is why the title virgin could be used of a goddess who entertained lovers. Her virginity signified she had retained freedom of choice: to take lovers or reject them.

"The use of the image survives. . . Elizabeth 1 was hardly entitled the Virgin Queen because she refused lovers – a succession of favourites characterizes her reign. For although she may have been technically chaste, her virginity principally indicated she could not be subjugated or possessed. In Christian times, however, virginity only rarely preserved the notion of female independence." (*Alone of All Her Sex*).

Thus the Christian Church widened the whole idea of virginity to embrace a philosphy of asceticism. "The interpretation of the virgin birth", argues Warner, "as the moral sanction of goodness of sexual chastity was the overwhelming and distinctive contribution of the Christian religion to the ancient mythological formula." It transformed the Virgin Mary into an effective instrument of asceticism and female subjection giving a very different image of the feminine ideal. For through virginity and self-inflicted hardship, the faults of female nature could be corrected. That virginity became to be seen as so important for women – but not for men – is also the result of the mental image the early fathers of the Church had of the female body. Virginity was perceived as having been created by God and was therefore holy. As Warner points out, the cult of Mary is inextricably interwoven with Christian ideas about the dangers of the flesh and their special connexion with women.

At the same time, virginity was thought to confer a great strength or power, echoing pre-Christian beliefs in its magical power. According to Warner, this idea "operates on two different planes. First, the early fathers taught that the virginal life reduced the special penalties of the fall in women and was therefore holy. Second, the image of the virgin body was the supreme image of wholeness and wholeness was equated with holiness." Once punctured, a woman became, like a seive, a very leaky VESSEL.

The C18th slang use of the term *her purse* for a woman's virginity can be seen as a more materialistic example of the power which was ascribed to it during a period when a definite defloration mania among men caused procurers of young girl PROSTITUTES to go to the most outrageous lengths to obtain virgins, as well as help the girls simulate virginity for their customers. At the same time, of course, virginity was an absolute necessity for the daughters and future wives of the whoremongers (see WHORE) just as chastity (ie, abstinence from illicit intercourse) was a requisite for their wives.

Kate Millett argues that virginity presents an interesting example of male ambivalence in patriarchal societies: "On the one hand, it is. . .a mysterious good because a sign of property received intact. On the other hand, it represents an unknown evil associated with the mana of blood and terrifyingly 'OTHER'." (*Sexual Politics*)

Examining the patriarchal model of the virgin female ideal Simone de Beauvoir notes the connexions between the psychological and material forces at work. Rational motives undoubtedly play a part, she argues, in the demand for virtue: "like the chastity of the wife, the innocence of the fiancée is necessary so that the father may run no risk, later, of leaving his property to a child of another. But virginity is demanded for more immediate reasons when a man regards his wife as his personal property. In the first place, it is always impossible to realize positively the idea of possession; in truth, one never has any thing or person; one tries then to establish ownership in a negative fashion. The surest way of asserting that something is mine is to prevent others from using it. And nothing seems to a man to be more desirable than what has never belonged to any human being: then the conquest seems like a unique and absolute event. Virgin lands have always fascinated explorers; mountain-climbers are killed each year because they wish to violate an untouched peak. . . An object that men have already used has become an instrument; cut from its natural ties, it loses its most profound properties: there is more promise in the untamed flow of torrents than in the water of public fountains." (*The Second Sex*).

But, as de Beauvoir shows, virginity has an erotic attraction only if it is in alliance with youth; otherwise its mystery becomes disturbing. "Many men today feel a sexual repugnance in the presence of maidenhood too prolonged. . . Unless feminine virginity has been dedicated to a god, one easily believes that it implies some kind of marriage with the demon. Virgins unsubdued by man, old women who have escaped his power, are more easily than others regarded as SORCERESSES; for the lot of woman being bondage to another, if she escapes the yoke of man she is ready to accept that of the devil."

Proof of her argument is the high proportion of old unmarried women persecuted as WITCHES during the C14th–C18th. "The male hesitation between fear and desire, between the fear of being in the power of uncontrollable forces and the wish to win them over" writes de Beauvoir, "is strikingly reflected in the myth of virginity. Now feared by the male, now desired or even demanded, the virgin would seem to represent the most consummate form of feminine mystery; she is therefore its most disturbing and at the same time its most fascinating aspect."

Jack Nichols adds another reason for the extreme importance men attach to virginity in their BRIDES: "It assures them that their virgin partner is ignorant of sexual matters herself and therefore not likely to make comparisons with their prowess." (*Men's Liberation*, 1975)

Vixen

The name for the female fox (originally spelled *fixen*) came to be used figuratively for an ill-tempered quarrelsome woman, a SHREW or a TERMA-GANT, towards the end of the C16th, eg: "O when she's angry, she is keene and shrewd, She was a vixen." (Shakespeare, *Midsummer Night's Dream*, 1590) Whereas the male of the species provides the image of craftiness, wiliness and cunning – not altogether negative qualities – the female's propensity for jealously guarding its young provides a totally negative image when applied to women: "She is a foole, a nasty queene [see QUEEN], a SLUT, a fixen, a scolde [see SCOLD]" (Robert Burton, *Anatomie of Melancholy*, 1621)

Vulva See PORCELAINE

Wanton

Middle English *wantoun* or *wantowen*, meaning unrestrained, is based on the root *wan-*, meaning lacking (hence present-day *wane* and want) and *teon*, which had a variety of related meanings including to draw together, restrain and educate. From c1386–c1560 *wanton* denoted unrestrained, and developed to mean sportive or playful and, of persons, jovial, given to broad jesting or waggish. It also meant free from care, with positive connotations discernible from Shakespeare's punning lines: "When we have laught to see the sailes conceive, And grow big bellied with the wanton wind." (*Midsummer Night's Dream*, 1596)

But a process of pejoration began in the C14th which resulted in today's negative sense of deliberately brutal, merciless and inhumane, as in *wanton destruction*, *wanton cruelty*, etc. Used of adults, *wanton* meant undisciplined, ungoverned, not amenable to control, unmanageable or rebellious; when used of children it meant naughty or unruly. (c1300–1697). *Wanton* also acquired mild sexual connotations in the sense of given to amorous dalliance. This was used originally only of women but later of both sexes with the more pejorative sense of lascivious, unchaste (see CHASTE) or lewd.

As a fairly weak term of opprobrium, *wanton* has been used to denote: spoiled or petulant (of children), hence self-indulgent, effeminate and luxurious (1538–1835); fastidious or dainty in appetite (1530–1727); luxurious (of clothing or diet) (1489–1825); capricious, frivolous or giddy (1538–1602). None of these human failings in themselves sound particularly fearsome or dangerous but they combined in the C16th to form a female archetype of the devil-inspired unruly, sexually expressive woman who was ultimately threatening to order. She was described by the English poet John Skelton (C1460–1529) as a fearsome creature indeed – every bit as bad as the SHREW, if not worse:

> Womanhod, wanton, ye want!
> Youre medlyng, mastres, is manerles;
> Plente of yll, of goodnes skant,
> Ye rayll at ryot, recheles.
> . . . .
> Youre key is mete for euery lok,
> Youre key is commen and hangyth owte;
> Youre key is redy, we nede not knok;
> Nor stand long wrestyng there aboute;
> Of youre doregate ye haue no doute:

But one thyng is, that ye be lewde!
Hold youre tong, now, all beshrewde!

In *Woman and the Devil in Sixteenth-Century Literature*, Lucy de Bruyn shows how the wanton contradicted the male ideal of womanhood. Far from being 'Faire, kinde and true' she was the woman who, false to her own nature, gloried in being tempted and in playing the temptress. The weapons and artifices invented by the devil for the downfall of the good woman were particularly designed for the weaker members of womankind and ingeniously contrived to please her. The outward signs of wantonness were easy to detect: a weakness for fashionable clothes and cosmetics; a tendency to go gadding abroad; and a taste for the dainty dish, luxury and lechery. The point was that man considered it likely that if woman indulged in her vanities, haunted public places rather than remained in the home and satisfied her appetite for luxury, she would be tempted to behave as a man, change her obedience to demand and take certain liberties that were otherwise denied her. "The essence of womanhood in the tradition of the time," notes de Bruyn, "is summed up in the free and loving submission to her lord's will, her selfless, courageous co-operation and merciful disposition and equally in her sense of initiative and unflinching stand in the face of danger." But once seduced by the devil, the wanton was capable only of a self-centred love which lacked all nobility. By seducing man's virtue, "She destroys not only her own womanhood but creates havoc all around her even to the wreck of society."

The deceiving, seducing, uncontrollable and untamable characteristics of the wanton woman were those which were feared and despised in the JILT, as well as the WHORE.

Weak See VESSEL

Weird

The origins of *weird* are strongly magical and pagan. In Old English, *wyrd* was the name given to the triple FATE goddesses of classical times who determined the course of human life – the ubiquitous VIRGIN/MOTHER/CRONE trinity of ancient mythology. The OED suggests that the word derives from a Germanic root meaning become. Another theory is that it derives from the Anglo-Saxon name of the death aspect of the triple-goddess, whose name has been variously given as *Wyrd*, *Wurd* or *Urd*, meaning both 'earth' and 'Word of Fate's Immutable Law'. In *Beowulf* (C8th), the word is used to denote the principle, power or agency by which events are predetermined: "Every man in this life will go lay him down on the bed where Wyrd has decided to nail him." This sense of *weird* as fate, or destiny, was much influenced by the Scottish and northern English use of the word, often in the archaic phrase *to dree one's weird*, meaning to endure one's fate, suffer or submit to one's destiny.

Shakespeare also influenced its development. He called his three WITCHES in *Macbeth* (C1605) the 'weird sisters', frequently using the spelling 'weyward'. The OED suggests this was the result of an association with *wayward* which in Middle English ws termed *awayward*, meaning turned away: an appropriate epithet for witches who were accused of turning away from God to the devil (or to the female goddessses of pagan religions).

By the C19th, with the Christian Church no longer obsessed by the need to protect itself from witches, *weird* lost most of its early supernatural meaning and female specificity. In UK and US usage it weakened in meaning, coming to denote merely strange, unusual or odd. Memories in Scotland are, perhaps, longer, for there *weirdless* continues to be used to mean ill-fated or unlucky, hence, since c1800, also to mean unbusinesslike, incapable or worthless, and *weirdly* is used to mean ghostly.

Wench

Wench is derived from an Indo-European root *weng*, meaning twist or bend. Presumably through the association of the malleability or unreliability of youth, this resulted in the Old English *wencel*, meaning a child of either sex, also a servant or slave or a common woman (c890–1300). *Wencel* was replaced in Middle English by *wenche*, with the specialised female-specific meaning of a GIRL, MAID, young woman or female child. The word had sufficient prestige to appear in Piers Plowman in the late C14th in the phrase 'Goddes Wench', a reference to the VIRGIN Mary. But degeneration was not far off: *wench* denoted a female peasant or servant child at the end of the C13th, and when used of an adult woman it acquired negative sexual connotations – first MISTRESS and then a WANTON woman. By the end of the C16th a *wencher* was a man who "associates with common women". Webster's is less euphemistic than this OED definition, stating baldly that *to wench* means "to consort with lewd women, especially to practice fornication [see FORNICATE]". In the USA *wench* retained its early associations with women at the bottom of the social scale: "Wench: A colored woman of any age; a negress or mulatress, especially one in service". (*The Century Dictionary*, 1891)

In current usage *wench* has ameliorated according to some etymologists; it is "used only humorously to refer to a woman, especially a BUXOM one and is regarded as having agreeably 'naughty' overtones". (Adrian Room, *Dictionary of Changes in Meaning*) However, not every woman described as a wench finds it particularly agreeable to have a word applied to her which suggests she is promiscuous.

Whore

Whore denoting a PROSTITUTE or HARLOT first appeared in written English in 1100. The late Old English *hore* is related to the Gothic *hors*, meaning adulterer. The Indo-European root of *whore* was *ka-* meaning to desire, which appears in Latin as *carus*, meaning dear or beloved. The present-day Italian word for prostitute, *carogna*, also comes from this base as does the Old Irish *cara*, meaning friend, and *caraim*, I love.

This etymological history plus the significant positions of power of the Harlot-Priestesses in ancient Greece and Rome have led some feminist linguists to suggest that the term *whore* once connoted love, respect and reverence, and that it was non-gender-specific. According to this thesis, it was when the early Christians began to vilify the sacred whores of pagan religions, that what had originally been a polite term of respect began a process of pejoration. As it underwent pejoration it narrowed to refer to women solely in derogatory terms and eventually became confined to coarse and abusive speech.

Whore has a wider meaning than merely a woman who prostitutes herself for hire: it is also used more generally of any woman who is considered unchaste (see CHASTE) or lewd, a fornicatress or adulteress (see FORNICATE) and, since 1205, it has been a term which, on occasions, has been applied opprobriously to a CONCUBINE or kept MISTRESS as well as to a catamite. No word exists expressing opprobrium for the male who keeps a concubine or mistress. The archaic term *whoremonger* (since 1521) for a male who fornicates with whores certainly contains some moral reproach but is now very rarely used. Women today who make no secret of their sexual desires are still likely to be widely regarded as SLUTS or whores; it is expected behaviour of males.

Like most of our vocabulary connected to male desire for illicit sex, the way in which *whore* has been used reveals an ambivalence: there is both an abhorrence of the flesh and a passion for it. These two feelings live side by side, unreconciled. Thus the word could be used in relatively polite (but male) society in the phrase *to go a-whoring*, eg: "The common Diversions of men of Fashion; that is to say, in Whoring, Drinking, and Gaming". (*Tatler,* 1709) However, from C14th–C19th the term *whorson* (ie, son of a whore) was a coarse epithet applied to a person or thing meaning vile, abominable, execrable and detestable. The son of a whore touches upon something most upsetting to the male psyche: the laws of inheritance in patriarchal society make it imperative that a man knows exactly who his son is.

Wicked

All wickedness is but little to the wickedness of a woman.
Ecclesiasticus 15:19

There are several theories about the origins of *wicked*. One suggestion is that the word derives from the Middle English *wikke*, meaning feeble – thus the wicked are weak and feeble in their resistance to sin. Another is that *wicked* meant lively and is connected to the *wick*, or live part, of a candle. *The Oxford Dictionary of English Etymology*, however, proposes that *wicked* was formed on *wick*, a dialect adjectival use of the Old English *wicce*, meaning WITCH. This ties in with the weak and feeble theory since witches were women who, as daughters of Eve, were thought to be less resistant to the temptations of the Devil than men. It was proposed by the authors of the *Malleus Maleficarum* 'Witches Hammer' (1498) that the very word *female* derived from *fe*, meaning faith, and *minus*, meaning less than.

Wicked entered English c1200 with wide application, but always of strong reprobation, implying a high degree of evil. The Devil – the consort of witches – was referred to as 'The Wicked One'.

In the 1920s, in wonderful disregard for earlier moral values, *wicked* came to be used in US slang to mean: "excellent in any way; potent, strong, capable". (*Dictionary of American Slang*) This is currently a very popular meaning in Anglo-American youth-culture jargon.

Widow

Since marriage has made two of one, a widow is a woman that has been emptied of herself.
Joseph T Shipley, Dictionary of Word Origins

. . .she was a widow, that strange feminine entity who had once been endowed with a dual personality and was now only half of what she had been.
Agnes Sligh Turnbull, The Flowering, 1972

Old English *widewe* or *widuwe* originated in the Indo-European root *widh-* or *weidh-*, meaning to be empty, to be separated, as in the Sanskrit *vidh*, meaning be destitute or lack. Hence the Latin *viduus*, meaning bereft, void or widowed, and *dividere*, denoting divide.

Widow entered English c825. It is one of the few female words in the English language which provides a base which is stronger than the corresponding male term *widower*, which did not appear until the second half of the C14th. Sex and marriage appear the only semantic area in which this occurs: PROSTITUTE denotes a female for which the corresponding masculine term is *male prostitute*; BRIDE is the base for *bridegroom*; *widow* is the base on which *widower* is formed. Most other terms, such as *author* or *actor*, are assumed to be male and the suffix *-ess* is generally added to form the feminine, AUTHORESS or ACTRESS.

The widow has always occupied an anomalous position in society. If the VIRGIN MAID was the property of her father, and the WIFE the property of her husband to whom did the widow belong and to what man did she owe obedience? The ideal was the woman who remained in CHASTE mourning, faithful to the memory of her late husband, until her own demise. But widowhood placed a woman, if she had any resources, in a position more powerful than other women, opening the possibility of the exercise of personal power. Far from becoming destitute, by common law the medieval widow became united with one-third of her husband's holding. Although she could not dispose of it, and her position could be fraught with the dangers of violence and intimidation being used to overturn her legal rights, "She regained her legal personality. . .and, for the first time in her life, could make independent decisions." (Margaret Wade Labarge, *Women in Medieval Life*)

In 1545 the now obsolescent word *relict* entered English as a synonym for a widow. It derived from the past participle of the Latin *relinquere*, meaning to leave behind or relinquish. From this it developed the obsolete senses of a deserted or discarded person (1592) and the remains, remnant or residue, and surviving part (1598). As Labarge notes, the poor widow without lands, rentals, trade or dutiful family was indeed a figure of destitution and great need, but the activities of the more financially fortunate widow "suggest that their new state of legal and personal freedom inspired fresh energy and competence". Hence, in the C17th *relict* acquired the sense of a thing left to one by inheritance.

In the mid-C16th the word *vidual*, adopted from the Latin *vidualis*, from *viduus*, meaning destitute, entered English denoting of, or belonging to, or befitting a widow or widowhood. But just what was befitting to the state of widowhood? On the one hand a widow was expected to conform to a passive code of behaviour: "Great difference then is there betwixt those widows who live alone, and those who frequent the company of men. For a widow to love society. . .gives speedy wings to spreading infamy. . .for in such meetings she exposeth her honour to danger, which above all she ought incomparably to tender." (Richard Brathwaite, *The English gentle-woman, Drawne out to the full Body: Expressing what Habilliments doe best attire her, what Ornaments doe best adorne her, what Complements doe best accomplish her*, 1641) On the other hand, it was also a commonly held assumption that a woman who had once experienced sex would wish to indulge in such pleasures as soon and as often as possible; the 'lusty widow', as the Duchess of Malfi was termed by her brother Ferdinand, must be ever on the lookout for sexual fulfilment.

The more wealthy the widow the less convenient it was to insist upon her chastity and fidelity. As Antonia Fraser writes in her study of women in the

C17th: "[to] those with something to gain from a woman's remarriage, notably her prospective second husband – no spectacle was more stirring than that of a wealthy widow. A Tally-Ho would go up when one of these creatures was sighted, followed by a pursuit which can only be compared to the contemporary chase after an heiress; except that the fox [see VIXEN] in this case was older and therefore wilier. . .the figure of the wealthy widow, that contemporary object of desire, begins to emerge as one VESSEL who was in practice by no means quite so weak as the rest of womankind." (*The Weaker Vessel*)

In the C20th, although C17th worries that remarriage to a widow might constitute bigamy – or even 'trigamy' in the case of the twice-widowed woman – had long since faded, concern about to whom the female survivor of a marriage belonged, remained. Amy Vanderbilt's *Complete Book of Etiquette*, (1952) is stern on this subject: on the vexatious issue of calling cards, "A widow shows respect for her husband by keeping his name on her cards and by using it socially in every way. She is Mrs George Grayson, not Mrs Alice Grayson, no matter how long she survives her husband."

The term *grass widow* first appeared in 1528 in a treatise by Sir Thomas More to denote "an unmarried woman who has cohabited with one or more men; a discarded mistress". (OED) Some etymologists have suggested that the term is a corruption of *grace widow*, but the more likely theory holds that 'grass' refers to a bed of straw, ie, not a legal marital bed. In the C19th the term was revived in Anglo-Indian usage for a married woman temporarily away from her husband, perhaps in the cooler 'grass' hills while he was elsewhere, on duty.

Wife

Wife and servant are the same
But only differ in the name.

When she the word 'obey' has said,
And man by law supreme has made,

Fierce as an Eastern prince he grows
And all his innate rigor shows.

Then shun, oh shun that wretched state
And all the fawning flatterers hate.

Value yourselves and men despise:
You must be proud if you'll be wise.

Lady Chudleigh, *To the Ladies*, 1703

According to one particular theory, *wife* originated in the Old English *wefan*, meaning to weave. This theory was used by many, including the English writer and art critic John Ruskin (1819–1900) to justify an insistence that a woman's place was in the home, claiming that *wife* originally meant 'she who weaves'. Today etymologists discount this theory and admit to not knowing the origins of the Old English *wif*, which has similarities in the Old Frisian and Old Saxon *wif* and the Old High German *wip*.

When *wif* first entered English in the early C8th, it meant woman, or an adult female, the feminine equivalent of *wer*, meaning adult male (which exists today only in *werewolf*). *Wife* later degenerated to mean a woman of humble rank or one of "low employment" (Samuel Johnson, 1755), especially one engaged in the sale of some commodity. In this last sense *wife* is no longer used, although the compound FISHWIFE, originally a woman seller of fish, is still used – now denoting a woman who uses coarse language.

In c888 *wife* specialised to mean a woman joined to a man by marriage, in other words, a married woman. Feminists have noted the inequality in the Christian marriage ceremony in which the couple are declared to be 'man and wife', pointing out the discrepancy between *man*, ie, one who is his own master, and *wife*, ie, a woman who belongs to a man. This formulation seems to be due to an error on the part of the early translators of the Bible: the Latin for both 'man' and 'husband' is *vir*, whereas two different words exist for 'woman' (*mulier*) and 'wife' (*uxor*) (see UXORIOUS). Around 1425 *wife* in this sense degenerated and became a euphemism for a kept MISTRESS or a CONCUBINE. Towards the end of the C16th *wife* briefly ameliorated and was applied as a term of affection to a female friend (presumably of a man, although the OED makes this masculist assumption by not specifying).

In the late C14th until 1620, *wife* came to denote a woman of fairly high status, the mistress of a household, or HOUSEWIFE, or the hostess or landlady of an inn. Derogatory attitudes towards wives can be seen in the C19th prison cant use of *wife* for a leg shackle and in male homosexual slang use of *wife* for the passive member of a GAY partnership.

The colloquial phrase *better half* for a wife has been in use since the late C16th. *The Penguin Dictionary of Historical Slang* claims it was used seriously in the C19th–C20th. If this is true, it perhaps points to the C19th tendency of men to place their wives on pedestals as 'naturally' the more continent, gentler and less belligerent SEX – thus justifying male philandering and adultery, and the insistence upon shackling (middle-class) wives to the home. This was not an invention of the C19th, as an old English proverb testifies: "A wife that expects to have a good name/Is always at home, as if she were lame."

If the term *better half* is serious, then the cockney rhyming slang term for a wife, *trouble and strife*, is, presumably, a joke.

Wimmin See HERSTORY

Wimp

The origins of *wimp* are uncertain. The OED suggests it was originally US slang; Webster's believes it originated in the UK. In 1917 the phrase *to go wimping* appeared as Oxford University slang meaning, for a male, to be on the look out for females for sexual gratification, in the 1920s *wimp* denoted a woman or girl. The word may be an abbreviated corruption of *women*, or it may have been formed on *whimper*; the OED invites us to compare it with the English dialect word *wimp*, meaning (of a dog) to whine (see BITCH).

Today, *wimp* is an abusive or contemptuous slang term for a weak or ineffectual person. It is used mostly of a man, when it is particularly insulting as it implies he is EFFEMINATE.

Witch

Everywhere the man strives to rid himself of women by objectifying it. "It is not",
he says "that I dread her; it is that she herself is malignant, capable of any crime,
a beast of prey, a vampire, a witch, insatiable in her desires. She is the very
personification of what is sinister."

Karen Horney (1885–1952)

When *witch* first entered written English c890 it denoted a man who practised witchcraft – a sorcerer or a wizard. By 1000 *witch* came to be used of a woman who practised witchcraft or magic, a sorceress. Some etymologists have proposed that *wicce* was a corruption of *witga*, meaning a seer or diviner, from the Old English *witan*, meaning to see or know. Similarly, Icelandic *vitkih*, a witch, came from *vita*, to know. In Middle Dutch a witch was a *wijsseggher*, a wiser-sayer, or soothsayer, hence the word *wiseacre*, meaning one who pretends to, or affects an air of, wisdom. In 1382 the term *wisewoman* entered English to refer to a woman skilled in the art of 'white' magic: one who dealt in charms against disease and misfortune, or malignant 'black' witchcraft, who dealt in healing in general and especially in midwifery. Towards the end of the C17th *sage woman* (from the Latin *sapere* meaning be wise) became a synonym for a MIDWIFE.

In her essay *Wisewoman and Medicine Man*, Ann Oakley writes: "Etymologically and historically, four words or roles have been closely related. These are WOMAN, WITCH, midwife and healer." In the transition from the traditional female control of medicine to male control, the C14th–C17th stand out as a landmark, when, "In Europe medicine emerged as a predominantly male professional discipline, and the traditional female lay-healer was suppressed. . . Women have a long history as community healers in pre-industrial Europe and colonial America. The 'good woman', 'CUNNING woman' or 'wisewoman' was the person to whom people turned in times of illness. . . Practising wisewomen-midwives had a generally respectable and sometimes high, status among the people they served. The negative appellation 'witch' was fostered by the medieval Church to whom disease was a god-given affliction, and thus a phenomenon which had to be under strict religious control."

At first the Christian Church was anxious to discredit the notion of witches and did not equate witchcraft with heresy until the mid-C13th when the Inquisition began witch trials, culminating in the mass persecution of witches in the C16th and C17th. Some estimates put the number of witches burnt, hanged or drowned as high as nine million. The majority of witches were women – King James 1 of England and 4 of Scotland (1566–1625) estimated that as many as nineteen out of every twenty were female. Thus, by the end of the C15th, *witch* came to denote a woman who supposedly had dealings with the devil or evil spirits who were able to perform supernatural acts. The corresponding male term was *wizard* or *warlock*.

In the light of the C20th jokey image of witches who adorn halloween parties, it is important to stress that a witch once represented all that was most evil; she was greatly feared and hated. This massive witch hunt (a term not coined until 1640 and which in the C20th came to mean "a single-minded and uncompromising campaign against a group of people with unacceptable views of behaviour, specifically communists; especially one regarded as unfair or malicious persecution". (OED)) was spear-headed by two Dominican Inquisitors, Heinrich Kramer and Jacobus Sprenger, in their book *Malleus Maleficarum* or 'Witches Hammer' (1487). They believed it was their task to rid Europe of any remaining pagan influence and defined witches as women who falsely imagined that during the night they rode abroad on their BESOMS with Diana – the Roman triple goddess whose cult was so widespread that early Christians saw her as their major rival and named her 'Queen of Witches'.

The Inquisitors inveighed against the power of witches – mostly old, muddle-headed WIDOWS and SPINSTERS, as well as midwives and healers – who, they claimed, had intercourse with the devil, and could cause any and every bodily infirmity – especially to men. As well as killing children, injuring cattle, raising and stirring up hailstorms and tempests and causing lightning to blast both men and beasts, witches were found guilty of causing confusion in men's minds and, with a spell or CHARM known as GLAMOUR, they could persuade a man that his penis had disappeared. The hostility between witchcraft and the Church, as the *Malleus Maleficarum* outlined it, focused on sentiments towards women and sexual practices; the two authors disclose unmistakably their phobia of women and their repugnance of sexual activity. The witch became the scapegoat for their MISOGYNY and was a useful weapon with which the Church attempted to maintain dominion at a time of unrest, when secular ideas began to challenge traditional knowledge, and when powerful central-ised monarchs of newly emerging nation states were replacing the authority of Rome. "Also, of course, the female healer challenged the male hegemony of the Church. . . The midwife's role in childbirth came in for particular attack. Any midwife was liable to be accused of being a witch, but particularly the unsuccessful among them. The *Malleus Maleficarum-* . . .charged the witch-midwife with various reproductive crimes. . .'No one' said the authors [Kramer and Sprenger] 'does more harm to the Catholic Faith than midwives.' " (Oakley)

Until the mid-C16th, a distinction was maintained between the good, or white, witch and the bad, or black, one. In 1542, a Tudor Witchcraft Act made witchcraft a felony punishable by death, and a further act six years later specifically listed the good witch as an unlicensed practitioner of medicine and distinguished between her activities and the necessarily evil acts of the bad witch. An act of 1563 abolished this distinction and declared that 'witchness' itself was a condition of the person accused.

As belief in witches waned and their persecution ended in the C18th, belief in the notions of evil in their once malevolent charm, glamour and enchantment (see ENCHANT) also diminished. The term *bewitch* (c1205) which originally meant to affect, usually injuriously, by witchcraft or magic, came "to mean to attract or please to such a degree as to take away all power of resistance or considered reservation". (Webster's) The 'glamour' of the C16th which once castrated the luckless male now gives potency by fascinating, enticing and alluring him. But in the abusive epithet *old witch* a sense of the evil HAG still survives, as it does in the term *witches' cauldron*, which denotes an unholy combination or set of circumstances and a turbid or menacing situation.

Wizard, the male practitioner of magic arts, was formed on Old English *wis*, meaning having sound judgment, or learned. The Middle English *warlow(e)*, later superseded by the Scottish spelling *warlock*, also denoted a male sorcerer or a wizard in the C14th. *Wizard* entered English in c1440 to mean a philosopher or sage. Although the term came to be synonymous with evil during the C16th, a connotation of wisdom has always been retained. Whereas in some uses *witch* has never completely lost connotations of evil, *wizard* began to be used figuratively with strong positive connotations in the early C17th of a man who did wonders in his profession. In the 1920s it became a slang term to express admiration for something considered excellent, marvellous or absolutely splendid, and *wizardry* in the 1950s came to mean skill or expertise.

Woman

Woman is from Old English *wifman*, formed on *wif*, meaning woman, and *man(n)*, meaning humankind, thus giving the meaning adult female person. *Waepman* was the male equivalent, meaning adult male person. The spelling of *wifman*, by dropping the 'f' and changing the 'i' to an 'o', evolved by the

C14th into *woman*. This formation is also found in the archaic word *leman* which developed from *leofman* from *lief*, meaning preferred, which came to mean first the non-gender-specific sweetheart, later narrowing and acquiring the specifically female and sexual meaning of MISTRESS.

Etymologists today confess to being baffled about the origins of *woman* but various theories, sometimes fuelled by the change in spelling and pronunciation, demonstrate a tendency to refer to the past to justify current beliefs. The American sociolinguist Mary Ritchie Key cites an erroneous etymological theory that *wifman* originally meant WIFE-man which is used to support the view that woman has no being apart from a husband, as an example of the way in which the (supposed) history of a word "is sometimes, and wrongly, used to control the dimensions of conduct permitted persons referred to by that word". (*Male/Female Language,* 1975)

Another theory claims *wif* derives from the Old English *wefan* meaning to weave, and this has provided 'evidence' that a woman's place was in the home, (ie, at her loom). A theory proposed by Samuel Purchas in 1619 was that a woman was "a house builded for generation and gestation, whence our language calls her woman, WOMB-man", echoing Protestant views about women such as those expounded by Martin Luther (1483–1546): "Men have broad shoulders and narrow hips, and accordingly they possess intelligence. Women have narrow shoulders and broad hips. Women ought to stay at home; the way they were created indicates this, for they have broad hips and a wide fundament to sit upon, keep house, and bear and raise children." (*Table Talk*)

An earlier attempt to justify a Christian belief that women were inferior to men by appealing to etymology is found in the C6th philosopher Isidore of Seville: "He is called 'man' (*vir*) because there is greater strength (*vis*) in him than in women: Whence 'virtue' takes its name. . . But 'woman' (*mulier*) comes from 'softness' (*a mollitie*). . .therefore there is greater virtue in man and less in woman." In like vein, the Dominican authors of *Malleus Maleficarum*, the late C15th handbook for WITCH hunters, insisted that *femina*, meaning woman, derived from *fe* (faith) and *minus* because their faith was less strong than that of the male sex. This explained why the preponderance of witches were female.

In the C16th and C17th punsters made the pseudo-etymological association with *woe* – whose woe depended upon the sentiments of the author: "Woman. . .soothe said I in prophesie when thou wast taken of my body, mans woe thou woldest be witlie, therefore wast thou so named." (*Chester Whitsun Plays,* 1500); "Man himselfe borne of a woman, is in deede a wo man, that is, ful of wo and miserie." (Sir Thomas More, *A Dialogue of Comfort Against Tribulation,* 1534); "A woman! As who saith, woe to the man!" (J Heywood, *Proverbs,* 1546); "Say of Woman worst ye can, What prolongs their woe, but man?" (Richard Flecknoe, 1653)

Old English *wifman* denoted both an adult female person and a female servant. In the C14th *woman* came to mean a LADY love, later a kept MISTRESS and, in the plural, it came to denote human females as partners in sexual intercourse "or irregularities" as Webster's euphemistically puts it. In the C15th it signified a wife. In the US in 1834 it was low colloquialism for a MOTHER. But the negative and sexual connotations never completely disappeared: since the early C17th *a woman of pleasure* meant one who is devoted to the pursuit of sensual pleasure and later, more specifically, a WANTON or a COURTESAN. By 1785 the *Dictionary of the Vulgar Tongue* defined both this phrase and a *woman of the town* as a PROSTITUTE. In the C19th *woman* became low slang for the female pudendum or VAGINA.

Towards the end of the C18th *woman* began to be used in contrast, explicit or implicit, with *lady*, eg, in 1847 the English journal *The Athenaeum* recorded that the "Defendant pleaded. . .that the person described as a woman was in fact a lady". Muriel R Schulz suggests that *woman* was avoided "probably as a Victorian sexual taboo, since it had acquired the meaning 'paramour or mistress' or the sense of intercourse with women when used in the plural, as in *Wine, Women, and Song*." But this cannot be the full explanation since *lady* in various compound terms, such as *lady of the night* and *ladybird*, had also meant a WHORE since the C16th and, by the C19th, was yet another synonym for the female genitalia. *Lady,* however, retained its connotations of superior gentility and had become identified with positive values of the feminine ideal: to be ladylike was, essentially, to be passive and CHASTE. It was not a quality possessed by working women – whose morals have always been considered suspect by the middle and upper classes.

FEMALE was another preferred substitute for *woman* during the C19th. This, however, also became contaminated by notions of indelicacy, possibly because of its associations with female biological function. It was so repugnant a word to Mrs Sarah Josepha Hale, editor of *Godey's Lady's Book*, that when the Vassar Female College was founded in 1861 she spent six years fighting to secure the removal of the offending adjective from the college sign.

The rivalry between the two words *woman* and *lady* continued into the C20th. Amy Vanderbilt's *Complete Book of Etiquette* (1954) introduces us to a prescriptive miasma of complicated usage: "A woman caller being announced in an office or in your home by an employee. . .is a 'lady', not a woman" And yet: "Remember, the King of England in his abdication speech referred to Wallis Simpson as 'the *woman* I love'. The word used properly has great dignity and meaning." Thus: "A man, speaking of his wife, should refer to her as a 'woman' to his friends, as a 'lady' only to tradespeople and various others in service capacities." On the other hand: "A gentleman stands behind a *lady's* chair until she is seated." However, Vanderbilt warned that the use of lady "is very limited, unless we wish to imply our own humbler position".

When defining the essential qualities (womanliness) of a woman, a consistently ambivalent and mostly derogatory stereotyped picture emerges from the major dictionaries: she is modest, delicate, tender, compassionate, sympathetic, gentle, affectionate, domesticated but she is also intuitive, changeable, capricious, submissive, prone to tears, fickle, superficial, foolish and lacking in promptness. Above all, she is weak, subordinate to man, and possesses qualities that have not been highly valued in a society which glorifies the characteristics connoted by manliness, ie, courage, valour, gallantry, strength, braveness, resoluteness, vigour, maturity, honour, dignity, nobility and authority. The worst that could be said of manliness, as recorded by the OED, is selfishness and pride. In some uses *man* can denote a human male who serves or is subordinate to another, as in *manservant* or the military term *men* (as opposed to officers). But it can also denote the opposite, ie, a master, overseer, foreman or boss. *Woman*, on the other hand, almost always connotes inferiority or subjection; the nonce-use of *woman* as a transitive verb (1595) meant "To make like a woman in weakness or subservience." (OED) *Womanish*, meaning characteristic of or proper to a woman, synonymous with *womanly* or *feminine* (c1374), became a derogatory term by 1390 that was still in use in the late C18th, eg: "She betrayed neither weakness, nor womanish submission." (Goldsmith, *History of England*. 1771) The phrase *to make a woman of you* (c1400) once meant specifically to deprive of virginity (see VIRGIN) and in modern usage means to bring into submission; *to make a man of you* implies releasing a male from his mother's EMASCULATING apron strings. A woman with manly attributes becomes the feared VIRGAO or AMAZON, but a man with womanly attributes is the despised EFFEMINATE, eg: "A woman impudent and mannish grown, Is not more loth'd than an effeminate man." (Shakespeare, *Troilus and Cressida*, 1606)

The history of *woman* and other related compound terms all point to a stereotyped view of woman as being weak and less than man; as the C20th psychiatrist Alfred Adler wrote: "All our institutions, our traditional attitudes, our laws, our morals, our customs, give evidence of the fact that they are determined and maintained by privileged males for the glory of male domination. . .That woman must be submissive, is an unwritten but deeply rooted law. . ." A law most clearly expressed in the Jewish morning prayer of males: "Blessed be God. . .that he did not make me a woman." Their wives, noted Simone de Beauvoir, "pray on a note of resignation 'Blessed be the Lord, who created me according to his will.' " (*The Second Sex*)

In the C20th *woman* has achieved a degree of amelioration, largely due to FEMINISM. This process began in the C19th when the word *womanfully* (1822), formed after *manfully*, was used to mean with womanly courage or perseverance, or like a woman of spirit. The term *new woman* (1894) was applied to women of so-called advanced views who advocated the independence of their sex and who defied patriarchal convention; it slowly began to be used with approval of the strong female characters in the novels of George Gissing, George Bernard Shaw, H G Wells, etc. The word was also claimed by those campaigning for the female franchise – at first called *womanists* (in the early C17th) and later called *feminists*, SUFFRAGETTES or *suffragists*.

In the C20th *womanist* became the preferred term among some Black women for a Black feminist: "Womanist is to feminist as purple is to lavender." (Alice Walker, *The Color Purple,* 1983) Among suffragettes, the term *woman's vote* became the accepted term – although it was an issue that most men (be they gentlemen or not) believed no 'lady' would get involved in. The same can be said of the term *Woman's Liberation* – depending upon the politics of the user, *woman* in this context can denote a strong (but not masculine) independently-minded female – or an unfeminine and therefore sexually unattractive (to men) female beyond the power of males to control. That the connotations of *woman* are socially constructed is clearly expressed by Simone de Beauvoir: "One is not born, but rather becomes a woman." (*The Second Sex*)

Womb

Women's brains are in a certain sense. . .in their wombs.

Havelock Ellis (1859–1939)

But if God had wanted us to think with our wombs, why did he give us a brain?

Clare Boothe Luce, *Slam the Door Softly,*1970

Old English *womb* or *wamb* is related to the Gothic *wamba*, of unknown origin. In Greek the root *-delph* signified womb: Delphi was the oldest and most revered of oracles in ancient Greece, where MOTHER Earth was worshipped under the name of Delphyne, or the 'Womb of Creation', hence the words DELPHIC and *delphian*, meaning obscure or ambiguous. From the same root came *delphax*, meaning young PIG. Possibly because the SOW and the human female are the only mammals with a hymen, pigs have always had strong associations with women and their sex organs. (See also PORCELAIN and MATRICULATE). One imaginative theory about the etymological source of *woman* suggested that "She is a house builded for generation and gestation, whence our language calls her woman, womb-man." (Samuel Purchas, *Microcosmus,* 1619)

Womb entered English in c825 to denote the uterus, but, just as was then believed a woman was made mentally unstable or hysterical (see HYSTERIA – derived from the Greek *hustera*, meaning womb) by her supposedly wandering womb, several meanings of *womb* wandered around the body. From c825–1684, the abdomen was called the *womb*, as was the stomach from c950–1756, the bowels from c1000–1544, and the belly-piece of a hide or skin from 1434–1612. In translations of the Latin Vulgate Bible, *venter*, in the sense of heart or soul, was translated as 'womb', and in 1398 the ventricle of the heart was translated as 'womb' in a medical treatise. In 1545 Thomas Raynalde in *Byrth of Mankynde* attempted to clarify the situation: "These thre woords, the MATRIX, the mother, and the wombe do signifie but one thynge." (*MOTHER* was another term for hysteria.)

Both the term and the psychoanalytic concept of womb-envy as a counterpart to penis-envy was introduced by Karen Horney in her essay *The Flight from Womanhood* (1926). Arguing that motherhood gives women "a quite indisputable and by no means negligible physiological superiority", she asks "Is not the tremendous strength in man of the impulse to creative work in every field precisely due to their feeling of playing a relatively small part in the creation of living beings, which constantly impels them to an overcompensation in achievement?"

Bibliography

Dictionaries and Encyclopedias

Attwater, Donald, *The Penguin Dictionary of Saints*. Penguin, London. 1965

Ayto, John *The Longman Register of New Words*. Longman, Harlow. 1989

Barney, Stephen A, *Word Hoard: An Introduction to Old English Vocabulary*. Yale University Press, Newhaven. 1985

Bottomore, Tom, *A Dictionary of Marxist Thought*. Harvard University Press, Harvard. 1983

Briggs, Katharine, *A Dictionary of Fairies*. Penguin, London. 1977

Bullock, Alan and Stalleybrass, Oliver (eds), *The Fontana Dictionary of Modern Thought*. Fontana, London. 1977

Bullock, Alan and Woodings, R B (eds), *The Fontana Biographical Companion to Modern Thought*. Fontana, London. 1983

Byrne, Josefa Heifetz, *Mrs Byrne's Dictionary of Unusual, Obscure and Preposterous Words*. Granada, London. 1979

Cohen, J M and M J, *The Penguin Dictionary of Modern Quotations*. Penguin, London. 1980

Cohen, J M and M J, *The Penguin Dictionary of Quotations*. Penguin, London. 1960

Cottle, Basil, *The Penguin Dictionary of Surnames*. Penguin, Harmondsworth. 1978

Diabolus, Dick, *Beelzebub's Beastly Barbs: A Cynics Dictionary*. Diabolus Press, London. 1982

Dutton, Dave, *Lanky Spoken Here: A Guide to the Lancashire Dialect*. M & J Hobbs/Michael Joseph, London. 1978

Enright, D J (ed), *Fair of Speech: The Uses of Euphemism*. OUP, Oxford. 1985

Evans, Ivor H (ed), *Brewer's Dictionary of Phrase and Fable*. Book Club Associates/Cassell, London. 1981

Fergusson, Rosalind, *The Penguin Dictionary of Proverbs*. Penguin, Harmondsworth. 1983

Fowler, H W *A Dictionary of Modern English Usage*. OUP, Oxford. 1983 (first published 1926)

Franklyn, Julian, *A Dictionary of Rhyming Slang*. Routledge & Kegan Paul, London. 1961

Gearrfhocloir Gaeilge-Bearla (Irish–English Dictionary). Department of Education, Dublin. 1981

Gove, Philip Babcock (ed), *Webster's Third New International Dictionary of the English Language*. G & C Merriam Co., Springfield, Mass. 1961

Green, Jonathon, *The Slang Thesaurus*. Elmtree, London. 1986

Green Jonathon, *The Dictionary of Contemporary Slang*. Pan, London. 1984

Grose, Francis, *1811 Dictionary of the Vulgar Tongue*. Papermac, London. 1982

Hall, J R Clark, *A Concise Anglo-Saxon Dictionary*. University of Toronto Press, Toronto. 1960

Hanks, Patrick (ed), *Collins Dictionary of the English Language*. Collins, London. 1979

Heller, Louis, Humez, Alexander and Dror, Malcah, *The Private Lives of English Words*. Routledge & Kegan Paul, London. 1984

Hilliam, David, *Chambers Wordlore*. Chambers, Edinburgh. 1984

Hornadge, Bill, *The Australian Slanguage*. Cassell, Melbourne. 1980

Hudson, Kenneth, *The Dictionary of the Teenage Revolution and its Aftermath*. Macmillan, London. 1983

Johnson, Samuel, *Dictionary of the English Language* (1755). Adler, New York. 1968

Kramerae, Cheris and Treichler, Paula A, *A Feminist Dictionary*. Pandora Press, London. 1985

Longman Dictionary of English Idioms. Longman, London. 1979

Longman Dictionary of the English Language. Longman, London. 1984

McConville, Brigid and Shearlaw, John, *The Slanguage of Sex*. Futura, London. 1985

Mencken, H L, *Dictionary of Quotations*. Collins, London. 1982

Monaghan, Patricia, *Women in Myth and Legend*. Junction Books, London. 1981

Morris, William (ed), *The American Heritage Dictionary of the English Language*. American Heritage Publishing Co/Houghton Mifflin. 1969

Murray, J A H, Bradley, H, Craigie, W A and Onions, C T, *The Oxford English Dictionary*. OUP, Oxford. 1933. Supplements 1972–86

Neaman, Judith S and Silver, Carole G, *Dictionary of Euphemisms*. Unwin, London. 1984

Onions C T (ed), *The Oxford Dictionary of English Etymology*. OUP, Oxford. 1966.

Partnow, Elaine (ed), *The Quotable Woman 1800–1981*. Facts on File, New York. 1982

Partridge, Eric, *A Dictionary of Slang and Unconventional English*. Routledge & Kegan Paul, London. 1961

Partridge, Eric, *The Penguin Dictionary of Historical Slang*. Penguin, Harmondsworth. 1972

Peter, Dr Lawrence, *Quotations for Our Time*. Magnum, London. 1980

Pierce, Ambrose, *The Devil's Dictionary* (1911) Dover, New York. 1958

Radford, Edwin and Smith, Arlen, *To Coin a Phrase: A Dictionary of Origins*. Papermac, London. 1981

Rodgers, Bruce, *Gay Talk: A Dictionary of Gay Slang*. Putnam, New York. 1972

Roget's Thesaurus of English Words and Phrases. Penguin, Harmondsworth. 1962

Room, Adrian, *Dictionary of Changes in Meaning*. Book Club Associates/ Routledge & Kegan Paul, London. 1986

Rycroft, Charles, *A Critical Dictionary of Psychoanalysis*. Penguin, Harmondsworth. 1972

Shapiro, Max S And Hendricks, Rhoda, *A Dictionary of Mythologies*. Granada, London. 1979

Shipley, Joseph T, *Dictionary of Early English*. Littlefield, Adams & Co, Totowa, New Jersey. 1968

Shipley, Joseph T, *Dictionary of Word Origins*. Philosophical Library, New York. 1945

Simpson, John, *The Concise Oxford Dictionary of Proverbs*. OUP, Oxford. 1982

Skeat, Walter W, *An Etymological Dictionary of the English Language*. Clarendon Press, Oxford. 1978

Sykes, J B (ed), *The Concise Oxford Dictionary of Current English*. OUP, Oxford. 1982

The Concise Oxford Dictionary of Quotations. OUP, Oxford. 1964

Thorne, J O and Collocott, T C (eds), *Chamber's Biographical Dictionary*. Chambers, Edinburgh. 1984

Todasco, Ruth (ed), *An Intelligent Woman's Guide to Dirty Words*. Loop Centre YWCA, Chicago. 1973

Tripp, Rhoda Thomas, *The International Thesaurus of Quotations*. Penguin, Harmondsworth. 1976

Tuttle, Lisa, *Encyclopedia of Feminism*. Longman, London. 1986

Uverov, E B, Champan, D R and Isaacs, Alan, *The Penguin Dictionary of Science*. Penguin, Harmondsworth. 1979

Walker, Barbara G, *The Woman's Encyclopedia of Myths and Secrets*. Harper & Row, San Francisco. 1983

Waring, Philippa, *Dictionary of Omens and Superstitions*. Souvenir Press, London. 1978

Wentworth, Harold and Flexner, Stuart Berg, *Dictionary of American Slang*. Crowell, New York. 1967

Williams, Raymond, *Keywords: A Vocabulary of Culture and Society*. Flamingo, London. 1983

Withycombe, E G, *The Oxford Dictionary of English Christian Names*. OUP, Oxford. 1977

Wright, Peter, *Lancashire Dialect*. Dalesman Books, Lancaster. 1980

Language
See all asterisked items in General list.

General
Abbott, Sidney and Love, Barbara, *Sappho Was A Right On Woman: A Liberated View of Lesbianism*. Stein & Day, New York. 1973

Adams, Carol, *Ordinary Lives*. Virago, London. 1982

* Aitchison, Jean, *Language Change: Progress or Decay?* Fontana, London. 1981

Alcott, Louisa May, *Work* (1882). Schocken, New York. 1977

Alexander, Sally, 'Women, Class and Sexual Differences in the 1980s and 1840s: Some Reflections on the Writing of a Feminist History', *History Workshop Journal* no 17. London. 1984

Alexander, Sally, 'Women's Work in Nineteenth Century London: A Study of the Years 1820–1850', in *The Rights and Wrongs of Women*, ed Juliet Mitchell and Ann Oakley

Alic, Margaret, *Hypatia's Heritage: A History of Women in Science from Antiquity to the Late Nineteenth Century*. The Women's Press, London. 1986

Appignianesi, Lisa, *Simone de Beauvoir*. Penguin, Harmondsworth. 1988

Arcana, Judith, *Our Mother's Daughters*. The Women's Press, London. 1979

Ardener, Shirley, (ed), *Perceiving Women*. Dent, London. 1975

Aries, Philippe, *Centuries of Childhood. A Social History of Family Life*. Random House, New York. 1962

Armstrong, Karen, *The Gospel According to Women*. Pan, London. 1986

Ashley, Maurice, *England in the Seventeenth Century*. Pelican, Harmondsworth. 1954

Austen, Jane, *Mansfield Park* (1814). Penguin, Harmondsworth. 1983

Bachofen, J J, *Myth, Religion and Mother Right* (1841). Princeton University Press, Princeton. 1973

Bamberger, Joan, 'The Myth of Matriarchy: Why Men Rule in Primitive Society' in *Woman Culture and Society*, eds Michelle Rosaldo and Louise Lamphere.

Banks, Olive, *Faces of Feminism*. Martin Robinson, Oxford. 1981

Barrett, Michele and Mary McKintosh, *The Anti-Social Family*. Verso, London. 1983

Barthes, Roland, *Mythologies*. Jonathan Cape, London. 1972

Beard, Mary, *Woman As Force in History*. Collier/Macmillan, London. 1946

Beauman, Nicola, *A Very Great Profession*. Virago, London. 1983

Behn, Aphra (see Morgan, Fidelis)

Belotti, Elena, *Little Girls*. Writers and Readers, London. 1975

Benjamin, J, 'Chodorow's Reproduction of Mothering: An Appraisal' , *Psychoanalytic Review* vol 69 no 1. 1982

Benjamin, Jessica, *The Bonds of Love: Psychoanalysis, Feminism and the Problem of Domination*. Pantheon, New York. 1988

Bernal, Martin, *Black Athena: The Afroasiatic Roots of Classical Civilization*. Free Association Books, London. 1987

Bettelheim, Bruno, *Symbolic Wounds: Puberty Rites and the Envious Male*. Collier, New York. 1962

Bettelheim, Bruno, *The Uses of Enchantment: The Meaning and Importance of Fairy Tales*. Peregrine, Harmondsworth. 1978

Bird, Caroline, *Born Female*. McKay, New York. 1968

Black, Clementina (ed), *Married Women's Work*. Virago, London. 1983

* Black, Maria and Coward, Rosalind, 'Linguistic, Social and Sexual Relations: A Review of Dale Spender's Man Made Language', *Screen Education* no. 39. SEFT, London. Summer 1981

* Bloomfield, L, *Language*. Allen & Unwin, London. 1933

* Bodine, Ann, 'Androcentrism in Prescriptive Grammar: Singular "They", Sex Indefinite "He" and "He" or "She" ', *Language in Society* vol 4 no 2. 1975

* Bodine, Ann, 'Sex Differentiation in Language' in *Language and Sex*, eds Barrie Thorne and Nancy Henley

Booth, Clare Luce, *The Women*. Random House, New York. 1937

Brecher, Edward, *The Sex Researchers*. Andre Deutsch, London. 1970

* Brend, Ruth M, 'Male–female Intonation Patterns in American English' in *Language and Sex*, ed Barrie Thorne and Nancy Henley

Briffault, Robert, *The Mothers: A Study of the Origins of Sentiments and Institutions*. Macmillan, New York. 1927

Brighton Women and Science Group (eds), *Alice Through the Microscope*. Virago, London. 1980

Bristol Women's Studies Group (eds), *Half the Sky: An Introduction to Women's Studies*. Virago, London. 1979

Brown, Judith C, *Immodest Acts*. OUP, Oxford. 1986

Brown, Rita Mae, *Rubyfruit Jungle*. Bantam, New York. 1975

Brown, Wilmette, *Black Women and the Peace Movement*. Falling Wall Press, Bristol. 1984

Brownmiller, Susan, *Against Our Will*. Secker and Warburg, London. 1975

Brownmiller, Susan, *Femininity*. Paladin, London. 1986

Bryan, Beverly, Dadzie, Stella and Scafe, Suzanne, *The Heart of the Race: Black Women's Lives in Britain*. Virago, London. 1985

Buckmaster, Henrietta, *Women Who Shaped History*. Collier Books, New York. 1974

Bullough, Vern and Bonnie, *Prostitution*. Crown, New York. 1978

* Burchfield, Robert, *The English Language*. OUP, Oxford. 1985

* Bynon, Theodora, *Historical Linguistics*. CUP, Cambridge. 1983

Cambridge Women's Studies Group (eds), *Women In Society*. Virago, London. 1981

* Cameron, Deborah, *Feminism and Linguistic Theory*. Macmillan, London. 1985

* Cameron, Deborah and Coates, Jennifer, 'Some problems in the Sociolinguistic Explanation of Sex Differences', *Language and Communication* vol 5 no 3. 1985

Caputi, Jane, *The Age of Sex Crime*. The Women's Press, London. 1988

Carpenter, Edward, *The Intermediate Sex*. Allen & Unwin, London. 1908

Carter, Angela, *Sadeian Women*. Virago, London. 1979

Cartledge, Sue and Ryan, Joanna (eds), *Sex and Love*. The Women's Press, London. 1983

Chamberlain, Mary, *Old Wives' Tales*. Virago, London. 1981

Chasseguet-Smirgel, Janine, *Female Sexuality*. Virago, London. 1981

Chatkiss, W (ed), *Loaded Questions: Women in the Military*. Transnational Institute, Amsterdam. 1981

Chaucer, Geoffrey, *Complete Works*. OUP, Oxford. 1912

* Cherry, Louise, 'Teacher–Child Verbal Interaction: An Approach to the Study of Sex Differences' in *Language and Sex*, Barrie Thorne and Nancy Henley

Chesler, Phyllis, *About Men*. The Women's Press, London. 1978

Chesler, Phyllis, *Women and Madness*. Avon Books, New York. 1972

Chicago, Judy, *The Dinner Party: A Symbol of Our Heritage*. Anchor Press, New York. 1979

Chodorow, Nancy, *The Reproduction of Mothering: Psychoanalysis and the Sociology of Gender*. University of California Press, Berkeley & London. 1978

* Chomsky, Noam, *Reflections of Language*. Fontana, London. 1976

Claremont de Castellejo, Irene, *Knowing Women*. Harper & Row, New York. 1974

Clark, Anna, *Women's Silence, Men's Violence: Sexual Assault in England 1770–1845*. Pandora Press, London. 1987

* Coates, Jennifer, *Women, Men and Language*. Longman, London. 1986

* Cohen, Marcel, *Language: Its Structure and Evolution*. Souvenir Press, London. 1975

Cohen, Stanley (ed), *Images of Deviance*. Pelican, Harmondsworth. 1971

Collins, Jackie, *Hollywood Wives*. Pan, London.

Cook, Pam, *The Cinema Book*. British Film Institute, London. 1985

Coontz, Stephanie and Henderson, Peta (eds), *Women's Work, Men's Property: The Origins of Gender and Class*. Verso, London. 1986

Coote, Anna and Campbell, Beatrix, *Sweet Freedoms*. Pan, London. 1982

Coote, Anna and Kellner, Peter, *Hear This, Brother: Women Workers and Union Power*. New Statesman, London. 1980

* Copley, J, *Shift of Meaning*. OUP, London. 1961

Coward, Rosalind, *Female Desire*. Paladin, London. 1984

Coward, Rosalind, *Patriarchal Precedents: Sexuality and Social Relations*. Routledge & Kegan Paul, London. 1983

* Coward, Rosalind, and Ellis John, *Language and Materialism: Developments in Semiology and the Theory of the Subject*. Routledge & Kegan Paul, London. 1977

* Culler, Jonathan, *Barthes*. Fontana, London. 1983

* Culler, Jonathan, *Saussure*. Fontana, London. 1976

Daly, Mary, *Beyond God the Father*. Beacon Press, Boston. 1974
* Daly, Mary, *Gyn/Ecology*. The Women's Press, London. 1979
Daly, Mary, *Pure Lust: Elemental Feminist Philosophy*. The Women's Press, London. 1984
Dangerfield, George, *The Strange Death of Liberal England 1910–1914*. Capricorn Books, New York. 1961
David, Elizabeth, *French Provincial Cooking*. Penguin, Harmondsworth. 1967
Davidoff, Leonore, *The Best Circles: Society, Etiquette and the Season*. Croom Helm, New York. 1973
Davies, Margaret Llewelyn (ed), *Maternity: Letters from Working Women* (1915). Virago, London. 1978
Davis, Elizabeth Gould, *The First Sex*. Penguin, Harmondsworth. 1975
Davis, Natalie Zemon, *Society and Culture in Early Modern France*. Stanford University Press, Berkeley, Ca. 1975
de Beauvoir, Simone, *Adieux: A Farewell to Sartre* (1985). Penguin, Harmondsworth. 1974
de Beauvoir, Simone, *All Said and Done*. Andrew Deutsch, London. 1974
de Beauvoir, Simone, *A Very Easy Death*. Penguin, Harmondsworth. 1969
de Beauvoir, Simone, *Memoirs of a Dutiful Daughter*. Penguin, Harmondsworth. 1963
de Beauvoir, Simone, *The Coming of Age*. Warner Books, New York. 1972
de Beauvoir, Simone, *The Prime of Life*. Penguin, Harmondsworth. 1963
de Beauvoir, Simone, *The Second Sex* (1949). Penguin, Harmondsworth. 1972
de Bruyn, Lucy, *Women and the Devil in Sixteenth-Century England*. The Compton Press, Tisbury, Wiltshire. 1979
de Lauretis, Teresa, *Alice Doesn't: Feminism, Semiotics, Cinema*. Macmillan, London. 1984
Delmar, Rosalind, 'What is Feminism?' in *What is Feminism?* eds Juliet Mitchell and Ann Oakley
de Pizan, Christine, *The Book of the City of Ladies* (1405). Pan, London. 1983
* de Saussure, Ferdinand, *Course in General Linguistics*. Fontana, London. 1974
Deutsch, Helene, *The Psychology of Women*. Grune & Stratton, New York. 1945
Diner, Helen, *Mothers and Amazons*. Julian Press, New York. 1965
Dinnerstein, Dorothy, *The Mermaid and the Minotaur: Sexual Arrangements and Human Malaise*. Harper & Row, New York. 1976; *The Rocking of the Cradle and the Ruling of the World*. The Women's Press, London. 1987
Dixon, Miriam, *The Real Matilda: Woman and Identity in Australia 1788–1985*. Pelican, Melbourne. 1976
Duby, Georges, *The Knight, the Lady and the Priest*. Peregrine, Harmondsworth. 1985
Dworkin, Andrea, *Intercourse*. Arrow Books, London. 1988
Dworkin, Andrea, *Pornography: Men Possessing Women*. The Women's Press, London. 1981

Dworkin, Andrea, *Woman Hating*. E P Dutton, New York. 1974

Easlea, Brian, *Science and Sexual Repression*. Weidenfeld & Nicolson, London. 1981

Ecker, Gisele (ed), *Feminist Aesthetics*. The Women's Press, London. 1985

Edwards, Susan, *Female Sexuality and the Law*. Martin Robinson, Oxford, 1981

Ehrenreich, Barbara and English, Deidre, *Complaints and Disorders*. Writers and Readers, London. 1973

Ehrenreich, Barbara and English, Deidre, *For Her Own Good: 150 Years of the Experts Advice to Women*. Pluto Press, London. 1979

Ehrenreich, Barbara and English, Deidre, *Witches, Midwives and Nurses*. Writers and Readers, London. 1973

Eichenbaum, Luise and Orbach, Susie, *Outside In Inside Out*. Penguin, Harmondsworth. 1982

Elgin, Suzette Haden, *Native Tongue*. The Women's Press, London. 1985

Ellis, Havelock, *Man and Woman* (1894). Heinemann, London. 1934

Ellis, Havelock, *The Erotic Rights of Women*. British Society for the Study of Sex Psychology, London. 1917

Engels, Frederick, *The Condition of the Working Class in England* (1845). Panther, St Albans. 1969

Engels, Frederick, *The Origin of the Family, Private Property and the State* (1884). Pathfinder Press, New York. 1972

Enloe, Cynthia, *Does Khaki Become You?*. Pluto Press, London. 1983

Enriques, Fernando Dr, *Modern Sexuality*. MacGibbon and Kee, London. 1968

Ettore, E M, *Lesbians, Women and Society*. Routledge & Kegan Paul, London. 1980

Evans, Mary (ed), *The Woman Question: Readings on the Subordination of Women*. Fontana, London. 1982

Faderman, Lillian, *Surpassing the Love of Men*. The Women's Press, London. 1985

Faust, Beatrice, *Women, Sex and Pornography*. Melbourne House, London. 1980

Fee, Elizabeth, 'A Feminist Critique of Scientific Objectivity', *Science for the People* vol 14 no 4. Science Resource Centre, Cambridge, Mass. July/Aug 1982

Fell, Christine, *Women in Anglo-Saxon England*. Basil Blackwell, Oxford. 1986

Feminist Anthology Collective, *No Turning Back: Writings from the Women's Liberation Movement 1975–80*. The Women's Press, London. 1981

Feminist Review, London. 1978–88

Feminist Review (ed), *Sexuality: a Reader*. Virago, London. 1987

Figes, Eva, *Patriarchal Attitudes*. Virago, London. 1978

Firestone, Shulamith, *The Dialectic of Sex: The Case for Feminist Revolution*. Paladin, London. 1972

Flexner, Eleanor, *Century of Struggle: The Woman's Rights Movement in the*

United States. Atheneum, New York. 1974
Formations, Routledge & Kegan Paul, London. 1983–87

Focault, Michel, *The History of Sexuality Vol 1: An Introduction.* Allen Lane, London. 1979
Frankfort, Ellen, *Vaginal Politics.* Bantam, New York. 1973
Frazer, Antonia, *The Weaker Vessel. Woman's Lot in Seventeenth-Century England.* Methuen, London. 1985
Fraser, Ronald, *Work* (2 vols). Penguin, Harmondsworth.
Frazier, Sir James G, *The Golden Bough.* Macmillan, New York. 1922
Frazier, Nancy and Sadker, Myra, *Sexism in School and Society.* Harper and Row, New York. 1973
French, Marilyn, *Beyond Power: On Women, Men and Morals.* Sphere, London. 1986
Freud, Sigmund, *Case Histories 1.* Pelican, Harmondsworth. 1977
Freud, Sigmund, *General Remarks on Hysterical Attacks.* Hogarth Press, London. 1948
Freud, Sigmund, *On Sexuality.* Pelican, Harmondsworth. 1977
Freud, Sigmund, *The Future of an Illusion.* Hogarth Press, London. 1961
Freud, Sigmund, *The Psychopathology of Everyday Life.* Pelican, Harmondsworth. 1975
Freud, Sigmund and Breuer, Joseph, *Studies on Hysteria.* Pelican, Harmondsworth. 1974
Friday, Nancy, *My Mother, Myself.* Dell, New York. 1977
Friday, Nancy, *My Secret Garden.* Virago/Quartet, London. 1976
Friedan, Betty, *The Feminine Mystique.* Penguin, Harmondsworth. 1965
Friedan, Betty, *The Second Stage.* Michael Joseph, London. 1982
* Fry, Dennis, *Homo Loquens: Man as a Talking Animal.* CUP, Cambridge. 1977

Gabor, Mark, *The Pin-Up: A Modest History.* Andre Deutsch, London. 1972
Gallop, Jane, *Feminism and Psychoanalysis: The Daughter's Seduction.* Macmillan, London. 1982
Gathorne-Hardy, Jonathan, *The History of the British Nanny*
* Gill, Gillian C, 'Women and Men Speaking by Cheris Kramerae; Sexist Language: A Modern Philosophical Analysis edited by Mary Vetterling-Braggin; Women and Language in Literature and Society edited by Sally McConnell-Ginet, Ruth Borker, and Nelly Furman', *Signs. Journal of Women in Culture and Society* vol 8 no 2. University of Chicago Press, Chicago. 1982
Gilman, Charlotte Perkins, *The Man-Made World: Our Androcentric Culture* Charlton, New York. 1914
Gold, Mick, 'The History of Nature' in *Geography Matters!* by Massey, Doreen and Allen, John. CUP, Cambridge. 1984
Goldsmith, Margaret, *Sappho of Lesbos.* Rich and Cowen, London. 1938
Gornick, Vivian and Moran, Barbara K (eds), *Woman in Sexist Society: Studies in Power and Powerlessness.* New American Library, New York. 1972
Gottlieb, Beatrice, 'Feminism in the Fifteenth Century' in *Women of the Medieval World,* eds Julius Kirshner and Suzanne F Wemple

* Graham, Alma, 'The Making of a Nonsexist Dictionary' in *Language and Sex*, by Barrie Thorne and Nancy Henley

* Grahn, Judy, *Another Mother Tongue: Gay Words, Gay Worlds*. Beacon Press, Boston, Mass. 1984

Graves, Robert, *The Greek Myths* (2 vols). Pelican, Harmondsworth. 1955

Graves, Robert, *The White Goddess*. Faber & Faber, London. 1961

Greave, Norma and Grimshaw, Patricia (eds), *Australian Women*. OUP, Melbourne. 1981

Greer, Germaine, *Sex and Destiny: The Politics of Human Fertility*. Picador, London. 1985

Greer, Germaine, *The Female Eunuch*. Paladin, London. 1971

Griffin, Susan, *Pornography and Silence*. Harper and Row, New York. 1981

Griffin, Susan, *Woman and Nature*. The Women's Press, London. 1984

Grosskurth, Phyllis, *Havelock Ellis: A Biography*. Quartet, London. 1981

Grosskurth, Phyllis, *Melanie Klein: Her World and Her Work*. Hodder and Stoughton, London. 1986

Gurko, Miriam, *The Ladies of Seneca Falls: The Birth of the Woman's Rights Movement*. Schocken Books, New York. 1976

Hall, Radclyffe, *The Well of Loneliness* (1928). Virago, London. 1982

Hall, Ruth (ed), *Dear Dr Stopes: Sex in the 1920s*. André Deutsch, London. 1978

Hall, Ruth, *Marie Stopes, A Biography*. Virago, London. 1978

Harding, M Esther, *Women's Mysteries*. Rider, London. 1971

* Harris, Marvin, *Cows, Pigs, Wars and Witches*. Vintage Books, New York. 1974

* Harris, Roy, *The Language Myth*. Duckworth, London. 1981

Hartman, Mary and Banner, Lois W (eds), *Clio's Consciousness Raised. New Perspectives on the History of Women*. Harper Colophon, New York. 1974

Haskell, Molly, *From Reverence to Rape: the Treatment of Women in the Movies*. Penguin, Harmondsworth. 1974

Hays, H R, *The Dangerous Sex: The Myth of Feminine Evil*. Putnam, New York, 1964

Haywood, Eliza, *The History of Miss Betsy Thoughtless* (1751). Pandora, London. 1986

Heilbrun, Carolyn, G, *Reinventing Womanhood*. W W Norton, New York. 1979

Heilbrun, Carolyn, G, *Toward a Recognition of Adrogyny*. Knopf, New York. 1973

* Hejinan, Lyn and Watten, Barrett (eds), 'Women and Language', *Poetics Journal* no 4. California. May 1984

* Henley, Nancy, 'Power, Sex and Nonverbal Communication' in *Language and Sex*, eds Barrie Thorne and Nancy Henley

* Henley, Nancy and Thorne, Barrie, *She Said/He Said. An Annotated Bibliography of Sex Differences in Language, Speech and Non-Verbal Communication*. Know Inc, Pittsburg, PA. 1975

Hernton, Calvin C, *Sex and Racism*. Paladin, St Albans. 1970

Herschberger, Ruth, *Adam's Rib*. Harper & Row, New York. 1970

Hewitt, Patricia, *Rights for Women*. NCCL, London. 1975

Hite, Shere, *The Hite Report: A Nationwide Study of Female Sexuality*. Macmillan, New York. 1976

Hite, Shere, *The Hite Report on Women and Love: A Cultural Revolution in Progress*. Viking, London. 1988

Hobsbawm, Eric, *The Age of Capital 1848–1875*. Penguin, Harmondsworth. 1975

Hoch, Paul, *White Hero Black Beast*. Pluto Press, London. 1979

Hodson, Phillip, *Men: An Investigation into the Emotional Male*. Ariel Books. London. 1984.

Holledge, Julie, *Innocent Flowers*. Virago, London. 1981

hooks, bell, *Feminist Theory: From Margin to Centre*. Southend Press, Boston, Mass. 1984.

Hooper, Anne, *Women and Sex*. Sheldon Press, London. 1986

Horn, Pamela, *The Rise and Fall of the Victorian Servant*. Gill & Macmillan, Dublin. 1975

Horney, Karen, *Feminine Psychology*. W W Norton, New York. 1973

Hughes, Anne, *The Diary of a Farmer's Wife 1796–1797*. Penguin, Harmondsworth. 1981

Ibsen, Henrik, *A Doll's House* (1879). Penguin, Harmondsworth. 1965

Jacobus, Mary, *Reading Woman: Essays in Feminist Criticism*. Methuen, London. 1986

James, Henry, *The Bostonians* (1886). Penguin, Harmondsworth. 1984

Janeway, Elizabeth, *Man's World, Woman's Place: A Study in Social Mythology*. Michael Joseph, London. 1972

Janssen-Jurreit, Marielouise, *Sexism: The Male Monopoly on History and Thought*. Farrar Straus and Giroux, New York. 1982

Jeffreys, Sheila, *The Spinster and Her Enemies: Feminism and Sexuality 1880–1930*. Pandora, London. 1985

* Jespersen, Otto, *Language: Its Nature, Development and Origin*. Allen and Unwin, London. 1922

* Jespersen, Otto, *The Growth and Structure of the English Language*. Methuen, London. 1986

Joans, Lynn (ed), *Keeping the Peace*. The Women's Press, London. 1983

Johnston, Jill, *Lesbian Nation: The Feminist Solution*. Simon & Schuster, New York. 1973

Jones, Gareth Steadman, *Outcast London: A Study in the Relationship Between Classes in Victorian Society*. Clarendon Press, Oxford. 1971

Jong, Erica, *Witches*. Granada, London. 1982

Joreen, 'The BITCH Manifesto' in *Notes From the Second Year*. New York. 1970

Jung, Carl, *Man and His Symbols*. Doubleday, New York. 1964

Jung, Carl, *Psychology and Religion*. Yale University Press, Newhaven. 1938

Kaplan, Cora, *Sea Changes: Essays on Culture and Feminism*. Verso, London. 1986

Kaplan, E Ann (ed), *Women in Film Noir*. British Film Institute, London. 1980

Kelly, Joan, *Women, History and Theory*. The University of Chicago Press, Chicago. 1984

* Key, Mary Ritchie, *Male/Female Language*. The Scarecrow Press, Metuchen, NJ. 1975

King, Josephine and Stott, Mary (eds), *Is This Your Life? Images of Women in the Media*. Virago/Quartet, London. 1977

Kinsey, A C, Pomeroy, W B Martin, C E, and Gebhard, P H, *Sexual Behaviour in the Human Female*. Saunders, Philadelphia & London. 1953

Kinzer, Nora Scott, *Put Down and Ripped Off: The American Woman and the Beauty Cult*. Crowell, New York. 1977

Kirshner, Julius and Wemple, Suzanne F (eds), *Women of the Medieval World*. Basil Blackwell. 1985

Koedt, Anne, 'The Myth of the Vaginal Orgasm' in *Radical Feminism*, eds Anne Koedt, Ellen Levine and Anita Rapone. Quadrangle/New York Times, New York. 1973

* Kramer, Cheris, 'Women's Speech: Separate But Unequal?' in *Language and Sex*, eds Barrie Thorne and Nancy Henley

Kramer, Heinrich and Sprenger, Jacob, *Malleus Maleficarum* (1486). Dover Publications, New York. 1971

* Kramerae, Cheris (ed), *The Voices and Words of Women and Men*. Pergamon Press, Oxford. 1980

* Kramerae, Cheris and Treichler, Paula (eds), *Women and Language News*. University of Illinois, Urbana, III. 1976

* Kristeva, Julia, *Desire in Language: A Semiotic Approach to Literature and Art*. Basil Blackwell, Oxford. 1981

Kristeva, Julia (see Moi, Toril)

Kuhn, Annette, *The Power of the Image*. Routledge & Kegan Paul, London. 1985

Labarge, Margaret Wade, *Women in Medieval Life*. Hamish Hamilton, London. 1986

* Lakoff, Robin, *Language and Woman's Place*. Harper Colophon, New York. 1975

Langland, William, *Piers the Ploughman*. Penguin, London. 1966

Latimer, Hugh, *Sermons*. J M Dent, London. 1906

Lawrence, Marilyn (ed), *Fed Up and Hungry: Women, Oppression and Food*. The Women's Press, London. 1987

Lee, Patrick C and Stewart, Robert Sussman, *Sex Differences*. Urizen Books, New York. 1976

Lefkowitz, Mary R, *Women in Greek Myth*. Duckworth, London. 1986

Legman, G, *Rationale of the Dirty Joke*. Grove Press, New York. 1968

Legman G, (ed), *The Limerick*. Jupiter Books, London. 1974

Lerner, Gerda, *The Creation of Patriarchy*. OUP, Oxford. 1986

Lerner, Gerda, *The Majority Finds Its Place: Placing Women in History*. New York. 1979

Liddington, Jill and Norris, Jill, *One Hand Tied Behind Us*. Virago, London. 1978

Lipschitz, Susan, 'The Witch and Her Devils: An Exploration of the Relationship between Femininity and Illness' in *Tearing the Veil*, ed Susan Lipschitz. Routledge & Kegan Paul, London. 1978

Lloyd-Jones, Hugh, *Females of the Species*. Duckworth, London. 1975

London Feminist History Group, The (eds), *The Sexual Dynamics of History*. Pluto Press, London. 1983

* Lyons, John, *Chomsky*. Fontana, London. 1977

* Lyons, John, *Introduction to Theoretical Linguistics*. CUP, Cambridge. 1968

* Lyons, John, *Language, Meaning and Context*. Fontana, London. 1981

* Lyons, John, *Semantics*. CUP, Cambridge. 1977

Maccoby, Eleanor and Jacklin, Carol, *The Psychology of Sex Differences*. Stanford University Press, California. 1974

MacCormack, Carol and Strathern, *Nature, Culture and Gender*. CUP, Cambridge. 1980

McCrindle, Jean and Rowbotham, Sheila (eds), *Dutiful Daughters*. Pelican, London. 1979

* McCrum, Robert, Cran, William and MacNeil, Robert, *The Story of English*. Faber and Faber, London. 1986

MacDonald, Holden Pat and Ardener, Shirley (eds), *Images of Women in Peace and War*. Macmillan, London. 1987

MacKenzie, Midge, *Shoulder to Shoulder*. Penguin, Harmondsworth. 1975

MacKenzie, Norman and Jeanne (eds), *The Diary of Beatrice Webb*. (4 vols) Virago, London. 1982–5

MacLeod, Sheila, *The Art of Starvation*. Virago, London. 1981

Maitland, Sarah, *A Map of the New Country: Women and Christianity*. Routledge & Kegan Paul, London. 1983

Maitland, Sarah and Garcia Jo (eds), *Walking on the Water: Women Talk About Spirituality*. Virago, London. 1983

Malinowski, Bronislaw, *Sex and Repression in Savage Society*. The Humanities Press, New York. 1927

Malinowski, Bronislaw, *Sex Culture and Myth*. Harcourt, Brace, New York. 1962

* Mandelbaum, David G (ed), *Selected Writings of Edward Sapir*. University of California Press, Berkeley, Ca. 1949

Marcus, Maria, *A Taste for Pain*. Souvenir Press, London. 1981

Marcus, Steven, *The Other Victorians*. Basic Books, New York. 1964

Markale, Jean, *Women of the Celts*. Gordon Cremonosi, London. 1975

Marks, Elaine and de Courtivron, Isabelle (eds), *New French Feminisms*. Harvester Press, Brighton. 1981

Martineau, Harriet, *Autobiography* (2 vols) (1855). Virago, London. 1983

* Martyna, Wendy, 'Beyond the "He-Man" Approach: The Case for Non-Sexist Language', *Signs: Journal of Women In Culture and Society* vol 5 no 3. University of Chicago Press, Chicago. 1980

Masters, William H and Johnson, Virginia E, *Human Sexual Inadequacy*. Little, Brown, Boston, Mass. 1970

Masters, William H and Johnson, Virginia E, *Human Sexual Response*. Little, Brown, Boston, Mass. 1966

Mead, Margaret, *Male and Female* (1949). Pelican, Harmondsworth. 1962

Mee, Arthur, *Talks To Boys*. Hodder and Stoughton, London. 1941

Mercer, Jan (ed), *The Other Half: Women in Australian Society*. Penguin, Melbourne. 1975

Merchant, Carolyn, *The Death of Nature*. Wildwood, London. 1982

Merck, Mandy, 'The City's Achievements: The Patriotic Amazonamachy and Ancient Athens' in *Tearing the Veil*, ed Susan Lipschitz. Routledge & Kegan Paul, London. 1978

m/f, London. 1978–87

Michalowski, H, 'The Army Will Make a "Man" Out of You' in *Reweaving the Web of Life: Feminism and Non-Violence*, ed P McAllister. New Society Publishers, Philadelphia. 1982

Mill, Harriet Taylor, *Enfranchisement of Women* (1851) Virago, London. 1983

Mill, John Stuart, *The Subjection of Women* (1869). Virago, London. 1983

Miller, Alice, *For Your Own Good*. Virago, London. 1987

Miller, Alice, *The Drama of the Gifted Child and Search for the True Self*, trans. Ruth Ward. Faber and Faber, London. 1983

Miller, Alice, *Thou Shalt Not Be Aware*. Pluto Press, London. 1985

* Miller, Casey and Swift, Kate, *The Handbook of Non-Sexist Writing for Writers, Editors and Speakers*. The Women's Press, London. 1981

* Miller, Casey and Swift, Kate, *Words and Women. New Language in New Times*. Victor Gollancz, London. 1977

Miller, Jane, *Women Writing about Men*. Virago, London. 1986

Miller, Jean Baker, *Toward a New Psychology of Women*. Beacon Press, Boston, Mass. 1976

Millett, Kate, *Sexual Politics*. Avon Books, New York. 1971

Millett, Kate, *The Prostitution Papers*. Paladin, St Albans. 1975

Millum, Trevor, *Images of Woman: Advertising in Women's Magazines*. Chatto and Windus, London. 1975

Mitchell, Juliet, *Pyschoanalysis and Feminism*. Pelican, Harmondsworth. 1975

Mitchell, Juliet, *Women: The Longest Revolution*. Virago, London. 1984

Mitchell, Juliet (ed), *The Selected Melanie Klein*. Peregrine, Harmondsworth. 1986

Mitchell, Juliet and Oakley. Ann (eds), *The Rights and Wrongs of Women*. Penguin, Harmondsworth. 1976

Mitchell, Juliet and Oakley, Ann (eds) *What is Feminism?* Basil Blackwell, Oxford. 1986

Mitchell, Margaret, *Gone With the Wind*. Macmillan, London. 1940

Moers, Ellen, *Literary Women: The Great Writers*. Doubleday, New York. 1976

Moi, Toril (ed), *The Kristeva Reader*. Basil Blackwell, Oxford. 1986

More, Thomas, *Utopia* (1516) Yale University Press, New Haven. 1964

Morgan, Elaine, *The Descent of Woman*. Bantam Books, New York. 1973

Morgan, Fidelis, *Female Wits: Women Playwrights on the London Stage 1660–1720*. Virago, London. 1981
Morgan, Robin (ed), *Sisterhood is Powerful*. Vintage, New York. 1970

Nabokov, Vladimir, *Lolita*. Penguin, Harmondsworth. 1980
Nead, Lynda, *Myths of Sexuality. Representations of Women in Victorian England*. Basil Blackwell, Oxford. 1988
Nelson, Sarah, *Incest: Fact and Myth*. Stramullian, Edinburgh. 1987
Neumann, Erich, *The Great Mother: An Analysis of the Archetype*. Princeton University Press, Princeton. 1974
Newton, Judith L, Ryan, Mary and Walkowitz, Judith (eds), *Sex and Class in Women's History*. Routledge & Kegan Paul, London. 1983.
Nicholson, Joyce, *What Society Does to Girls*. Virago, London. 1977
* Nilsen, Alleen Pace, 'Linguistic Sexism as a Social Issue' in *Sexism and Language*, ed Alleen Pace Nilsen et al. NCTE, Urbana, Ill. 1977
Nowak, Mariette, *Eve's Rib*. St Martins Press, New York. 1980

Oakley, Ann, *Housewife*. Pelican, Harmondsworth. 1976
Oakley, Ann, *Subject Women*. Martin Robinson, Oxford. 1981
Oakley, Ann, *Taking it like a Woman*. Jonathan Cape, London. 1984
Oakley Ann, *The Sociology of Housework*. Pantheon, New York. 1974
O'Faolain, Julia and Martines, Lauro, *Not in God's Image: Women in History*. Virago, London. 1979
Okely, Judith, *Simone de Beauvoir*. Virago, London. 1986
Olsen, Tillie, *Silences*. Virago, London. 1980
Orbach, Susie, *Fat is a Feminist Issue*. Paddington Press, London. 1978
Ortner, Sherry B, 'Is Female to Male as Nature is to Culture?' in *Woman, Culture and Society*, eds Michelle Zimbalist Rosaldo and Louise Lamphere
* Orwell, George, 'Politics and the English Language' in *Collected Essays*. Secker Warburg, London. 1961
* Osman, Sona et al, 'A to Z of Feminism', *Spare Rib*. London. Nov 1983 – Jan 1984

Pankhurst, Emmeline, *My Own Story* (1914). Virago, London. 1979
Pankhurst, Sylvia, *The Suffragette Movement* (1931), Virago, London. 1977
Pomeroy, Sarah B, *Goddesses, Whores, Wives and Slaves. Women in Classical Antiquity*. Schocken, New York. 1975

Quinn, Susan, *A Mind of Her Own: The Life of Karen Horney*. Macmillan, London. 1988

Radical Science Collective (ed), *Free Associations*. Free Association Books, London. 1984–86
Raeburn, Antonia, *The Militant Suffragettes*. Michael Joseph, London. 1973
Ramelson, Marian, *The Petticoat Rebellion*. Lawrence and Wishart, London. 1976

Reed, Evelyn, *Problems of Womens' Liberation*. Pathfinder Press, New York. 1970

Reeves, Maude Pember, *Roundabout a Pound a Week* (1913). Virago, London. 1979

Reik, Theodor, *The Creation of Woman*. George Braziller, New York. 1961

Rice, Margery Spring, *Working Class Wives* (1939). Virago, London. 1981

Rich, Adrienne, *Blood, Bread and Poetry*. Virago, London. 1987

Rich, Adrienne, *Of Woman Born: Motherhood as Experience and Institution*. Virago, London. 1977

Rich, Adrienne, *On Lies, Secrets and Silence*. Virago, London. 1980

Richards, Janet Radcliffe, *The Sceptical Feminist*. Pelican, Harmondsworth. 1982

Riley, Denise, *War in the Nursery*. Virago, London. 1983

Roberts, Helen (ed), *Doing Feminist Research*. Routledge & Kegan Paul, London. 1981

Robertson, Geoffrey, *Obscenity: An Account of Censorship Laws and their Enforcement in England and Wales*. Weidenfeld and Nicolson, London. 1979

Rogers, Katharine M. *Feminism in Eighteenth-Century England*. University of Illinois Press, Urbana, Ill. 1982

Rosaldo, Michelle Zimbalist and Lamphere, Louise (eds), *Woman, Culture and Society*. Stanford University Press, Stanford, Ca. 1974

Rosen, Marjorie, *Popcorn Venus*. Avon Books, New York. 1973

Rossi, Alice S (ed), *The Feminist Papers*. Bantam, New York. 1974

Rousseau, Jean Jacques, *Emile; or, a Treatise on Education* (1726). Dent, London. 1984

Rowbotham, Sheila, *Dreams and Dilemmas*. Virago, London. 1983

Rowbotham, Sheila, *Hidden from History*. Pluto Press, London. 1974

Rowbotham, Sheila, *Woman's Consciousness, Man's World*. Penguin, Harmondsworth. 1973

Rowbotham, Sheila, Segal, Lynne and Wainwright, Hilary, *Beyond the Fragments*. Merlin Press, London. 1979

Rowbotham, Sheila and Weeks, Jeffrey, *Socialism and the New Life: the Personal and Sexual Politics of Edward Carpenter and Havelock Ellis*. Pluto Press, London. 1977

Rowe, Marsha, *Spare Rib Reader*. Penguin, Harmondsworth. 1982

Rowland, Judith, *Rape: The Ultimate Violation*. Pluto Press, London. 1986

Rush, Florence, *The Best Kept Secret: the Sexual Abuse of Children*. McGraw-Hill, New York. 1981.

Ruskin, John, *Sesame and Lillies* (1865). Homewood, Chicago. 1902

Russ, Joanna, *How to Supress Women's Writing*. The Women's Press, London. 1984

Russell, Diana E H, *The Politics of Rape*. Stein and Day, New York. 1975.

Sachs, Albie and Wilson, Joan Hoff, *Sexism and the Law*. Martin Robertson, Oxford. 1978

* Sachs, Jacqueline, 'Cues to the Identification of Sex in Children's Speech' in *Language and Sex*, eds Barrie Thorne and Nancy Henley

Sacks, Karen, 'Engels Revisited: Women, the Organisation of Production and Private Property' in *Woman, Culture and Society*, ed Michelle Zimbalist Rosaldo and Louise Lamphere

Saffioti, Heleieth I B, *Women in Class Society*. Monthly Review Press, New York. 1978

Sapir, Edward (see Mandlebaum, David G)

Sappho, *Poems and Fragments* (C6th BC), trans. Josephine Balmer. Brilliance Books, London. 1984

Sargant, Lydia (ed), *Women and Revolution: A Discussion of the Unhappy Marriage of Marxism and Feminism*. Southend Press, Boston, Mass. 1981

Sartre, Jean-Paul, *Being and Nothingness*. Metheun, London. 1965

Sayers, Janet, *Biological Politics: Feminist and Anti-Feminist Perspectives*. Tavistock, London. 1982

Sayers, Janet, *Sexual Contradictions*. Tavistock Publications, London. 1986

* Schulz, Muriel R, 'The Semantic Derogation of Woman' in *Language and Sex*, eds Barrie Thorne and Nancy Henley

Seager, Joani and Olson Ann, *Women in the World: An International Atlas*. Pluto/Pan, London. 1986

Segal, Hanna, *Klein*. Fontana, London. 1979

Segal, Lynne (ed), *What is to be done about the Family?* Penguin, Harmondsworth. 1983

Semonides (see Lloyd-Jones, Hugh)

Sevely, Josephine Lowndes, *Eve's Secrets: A New Perspective on Human Sexuality*. Bloomsbury, London. 1987

Shahar, Shulamith, *The Fourth Estate: A History of Women in the Middle Ages*. Methuen, London. 1983

Shakespeare, William, *Complete Works*. Spring Books, New York. 1948

Sharpe, Sue, *'Just Like a Girl': How Girls Learn to be Women*. Penguin, Harmondsworth. 1976

Sheehy, Gail, *Passages*. E P Dutton, New York. 1976

Shorter, Edward, *A History of Women's Bodies*. Penguin, Harmondsworth. 1984

Showalter, Elaine, *A Literature of Their Own: British Women Novelists from Brontë to Lessing*. Virago, London. 1978

Showalter, Elaine, *The Female Malady*. Virago, London. 1987

Showalter, Elaine (ed), *The New Feminist Criticism: Essays on Women, Literature and Theory*. Virago, London. 1986

Shulman, Alix Kates, *Memoirs of an ex-Prom Queen*. Bantam, New York. 1973

Shuttle, Penelope and Redgrove, Peter, *The Wise Wound*. Penguin, Harmondsworth. 1980

Simpson, Ruth, *From the Closet to the Courts: The Lesbian Transition*. Penguin, Harmondsworth. 1977

Smart, Carol, *Women, Crime and Criminology: A Feminist Critique*. Routledge & Kegan Paul, London. 1976

Smart, Carol and Barry (eds), *Women, Sexuality and Social Control*. Routledge & Kegan Paul, London. 1978

* Smith, Philip M, *Language, The Sexes and Society*. Basil Blackwell, Oxford. 1985

Smith-Rosenberg, Carroll, *Disorderly Conduct: Visions of Gender in Victorian America.* Knopf, New York. 1985

Snitow, Ann, Stansell, Christine and Thompson, Sharon (eds), *Desire: The Politics of Sexuality.* Virago, London. 1984

Solanas, Valerie *SCUM Manifesto.* The Olympia Press, New York. 1967

Solomon, Barbara H and Bergren Paula S, *A Mary Wollstonecraft Reader.* Mentor, New York. 1983

Sontag, Susan, *Illness as Metaphor.* Random House, New York. 1977

Spender, Dale, *Invisible Women.* Writers and Readers, London. 1982

* Spender, Dale, *Man Made Language.* Routledge & Kegan Paul, London. 1980

Spender, Dale (ed), *Men's Studies Modified.* Pergamon Press, Oxford. 1981

Spender, Dale, *There's Always Been a Women's Movement This Century.* Pandora, London. 1983

Spender, Dale, *Women of Ideas and What Men Have Done to Them.* Ark, London. 1983

Stanley, Autumn, 'Behind the Bronze Curtain or What the Farmer Saw: A Review of Gerda Lerner's *The Creation of Patriarchy*' (Forthcoming). 1988

Stanton, Elizabeth Cady, *The Woman's Bible* (1895–88). Polygon Books, Edinburgh. 1985

* Steedman, Carolyn, Irwin, Cathy and Walkerdine, Valery (eds), *Language, Gender and Childhood.* Routledge & Kegan Paul, London. 1985

Stefan, Verena, *Shedding.* The Women's Press, London. 1979

Stein, Sarah, *Girls and Boys.* Hogarth Press, London. 1984

Steinem, Gloria, *Outrageous Acts and Everyday Rebellions.* Flamingo, London. 1984

* Steiner, George, *Language and Silence.* Peregrine, Harmondsworth. 1969

Stewart-Park, Angela and Cassidy, Jules, *We're Here: Conversations with Lesbian Women.* Quartet, London. 1977

Stone, Lawrence, *The Family, Sex and Marriage in England 1500–1800.* Pelican, Harmondsworth. 1979

Stone, Merlin, *The Paradise Papers: The Suppression of Women's Rites.* Virago/Quartet, London. 1976

Storr, Anthony, *Human Aggression.* Pelican, Harmondsworth. 1970

Storr, Anthony, *Sexual Deviation.* Pelican, Harmondsworth. 1964

Storr, Anthony, *The Art of Psychotherapy.* Secker and Warburg/Heinemann, London. 1979

Storr, Anthony, *The Dynamics of Creation.* Secker and Warburg, London. 1972

Strachey, Lytton, *Eminent Victorians.* Collins, London. 1959 (first published 1918)

Strachey, Ray, *The Cause: A Short History of the Women's Movement in Great Britain* (1928). Virago, London. 1978

* Strainchamps, Ethel, 'Our Sexist Language' in *Women in Sexist Society*, eds Vivian Gornick and Barbara K Moran

Summers, Anne, *Damned Whores and God's Police: the Colonization of Women In Australia.* Penguin, Melbourne. 1975

* Swacker, Marjorie, 'The Sex of the Speaker as a Sociolinguistic Variable' in *Language and Sex*, eds Barrie Thorne and Nancy Henley

Tannahill, Reay, *Sex in History*. Hamish Hamilton, London. 1980
Taylor, Barbara, *Eve and the New Jerusalem*. Virago, London. 1983
Taylor, Debbie et al (eds), *Women: A World Report*. Methuen, London. 1985
Teale, Ruth (ed), *Colonial Eve: Sources on Women in Australia. 1788–1914*. OUP, Melbourne. 1978
Thompson, Dorothy (ed), *Over Our Dead Bodies*. Virago, London. 1983
Thompson, E P, *The Making of the English Working Class*. Pelican, Harmondsworth. 1968
Thompson, William, *Appeal of One Half of the Human Race, Women, Against the Pretentions of the Other Half, Men. To Retain them in Political and Hence in Civil and Domestic, Slavery* (1825). Virago, London. 1883
* Thorne, Barrie and Henley, Nancy (eds), *Language and Sex. Difference and Dominance*. Newbury House, Rowly, Mass. 1975
* Thorne, Barrie and Henley, Nancy, 'Difference and Dominance: An Overview of Language, Gender, and Society' in *Language and Sex*, eds Barrie Thorne and Nancy Henley
Tomalin, Claire, *The Life and Death of Mary Wollstonecraft*. Pelican, Harmondsworth. 1977
Trevor-Roper, Hugh, *Witchcraze of the Sixteenth and Seventeenth Centuries*. Pelican, Harmondsworth. 1969
Tristan, Flora, *The London Journal* (1842). Virago, London. 1982
Trotsky, Leon, *Women and the Family* (1923–36). Pathfinder Press, New York. 1970.
* Trudgill, Peter, 'Sex, Covert Prestige, and Linguistic Change in the Urban British English of Norwich' in *Language and Sex*, eds Barrie Thorne and Nancy Henley
* Trudgill, Peter, *Sociolinguistics: An Introduction to Language and Society*. Pelican, Harmondsworth. 1989
Tuchman, Gaye, Daniels, Arlene Kaplan and Benet, James (eds), *Hearth and Home: Images of Women in the Mass Media*. OUP, New York. 1978
Turner, Ian, Factor, June and Lowenstein, *Cinderella Dressed in Yella*. Heinemann Educational, Richmond, Australia. 1978

Ullman, Walter, *A History of Political Thought: The Middle Ages*. Pelican, Harmondsworth. 1965

Vanderbilt, Amy, *Complete Book of Etiquette: A Guide to Gracious Living*. Doubleday, New York. 1954
Vicinius, Martha, *Independent Women. Work and Community for Single Women 1850–1920*. Virago, London. 1985

Walkowitz, Judith, 'Male Vice and Feminist Virtue: Feminism and the Politics of Prostitution in Nineteenth Century Britain', *History Workshop Journal* 13. London. 1982

Walkowitz, Judith, *Prostitution and Victorian Society, Women, Class and State*. CUP, Cambridge. 1980

Walkstein, Diane and Kramer, Samuel Noah, *Inanna: Queen of Heaven and Earth*. Harper and Row, New York. 1983

Walters, Margaret, *The Nude Male*. Paddington Press, London. 1978

Walters, Margaret, 'The Rights and Wrongs of Women: Mary Wollstonecraft, Harriet Martineau, Simone de Beauvoir' in *The Rights and Wrongs of Women,* eds Juliet Mitchell and Ann Oakley

Wandor, Michelene (ed), *On Gender and Writing*. Pandora Press, London. 1983

Ward, Elizabeth, *Father-Daughter Rape*. The Women's Press, London. 1984

Warner, Marina, *Alone Of All Her Sex: the Myth and the Cult of the Virgin Mary*. Quartet Books, London. 1978

Warner, Marina, *Joan of Arc*. Weidenfeld and Nicolson, London. 1981

Warner, Marina, *Monuments and Maidens*. Weidenfeld and Nicolson, London. 1985

Webb, Beatrice, see MacKenzie, Norman and Jeanne

Weedon, Chris, *Feminist Practice & Poststructuralist Theory*. Basil Blackwell, Oxford, 1987

Weibel, Kathryn, *Mirror, Mirror: Images of Women Reflected in Popular Culture*. Anchor Press, New York. 1977

Weideger, Paula, *Female Cycles*. The Women's Press, London. 1978

West, Rebecca, *The Strange Necessity* (1928). Virago, London. 1987

West, Rebecca, *The Young Rebecca*. Virago, London. 1983

Williams, Raymond, *The Long Revolution*. Penguin, Harmondsworth. 1975

Williamson, Judith, *Consuming Passions*. Marion Boyars, London. 1986

Williamson, Judith, *Decoding Advertisements*. Marion Boyars, London. 1978

Wilson, Amrit, *Finding a Voice: Asian Women in Britain*. Virago, London. 1978

Wilson, Elizabeth, *Adorned in Dreams*. Virago, London. 1985

Winnicott, D W, *Playing and Reality*. Penguin, Harmondsworth. 1980

Winnicott, D W, *The Child, The Family and The Outside World*. Pelican, Harmondsworth. 1964

Winnicott, D W, *The Piggle*. Penguin, Harmondsworth. 1980

* Wittig, Monique and Zeig, Sande, *Lesbian Peoples: Materials for a Dictionary*. Virago, London. 1980

Wollstonecraft, Mary, *A Vindication of the Rights of Woman* (1792). Everyman's Library, London. 1929

Woolf, Virgina, *A Room of One's Own* (1928) Penguin, Harmondsworth. 1945

Woolf, Virgina, *Three Guineas* (1938). Penguin, Harmondsworth. 1977

Young, Robert (ed), *Sexual Difference*. The Oxford Literary Review, Oxford. 1986

Zaretski, Eli, *Capitalism, the Family and Personal Life*. Pluto Press, London. 1976

Zilbergeld, Bernard, *Men and Sex*. Fontana, London. 1980

* Zimmerman, Don H, and West, Candace, 'Sex Roles, Interruption and Silences in Conversations' in *Language and Sex*, eds Barrie Thorne and Nancy Henley